2014
2017
2019

MILESTONES
OF F

D0851699

MILESTONES OF FLIGHT

MICHAEL J.H. TAYLOR & DAVID MONDEY

JANE'S

INTRODUCTION

Can you tell me when . . . what was the date . . . when did . . are all precursors to questions of time. They come in many other forms also, but all seek to establish a reliable date for some occurrence which, in the case of the authors of this book, applies to aerospace events. It is surprising how wide is the occupational field from which such enquiries come but, of course, people connected directly or indirectly with the world's aerospace industry are those who most frequently need to find an answer to such questions.

The authors' experience brought an appreciation that an up-to-date aerospace chronology would be a valuable tool for a wide variety of people. But, perhaps more importantly, the compilation of this book has produced a condensation of fascinating highlights of man's efforts to gain wings and to reach out into space. It provides a running history of the development of aviation and spaceflight which, interspersed with a background of important international events, makes fascinating reading. Like many collections of facts, it gives an unspoken commentary on the ingenuity and frailties of man.

The layout is purely chronological and a simple convention has been adopted for dates. For example, January 1 covers an event on that specific date; January 1-5 refers to one which occurred during that period of time, and January 1/2 means that it happened during the night separating those two dates. The comprehensive index is intended to make it easy to locate the event or item for which you need a date.

BALDVOVS VOLARE COИATVS COLLVM FRAИGIT.

The Temple of Apollo

863 BC
Bladud, the ninth king of Britain, comes to the throne. He is killed when he attempts to fly from the Temple of Apollo in Trinavantum (London) using wings covered with feathers, probably in 843 BC.

470 – 391 BC
Mo Ti (Tzu) lives in China. He is said to have invented the kite, having constructed one of wood. China in the 4th century BC is recognised as the birth place of the kite for pleasure and war.

c.400 – 350 BC
Archytas of Tarentum, Italy, is a Greek-born scientist, philosopher and mathematician. He builds a small wooden bird, which is suspended from the end of a pivoted arm. The bird is propelled on the arm by a steam or compressed air jet.

c.200 BC
Chinese General Han Hsin uses kites in warfare, to measure distances between his forces and the enemy.

c.6th Century
Kites are used in China for signalling military instructions by semaphore.

c.1020
An English Benedictine monk, known as Oliver of Malmesbury 'The Flying Monk', attempts to fly from Malmesbury Abbey using wings. He breaks his legs in the attempt.

1042
Tseng Kung Liang of China tells of the use of rockets in war. These early projectiles are fuelled with gunpowder.

c.11th Century
Saracen of Constantinople attempts to fly from a building using a cloak fitted with ribs. He dies in the attempt, when one rib snaps and he plunges to the ground.

c.12th Century
The first Chinese rocket is launched. (q.v. 1232)

12th – 14th Century

The first model helicopters are flown as string-pull toys. One is illustrated in a Flemish manuscript of c.1325, while a painting of 1460 depicts a toy helicopter. (q.v. April 28, 1784)

1232

The defenders of the Chinese city of Peiping repel Mongol forces with artillery rockets.

1250

Roger Bacon, an English Franciscan monk, completes a book entitled *Secrets of Art and Nature*. In it he makes the first known reference to a flying machine with 'artificiall Wings made to beat the Aire', known today as an ornithopter.

1258

Europe first hears of artillery rockets for war.

14th Century

Marco Polo, his father and an uncle witness man-carrying kites being flown by sailors in Cathay (China).

1306

Parachute jumps are made in China during the coronation of Fo-Kin.

1326-27

Bomb-carrying pennon-type kites are illustrated in Europe.

c.1420

Italian Joanes Fontana designs the first rocket-powered aeroplane, configured as a model bird. This is illustrated in a manuscript in the state library at Munich.

1452 – 1519

The Italian artist and inventor Leonardo da Vinci produces several designs for aviation-related machines during his lifetime. Between 1483 and 1497 he designs a parachute, ornithopter, helicopter and powered aeroplane.

1503

An Italian named G.B. Danti survives his attempt to fly at Perugia using inadequate wings.

1507

John Damian breaks his thigh bone after attempting to fly from a wall at Stirling Castle, Scotland, using feather-covered wings.

1647

Italian Titus Livio Burattini, who is at the Polish court of King Wladyslaw IV, makes and flies a model aeroplane. It has four sets of wings, two sets beating as those of an ornithopter.

1655

Englishman Robert Hooke builds and flies a model ornithopter.

1670

Jesuit priest Francesco de Lana designs a lighter-than-air machine. This is basically a boat hull fitted with a mast and sail, lifted by four rope-tethered copper spheres from which the air has been extracted.

1678

French locksmith Besnier attempts unsuccessfully to fly at Sablé using two paddle-like wings hand-held across his shoulders, driven up and down in flapping motion by rods attached between his ankles and one end of each wing. Two pairs of hinged surfaces on a pole make up each wing, these surfaces spreading during the downward motion and folding during the upward.

1680

The Italian Giovanni Borelli outlines his theories of why man cannot achieve flight without mechanical aid in a book entitled *De Motu Animalium*.

1687

M. de la Loubères visits Siam and mentions in a history 'an ingenious athlete who exceedingly diverted the King and his Court by leaping from a height and supporting himself in the air by two umbrellas, the handles of which were affixed to his girdle.'

c.17th Century

Hezarfen Celebi of Turkey attempts to fly from a tower in Galata. He is said to have glided some distance.

1709

August 8 Father Bartolomeu de Gusmão demonstrates a small model hot-air balloon in the Ambassador's drawing room at the Casa da India, Lisbon, to King John V of Portugal and other dignitaries. The balloon lifts to a height of 3.5m (12ft) before being destroyed to prevent it setting the curtains on fire. He later constructs a model glider.

1742

The Marquis de Bacqueville attempts to fly across the river Seine from the roof of a Paris hotel using multi-wings. Some gliding flight is achieved.

1754

Russian Michael Vasilyevitch Lomonosov flies a model helicopter powered by clockwork.

1763

July Melchior Bauer of Germany designs a heavier-than-air aircraft intended as a military bomber. His aircraft is named *Sky Wagon* and is intended to carry a pilot plus approximately 45kg (100lb) of weapons. Power is provided by the pilot flapping two wings, while the main fixed wing is a lightweight structure of silk-covered pinewood with brass wire strengthening. Expected to be constructed on a mountain top, for the convenience of flight testing, it is probably never built.

1766

Henry Cavendish isolates hydrogen and refers to it as Phlogiston. He informs the Royal Society that Phlogiston is much lighter than atmospheric air.

1772

Canon Desfarges constructs an ornithopter, but this proves unsuccessful.

1780

Hyder Ali of Mysore, India, repels British forces at Guntur with iron-cased artillery rockets.

Brother Cypian, an east-European monk, claims to have achieved gliding flight from a mountain.

1781

In Austria, Karl Friedrich Meerwein designs and builds an advanced form of glider, for which a proper area of wing has been calculated for manned flight. It is said to have flown on at least two occasions. Some propulsion is claimed by an up-and-down movement of the oval wing.

1782

The French Montgolfier brothers demonstrate a model hot-air balloon.

1783

Frenchman Sebastien le Normand jumps from the height of a first storey at Montpellier grasping a 76cm (30in) diameter parachute.

April 25 A full-size but unmanned Montgolfier hot-air balloon rises to an altitude of about 300m (1,000ft).

June 4 The Montgolfier brothers demonstrate in public at Annonay a small hot-air balloon of 11m (36ft) diameter.

August 27 Jacques Alexandre César Charles releases a 3.5m (12ft) diameter unmanned hydrogen balloon from Champ-de-Mars, Paris, which makes a 45 minute flight to Gonesse. On landing it is attacked and destroyed by villagers who believe it to be a monster, the evil smell coming from its punctured envelope adding credence to this theory.

September 19 A sheep, cock and duck ascend in a 13m (41ft) Montgolfier hot-air balloon at the Court of Versailles. It comes to rest 3.2km (2 miles) away in the Forest of Vaucresson.

October 15 François Pilâtre de Rozier ascends in a tethered Montgolfier hot-air balloon to become the first aeronaut. He rises to an altitude of about 25 metres (82ft).

November 21 François Pilâtre de Rozier and the Marquis d'Arlandes make the first free flight by balloon

Charles and Robert ascend in a hydrogen balloon, December 1 1783. (*Science Museum, London*)

(Montgolfier), from the Château la Muette to the Butte-aux-Cailles, remaining airborne for 25 minutes. They become the world's first pilot and passenger and the first men to make a journey by air.

December 1 Jacques Alexandre César Charles and M. Robert become the first men to make a free flight in a hydrogen balloon, flying 43km (27 miles) from Les Tuileries, Paris, to Nesles.

1784
Frenchman Lt Jean-Baptiste Marie Meusnier shows his design for a dirigible.

A Frenchman named Gérard designs and builds an ornithopter with a gunpowder engine to drive the wings. Flight is not achieved.

February 4 Irishman Riddick releases an unmanned hot-air balloon from the Rotunda Gardens, Dublin.

February 25 The first balloon ascent (Montgolfier) is made in Italy by the Chevalier Paolo Andreani, Charles Gerli and Augustin Gerli.

April 15 Irishman Rosseau and a small boy make a flight in a balloon lasting two hours. This is the first manned flight in Ireland.

April 28 Frenchmen Launoy and Bienvenu demonstrate the first known self-propelled model helicopter. It uses a two-blade propeller at each end of a stick, powered by a bowdrill system. (q.v. 1796)

May 20 Marchioness de Montalembert and three others became the first women to fly, ascending from the Faubourg-Saint-Antoine, Paris, in a tethered Montgolfier hot-air balloon.

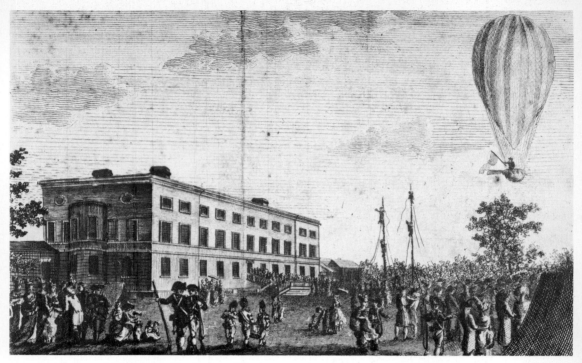

June 4   Madame Thible makes the first free flight by a woman in a hot-air balloon, from Lyon, France.

August 25   James Tytler makes a flight at Edinburgh in a Montgolfier-type hot-air balloon. Tytler had previously flown on the 7th from the Comely Gardens, Edinburgh.

September 15   The first journey of significance in a hydrogen balloon is made by Vincenzo Lunardi of Lucca, who makes a flight in England from the Honourable Artillery Company's Moorfields ground to Standon Green End, Hertfordshire.

October 4   James Sadler becomes the first English aeronaut, going aloft in a Montgolfier-type hot-air balloon in Oxford.

October 16   Jean-Pierre Blanchard attempts to propel his balloon by hand-turning a six-blade propeller fitted to the basket.

1785

January 7   Jean-Pierre Blanchard and American Dr John Jeffries fly across the English Channel in a hydrogen balloon from Dover, England, to Forêt de Felmores, France, the journey taking about two and a half hours.

January 19   Irishman Richard Crosbie attempts the first aerial crossing of the Irish Sea by hydrogen balloon. But, once airborne, he decides that a night crossing might be too dangerous and lands again.

May 12   A second attempt by Richard Crosbie to cross the Irish Sea fails when the hydrogen balloon proves to be insufficient to lift him. A volunteer from the onlookers, Richard McGwire, takes his place (as a lighter man) but alights in the sea some ten miles from Howth.

June 15   François Pilâtre de Rozier and Jules Romain are killed while trying to fly across the English Channel in a composite hot-air and hydrogen balloon.

July 19   Richard Crosbie makes a third attempt at an aerial crossing of the Irish Sea. His journey is full of event and he is eventually rescued by the barge *Captain Walmitt* as he heads away from the Welsh Coast during a storm.

1785-89

Jean-Pierre Blanchard undertakes balloon flights throughout Europe, including first flights in Belgium, Germany and Switzerland.

1790

French chemist Lavoisier refers to Cavendish's 'inflammable air' as hydrogen.

1791

August 2   Blanchard drops animals by parachute from a balloon flying over Vienna.

1793

Blanchard makes a parachute descent at Basle but breaks a leg. This followed an earlier experiment in which he released a dog from a balloon flying at a height of 1,830m (6,000ft) over Strasbourg. The dog landed without injury. (q.v. August 2, 1791)

January 9   Blanchard makes the first balloon ascent in the United States of America, flying in a hydrogen balloon from the Walnut Street Prison, Philadelphia, to

Gloucester County, New Jersey. The journey lasts 46 minutes.

1794

June 26   Captain Coutelle of the French Republican Army ascends in a tethered hydrogen balloon at Maubeuge, Belgium, during the Battle of Fleurus. The balloon, named *Entreprenant*, is the first balloon used in war.

1796

George Cayley builds a bowdrill-powered model helicopter similar to that of Launoy and Bienvenu in France. It uses four-blade rotors made from bird's feathers.

1797

October 22   André Jacques Garnerin makes the first parachute jump from a balloon at considerable height (about 900m; 3,000ft). Garnerin eventually loses his life during a descent in France. (q.v. September 21, 1802)

1798

November 10   Madamoiselle Labrosse and Madamoiselle Henry ascend in a balloon at Paris. Madamoiselle Labrosse later becomes Madame Garnerin.

1799

George Cayley produces the first known design for an aeroplane incorporating fixed wings, a cruciform tail unit, and a propulsion system (paddles). The design is engraved on a silver disc.

British forces again face a rocket barrage in India, this time from Tipu Sultan.

Napoleon orders disbandment of the two French balloon companies.

1802

September 21   André Jacques Garnerin makes the first parachute descent in England, but is injured when one of the straps attaching the parachute to the basket gives way.

1804

George (later Sir George) Cayley constructs his first monoplane model glider. It incorporates such modern features as a monoplane wing of large area, mounted about a third of the way along the single-rod fuselage, and small cruciform horizontal and vertical tail surfaces.

1805

British Colonel William Congreve first tests his developed artillery rocket at the Royal Laboratory, Woolwich.

1806

October 8   The Royal Navy fleet sailing for Boulogne during the Napoleonic war includes 24 ships carrying Congreve rockets. These rockets do great damage to Boulogne and French naval vessels.

1807

Some 25,000 Congreve rockets are fired against Copenhagen by the Royal Navy, each with a range of up to 3.2km (2 miles).

1808

July 24   R. Jordarki Kuparanto becomes the first man to bale out of a damaged aircraft with a parachute, when his Montgolfier hot-air balloon catches fire over Warsaw.

1809

George Cayley completes his first full-size glider and flies it without a pilot.

Jacob Degen of Switzerland makes hop flights using an ornithopter fitted with a fairly small hydrogen balloon for extra lift. By itself the ornithopter would be unsuccessful.

March 7   Jean-Pierre Blanchard dies of a heart attack while aloft in a balloon.

1811

German Albrecht Berblinger attempts to fly across the River Danube using an ornithopter based on a design by Jacob Degen. His attempt is unsuccessful.

1812

October 1   James Sadler attempts to make the first air crossing of the Irish Sea. He leaves Dublin in a hydrogen balloon and successfully flies to Anglesey, but is blown out to sea again. He is later rescued. (q.v. July 22, 1817)

1815

A Rocket Brigade of the British Army is used during the Battle of Waterloo.

September   Eliza Garnerin, André Jacques Garnerin's niece, ascends in a balloon at Paris and then makes the first parachute descent by a woman.

1816

Jacob Degen builds a clockwork model helicopter with contra-rotating rotors.

James Sadler as engraved for the Dublin Magazine. (*National Library of Ireland*)

THE PENNY MECHANIC,
AND THE CHEMIST.

No XL.]   SATURDAY, JULY 29, 1837.   [Vol 1.

MR. COCKING'S PARACHUTE.

Robert Cocking about to attempt a parachute descent from the *Great Nassau Balloon,* **July 24 1837.** (*Science Museum, London*)

1817
July 22 Windham Sadler, son of James Sadler, makes the first aerial crossing of the Irish Sea, flying in a balloon from Portobello Barracks to Holyhead, Wales.

1819
July 7 Madame Blanchard becomes the first woman to die in a flying accident when her hydrogen balloon catches fire during a firework party in Paris.

August 2 Charles Guille makes the first parachute jump from a balloon in the USA, descending from a height of 2,440m (8,000ft) over New Bushwick, Long Island, NY.

1825
A school teacher from Bristol, England, named George Pocock is said to have lifted his daughter Martha off the ground using a kite designed by himself.

1827
George Pocock demonstrates the effectiveness of his kites by tying one to a carriage. With this arrangement Pocock is pulled from Bristol to Marlborough at speed.

1828
Englishman Mayer builds a full-size man-powered helicopter. It is unsuccessful.

Italian Vittorio Sarti designs a helicopter with contra-rotating blades.

1832
May 14 Probably the first aeronaut to reach a century of flights is Charles Green, who on this day takes off for his 100th flight from the Mermaid Tavern, Hackney, England.

1836
August The *Royal Vauxhall Balloon*, sometimes referred to as the *Nassau*, is flown for the first time.

November 7-8 Charles Green, Robert Holland and Monck Mason ascend from Vauxhall Gardens, London, in the balloon *Royal Vauxhall Balloon* and travel 772km (480 miles) to a location close to Weilberg, Duchy of Nassau.

1837
July 24 Briton Robert Cocking attempts to make a descent from the *Great Nassau Balloon* using a parachute of his own design. Its main feature is the new canopy, which is turned upside down in order to prevent the oscillations of earlier parachutes. At an altitude of about 2,000m (6,600ft) the parachute is released from under the balloon. After steady descent the upper rim of the parachute collapses and Cocking is killed.

1842
Englishman W.H. Phillips builds a powered model helicopter which flies. It is powered by a steam pressure-jet system through the rotor-tips.

1843
Englishman William Samuel Henson patents the design of his passenger-carrying steam-powered aeroplane known successively as the *Aerial Steam Carriage* and the *Ariel.*

Henson's *Ariel,* **1843.** (*Science Museum, London*)

Henri Giffard makes the first powered flight in a dirigible, September 24 1852. (*Science Museum, London*)

Englishman Bourne flies a model helicopter powered by springs.

1847

Henson's 6.10m (20ft) – span model of the *Aerial Steam Carriage*, driven by a steam engine, is built. During flight trials, a launching ramp is eventually used to help gather speed prior to take off, but the carriage is incapable of sustaining flight.

Cayley's sketch of his boy-carrying aeroplane, drawn in 1853. (*Science Museum, London*)

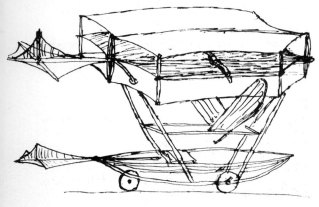

1849

A young boy makes a tethered flight in a glider designed and constructed by Sir George Cayley, to become the first person to fly in a heavier-than-air aircraft.

August 22 Austrian pilotless hot-air balloons are launched against defending forces in Venice. Each balloon carries a light bomb and fuse.

October 7 M.F. Farban makes the first balloon flight over the Alps, travelling from Marseille to Turin.

1852

September 24 Henri Giffard makes the first powered flight in a dirigible, flying from the Hippodrome in Paris to Trappes (a distance of about 27km; 17 miles). Power is provided by a 2.24kW (3hp) steam engine driving a large three-blade propeller.

1853

June Sir George Cayley's coachman flies in a Cayley glider at Brompton Hall, Scarborough, England.

1854

June 27 Frenchman Louis Charles Letur is fatally injured in a parachuting accident in England. He had previously made several successful descents in his controllable parachute.

1856

Frenchman L.P. Mouillard, author of *L'Empire de l'Air*, attempts to fly a model glider. It is unsuccessful. Other model gliders follow, but are equally unsuccessful.

Viscount Carlingford tests his full-size aeroplane (later expected to make a powered flight) in Ireland as an unmanned glider. Development ends before a powered flight is attempted.

1857
J.M. le Bris completes a short free flight in a glider launched from a moving horse-drawn cart.

December 15 Sir George Cayley, the so-called 'father' of heavier-than-air aviation, dies.

1857-8
Félix du Temple de la Croix flies a model aeroplane powered by a clockwork and later a steam, engine. (q.v. 1874)

1858
Frenchman Félix Tournachon (Nadar) takes the earliest known aerial photograph, depicting part of Paris, from a tethered balloon.

March 29 The first ascent by a hydrogen balloon in Australia is made from the Cremorne Gardens, Melbourne.

1859
July 2 John Wise, O. Gager and John La Mountain fly 1,800km (1,120 miles) from St Louis, Missouri, to Henderson, New York, USA, in a hydrogen balloon. (q.v. 1873)

E. Cordner flies a man-carrying sea rescue kite in Ireland.

1860
Frenchman Etienne Lenoir invents the gas engine.

1861
June 18 American Thaddeus Sobieski Constantine Lowe pilots the balloon *Enterprise*, from which the first aerial telegraph message is transmitted.

October 1 The American Army Balloon Corps is formed, comprising five balloons and fifty men.

November *G.W. Parke Custis*, a converted coal barge, becomes the world's first operational aircraft carrier (carrying balloons) when it enters service with General McClellan's Army of the Potomac during the American Civil War.

1862
May 31 – June 1 The hydrogen balloon *Intrepid* is used for observation duties during the Battle of Fair Oaks in the American Civil War.

December 11 A balloon of the American Army Balloon Corps is used during the crossing of the river Rappahannock.

1863
Ponton d'Amécourt tests unsuccessfully a model helicopter. Power is provided by a steam engine, driving two two-blade rotors.

Hydrogen balloon *Intrepid***, 1862. (***US National Archives***)**

April 30 – May 5 The battle of Chancellorsville is fought during the American Civil War, with balloons being used for observation and artillery direction.

The American Balloon Corps is disbanded.

1864-70
Manned balloons are first used in a South American war when forces from Argentina, Brazil and Uruguay go to war against Paraguay. The joint air operations are made by the Brazilian Marquis de Caxias.

1865
Frenchman Charles de Louvrie produces the first design for a jet-propelled aeroplane (the *Aéronave*). This uses a canopy-type wing above a four-wheel cart supporting the motor.

1865-72
Austrian Paul Hänlein produces a gas-driven internal combustion engine with four horizontally-opposed cylinders, intended for motive power.

1866
January 12 The Aeronautical Society of Great Britain is founded. (q.v. June 25, 1918)

1867

Englishmen J.W. Butler and E. Edwards patent the design of a delta-winged powered aeroplane.

1868

June The Aeronautical Society of Great Britain holds the first aeronautical exhibition at the Crystal Palace, England.

1870

Gustave Trouvé flies successfully a model ornithopter which uses revolver parts to beat the wings up and down.

The Prussian Army forms two Luftschiffer detachments to operate lighter-than-air craft during the Franco-Prussian war. These are organised by Englishman Henry Coxwell, but soon disband.

September 23 Jules Duroug ascends from Paris in a hastily made balloon following the surrounding of the city by the Prussian Army during the Franco-Prussian War. Construction of balloons continues, and by January 28 1871 some 66 balloon flights have been made, carrying 155 persons, nearly 3 million letters and other cargo out of Paris.

1870-76

During 1870-71 Alphonse Pénaud demonstrates several model helicopters with rotors driven by twisted rubber. He also flies a model aeroplane with built-in stability. In 1876 he also designs the first amphibian, becoming second only to Sir George Cayley in early aeronautics.

1871

In Britain, Francis H. Wenham and John Browning build the first wind tunnel.

Frenchman Charles Renard flies a multi-wing model glider. It features movable winglets for stability in flight.

1872

Austrian Paul Hänlein demonstrates his 50m-long dirigible with a number of tethered flights. Power is provided by a single 3.7kW (5hp) Lenoir engine, fuelled by hydrogen from the envelope.

1873

John Wise pilots a very large hydrogen balloon on the start of the first attempted transatlantic air crossing. Financed by the *New York Daily Graphic*, the balloon crashes after only 66km (41 miles) has been flown.

1874

French Navy officer Félix du Temple de la Croix makes a 'hop' flight at Brest in his bird-like aeroplane, having used a ramp to gather pace.

1875

Thomas Moy's unmanned powered aeroplane *Aerial Steamer* lifts itself off the ground at the Crystal Palace, England.

1876

Nikolaus Otto of Germany patents a four-stroke cycle gas-fuelled engine. (q.v. 1877).

American J.B. Ward designs a helicopter-cum-hovercraft.

1877

Nikolaus Otto invents the four-stroke petrol-fuelled internal combustion engine. Director of the Otto engine factory is Gottlieb Daimler who, in 1884, designs the first petrol-fuelled internal combustion engine to be put to practical use. A single-cylinder engine, it is used by Karl-Friedrich Benz to power the first motorcycle proper of 1885.

The French Établissement Aérostatique Militaire is set up at Meudon.

1878

The first British government funding of aircraft takes place with the allocation of £150 for the construction of a hydrogen balloon. The resulting coal-gas balloon costs £71 and is named *Pioneer*.

1879

In France, Victor Tatin flies a model aeroplane powered by a compressed air motor. It is of advanced concept, with monoplane wings, a tailplane and two four-blade tractor-mounted propellers.

The dirigible hangar completed at Chalais-Meudon for an exhibition of 1878 is officially taken over as hangar Y. The French State Airship Factory is operated at Chalais-Meudon from the 1880s until 1940.

July 31 The first ascent of a hydrogen balloon in Canada takes place at Montreal.

1880

June 1 Russian Alexander Fedorovich Mozhaiski patents his original 'flying machine' powered by a steam engine. (q.v. 1884 and March 1890)

Dr Karl Wölfert and Herr Baumgarten of Germany ascend in a dirigible fitted with a small engine. Poor load distribution causes it to crash. Baumgarten leaves the project.

June 24 A balloon detachment of the British Army takes part in manoeuvres at Aldershot.

1882

March 5 Dr Karl Wölfert of Germany tries to propel an airship with a hand-turned propeller at Charlottenburg. The attempt is unsuccessful.

1883

October 8 Frenchman Gaston Tissandier becomes the first to fit an electric motor (Siemens) to an airship, powered by 24 bichromate of potash batteries.

The School of Ballooning is founded at Chatham, Kent, England.

1884

Alexander Fedorovich Mozhaiski completes his 14m (46ft)-chord steam-engined monoplane. Piloted by I. Golubev, it makes a 'hop' flight after a ramp launch.

August 9 Capt Charles Renard and Lt Arthur Krebs, French Corps of Engineers, fly the dirigible *La France* from and back to Chalais-Meudon, the journey taking 23 minutes and covering 8km (5 miles). *La France*, powered by a 6.7kW (9hp) Gramme electric motor, thus becomes the first fully controllable dirigible to fly.

November 26 A balloon detachment of the British Army leaves Britain to accompany the infantry to Cape Town during the expedition to Bechuanaland. It arrives on December 19.

1885
February 15 A balloon detachment of the British Army leaves Britain to accompany the infantry as part of the expeditionary force to the Sudan.

The Prussian Airship Arm is made into a permanent air arm with the founding of the Preussische Luftschiffer-Abteilung. Based at Berlin-Schöneberg, it operates tethered and kite balloons for four years.

1888
August 12 Dr Wölfert flies a balloon fitted with a 1.5kW (2hp) Daimler petrol engine at Seelberg, Germany.

1889
German engineer Otto Lilienthal has *Der Vogelflug als Grundlage der Fliegekunst* (The Flight of Birds as the Basis of the Art of Flying) published.

Percival Spencer makes a parachute jump from a balloon at Clonturk Park, Drumcondra. This marks the first parachute descent in Ireland.

1890
Königliche Bayerische Luftschiffer-Abteilung is formed as a separate force to Preussische Luftschiffer-Abteilung, remaining active until 1919.

May The Balloon Section of the Royal Engineers is formed as part of the British Army.

Model of Ader's *Eole* showing the steam engine and wing mechanism, October 9 1890. (*Science Museum, London*)

October 9 Frenchman Clément Ader makes the world's first powered 'hop' from level ground in his bat-like steam-powered *Eole* monoplane at Château Pereire, Armainvilliers. A distance of about 50m (165ft) is covered.

1891
Sir Hiram Maxim begins fabrication of components for his huge 371.61m² (4,000 sq ft) wing area test-rig bi-plane.

American physicist Samuel Pierpont Langley begins designing and building model aeroplanes with steam engines. Each is later launched from a catapult mounted on the roof of a houseboat on the Potomac River, Washington, D.C. The aeroplanes are known under the collective name *Aerodrome*. (q.v. 1896).

The Balloon School and Factory, supporting the Balloon Section of the Royal Engineers, is moved to a new location at Farnborough, Hants, England.

1892
Austria's first air section is formed as the K.u.K. Militäräronautische Anstalt.

February 3 The French Minister of War contracts Clément Ader to build and supply a military aeroplane. It has to be a two-seater capable of carrying 75kg (165lb) of bombs.

May A balloon factory is founded at Aldershot, England.

1893

Australian Lawrence Hargrave originates the box-kite structure.

Horatio Phillips is said to have flown (unmanned) an early *Multiplane* aeroplane at Harrow, England. A 33kg (72lb) weight represented the pilot.

1894

French born American railroad engineer Octave Chanute has *Progress in Flying Machines* published.

August von Parseval and Premierleutnant Bartsch von Sigfeld demonstrate the first German kite balloons.

Czesław Tański flies a model aeroplane. This is the first successful Polish heavier-than-air aircraft. From 1896 he flight tests various full-size hang gliders.

Count Ferdinand von Zeppelin's first passenger-carrying airship design is rejected by the German government's technical commission.

July 31 Sir Hiram Maxim's huge biplane test rig, powered by two 134kW (180hp) steam engines and with 371.61m² (4,000 sq ft) of wing area, lifts off the ground during a test run. The 'flight' is restricted to a height of about 0.61m (2ft) by restraining guard rails positioned above the launching rails. One guard rail is smashed by the impact of the lifting biplane.

1895

British marine engineer Percy S. Pilcher completes his *Bat* monoplane glider. The *Bat* is subsequently fitted with a tail unit following his visit to Germany at the invitation of Otto Lilienthal.

Count Ferdinand von Zeppelin is granted the first patent for his method of rigid airship construction.

Otto Lilienthal with his 1895 glider. (*Science Museum, London*)

Irishman Professor George Francis Fitzgerald attempts to fly using towed gliders. His experiments are unsuccessful despite the modern appearance of his aircraft, which look similar to those flown successfully by Lilienthal in Germany.

1896

The last of Percy Pilcher's four gliders is completed as the *Hawk*. This has a twin-wheel forward landing gear with shock absorbers. *Hawk* proves very successful.

The Spanish Servicio Militar de Aerostación is formed.

Count Ferdinand von Zeppelin raises 800,000 Reichsmarks for the 'Joint Stock Company for Promotion of Airship Flight'.

Octave Chanute begins designing and constructing gliders, eventually producing the classic constant-chord biplane configuration.

May 6 American Samuel Pierpoint Langley flies the first model *Aerodrome* from a houseboat on the Potomac River. This model is steam-powered.

August 10 Otto Lilienthal dies of his injuries, caused by a crash in one of his gliders on the Rhinower Hills the previous day. Since 1891 Lilienthal had flown two biplane and five monoplane gliders with outstanding success.

1897

June 14 The first deaths in a dirigible accident are recorded, when Wölfert and his mechanic Herr Knabe are killed in Germany. The engine vaporiser on *Deutschland* sets fire to the dirigible's envelope, causing the gas to explode.

July 11 Salomon August Andrée, Nils Strindberg and Knut Fraenkel of Sweden start off from Danes Island, Spitzbergen, on the first attempt to fly over the North Pole by balloon. The attempt ends three days later when the balloon descends and all three men die. (q.v. August 6, 1930)

Professor George Francis Fitzgerald attempting to fly at College Park, Dublin, 1895. (*Aer Lingus*)

Percy Pilcher flying the *Hawk*, 1896. (*Science Museum, London*)

August 12-14 Clément Ader makes two attempts to fly his new *Avion III* aeroplane, basically a twin-engined *Éole*. No flight is achieved.

October 14 Clément Ader's military aeroplane attempts a flight at Satorg, France, but crashes. Official backing is withdrawn.

November 3 The German Schwartz *Metallballon* all-metal airship makes its first and last flight, piloted by a soldier.

1898

A carved wooden bird dating from the 3rd or 4th century BC is found in Egypt. This has many features of a model glider, including a thin and tapering body, straight wings and a horizontal tail.

Russian Konstantin E. Tsiolkovsky puts forward the concept of using liquid hydrogen and oxygen as rocket fuels.

Brazilian Alberto Santos-Dumont moves to Paris. (q.v. October 19, 1901 and September 13, 1906).

The Aéro Club de France is established.

Langley receives a $50,000 subsidy from the US government to continue his experiments with *Aerodromes*, but now in full-size form.

1899

August The brothers Orville and Wilbur Wright, bicycle makers, use a 1.5m (5ft)-span biplane kite to test control by wing warping.

Cody man-lifting kite, 1899.

American-born Samuel Franklin Cody begins his experiments with man-lifting kites.

Work begins on an airship hangar for Count von Zeppelin, which will be anchored on Lake Constance and resting on 95 floats.

September 30 Percy Pilcher crashes at the home of Lord Braye at Market Harborough, when a bamboo strut in the tail unit of *Hawk* breaks while airborne. He dies two days later, the first Briton to die in a heavier-than-air aircraft accident.

1900
The Wright brothers produce their No.1 glider. This biplane is successful but is considered to have too little span.

Three Balloon Sections of the Royal Engineers are operated in South Africa during the Boer War.

July 2 Count Ferdinand von Zeppelin takes up five other people on the initial flight of his first airship LZ 1. The flight, from the airship's floating hangar on Lake Constance, lasts about 20 minutes.

1901
The Wright brothers produce their No.2 glider, with a new wing aerofoil and greater span. Tests at Kill Devil Hills prove disappointing.

Austrian Wilhelm Kress begins trials with his tandem triplane-winged seaplane. It eventually achieves the first 'hop' from water before capsizing.

June Langley flies a petrol-engined quarter-scale model of his projected full-size *Aerodrome*. This is the first aeroplane with a petrol engine to achieve level flight. It flies three times in June. (q.v. August 8, 1903)

August 14 Gustav Whitehead, a Bavarian who had emigrated to the USA, reportedly flies an aeroplane of his own design at Bridgeport, Connecticut. The aeroplane, with one engine to drive the wheels of the landing gear and the other to power the propellers, makes a flight of approximately 270m (880ft) at an altitude of 15m (50ft). It lands safely, having navigated around trees in the flight path. This powered and sustained flight is not recognised officially as the first powered flight, possibly through lack of publicity. A second flight is achieved the same day.

October 19 Brazilian Alberto Santos-Dumont wins a cash prize by flying his No.6 airship round the Eiffel Tower.

October 29 The Aero Club is established in Britain. (q.v. February 15, 1910)

1902
January 17 Gustav Whitehead reportedly flies the world's first flying-boat, covering a circular distance of approximately 11km (7 miles) and alighting on water. Produced from components stripped from his earlier landplane (q.v. August 14, 1901), it uses two engines and is fully-controllable. This flight, and those that follow, are not recognised officially, possibly through lack of publicity.

September – October The Wright brothers flight test their No.3 glider, the design of which has been based

Langley's full-size *Aerodrome* drops into the river, October 7 1903. (*Smithsonian Institution*)

not on previously published material but on original research of their own. During these months No.3 is flown on nearly 1,000 occasions and proves very successful.

1903

March 23 The Wright brothers file a patent for an aeroplane based on the No.3 glider.

August 8 Langley flies his petrol-engined quarter-scale *Aerodrome* fully successfully for the first time. (q.v. June 1901).

August 18 German Carl Jatho 'hops' his aeroplane for a distance of 18m (59ft). It is powered by a 6.7kW (9hp) petrol engine.

October 7 Langley's full-size *Aerodrome*, piloted by Charles M. Manly (creator of the 39kW/52hp Manly-Balzer petrol engine that powers the aircraft) attempts a flight from the houseboat launcher. The *Aerodrome* fouls the launcher and drops into the river below.

November 12 The Lebaudy brothers fly their airship between Moisson and Champ-de-Mars, a distance of 60km (37 miles).

The Wrights achieve real flight, December 17 1903.

December 8 The second attempted launch of the *Aerodrome* takes place, again with Manly at the controls. Its rear wing fouls the launcher and the *Aerodrome* is badly damaged as it falls tail-first into the river. Official support for the project is withdrawn.

December 14 Wilbur Wright fails in his attempt to make a sustained flight with the *Flyer*, and the aircraft is slightly damaged.

December 17 At 10.35 am at Kill Devil Hills, Kitty Hawk, North Carolina, Orville Wright pilots the Wright *Flyer* on a 36.5m (120ft) flight lasting twelve seconds, achieving the world's first manned, powered, sustained and controlled flight by a heavier-than-air aircraft. Three further flights are made, the longest lasting nearly a minute.

1904

German Christian Hülsmeyer patents a design for a radar instrument.

Frenchman Robert Esnault-Pelterie flies a glider with ailerons for control. This is the first full-scale aeroplane to feature this innovation. He later becomes famous for his REP powered monoplanes, the most important of which is the REP 2 *bis* (flown in 1909).

May 26 The Wright brothers make the first of 105 flights with *Flyer No II*.

September 20 Wilbur Wright makes the first ever circuit flight in an aeroplane.

November 9 Wilbur Wright flies 4.43km (2.75 miles) at Dayton, recording the first aeroplane flight of more than five minutes.

1905

January 18 Initial discussions for the purchase of an aeroplane are conducted between the Wright brothers and the US government. (q.v. December 23, 1907)

April 29 American Daniel Maloney makes the first glider flight from a tethered balloon. The glider was designed by John Montgomery. Maloney is killed in a similar flight on July 18.

June 6 Gabriel Voisin lifts off the River Seine in his 'boxkite' glider, which is towed by a motorboat.

June 23 The first flight of the Wright *Flyer III* is made, the first practical version of the *Flyer*. It is fully controllable.

October 5 Wilbur Wright pilots the *Flyer No III* during a flight covering nearly 39km (24.2 miles) and lasting 38 minutes.

October 14 The FAI (Fédération Aéronautique International) is established in France.

October 16 The Wright brothers make their last flight for nearly three years. (q.v. May 6, 1908)

Santos Dumont 14-bis during tethered trials. (Musée de l'Air)

November 30 An attempt to launch Zeppelin LZ 2 from Lake Constance results in damage to the airship before flight is achieved

The Aero Club of America is founded.

1906

Harry Harper of the *Daily Mail* is made the first full-time air correspondent of a newspaper anywhere in the world.

January 17 Zeppelin LZ 2 is launched successfully but has to land at Kisslegg due to fuel system problems.

January 18 LZ 2 is destroyed in a gale while moored at Kisslegg.

February 27 Samuel Pierpoint Langley dies at Aiken, South Carolina.

March 18 Romanian Trajan Vuia hops his No 1 monoplane for the first time. It features a tractor-mounted engine, variable-incidence wing and an undercarriage with pneumatic tyres.

July 7 The first officially-recognised balloon race in Britain begins at Barns Elms, London.

August 11 Mrs C.J. Miller becomes the first American woman passenger in a dirigible.

August 16 Jacob C.H. Ellehammer of Denmark hops his semi-biplane for the first time.

Phillips *Multiplane*, 1907.

September 12   Ellehammer makes a tethered hop of about 43m (140ft) in his semi-biplane, which is powered by a 15kW (20hp) engine of his own design (q.v. June 28, 1908)

September 13   Santos-Dumont's 14-*bis* biplane 'hops' for a distance of 7m (23ft).

September 30   The first international balloon race starts at Les Tuileries, Paris, and 16 entrants compete for the Gordon Bennett Trophy. It is won by Lt Frank P. Lahm, US Army, who flies the balloon *United States* 647km (402 miles) to Fylingdales Moor, England.

October 9   Zeppelin LZ 3 flies. It subsequently becomes the first military Zeppelin as the Army Z1 (q.v. November 7, 1908 and June 20, 1909)

October 23   Alberto Santos-Dumont flies his biplane 14-*bis* nearly 60m (197ft) to win the 3,000-franc Archdeacon Prize for a flight of more than 25m (82ft).

November 12   Alberto Santos-Dumont makes the first officially recognised sustained flight by a piloted and powered aeroplane in Europe, flying his tail-first biplane 14-*bis* 220m (722ft) in just over 21 seconds. This becomes the first internationally-ratified world distance record for aeroplanes.

1907

Horatio Phillips flies his *Multiplane* aircraft for about 152m (500ft) at Streatham. Although this is the first flight of a piloted and powered aeroplane in Great Britain, it is not officially accredited as such. The *Multiplane* has more than 160 very narrow-chord wings.

The Séguin brothers in France begin their development work on the Gnome rotary aero engine.

Hugo Junkers in Germany patents his original 'opposite piston' diesel-type engine, the start of a long line of diesel engines as motive power.

March 16 – April 13   The French brothers Charles and Gabriel Voisin produce a biplane for Léon Delagrange, which performs six flights at Bagatelle between these dates, the best of 60m (197ft). The Voisin-Delagrange No1 is destroyed on November 3, following a period as a floatplane.

April 5   Louis Blériot makes a brief flight in his tail-first pusher-engined Type V monoplane.

April 6   The *Daily Mail* newspaper sponsors a model aircraft exhibition at the Agricultural Hall, London. The best flying models are taken for a 'fly off' competition at Alexandra Palace. This is won by Alliott Verdon Roe, who wins a reduced prize of £75. With this Roe partly finances his first full-size aeroplane. This is the first of many *Daily Mail* newspaper prizes for air achievements. (q.v. June 8, 1908)

A. V. Roe with his model aeroplane at Alexandra Palace, photographed by Samuel Cody, April 6 1907. (*Fitz-Cowley*)

July 11 Louis Blériot's tandem-wing Type VI *Libellule* flies about 25m (80ft). It features the first cantilever wings to be tested and wingtip-type ailerons. During July and August it makes eleven take-offs, six of the flights covering distances of more than 100m (328ft).

August 1 The Aeronautical Division, US Signal Corps, is formed.

September 10 The British Army Dirigible No 1 *Nulli Secundus* flies for the first time at Farnborough.

September 29 The Bréguet-Richet helicopter lifts into the air at Douai, France, but has to be steadied by ground crew with poles. Power comes from a 37kW (50hp) Antoinette engine.

September 30 The first flight takes place of the Voisin-Farman I biplane. Between this date and November 23 this aircraft performs about twenty flights at Issy-les-Moulineaux, the one on November 9 of 1,030m (3,379ft) and lasting 1min 14sec.(q.v. January 13, 1908)

October 1 Dr Alexander Graham Bell, in the USA, heads the newly formed Aerial Experiment Association. Members include Glenn Curtiss and Lieut Thomas Selfridge. (q.v. September 17, 1908)

October 10 *Nulli Secundus* has to be split at its temporary mooring at Crystal Palace, to prevent it tearing away in the wind. It later emerges as *Nulli Secundus II*.

Nulli Secundus, September 10 1907. (*Science Museum, London*)

Bréguet-Richet helicopter, September 29 1907.

October 12-13 A.F. Gaudron and two crew members make the first crossing of the North Sea by air in the *Mammoth* hydrogen balloon, travelling about 1,160km (721 miles) from Crystal Palace, England, to Lake Vänern, Sweden.

October 26 Henry Farman sets an officially recognised distance record in the Voisin-Farman I, of 771m (2,530ft).

November 10 Louis Blériot makes a first flight in his Type VII monoplane. This is the ancestor of the modern tractor monoplane, and is followed by the Type VIII and eventually the highly-successful Type XI.

November 13 Paul Cornu makes the first free flight in a helicopter at Lisieux, France. This twin rotor machine is powered by an 18kW (24hp) Antoinette engine. The flight lasts 20 seconds, at a height of 0.30m (1ft).

Henry Farman inspecting his Voisin Farman I, 1907.

Gnome rotary engine, 1908. (Lent to *Science Museum, London*)

November 16 The Frenchman Robert Esnault-Pelterie flies 600m (1,968ft) in his R.E.P.1 monoplane.

November 30 Glenn Curtiss forms the first aeroplane company in the United States of America.

December 3 The *Cygnet I*, Dr Alexander Graham Bell's extraordinary tetrahedral-cell 'aerodrome' kite, is first flight tested. It is towed by a motorboat.

December 6 Dr Alexander Graham Bell's tetrahedral kite is towed for a second time, but is wrecked. Its pilot, Lt Selfridge, is unhurt.

December 23 Brigadier-General James Allen, Chief Signal Officer, US Army, produces the first specification for a military aeroplane. Tenders are requested. This is the first specification for a military aeroplane issued for commercial tender, but not the first official military aeroplane specification. (q.v. February 3, 1892)

1908

The Lebaudy dirigible *République* is the first to be used by the French Army on manoeuvres.

The Brazilian Army Balloon Corps is formed.

The first Gnome rotary aero-engine appears, giving an output of 37.25kW (50hp). The rotary engine had been invented, however, as long ago as the 1880s.

January 13 Henry Farman wins the Deutsch-Archdeacon Prize of 50,000 francs for the first officially observed circular flight of 1km in Europe.

February 6 The US Army accepts tenders from the Wright brothers, A. Herring and J. Scott for military aeroplanes. Only the Wrights eventually deliver an aeroplane.

February 10 The US Army signs a contract for the construction of a Wright Model A biplane as its first military aeroplane. This is just one of three contracts signed. (q.v. December 23, 1907, and February 6, 1908)

February 15 Capt Thomas Baldwin submits a tender for the first US Army dirigible.

March 12 The Aerial Experiment Association's first aeroplane to fly successfully is the *Red Wing*, designed by Lieut Thomas Selfridge. (q.v. October 1 and December 3 and 6, 1907)

April 11 Lieut Frank P. Lahm becomes head of the Aeronautical Division, US Signal Corps.

May Frenchman Léon Delagrange makes the first aeroplane flight in Italy.

Goupy I triplane, September 5 1908.

Henry Farman makes the first aeroplane flight in Belgium.

May 6 The Wright brothers begin flying again after nearly three years. They have now lost their technical lead over other pioneers and never regain it.

May 14 Charles W. Furnas becomes the first passenger to fly in an aeroplane when he is taken up by Wilbur Wright for a 29-second flight.

May 29 Ernest Archdeacon becomes the first aeroplane passenger in Europe when he is taken up by Henry Farman in France.

May 30 The first British-held international balloon race attracts thirty starters.

June 8 A.V. Roe makes a 'hop' flight in his full-size biplane (18kW; 24hp Antoinette engine) at Brooklands, England.

June 10 The first US Aeronautical Society is established in New York.

June 20 Glenn Curtiss follows the much earlier success of the Wright brothers by flying his biplane *June Bug*, so becoming America's third aviation pioneer. *June Bug* is the Aerial Experiment Association's third aeroplane.

Zeppelin LZ 4 flies for the first time. It begins Army trials on August 4 but after flying for 20 hours makes an emergency landing at Echterdingen.

June 21 A suffragette drops leaflets on to the House of Commons, England from a dirigible.

June 28 Dane J.C.H. Ellehammer makes the first aeroplane flight in Germany, at Kiel.

July 4 Glenn Curtiss wins the *Scientific American* Trophy by flying nearly 1.6km (1 mile) in his biplane *June Bug*.

July 8 Frenchwoman Madame Thérèse Peltier becomes the first woman to fly as passenger in an aeroplane when she is taken up by Frenchman Léon Delagrange in a Voisin biplane.

July 23 Thomas Baldwin delivers a dirigible and gas plant to the US Army at Fort Myer. (q.v. February 15, 1908)

August 4 Flight trials of Baldwin's US Army Signal Corps' No 1 dirigible begin at Fort Myer.

August 5 Zeppelin LZ 4 is destroyed by fire after striking electrical wires while anchored during trials for the Army. Subsequent 'Zeppelin Donation Fund' raises over 6,000,000 Reichsmarks in voluntary contributions and allows Count von Zeppelin to continue his work.

August 8 Wilbur Wright flies at Le Mans, France in the new two-seat Model A.

August 29 The Curtiss *Golden Flyer* wins the Coupe Gordon Bennett speed prize, attaining 75.7km/h (47mph).

September 3 Flight trials of the Wright brothers' aeroplane at Fort Myer begin. (q.v. February 10, 1908)

September 5 The French *Goupy I* flies for the first time. It is the first full-size triplane to fly.

September 6 Frenchman Léon Delagrange flies for 29min 53 seconds at Issy-les-Moulineaux, covering a distance of more than 24km (15 miles). This is the first half-hour flight in Europe.

September 17 Lieutenant Thomas Etholen Selfridge, US Army Signal Corps, becomes the first person to be killed in a powered aeroplane when the Wright biplane in which he is a passenger crashes at Fort Myer, Virginia. The pilot, Orville Wright, is badly injured.

September 21 Wilbur Wright performs the first significant endurance flight, remaining airborne in France over a distance of 66.5km (41.3 miles).

October Hans Grade becomes the first German pilot. (q.v. January 12, 1909)

October 8 Griffith Brewer becomes the first Briton to fly as a passenger in an aeroplane when he is taken up by Wilbur Wright in France.

October 16 American-born Samuel Franklin Cody makes the first officially recognised aeroplane flight in Great Britain, piloting the British Army Aeroplane No 1 during a flight of 424m (1,390ft) at Farnborough, England.

October 30 Henry Farman makes the first cross-country flight in Europe, flying about 26km (16 miles) from Châlons to Reims in a Voisin.

November 7 Zeppelin LZ 3 flies to Donaueschingen with the German Crown Prince on board.

December 4 J.T.C. Moore-Brabazon makes a flight of 410m (1,350ft) in a Voisin while taking flying instruction at Issy-les-Moulineaux.

December 31 Wilbur Wright wins the Michelin prize with a flight of 124km (77 miles) at Camp d'Auvours, France.

Wright biplanes under construction at Short Brothers, February 1909.

1909

The Austrian K.u.K. Luftschifferabteilung is formed from the previous air section.

Yakov M. Gakkel flies the first successful Russian-built aircraft, the Gakkel-3 of his own design.

The first edition of *Jane's All the World's Aircraft* is published, with Fred T. Jane as its first editor.

Hans Grade begins a privately-run airmail service in Germany, between Borck and Brück.

January 12 Hans Grade flies his triplane, the first successful German aeroplane.

January 23 The Blériot Type X1 makes its first flight, powered by a 21.5kW (30hp) REP engine.

February Shellbeach, Isle of Sheppey, becomes Britain's first aerodrome proper.

Eustace Short concludes an agreement with Wilbur Wright to build six Wright aircraft under licence in Britain. The Short brothers become, therefore, the first to manufacture aeroplanes in series.

February 23 J.A.D. McCurdy flies the Aerial Experimental Association's *Silver Dart* over Baddeck Bay in Nova Scotia. This records the first aeroplane flight in Canada and the first sustained flight in the British Empire.

March 9 The French *Goupy II* flies for the first time. It is the first fully successful tractor-engined biplane.

April Frenchman Legagneux makes the first aeroplane flight in Austria.

April 24 Wilbur Wright pilots a Wright biplane at Centocelle, Italy, from which the first aerial cinematograph film is taken.

April 30 J.T.C. Moore-Brabazon makes the first accredited aeroplane flight by an Englishman in England, flying his Voisin biplane over a distance of about 137m (450ft) at Leysdown, Isle of Sheppey.

British Army Aeroplane No I, May 14 1909.

May 14 Samuel Cody flies for a distance of more than one mile, from Laffan's Plain, Hampshire, in the British Army Aeroplane No 1.

May 20 Frenchman Paul Tissandier makes the first one hour flight in France, in a Wright biplane. Paul Tissandier was the second pupil to be taught to fly in France in 1908 by Wilbur Wright.

Paul Tissandier sets the first officially recognised (by FAI) world speed record for aeroplanes in a Wright biplane, achieving 54.77km/h (34.03mph).

May 26 Zeppelin LZ 6 is launched and flies successfully.

June 5
John Berry and Paul McCullough win the first National Balloon Race in America, covering about 608km (378 miles).

June 12 The Blériot XII becomes the first aeroplane to fly with two passengers (Santos-Dumont and Fournier) at Issy-les-Moulineaux.

June 20 Zeppelin LZ 3 is delivered to the German Army.

July 13 Alliot Verdon Roe becomes the first Briton to fly in a British aeroplane, covering 30m (100ft) in his paper-covered triplane at Lea Marshes, Essex.

Roe paper-covered triplane, July 13 1909.

Louis Blériot sets off across the English Channel, July 25 1909. (*Science Museum, London*)

July 19 Wireless telegraphy is used to relay information to Dover on the French weather situation prior to Latham's flight.

Englishman Hubert Latham attempts to be the first man to cross the English Channel by aeroplane, but ditches his Antoinette IV following engine trouble.

July 23 A. V. Roe flies 274m (900ft) in his triplane at Lea Marshes, Essex, England.

July 25 Frenchman Louis Blériot becomes the first man to fly across the English Channel by aeroplane (Blériot XI monoplane), taking off from Les Baraques, near Calais, at 4.41am and landing at Northfall Meadow by Dover Castle, 36½ minutes later. Blériot wins the £1,000 prize offered by the *Daily Mail*.

July 27 Latham makes a second attempt to fly the Channel from Cap Blanc Nez to Dover, but ditches in the sea 1.6km (1 mile) from the English coast.

The first flight takes place of the French Antoinette VII monoplane.

July 29 Frenchman Legagneux makes the first aeroplane flight in Sweden.

July 30 The Rinji Gunyo Kikyu Kenkyu Kai (Provisional Committee for Military Balloon Research) is formed in Japan.

July – October The first International Airship Exhibition (I.L.A.) is held at Frankfurt/Main. Count Ferdinand von Zeppelin lands his LZ 5 in the grounds.

August 2 The American Government buys its first aeroplane, a Wright Model A biplane later named *Miss Columbia*. The cost of the aeroplane is $25,000, not including a $5,000 bonus paid because it exceeds the official specification.

August 22 The first international meeting for aeroplanes is held at Reims, France. Twenty-three aircraft compete for cash prizes in speed, distance and duration competitions.

August 23 Glenn Curtiss flies the *Golden Flyer* at the Reims International Meeting, setting a record for speed at 69.821 km/h (43.385 mph).

August 24 Louis Blériot flies at Reims in his Type XI at a speed of 74.318 km/h (46.179 mph).

August 26 Hubert Latham gains a distance in a closed circuit record at Bétheny of 154.620km (96.076 miles), flying an Antoinette IV.

August 27 Henry Farman makes the first aeroplane flight of more than 100 miles, covering 180km (111.847 miles) in a closed circuit during the Reims International Meeting.

August 29 Glenn Curtiss wins the speed prize at the Reims International Meeting with a flight at 75.7 km/h

Ticket for a flight on board Delag Zeppelin *Viktoria Luise* dated April 21 1913, (*Science Museum, London*)

(47 mph) in the *Golden Flyer*. He also wins the Coupe Gordon Bennett.

Hubert Latham wins the altitude competition at the Reims International Meeting in his Antoinette, attaining 155m (508.5ft).

September Delagrange makes the first officially recognised aeroplane flight in Denmark.

September 7 Eugène Lefebvre crashes his Wright Model A at Port Aviation Juvisy and is killed, becoming the first pilot of a powered aeroplane to die while flying.

September 8 Cody makes the first flight in Great Britain of more than one hour's duration.

September 22 Captain Ferdinand Ferber is killed at Boulogne while attempting to take off in a Voisin. He is the second pilot to be killed in a powered aeroplane.

September 25 Four people are killed when the gasbag of the French dirigible *République* is pierced at an altitude of 122m (400ft) over Avrilly, France.

October 15 The first aviation meeting proper in Britain begins at Doncaster.

October 16 Count Ferdinand von Zeppelin forms Delag (Die Deutsche Luftschiffahrt Aktiengesellschaft) as the world's first commercial airline company. Using airships, Delag carries more than 34,000 passengers from 1910 to November 1913 between German cities, 19,100 of them flown from March 1912. Although the services are without injury, only three of the original six airships survive to the end.

October 27 Mrs Ralph H. van Deman becomes the first American woman passenger in an aeroplane, being taken aloft briefly by Wilbur Wright.

October 30 Moore-Brabazon wins the *Daily Mail* prize of £1,000 as the first Briton to fly for one mile in a British aeroplane (Short-built Wright biplane).

November The first flight takes place of the Etrich *Taube*, the first Austrian-designed and built aeroplane to

Etrich *Taube*, November 1909.

Madame la Baronne de Laroche, March 8 1910.

be flown in Austria. A bird-like monoplane, versions become early military aircraft in Austria and Germany.

December Frenchman Meurisse takes still photographs from an Antoinette monoplane, showing areas of Mourmelon and Châlons.

Geoffrey de Havilland's first aeroplane makes one flight. It is a 33.5kW (45hp) de Havilland/Iris Motor Company-engined biplane.

December 9 Colin Defries makes the first aeroplane flight in Australia.

December 31 Harry Ferguson makes the first aeroplane flight in Ireland, in a machine of his own design.

1910

The Imperial Russian Flying Corps is founded.

The *Golub* (Pidgeon), the first Russian-designed non-rigid airship, joins the Russian army at Lida.

The Russian Naval Aviation School is formed.

August Euler is awarded the first pilot's licence in Germany.

Romania establishes a Flying Corps.

January 7 Hubert Latham makes the first flight at an altitude of 1,000m (3,281ft) at Châlons, France, in an Antoinette VII.

January 10 The first aeroplane meeting in the USA is held at the Dominguez Field, Los Angeles, under the control of the Aero Club of California. During the event the first great American barnstormer, Charles F. Willard, wins the spot landing competition.

January 19 Lt Paul Beck drops dummy bombs (sandbags) over Los Angeles from an aeroplane piloted by Louis Paulhan.

February 15 The Aero Club of Great Britain becomes the Royal Aero Club.

March 8 Moore-Brabazon is given the first Aviator Certificate by the Royal Aero Club of Great Britain.

March 8 Madame la Baronne de Laroche becomes the first certificated woman pilot and the 36th French pilot.

March 10 Frenchman Emil Aubrun makes night flights in a Blériot monoplane at Villalugano, Buenos Aires, Argentina.

March 13 Captain Engelhardt makes the first aeroplane flight in Switzerland.

March 28 Frenchman Henri Fabre performs the first take-off from water in a powered seaplane, the *Hydravion*, at La Mède harbour, Martigues, France.

April The French Service Aéronautique is formed as part of the Army.

April 27/28 Claude Grahame-White makes the first night flight in the UK, performed during the *Daily Mail* £10,000 London to Manchester race. However, the race is won by Louis Paulhan, who is first to comply with the rules to fly from a point near the newspaper's London office to a point near its Manchester office.

June 2 The Hon. C.S. Rolls flies a Wright biplane across the English Channel and back, dropping a letter for the Aéro Club de France just before the return journey.

June 3 The British Army dirigible *Beta 1* flies for the first time. Actually the lengthened *Baby*, which had followed *Nulli Secundus*, *Beta 1* was the first British airship to be installed with WT and the first non-rigid airship anywhere to be moored by mast.

June 9 A Henry Farman, piloted by Lieut Féquant, undertakes the first French photographic reconnaissance flight.

June 10 A Wright biplane is taken into French Army service.

June 13
The *New York Times'* $10,000 prize for a return flight between New York and Philadelphia is won by Charles Hamilton .

June 17 First flight of the *Vlaicu I* parasol monoplane designed by Aurel Vlaicu in Romania. This date is still celebrated as the National Aviation Day in Romania.

Zeppelin LZ 7 *Deutschland,* operated by the airline Delag, begins passenger services between Frankfurt, Baden-Baden and Düsseldorf.

June 24 A.V. Roe flies his Roe III. This represents an advanced triplane design and four are built. Three are powered by 26kW (35hp) Green engines and all introduce trailing-edge ailerons, tail unit elevators and large-area rudders.

LZ 7 *Deutschland* makes a commercial return flight between Essen, Bochum and Dortmund, carrying 32 passengers.

June 28 LZ 7 *Deutschland* is wrecked in a gale at Teutoburger Wald but all 20 passengers survive.

June 30 American Glenn Hammond Curtiss drops dummy bombs on the shape of a battleship marked out on Lake Keuka.

July 10 Walter Brookins becomes the first pilot to fly at an altitude of more than one mile. His flight at Indianapolis, USA, is in a Wright biplane. The actual height achieved is 1,900m (6,234ft).

July 12 The Hon. Charles Rolls is killed during the Bournemouth Aviation Week in his Wright biplane.

July 13 Five people die when a German Erbslön non-rigid dirigible explodes near Opladen. It was powered by a 21kW (28hp) Benz engine.

July 21 The Wright brothers begin experimenting with wheeled landing gears.

July 24 German August Euler patents an aeroplane/ fixed machine-gun armament arrangement, which he later demonstrates on his biplane *Gelber Hund*. (Prior to the start of the First World War another German named Franz Schneider produces the first synchronised gun arrangement for an aeroplane).

Harry Ferguson and Rita Marr, August 1910. (*Aer Lingus*)

July 31 The Bristol Boxkite flies for the first time.

August Harry Ferguson carries a woman passenger (Rita Marr) in his aeroplane, the first passenger flight performed in Ireland.

August 10 Claude Grahame-White attempts to carry mail in his Blériot monoplane from Squires Gate, Blackpool, to Southport, but lands short.

August 17 Franco American John Moisant's mechanic becomes the first passenger to fly across the English Channel (Blériot monoplane).

August 20 Lt Jacob Earl Fickel, US Army, fires his Springfield rifle from the passenger seat of a Curtiss biplane at a target at Sheepshead Bay, New York State.

August 27 American James McCurdy transmits and receives radio messages between his Curtiss biplane and the ground.

August 28 Armand Dufaux flies over Lake Geneva in his tractor biplane.

September 2 Blanche Scott becomes the first American woman pilot to fly solo.

Walter Wellman and crew being rescued by the crew of SS *Trent,* **October 15 1910.** (*Science Museum, London*)

September 8   The first recorded air collision takes place between aircraft flown by two brothers named Warchalovski in Austria.

September 11   Robert Loraine flies a Farman biplane from Holyhead to the coast of Howth, making the first recognised aeroplane flight across the Irish Sea. During the flight his engine cut out on six occasions and he actually failed to reach the Irish coast by a few hundred metres.

September 14   Zeppelin LZ 6 is destroyed by fire at its hangar at Boden-Oos.

September 23   Peruvian Georges Chavez flies a Blériot monoplane over the Alps from Brig to Domodossola but is killed when he crash-lands.

September 27   Roger Sommer makes a flight in his unique twin-engined biplane.

October 1   Hendon aerodrome, North London, England, is opened.

October 2   The first properly recorded mid-air collision between two aeroplanes happens at Milan, when a Henry Farman biplane piloted by Englishman Capt Bertram Dickson is struck by an Antoinette flown by H. Thomas. Both pilots survive the accident. Dickson is also remembered as the first to fly an aeroplane with a passenger for two hours, on June 6, 1910.

October 15   American journalist Walter Wellman sets off from Atlantic City in his hydrogen-filled dirigible *America*, in an attempt to cross the North Atlantic. After two days and nights of flight, experiencing engine problems and other difficulties, Wellman and his crew of five (plus dog) are rescued at sea by the British ship SS *Trent*. This followed an earlier unsuccessful attempt to reach the North Pole by dirigible.

October 22   The Aéronautique Militaire is formed from the French Service Aéronautique.

Thomas O.M. Sopwith begins his flying career by crashing in a Howard Wright monoplane while attempting his first ever flight as a pilot. (q.v. December 18, 1910)

Ely takes off from USS *Birmingham*, November 14 1910. (*US Navy*)

October 28 M. Tabuteau, flying a Maurice Farman biplane at Etampes, France, sets up a distance in a closed circuit record of 465.72km (289.38 miles). The supremacy in performance of the Wright biplanes is over.

October 29 Claude Grahame-White wins the first Gordon Bennett international air race.

November 4 Briton E.T. Willows makes the first airship flight from England to France in his *Willows III*.

November 14 American Eugene B. Ely becomes the first man to fly an aeroplane from a ship when he takes off in his Curtiss pusher from the 25m (83ft) platform constructed over the bows of the anchored US Navy cruiser USS *Birmingham*.

November 23 Octave Chanute dies, having contributed much to the advancement of aviation.

December 10 Romanian Henri Coanda hops the world's first jet-powered aeroplane. It is powered by a 37.25kW (50hp) Clerget piston engine driving a centrifugal air compressor.

December 18 Thomas O.M. Sopwith makes a flight of 285km (177 miles) to win the Baron de Forest Prize of £4,000. His flight is from Eastchurch, England to Beaumont, Belgium, the longest straight line flight into Europe by a British pilot in a British aeroplane in 1910. His aircraft is a modified Howard Wright biplane.

1911

The Romanian Aviation Group is formed at Chitila.

January 7 Lt Myron S. Crissy, US Army, drops a live bomb on a target in San Francisco from a Wright biplane piloted by Philip Parmelee.

January 18 E.B. Ely becomes the first man to land an aeroplane on a ship when he lands his Curtiss pusher on the 36m (119ft) platform constructed on the stern of the anchored cruiser USS *Pennsylvania*.

January 26 Glenn Curtiss takes off in his hydro-aeroplane and then alights on the water of San Diego Harbor, performs taxi manoeuvres and takes off again. (q.v. February 17, 1911)

February 5 Vivian Walsh makes the first aeroplane flight in New Zealand.

February 7 The first French military flying certificate is awarded to Lieut de Rose.

February 17 Glenn Curtiss flies his seaplane to USS *Pennysylvania* in San Diego Bay, taxis alongside and is hoisted on board by crane. He is subsequently returned to the water and flies back to land.

February 18 Henri Pequet flies his Humber biplane from Allahabad to Naini Junction, India, on the first official airmail flight.

February 22 Pequet and Capt W.G. Windham begin a regular service between Allahabad and Naini Junction to coincide with the Universal Postal Exhibition being

Curtiss is hoisted on board USS *Pennsylvania,* **February 17 1911.** (*US Navy*)

held in Allahabad. The special envelopes carried are marked First Aerial Post.

March The Aeronáutica Militar Española is formed in Spain.

Captain Chambers, Bureau of Navigation, is ordered to help establish an aviation branch of the US Navy.

March 2 Four Royal Navy officers begin flying training at Eastchurch, Isle of Sheppey, Kent, England.

March 3 Philip Parmelee and passenger Lieut B. Foulois fly from Laredo on the Mexico/Texas border to Eagle Pass, Texas. During the course of the flight they receive radio messages and drop written messages to Army units.

March 5 The Belgian Army Balloon Company is formed as the Compagnie des Ouviers et Aérostiers.

March 17 The Curtiss D pusher-engined biplane with a tricycle landing gear is demonstrated to the US Army. It subsequently becomes Army aeroplane No 2.

March 23 Louis Bréguet carries eleven passengers for a distance of 5km (3.1 miles) in a huge parasol-winged monoplane of his own design.

March 24 Roger Sommer carries twelve passengers on a flight covering 800m (2,625ft) in an aircraft of his own design.

April 1 The Air Battalion of the Royal Engineers is formed in the UK.

April 11 The College Park US Army flying school is authorised.

April 12 Pierre Prier flies his Blériot monoplane from Hendon, London, to Issy-les-Moulineaux, Paris, non-stop in 3 hours 56 minutes.

May The British Army receives a Bristol Boxkite for army co-operation duties, following trials during manoeuvres.

May 16 Delag passenger-carrying airship Zeppelin LZ 8 *Ersatz Deutschland* is wrecked while docking but there are no casualties. (LZ 8 had entered service in March 1911).

June 18 The Circuit of Europe air race begins. It is won on July 7 by Lieutenant de Vaisseau Conneau in a Blériot monoplane. The race starts and finishes in Paris.

July 1 The first US Navy aeroplane, a Curtiss A-1 Triad hydroaeroplane, is flown.

July 4 Horatio Barber is paid £100 by the General Electric Company to carry a box of Osram lamps in his

Curtiss A-1 Triad hydroaeroplane, July 1 1911. (*US National Archives*)

Valkyrie monoplane from Shoreham to Hove and thus completes the first air cargo flight in the UK. Previously, the Wright brothers had carried cargo.

July 22 The *Daily Mail* newspaper £10,000, five-day 'Round Britain' air race starts at Brooklands. It is eventually won by Lieutenant de Vaisseau Conneau, French Navy, flying a Blériot XI monoplane.

August The first of Anthony Fokker's *Spider* monoplanes appears.

August 2 Harriet Quimby gains her licence to become the first American woman pilot.

August 3 A Voisin biplane takes off from the airfield at Issy-les-Moulineaux and alights on the River Seine using the aircraft's amphibious landing gear, thereafter returning to Issy.

August 18 The Royal Aircraft Factory F.E.2 pusher-engined biplane flies for the first time. Designed by Geoffrey de Havilland, this forms the general configuration for the wartime F.E.2a/b/c/d fighters and bombers.

September 9 British-born Gustav Hamel, flying a Blériot XI monoplane, makes the initial flight of the first official airmail service in Great Britain, from Hendon to Windsor, under the auspices of the Blériot and Grahame White flying schools. The service lasts until September 26.

September 17 – November 5 The first coast-to-coast flight across the USA is made by Calbraith P. Rodgers in a Burgess-Wright aeroplane, between New York and Pasadena.

September 18 The first aeroplane to fly with three propellers is the Short Triple Twin. A two-seater, it uses

Short Triple Twin, September 18 1911.

two 37kW (50hp) Gnome rotary engines, one mounted as a pusher driving one propeller and one as a tractor driving two propellers.

September 19 The first Italian airmail service starts between Bologna, Venice and Rimini.

September 23 Earle L. Ovington carries the first official consignment of air mail in the USA, flying in a Blériot-type monoplane (known as a Queen monoplane) from Nassau Boulevard, Mineola, Long Island. He is made Air Mail Pilot No. 1 by Postmaster-General Hitchcock.

September 24 Britain's first rigid airship, the R1 *Mayfly*, is destroyed in an accident before making a flight.

September 26 Britain's first airmail service is suspended.

October 11 The first flight is made of the Short Tandem Twin or *Gnome Sandwich*, a biplane with pusher and tractor-mounted 37kW (50hp) Gnome rotary engines. Either engine could be switched off in flight, making it a 'safe' aeroplane.

October 22 Capitano Piazza, Italian Air Flotilla, flies a Blériot monoplane from Tripoli to Azizia to make a reconnaissance of the Turkish forces. This is the first use of an aeroplane in war.

November 1 2nd Lt Giulio Gavotti, Italian Air Flotilla, drops Cipelli grenades on Turkish forces at Taguira Oasis and Ain Zara. This is the first time that bombs have been dropped from an aeroplane in war.

November 4 France grants Germany control of a portion of the Congo, thus allowing the French government to continue helping the Sultan of Marrakech to control belligerents in Morocco. Germany had previously threatened French interests by anchoring a cruiser off the coast of Agadir.

November 18 Cmdr Oliver Schwann performs the first take off from water in Britain.

December A Naval flying school is formed at Eastchurch, Kent.

December 27 The Royal Aircraft Factory B.E.1 two-seater flies for the first time. From it is developed the wartime B.E.2 reconnaissance biplane.

1912

The Danish Navy Flying School is established.

Edmond Audemars of Switzerland makes the first flight from Paris to Berlin in a Blériot monoplane.

The Turkish Army Aviation Section is formed.

The Campo do Seixcal is formed as the Portuguese air arm.

The US Army purchases six Burgess Model H biplane trainers. These are its first aeroplanes with tractor-mounted engines. Burgess also builds under licence (four years later) two British Dunne swept wing and tailless seaplanes for the US Navy, on which that service carries out its initial air-gunnery experiments.

The Bulgarian Army Aviation Corps is formed.

Frenchmen Ponche and Primard fly the world's first all-metal aeroplane, the Tubavion monoplane.

The Japanese Naval Air Service is formed.

January 10 Lt Charles Rumney Samson takes off in the Short S.38 from a specially-built wooden platform on board the battleship HMS *Africa*.

Glenn Curtiss makes a flight in the first flying-boat proper, a converted Curtiss A-2.

February 17 French military aircraft make their first flights in Algeria.

March The German Aviation Experimental Establishment (DVL) is founded at Berlin-Adlershof.

The first competition for seaplanes is held at Monaco.

The French government orders Blériot monoplanes to be grounded whilst investigations are made into the structural failures of several machines. Louis Blériot instigates the inquiry, which boosts his reputation. The ban lasts just two weeks.

March 1 Capt Albert Berry makes the first parachute jump from an aeroplane (Benoist) in the USA, descending over Jefferson Barracks, St. Louis.

March 3 The prototype Avro 500 is flown at Brooklands. Production examples of this two-seat biplane trainer enter service with RFC and Navy units.

March 12 The French Service de l'Aéronautique de la Marine is formed.

March 15 The newly-formed Turkish Army Aviation Section receives its first two French-built aircraft at Yesilköy.

March 29 Authorisation is given for the reorganisation of the French Aéronautique Militaire into three Groupes, based at Lyon, Reims and Versailles.

April 16 American Harriet Quimby flies the English Channel in a Blériot monoplane, taking off from Deal and landing at Cap Gris-Nez.

April 20 The first Hendon flying display is held.

April 22 Englishman Denys Corbett Wilson flies the St Georges Channel, recording the first aeroplane crossing between Great Britain and Ireland. (q.v. September 11, 1910)

May 1 A.V. Roe flies the Avro Type F, the first monoplane with a fully-enclosed cabin for the pilot

May 9 Cdr Samson of the Royal Navy becomes the first man to take off from a moving ship when he flies a Short pusher amphibian from the battleship HMS *Hibernia* during the Naval Review off Portland.

May 13 The Royal Flying Corps is inaugurated officially, comprising one airship and man-carrying kite squadron and two aeroplane squadrons. The same day the Flying Corps Naval Wing is inaugurated.

SHORT Biplane fitted with Air-Bags, 1912

H.M.S. 'Hibernia', with SHORT Biplane S.38 on special...

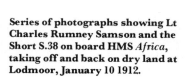

Series of photographs showing Lt Charles Rumney Samson and the Short S.38 on board HMS *Africa*, taking off and back on dry land at Lodmoor, January 10 1912.

S.38 rising from ship

Commander Samson landing at Lodmoor

May 16   A third aeroplane squadron becomes operational with the RFC as No 4 Squadron.

May 22   A US Marine Corps officer is ordered to begin flying.

May 30   Pioneer aviator Wilbur Wright dies from typhoid fever.

June   The new Royal Aircraft Factory B.E.2 two-seat observation biplane sets up a British altitude record of 3,219m (10,560ft) over Salisbury Plain.

June 2   Capt Charles de Forest Chandler, US Army Signal Corps, fires a machine-gun from a Wright Model B biplane being piloted by Lt Thomas de Witt Milling.

Capt Charles de Forest Chandler and Lt Thomas de Witt Milling with the Lewis machine-gun, June 2 1912. (*USAF*)

F.K. McClean flies through Tower Bridge, August 10 1912.

June 10 Airships *Schwaben* and *Gelber Hund* are used to carry the first German airmail, between Darmstadt and Frankfurt/Main. The experimental service lasts just twelve days.

June 19 The Central Flying School is established at Upavon, England.

June 21 Tina Broadwick becomes the first American woman to make a parachute descent in the USA.

June 26 The Kaigun Kokujutsu Kenkyu Kai (Naval Committee for Aeronautical Research) is formed in Japan.

June 27 The Italian Aviation Service is formed from the Battaglione Aviatori.

June 28 Delag passenger-carrying airship Zeppelin LZ 10 *Schwaben* is destroyed by fire while in its shed.

July 2 The Danish Army Flying School is established.

July 20 The Prince of Wales flies as a passenger on board the non-rigid airship *Beta 1*.

July 31 Lieut T.G. Ellyson is catapult-launched in an aeroplane from a wall platform at Annapolis, USA. This follows an earlier launch in September 1911 from a ground platform.

August The first British military aeroplane trials are held. The prize in the speed competition (considered the most important) is won by Cody in his primitive but highly powered Cathedral, although more advanced aircraft are displayed.

Following on from five Short biplanes, the sixth Royal Navy aircraft (and first French built aircraft to be acquired by the service) is a Bréguet biplane with a 59.7 kW (80 hp) Chenu engine.

August 10 F.K. McClean flies under the Thames bridges in London in a Short S.33 pusher biplane.

US Army Signal Corps aeroplanes fly during Army manoeuvres for the first time.

The Servicio Aeronautico del Ejercito (Military Aviation Service) is formed in Argentina.

August 25 Lt Wilfred Parke, Royal Navy, makes the first recorded recovery from a spin while flying an Avro biplane.

September The Air Squadron of the Royal Hellenic Army is formed.

The Australian Army Aviation Corps is formed.

September 19 Zeppelin LZ 13 *Hansa*, operated by Delag, starts the world's first international commercial service by an airship, flying between Hamburg, Copenhagen and Malmö.

October 1 The Military Aviation Service is formed in Germany. It is disbanded in 1919.

October 26 American Lt John H. Towers begins trials to determine the aeroplane's capability for anti-submarine warfare. (q.v. May 8, 1919)

November 12 A Curtiss A-1 Triad hydroaeroplane, piloted by Lt T. Ellyson, becomes the first aeroplane to be successfully catapult-launched from an anchored ship, at Washington Navy Yard.

November 19 The Italian Servizio d'Aviazione Coloniale is formed.

The British Admiralty awards Vickers a contract to design and build a prototype fighting aeroplane, which becomes the E.F.B.1. (q.v. February 1913).

November 27 A Curtiss F two-seat biplane becomes the US Army Signal Corps' first flying-boat. The Army eventually purchases three and others are built for the Navy and for private pilots.

November 28 Flotta Aerea d'Italia is formed.

December 5 Frenchman Jacques Schneider announces his intention to sponsor an international competition to encourage the development of seaplanes.

1913

The Serbian Military Air Service is formed.

Americans Lawrence Sperry and Lt Bellinger demonstrate the world's first gyroscopic automatic stabiliser in a Curtiss F flying-boat.

A German engineer named Schneider submits a patent application for his original synchronisation mechanism for a fixed machine-gun installation.

The Oberursel engine works in Germany acquires a licence to build French Gnome rotary aero engines.

The first armed aircraft to be built in Russia flies as the Dux 1. This pusher-engined biplane carries a machine-gun in the nose for ground attack.

January The Australian Flying Corps is formed.

Aircraft accompany US naval vessels for the first time during winter manoeuvres, under the command of Lt Towers.

February The Spanish air arm is renamed as the Servicio de Aeronáutica Militar Española.

Vickers Ltd displays the Destroyer E.F.B.1 armed biplane fighter at the Olympia Aero Show, England.

February 11 The Escuela de Aeronautica Militar is formed as the air service in Chile.

March Russian-born Igor Sikorsky produces his twin-engined *Bolshoi Bal'tisky* (The Great Baltic) or *Grand* RBVZ, which makes its first flight early this month.

March 5 The 1st Aero Squadron, US Army, is formed.

April 3 The second competition for seaplanes is held at Monaco.

April 16 Compagnie des Aviateurs is formed in Belgium from the previous Balloon Company.

The first Schneider Trophy race, contested over twenty-eight 10km circuits, is held at the Monaco seaplane meeting. It is won by Maurice Prévost in a Deperdussin, at an average speed of 73.63 km/h (45.75 mph).

April 16/17 Lt R. Cholmondeley of No 3 Squadron, makes the first night flight by a pilot of the RFC.

April 17 Gustav Hamel makes the first non-stop flight by aeroplane from England to Germany, taking 4 hours 18 minutes to fly his Blériot XI from Dover to Cologne.

May 10 Didier Masson, supporter of General Alvarado Obregon, drops bombs from an aeroplane on Mexican government gunships in Guaymas Bay.

May 13 Igor Sikorsky makes the first flight in the world's first four-engined aeroplane, the *Le Grand*. (*Russky Vityaz* or **Russian Knight**). This was not merely the *Bolshoi Bal'tisky* with two extra engines, as sometimes thought, but a new aircraft with four engines in tandem pairs. The first flight lasts less than ten minutes. However, the engine arrangement does not prove satisfactory and in June *Le Grand* is modified to have all four engines mounted in tractor configuration.

May 17 Domingo Rosillo flies a French Morane-Saulnier monoplane from Key West, Florida to Havana, Cuba.

May 28 The full-size Langley *Aerodrome* is flown briefly, having been modified during reconstruction.

June 21 Georgia Broadwick becomes the first woman to descend by parachute from an aeroplane, when she jumps over Los Angeles.

July 1 The Luchtvaartafdeling is formed in the Netherlands.

RBVZ *Le Grand*, **August 2 1913.**

August 2   The Sikorsky *Le Grand (Russky Vityaz)* makes a flight of 1 hour 54 minutes with eight passengers on board.

August 7   One of Britain's most famous pioneer aviators, Samuel F. Cody, is killed in a crash on Laffan's Plain, Farnborough.

August 16   The *Daily Mail* Hydro-Aeroplane Trial for seaplanes begins, the competitors setting out to fly 2,478 km (1,540 miles) round the United Kingdom. Only Harry Hawker starts the journey, which has to be completed by 30 August and flown in a British aeroplane, but crashes near Dublin. He receives a consolation prize of £1,000.

August 27   Lt Nesterov, Imperial Russian Army, flying a Nieuport Type IV monoplane over Kiev, performs the first loop.

September 2   Four aircraft of No 2 Squadron make the first sea crossing by the Royal Flying Corps, when they fly to the Rathbane Camp, County Limerick, for manoeuvres.

September 9   Zeppelin LZ 14 (L 1), the first German Navy airship, crashes into the North Sea off Heligoland and most of the crew of 20 are killed.

September 18   The prototype Avro 504 reconnaissance biplane flies for the first time. It competes in the 1913 Aerial Derby two days later.

September 20   The *Daily Mail* Aerial Derby is won by Gustav Hamel.

September 21   Adolphe Pégoud deliberately flies his Blériot monoplane upside-down, so making the first sustained inverted flight.

September 23   Roland Garros makes the first crossing of the Mediterranean by air, flying his Morane-Saulnier monoplane from Saint-Raphaël to Bizerte, Tunisia.

September 29   Maurice Prévost, flying the Deperdussin 'monocoque' (1913) at Reims, sets the first over 200 km/h speed record. He achieves 203.850 km/h (126.666 mph), the last speed record before the First World War.

October 13   M. Seguin and Farman (France) fly 1,021 km (634 miles), establishing the last international distance record before the First World War.

October 17   Zeppelin LZ 18 (L 2) burns while airborne at Johannisthal and there are no survivors from a crew of 28.

November   Mexico becomes the scene of the first ever aerial combat, when an aeroplane flown by Dean Ivan

Lamb for the army of Venustiano Carranza exchanges handgun shots with an aeroplane flown by Phillip Rader for General Huerta.

November 29 – December 29 Frenchman Jules Védrines makes the first flight from France to Egypt. His aeroplane is a Blériot monoplane.

December 28 Georges Legagneux sets the first altitude record for aeroplanes of more than 20,000ft, attaining 6,120m (20,079ft) in a Nieuport Type IIN at St. Raphaël, France.

1914

The Chinese Army Air Arm is formed. French Caudron biplanes were ordered in 1913.

The second Schneider Trophy contest is flown at Monaco. It is won by Briton C. Howard Pixton flying a modified Sopwith Tabloid at an average speed of 139.66 km/h (86.78 mph).

The Turkish Flying Corps is formed from the Army Aviation Section.

January The first US Navy air station is established at Pensacola.

First flight is made of the four-engined Sikorsky *Ilya Mourometz*, the first of series of bombers built under the same name.

January 1 Anthony Jannus of the Benoist Company flies a passenger from St. Petersburg to Tampa, Florida, in a Benoist flying-boat, completing the first scheduled service by an airline using aeroplanes.

Series of photographs showing McClean's Short biplane being transported to, and at, Alexandria. A crew of four is used. January 3 1914.

January 3 Frank K. McClean begins the first flight along the river Nile, leaving Alexandria in a Short biplane. The journey ends at Khartoum.

February 12 The first Russian *Ilya Mourometz* giant biplane carries sixteen passengers and a dog to a height of 2,000m (6,560ft), setting a world load-to-altitude record.

February 23 The prototype of the Bristol Scout single-seat biplane flies. Well ahead of its time in respect of design, the 'Baby Biplane' (as it is sometimes called) is capable of 153 km/h (95 mph). The improved Scout D production aircraft of 1916 carries a synchronised Vickers machine-gun.

March 23 The Royal Siamese Flying Corps is formed.

April The Fokker M.5K appears. It becomes the prototype of the famous Fokker Eindecker fighter.

April 25 Lt P.N.L. Bellinger makes the first American operational sortie by aeroplane when he searches for sea mines during the Vera Cruz incident. (A total of five Curtiss AB flying-boats are involved in this operation, flying from the battleship USS *Mississippi* and cruiser USS *Birmingham* operating on 43 consecutive days).

May 6 Lt P.N.L. Bellinger's Curtiss AB flying-boat is hit by rifle fire while on a reconnaissance flight during the

Vera Cruz incident, making it the first US Military aircraft to be struck by enemy gunfire.

May 9 W. Newell becomes the first person to descend by parachute from an aeroplane in the UK.

May 23 Gustav Hamel dies in an aeroplane accident after taking off from Calais, France.

June 22 The Curtiss flying-boat to attempt the first non-stop crossing of the Atlantic is officially named *America*. The date August 5 is set for the start of the flight.

June 28 Archduke Franz Ferdinand, heir to the Austria-Hungary throne, is assassinated in Sarajevo. The mobilisation of the armed forces of several countries begins soon after.

July R. Böhm (Germany), flying an Albatros B.I, remains airborne for 24 hr 12 min, establishing the last international flight endurance record before the First World War.

H.Oelerich (Germany), flying a DFW B.I, reaches an altitude of 8,150m (26,740ft), establishing the last international altitude record before the First World War.

July 1 The Naval Wing of the Royal Flying Corps separates and eventually forms the basis of the Royal Naval Air Service (RNAS).

July 7 Dr Robert H. Goddard in the USA receives a patent for his two-stage rocket that burns solid fuel.

July 18 The Aviation Section of the US Army Signal Corps is formed.

July 23 Austria-Hungary sends an ultimatum to Serbia following the events of June 28. It gives Serbia two days to accept peace terms that transgress its sovereignty. Nevertheless Serbia accepts.

July 27 Short brothers' test pilot Gordon Bell becomes the first pilot to drop a standard naval torpedo from an aeroplane, releasing a 14in torpedo from a Short tractor seaplane.

July 28 Sqn Cdr A. Longmore becomes the first Royal Navy pilot to drop a standard naval torpedo from an aeroplane when he releases a 14in (356mm) torpedo from a Short tractor seaplane.

July 30 Norwegian Tryggve Gran makes the first flight across the North Sea by aeroplane (Blériot monoplane).

July 31 The Swiss air arm is formed as the Flieger-truppe.

August The *Ilya Mourometz* is officially accepted for active service by the Russian Army.

August 1 Germany declares war on Russia.

France requisitions fifty Morane-Saulnier two-seat Parasols destined for export to Turkey. These equip French escadrilles MS 23 and MS 26.

August 2 German military forces invade Luxembourg and the first World War begins in earnest.

August 3 Germany declares war on France.

German forces invade Belgium after permission for free passage of its troops through Belgian territory had been denied.

August 4 Great Britain declares war on Germany after refusing German requests to approve its forces entering Belgium. At midnight war is declared after Germany fails to guarantee Belgian neutrality.

August 5 Austria-Hungary declares war on Russia.

August 6 Serbia declares war on Germany.

August 8 The observer of a French aircraft flown on a reconnaissance flight by Sadi Lecointe is wounded by a German rifleman, the first French casualty of the air war.

August 10 France declares war on Austria-Hungary.

German cruisers *Goeben* and *Breslau* anchor in the Dardanelles after a chase by Royal Navy vessels under the command of Admiral Troubridge.

August 11 RFC personnel leave Southampton for Amiens, France, to prepare for the arrival of RFC aircraft a few days later.

August 12 Great Britain declares war on Austria-Hungary.

Oberleutnant Reinhold Jahnow, German Air Service, is the first German airman to lose his life on active service. He is killed at Malmédy, Belgium.

2nd Lt R. Skene and R. Barlow of No 3 Squadron become the first members of the RFC to be killed while on active service. They crash their Blériot monoplane while flying to Dover for the crossing to France by the first British warplanes.

Sgt Bridou becomes the first French aviator to be killed in action, when he has an accident while returning from a reconnaissance mission.

August 13 Nos 2, 3, 4 and 5 squadrons, RFC, begin crossing the English Channel to France. The first aircraft to land is a Royal Aircraft Factory B.E.2a, piloted by Lt H.D. Harvey-Kelly.

August 14 Lt Cesari and Corporal Prudhommeau, French Air Force, attack the Zeppelin sheds at Metz-Frescaty.

August 19 Lt G. Mapplebeck, flying a Royal Aircraft Factory B.E.2a, and Capt P. Joubert de la Ferté, flying a Blériot monoplane, carry out the first RFC reconnaissance flight over German positions.

August 20 German forces march through Brussels.

August 22 RFC aeroplanes on reconnaissance duty locate von Kluck's forces as they advance through Belgium.

Lt V. Waterfall, RFC, is the first British airman to be shot down when his Avro 504 is hit by rifle fire in Belgium.

August 23 Japan declares war on Germany.

Lt H.D. Harvey-Kelly rests, having flown B.E.2a *347* across the Channel, August 13 1914. (*Imperial War Museum*)

The Battle of Mons starts with the British Expeditionary Force temporarily stopping von Kluck's army. This was the British Army's first major engagement. The BEF's planned retreat begins thereafter as von Kluck goes around the left flank.

Zeppelins LZ 22 (ZVII) and LZ 23 (ZVIII) are shot down.

August 24 French airship *Dupuy-de-Lôme* is shot down mistakenly by French ground troops.

August 25 Lt H.D. Harvey-Kelly and two other RFC pilots flying unarmed aircraft force a German two-seat reconnaissance aircraft to land.

Austria-Hungary declares war on Japan.

August 26 Staff Captain P.N. Nesterov, Imperial Russian Army, brings down an Austrian aircraft flown by Leutnant Baron von Rosenthal by ramming it with his unarmed Morane Type M monoplane. The Austrian aeroplane had been attacking Nesterov's airfield at Sholkiv. Both Nesterov and von Rosenthal are killed.

August 27 Wg Cdr C.R. Samson heads the first RNAS squadron to fly to France. The Eastchurch Squadron comprises a mixture of ten aeroplanes, including Sopwith Tabloids, Royal Aircraft Factory B.E.2s, Blériot monoplanes, a Short seaplane, Bristol and Farman biplanes, and the Astra-Torres No 3 airship.

August 28 Austria-Hungary declares war on Belgium.

August 30 Paris is bombed for the first time by a German Taube monoplane flown by Lt Ferdinand von Hiddessen. The five bombs, dropped on the Quai de Valmy, kill a woman and injure two others.

September The German Air Service adopts the Iron Cross insignia for its aircraft.

September 6 The Battle of the Marne begins and aeroplanes are used widely for reconnaissance purposes.

September 16 Approval is given for the founding of the Canadian Aviation Corps. Its only aeroplane is a Burgess-Dunne biplane.

September 22 Four aircraft of the Eastchurch Squadron, RNAS, attack German airship sheds at Düsseldorf and Cologne. Only the three 20lb (9kg) Hales bombs dropped by Flt Lt Collet hit a shed (at Düsseldorf) but do not explode.

September 27 The first French bomber Groupe is formed, equipped with Voisin 'Chicken Coop' biplanes.

October The first flight takes place of a three-engined Caproni bomber, eventually put in production as the Caproni 300HP.

Fokker M.8 two-seat high-wing monoplanes are accepted by the German military aviation service.

The French Aéronautique Militaire has expanded to 34 escadrilles, by far the largest air arm in the world.

Avro 504 which took part in the raid on the Zeppelin sheds at Friedrichshafen, piloted by Wg Cdr E.F. Briggs, November 21 1914.

October 5 Sgt Joseph Frantz and Caporal Quénault, French Air Force, shoot down a German Aviatik two-seater over Jonchery, Reims, with the machine-gun fitted to their Voisin biplane.

October 8 Sqn Cdr D.A. Spenser-Grey and Flt Lt R.L.G. Marix, Eastchurch Squadron, RNAS, take off to make a second attack on the airship sheds at Düsseldorf and Cologne. Spenser-Grey attacks Cologne railway station instead, but Marix hits and destroys a shed at Düsseldorf and Zeppelin LZ 25 (Z IX) inside. Marix is shot down on the return flight to Antwerp but returns safely to his squadron by road.

October 12 The first battle of Ypres begins, with Joffre striking for Lille between La Bassée and Ypres.

October 26 RNAS aircraft are ordered to carry Union Jack insignia.

October 31 Russia declares war on Turkey after Turkish naval vessels had shelled Russian ports two days earlier.

November 5 Great Britain declares war on Turkey.

November 21 Three Avro 504s of the RNAS attack the Zeppelin sheds at Friedrichshafen. Each aircraft carries four 20lb (9kg) Hales bombs. One Zeppelin is destroyed in its shed and the associated gasworks is badly damaged.

December 4 The German Navy forms its first seaplane unit.

December 6 The German Navy seaplane unit begins operations from its new base at Zeebrugge.

December 9 Leutnant Oswald Boelcke receives a Fokker A.1 reconnaissance monoplane.

December 10 Formation date of the Russian Army 'Flotilla of Flying Ships' (EVK), equipped with the first *Ilya Mourometz* long-range reconnaissance bombers. From then on all IM series aircraft are sent to this unit which, in time, comprise some 40-50 aircraft.

December 11 The RNAS adopts the roundel insignia in place of the Union Jack. The roundel has a white centre and red outer ring.

December 16 Two US Army lieutenants demonstrate two-way radio between the ground and an aeroplane. The aeroplane used is a Burgess-Wright.

December 21 A German aeroplane, probably a Taube monoplane, makes the first air attack on Britain, dropping two bombs into the sea off Admiralty Pier, Dover.

December 24 A bomb dropped from a German aeroplane explodes near Dover Castle.

December 25 Seven RNAS seaplanes are launched from seaplane carriers HMS *Empress*, *Engadine* and *Riviera* from a position north of Heligoland to attack the Zeppelin sheds at Cuxhaven.

1915

The Romanian Flying Corps is reorganised as the Corpul Aerian Româna.

The South African Aviation Corps is formed.

The Mexican Aviation Corps is formed.

The Haerens Flyvåpen (Army Air Force) and Marinens Flyvevaesen (Naval Air Service) are formed in Norway.

January The prototype Airco D.H.1 two-seat pusher-engined reconnaissance biplane flies for the first time.

Sikorsky S-16 two-seat armed biplanes appear, the first Russian aircraft designed specifically for aerial combat. Early examples are sent in March to the EVK unit operating *Ilya Mourometz* bombers, for experimental trials. The synchronised machine-gun proves troublesome.

January 7 The Italian Corpo Aeronautico Militare is formed.

January 19 Two German Navy Zeppelins, LZ 24/L 3 and LZ 27/L 4 (LZ 31/L 6 returns early because of engine trouble), make the first airship raid on Great Britain, having taken off from Fuhlsbüttel and Nordholz. L 3 drops bombs on Great Yarmouth, while L 4 drops incendiary and high-explosive bombs on Sheringham, Thornham, Brancaster, Hunstanton, Heacham, Snettisham and King's Lynn. Several British civilians are killed or injured in the raids.

January 23 Reconnaissance aircraft spot Turkish forces massing for an attack on the Suez Canal area.

February The Russian *Ilya Mourometz* IM-V series four-engined reconnaissance-bombers are armed with three machine-guns, mainly for use against ground targets.

Armed Vickers F.B.5 'Gun Bus' pusher biplane fighters enter service on the Western Front.

February 3 Turkish forces attack the Suez Canal area.

February 15 Sikorsky *Ilya Mourometz* reconnaissance-bombers attack targets in the Vistula-Dobrzhani area, Poland.

February 17 Zeppelin LZ 24 (L 3) is stranded and destroyed on the coast of Jutland during a gale.

HMS *Ark Royal* arrives off the Dardanelles and launches a seaplane to make a reconnaissance of Turkish ground forces. *Ark Royal* was designed as a merchant ship but converted in late 1914 to carry seaplanes, the first ship to be converted for this role.

March 3 The US National Advisory Committee for Aeronautics (NACA) is founded.

March 5 Zeppelin LZ 33 (L 8) crashes near Ostend after being hit by gunfire over Nieuport during a mission to attack England.

March 7 German Zeppelins raid Paris and its suburbs.

March 10 British aircraft bomb railway targets in Menin and Courtrai to prevent reinforcements from reaching German front-line positions.

March 20 The Belgian Aviation Militaire is formed.

April 1 Lt Roland Garros shoots down a German Albatros two-seater with the Hotchkiss machine-gun fitted to his Morane-Saulnier Type L monoplane. Steel wedge deflectors attached to the propeller protect the blades from damage as bullets pass through the propeller arc.

April 11 The first flight of the Zeppelin V.G.O.I prototype giant bomber is made at the hired Gotha works. This becomes the Zeppelin Staaken R.I., the first of 32 R-series bombers built by Zeppelin Staaken during the First World War.

April 16 Lt P.N.L. Bellinger in a US Navy AB-2 flying-boat is catapult launched from a barge. This follows earlier ground and wall experiments.

Morane-Saulnier monoplane fitted with deflector plates for the forward firing machine-gun. (*Imperial War Museum*)

SS *Lusitania*, **May 7 1915.** (*US National Archives*)

April 19   Lt Garros is forced down behind enemy lines and the details of the machine-gun arrangement on his Morane-Saulnier are studied by the Germans.

April 26   2nd Lt W.B. Rhodes-Moorhouse, RFC, is killed after making a low-level bombing attack on the railway station at Courtrai in a Royal Aircraft Factory B.E.2c. He is posthumously awarded the Victoria Cross.

April 30   Allied aeroplanes arrive in South West Africa to join the Union Expeditionary Force. These are used against German forces.

German Navy Zeppelin L 9 commanded by Kapit-änltn Mathys attacks three British submarines within three hours, damaging the conning tower of one (*D4*).

May 7   The liner *Lusitania* is sunk by the German submarine *U-20*.

May 11   The German High Command orders continuous airship raids on England to bomb the country into submission.

May 24   Italy declares war on Austria-Hungary.

May 26   Seventeen French Voisin biplanes of Groupe de Bombardement I attack a strategic military target at Ludwigshafen, near Mannheim.

A Halberstadt C-type flown by Oberleutnant Kästner, and with Leutnant Georg Langhoff as observer/gunner, makes the first intended German air attack on another armed aircraft, the latter a French Voisin making an armed reconnaissance flight over the airfield at Douai. The Voisin is shot down but the crew survive.

May 27   An Austrian Löhner L.1 flying-boat is captured off the Italian coast. The Italian company Società Anonima Nieuport-Macchi produces a similar aircraft, which starts the company in the flying-boat business.

May 31   Zeppelin LZ 38 makes the first bombing raid on London, killing seven civilians and injuring 14.

June   René Paul Fonck, subsequently the highest-scoring Allied pilot of the First World War, joins Escadrille C47 to fly Caudron G.IV bombing and reconnaissance aircraft.

June 1   The prototype Airco (de Havilland) D.H.2 makes its maiden flight. In production form the D.H.2 becomes the RFC's first true single-seat fighter and helps end the 'Fokker Scourge'.

A contract is signed by the US Navy for the Al(DN-1) dirigible from the Connecticut Aircraft Company. Launched in 1917 (in modified form), it makes three flights from Pensacola during April. It is the Navy's first dirigible.

June 6/7   Flt Sub-Lt R.A.J. Warneford of No 1 Squadron, RNAS, wins the Victoria Cross when he destroys Zeppelin LZ 37. Warneford flies his Morane-Saulnier parasol monoplane above LZ 37 and drops six 20lb (9kg) Hales bombs on the airship, the last exploding and causing it to fall at Ghent.

Airco (de Havilland) D.H.2, June 1 1915.

June 19 Flt Sub-Lt Warneford VC is killed when his Farman biplane breaks up in mid-air.

June 22 A forest fire (in Wisconsin) is observed from an aeroplane for the first time in the USA.

July German Fokker E.I monoplane fighters arrive on the Western Front for operational trials. These are the first fighters with synchronized machine-guns, able to fire through the propeller arc. They are flown by a small number of pilots from Douai airfield.

July 1 The Office of Naval Aeronautics is formed to oversee the air operations of the US Navy.

Leutnant Kurt Wintgens destroys a French Morane-Saulnier monoplane while flying a Fokker M.5K fitted with a machine-gun with synchronization gear.

July 5 German Army airship Schütte-Lanz SL5 is wrecked after a forced landing in a gale.

July 19 Georges Marie Ludovic Jules Guynemer, destined to become the second highest-scoring French pilot of the First World War, gains his first aerial victory while flying a two-seat Morane-Saulnier Parasol monoplane.

July 25 Major L.G. Hawker, RFC, gains victories over three armed German two-seat Albatros biplanes, flying a Bristol Scout C armed only with a hastily fitted cavalry carbine mounted at an angle to fire outside the propeller arc.

July 30 Leutnant Max Immelmann flies a Fokker M.8 in preparation for his first flight in an armed E.I fighter the next day.

August A French strategic bomber escadrille at Malzeville is disbanded following the loss of nine French aircraft of a similar escadrille to Fokker Eindeckers on August 2.

August 1 Leutnant Max Immelmann, soon known as 'The Eagle of Lille', gains his first aerial victory by shooting down an enemy aircraft while flying a Fokker E.I monoplane.

August 6 Germany Navy Zeppelin LZ 28 (L 5) has to make a forced landing in Russia after being hit by groundfire.

August 10 German Navy Zeppelin LZ 43 (L 12) is damaged while on a raid over England. It is towed back to Ostend but is accidentally destroyed.

August 12 Flt Cdr C.H. Edmonds, RNAS, flying a Short 184 seaplane from the seaplane carrier HMS *Ben-My-Chree*, makes the first air attack with a torpedo and sinks a Turkish supply ship in the Sea of Marmara during the Dardanelles campaign.

August 17 Flt Cdr Edmonds sinks a second Turkish ship off the Dardanelles with a torpedo. Flt Lt G.B. Dacre also sinks a Turkish boat, using a torpedo released from his aircraft while taxiing on the water.

August 19 Col Hugh Trenchard takes command of the RFC in France.

August 20 Italian Caproni Ca.2 triple-engined biplanes begin the first sustained bombing offensive against Austria-Hungary.

August 23 Capt A.J. Liddell, RFC, is awarded the Victoria Cross for valour while flying a Royal Aircraft Factory R.E.5.

Fokker E.III Eindecker, September 1915.

August 24 Maj L.G. Hawker, RFC, receives the Victoria Cross, for valour while flying a Bristol Scout. (q.v. July 25, 1915)

September The improved Fokker E.II monoplane fighter enters service, followed by the E.III.

September 3 Zeppelin LZ 40 (L 10) is struck by lightning and destroyed off Neuwerk Island.

September 14 Bulgaria declares war on Serbia.

September 15 Great Britain declares war on Bulgaria.

September 16 France declares war on Bulgaria.

Autumn-Winter The 'Fokker scourge' begins and lasts throughout the winter, as Fokker monoplane fighters with synchronized machine-guns shoot down large numbers of Allied aircraft.

October The Bulgarian Army Aviation Corps, disbanded after the Balkan War of 1912-13, is revived.

October 1 Passenger airship LZ 11 *Viktoria Luise* is wrecked while docking.

November 3 Flt Sub-Lt H.F. Towler, RNAS, takes off in a Bristol Scout C from the seaplane carrier HMS *Vindex* during launching experiments, subsequently ditching in the sea. This was the first occasion an aeroplane with a wheeled landing gear had taken off from a ship specifically designed as an aircraft (seaplane) carrier.

November 5 A Curtiss AB-2 flying-boat becomes the first aircraft to be catapult-launched from an anchored American battleship, USS *North Carolina* at Pensacola Bay, Florida.

November 6 A Curtiss AB-2 flying-boat, piloted by Lieut Cmdr Henry Mustin, is catapult-launched from USS *North Carolina* while underway. This is the first time an aeroplane has been so launched from a moving ship.

November 17 Zeppelin LZ 52 (L 18) is accidentally burned in its shed at Tondem.

November 18 German Navy Schütte-Lanz airship SL 6 (D 1) explodes while airborne and all the crew are killed.

December 11 German Navy Schütte Lanz airship SL 4 (C 2) is wrecked in its shed in a storm.

December 12 The Junkers J1 *Blechesel* ('Tin Donkey') all-metal reconnaissance and close-support monoplane flies in Germany.

December 17 The prototype Handley Page O/100 twin-engined heavy bomber flies for the first time.

December 23 Lt G.S.M. Insall, RFC, is awarded the Victoria Cross, for valour while flying a Vickers F.B.5.

Winter 1915-16 Formation of the first Russian Fighter Aviation Detachments.

1916

Kampfgeschwader Nr 1, the first German bomber wing, formed in November 1914 under the cover name *Brieftauben Abteilung Ostende* (Ostend Carrier Pigeon Detachment), receives Gotha IV bombers.

January Blueprints of the Russian Scarff-Dibovski machine-gun synchronization mechanism are sent on request to the British naval aviation authorities. Suitably adapted, this type of synchro mechanism is later favoured for use on the Sopwith 1½ Strutter and several other fighters.

January 1 Lt. R.B. Davis, RNAS, is awarded the Victoria Cross, for valour while flying a Nieuport fighter.

January 10 German Army airship Schütte-Lanz SL 2 is wrecked in a storm, having served on both the Eastern and Western fronts.

January 12 German fighter aces Max Immelmann and Oswald Boelcke receive the Pour le Mérite.

January 14 The RFC is ordered to escort each reconnaissance aeroplane with a minimum of three fighters because of the Fokker Eindecker menace.

February No 24 Squadron, RFC, stationed on the Western Front, is equipped with Airco (de Havilland) D.H.2 pusher-engined fighters.

February 2 German Navy Zeppelin LZ 54 (L 19) is shot down by British aircraft over the North Sea following a raid on England.

February 6 Max Immelmann goes into action flying a specially-prepared three-gun Fokker E.IV for the first time.

February 21 Zeppelin LZ 47 is attacked during a raid and bursts into flames.

The battle of Verdun starts. This battle sees the first major use of large formations of fighter planes.

April The Japanese Naval Air Corps is formed.

April 1 German Navy Zeppelin LZ 48 (L 15) is struck by ground fire over England and alights off the coast at Knock Deep, but sinks. All but one of the crew of 18 survive.

April 20 The Escadrille Américaine is established as an American volunteer unit flying with the French Aéronautique Militaire on the Western Front during the First World War. It later becomes the famed *Lafayette Escadrille*.

May The first American volunteer pilot serving with the French Aéronautique Militaire to receive the Médaille Militaire is Sgt Maj E. Cowdin, one of the seven original pilots. The 'American Squadron' had been formed on April 20, equipped with Nieuport 11 'Bébés'.

The prototype Armstrong Whitworth F.K.8 reconnaissance and light bombing biplane appears. No 35 Squadron, RFC, becomes the first to operate the 'Big Ack' on the Western Front, from early 1917.

May 1 German Navy's Schütte-Lanz airship (SL 3) (C 1) crashes near Gotland.

May 4 German Navy Zeppelin LZ 32 (L 7) is shot down by the cruisers HMS *Phaeton* and *Galatea* and is finished off by British submarine *E 31*.

May 17 Experiments with parasite fighters begin with the air-launching of a Bristol Scout from a Porte Baby three-engined flying-boat.

May 18 Lt Kiffin Rockwell, a pilot with the Escadrille Américaine, gains his first air victory while on a bomber escort mission near Mulhouse. Rockwell is killed in action on September 23.

May 22 Capt Albert Ball gains his first two aerial victories.

May 28 The prototype Sopwith Triplane 'Tripehound' single-seat fighter flies for the first time. Production Triplanes enter service with the RNAS.

May 31 German warships are shadowed by British seaplanes before and during the Battle of Jutland.

June 18 Oberleutnant Max Immelmann, 'The Eagle of Lille', is killed while flying his Fokker E.III in action against an F.E.2b of No 25 Sqn crewed by 2nd Lt. McCubbin and Corp J.H. Waller, RFC.

H. Clyde Balsley becomes the first American volunteer pilot serving with the *Lafayette Escadrille* to be shot down in action, near Verdun. He survives the incident.

June 23 Victor Emmanuel Chapman, flying with the famous volunteer fighter group *Lafayette Escadrille*, is the first American pilot to be killed in action when he is shot down near Verdun.

June 29 The first Boeing-built aeroplane flies as the B & W. Conceived by William Boeing and Commander G. Conrad Westervelt, US Navy, it is a 93kW (125hp) Hall-Scott A-5–engined training and sporting biplane.

July No 3 Wing, RNAS, becomes the first British strategic bombing unit, flying Sopwith 1½-Strutters.

July 1 The Battle of the Somme begins and both sides fight to gain air superiority. As the battle drags on for weeks and then months, the Allies begin to take control and are able to make successful sorties over enemy positions.

The Russian Aviation Experimental Bureau (RIB) is formed as part of the Moscow Higher Technical School

July 14 The Bristol M.1A monoplane scout flies as a prototype. In its later M.1C form it is ordered in limited numbers and serves in Macedonia and the Middle East but not on the Western Front despite an excellent speed of 209km/h (130mph).

July 15 William E. Boeing forms Pacific Aero Products.

August The prototype Airco (de Havilland) D.H.4 day bomber flies for the first time.

August 2/3 German Army airship Schütte-Lanz SL 11 is shot down over London and there are no survivors. (q.v. September 5, 1916)

August 5 Maj L.W.B. Rees, RFC, is awarded the Victoria Cross, for valour while flying an Airco D.H.2 fighter.

August 6 Capitaine René Paul Fonck forces down a German Rumpler biplane, his first confirmed victory.

August 26 The Brazilian Naval Aviation School is formed.

August 27 Italy declares war on Germany.

August 28 Germany declares war on Romania.

August 29 The US Naval Flying Corps is formed.

August 30 Turkey declares war on Romania.

September   The French Spad VII single-seat fighter enters service and contributes greatly to Allied aerial superiority. It eventually equips squadrons of eleven nations.

The Bristol F.2A Fighter flies. In production form the Fighter goes to the Western Front in April 1917, becoming one of the 'greats' of the war.

September 1   Bulgaria declares war on Romania.

September 5   Lt William Leefe Robinson, RFC, is awarded the Victoria Cross for destroying German airship Schütte-Lanz SL 11 over Cuffley on the night of 2/3 August, while flying a B.E.2c. (The destruction of SL 11 had far-reaching effects. It demoralised airship crews and, although not preventing large formations of German airships from attacking England, it did stop the expected large-scale raid on London by demonstrating the effectiveness of the defences).

September 12   The Hewitt-Sperry radio-guided flying bomb is flight tested in America. It is powered by a 29.75kW (10hp) engine and carries 140kg (308lb) of explosives.

September 15   French submarine *Foucault* is sunk by an Austrian Löhner flying-boat.

September 16   German Navy Zeppelin LZ 31 (L 6) is destroyed in its shed at Fuhlsbüttel when it catches fire while being inflated. LZ 36 (L 9) burns with it.

September 17   German Albatros D series fighters are flown on their first mission, under the command of Oswald Boelcke.

Rittmeister Manfred Frhr von Richthofen gains his first combat victory, bringing down an F.E.2b of No 11 Squadron, RFC. Richthofen's aircraft is an Albatros D.II.

September 23/24   Eleven Zeppelin airships raid England, three heading for London. LZ 76 (L 33), on its first mission, is badly damaged by anti-aircraft fire and is forced to land at Little Wigborough. LZ 74 (L 32) is attacked by 2nd Lt F. Sowrey and catches fire, falling at Great Burstead. There are no survivors.

September 24   The British Sopwith Pup single-seat biplane fighter claims its first victim, a German LVG two-seat biplane.

September 26   Hauptmann R. Berthold is awarded the Pour le Mérite.

October 2   German Navy Zeppelin LZ 72 (L 31) is shot down by British aircraft at Potters Bar.

October 5   The first British airline, Aircraft Transport and Travel Ltd, is registered in London.

October 12   Raymond Collishaw gains his first aerial victory. He eventually becomes the highest-scoring RNAS pilot with 60 victories.

October 14   Zeppelin LZ 39 is wrecked during a forced landing following a raid.

October 28   German fighter ace Hauptmann Oswald Boelcke is killed when the wing of his Albatros scout is struck by the undercarriage of another Albatros flown by Leutnant Boehme.

November 1916 – February 1918   A Friedrichshafen 33e floatplane named *Wölfchen* (Wolf Cub) is carried by the German auxiliary cruiser *Wolf* operating in the Indian and Pacific oceans. It is used mainly for reconnaissance purposes, but occasionally also to direct enemy ships towards its own vessel to secure their capture.

November   A German Rumpler crewed by Leutnants Falk and Schultheis, operating in support of Turkish forces from Beersheba, drops some light bombs on the Cairo railway station.

Handley Page O/100 heavy biplane bombers enter service with the RFC.

November 20   The Uruguayan Escuela Militar de Aéronautica is formed.

November 21   The prototype Bréguet 14 flies as a two-seat day bomber and reconnaissance biplane. It becomes one of the outstanding aircraft of the First World War.

November 23   Manfred von Richthofen shoots down Maj Lanoe G. Hawker, V.C., who is flying a D.H.2.

November 27   German Navy Zeppelin LZ 78 (L 34) is shot down off Hartlepool, England.

November 28   German Navy Zeppelin LZ 61 (L 21) is shot down by British fighters off Lowestoft.

Deck Offizier R. Brandt, flying an LVG C.II, drops six bombs near Victoria Station, London.

December 28   German Navy Zeppelins LZ 53 (L 17) and LZ 69 (L 24) are destroyed after L 24 breaks its back across the entrance to its shed at Tondem and catches fire, igniting L 17 in turn. The same day Schütte-Lanz SL 12 (E 5) is wrecked at its shed.

December 29   German Navy Zeppelin LZ 84 (L 38) makes a forced landing in Russia.

1917

The Air Squadron of the Royal Hellenic Army becomes the Hellenic Army Air Force.

One of the final series of Russian *Ilya Mourometz* bombers, the IM-Ye2, is defensively armed with one light cannon and eight machine-guns.

The Spanish Aeronáutica Naval is formed.

The Turkish Army Air Service is formed.

The Portuguese Arma da Aeronáutica and Aviacão Maritima are formed.

The Hellenic Naval Air Force is formed.

The Cuerpo de Aviación is formed as the Cuban air arm.

January 16   Rittmeister Manfred Frhr von Richthofen receives the Pour le Mérite. (His brother Lothar receives the decoration the same year).

February The first flight is made of the Junkers J4 armoured close-support biplane, featuring corrugated duralumin skinning. As the JI, it enters service in the late summer of 1917 and 227 are built.

February 7 German Navy Zeppelin LZ 82 (L 36) makes a forced landing at Rehben-an-der-Aller in fog and is wrecked.

February 11/12 In the first (unintentional) successful night fighting between aircraft, Leutnants Peter and Frohwein in a DFW C.V shoot down two enemy bombers as they are coming in to land at Malzeville. The C.V remains in use into 1918 and is extremely successful in reconnaissance and army co-operation roles.

February 12 Sgt T. Mottershead receives the Victoria Cross, for valour while flying in an F.E.2d

March First flight of the Caudron R.11 twin-engined three-seat escort fighter. Developed from the Caudron R.4, the R.11 is the first of the French multi-seat fighters and proves quite successful in service.

Royal Aircraft Factory S.E.5 single-seat biplane fighters enter service with the RFC.

Authority is given to convert the battle-cruiser being built as HMS *Furious* into an aircraft carrier.

An 'AT' remotely controlled pilotless bomber is tested unsuccessfully at the RFC's flying school, Upavon. The aircraft is a monoplane designed by Geoffrey de Havilland.

Albatros D.III fighters at Douai airfield, home of the 'Richthofen Flying Circus', April 1917.

March 6 Airco (de Havilland) D.H.4s arrive in France, first going to No 55 Squadron, RFC.

March 8 Count Ferdinand von Zeppelin dies, the pioneer designer of large rigid airships.

March 17 German Navy Zeppelin LZ 86 (L 39) is shot down by anti-aircraft guns over Compiègne, France.

March 21 No 100 Squadron, RFC, goes to France. It is the first British squadron to be formed for night bombing operations and is equipped with F.E.2b and B.E.2e biplanes.

March 25 Canadian William Avery Bishop gains his first aerial victory, over an Albatros. He ends the war with 72 victories.

March 30 German Navy Schütte-Lanz airship SL 9 (E 2) is destroyed in a storm and all 23 crewmembers are killed.

April Leutnant W. Voss receives the Pour le Mérite.

The first two weeks of 'Bloody April' see the loss of nearly 140 RFC aircraft brought together for an offensive. The main culprit is the German Albatros D.III fighter, which makes short work of several British types (especially the B.E.2c).

April 5/6 No 100 Squadron, RFC, makes its first raid, hitting Douai airfield.

French-built Spad XIII fighter operated by the American 2nd Pursuit Group.

First planned night interception. Leutnant Frankl of Jasta 4, flying an Albatros D.III, shoots down a British B.E.2c of No 100 Sqn over Ouiéry la Motte.

April 6 The United States of America declares war on Germany.

April 12 The French Aéronautique Militaire receives its first Bréguet 14s for use on the Western Front.

April 20 The first non-rigid airship to be built for the US Navy flies as the A1 (DN-1) at Pensacola, Florida.

April 26 Boeing Airplane Company is founded out of the Pacific Aero Products company.

April 29 US Navy airship A1 (DN-1) is abandoned after just three flights.

May French escadrilles begin to receive Spad XIII single-seat fighters. The Spad XIII is one of the fastest fighters of the First World War.

The German Friedrichshafen FF 49c flies as a reconnaissance seaplane. More than 230 are built, achieving great success. After the Armistice some are modified into makeshift airliners, with enclosed accommodation for three passengers.

May 6 Capt Albert Ball gains his 47th aerial victory, an Albatros fighter of Jasta 20.

May 7 Capt Albert Ball, Britain's first really great fighter ace, dies when he dives his S.E.5 into cloud while chasing a German aircraft. The cause of his death is never established.

Edward 'Mick' Mannock, RFC, gains his first aerial victory, destroying a balloon.

May 14 German Navy Zeppelin LZ 64 (L 22) is shot down by a British flying-boat and all the crew of 21 are killed.

May 15 Leutnant H. Gontermann receives the Pour le Mérite.

May 20 The first German submarine to be sunk by aeroplane (*U-36*) is destroyed in the North Sea by a Large America flying-boat commanded by Flt Sub Lt C.R. Morrish, RNAS.

May 22 Italian mail services by aeroplane begin with an official military service between Turin and Rome.

May 25 The first mass bombing raid on England by German aeroplanes takes place during daylight hours. The 21 Gotha bombers attacking Folkestone, Shorncliffe and elsewhere kill 95 people and injure 260 more.

May 31 First defensive success against enemy night bombers over Austro-Hungarian territory: Austrian Linienschiffleutnant G. Banfield flying a Pfalz A.II single-seater forces down an Italian seaplane. For this deed Banfield is awarded the Maria-Theresa Order which carries with it a hereditary peerage.

June The first of the German Staaken R.VI four-engined bombers is delivered to an operational unit.

Capt Albert Ball in the cockpit of an S.E.5, May 7 1917. (*Imperial War Museum*)

June 5 Twenty-two Gotha bombers attack Sheerness, England.

The US Army's First Aeronautic Detachment arrives in France.

June 8 Lt F.H. McNamara and Capt Albert Ball are awarded Victoria Crosses for valour.

June 13 Fourteen Gotha bombers carry out the first large-scale bombing raid on London, killing 162 people and injuring 432 others in an area around Liverpool Street Station. The casualties of this raid constitute nearly 20% of all British civilians killed or injured in bombing raids by aeroplanes during the 1914-18 war.

Hauptmann Ernst von Brandenburg wins the Pour le Mérite for leading the mass Gotha bombing raids on England.

June 14 Leutnant K. Allmenröder is awarded the Pour le Mérite.

German Navy Zeppelin LZ 92 (L 43) is shot down over the North Sea by British aeroplanes.

June 17 German Navy Zeppelin LZ 95 (L 48) is shot down over Suffolk, England, by British aeroplanes.

German Navy Zeppelin LZ 28 (L 40) is wrecked at Neuenwald.

June 28 Commercial airmail services in Italy begin with a flight from Naples to Palermo by Società Industrie Meridionali.

June 30 Lt Col William 'Billy' Mitchell takes over as Aviation Officer, American Expeditionary Forces.

July The prototype Airco (de Havilland) D.H.9 bomber flies for the first time.

Sopwith Camel single-seat biplane fighters go into action with the RFC for the first time.

July 7 A mass formation of Gotha and Friedrichshafen bombers of KG 3 based at Ghent attacks London during daylight hours, killing 57 people and injuring many others.

July 26 Formation date of German Jagdgeschwader Nr 1 (Jastas Nos. 4, 6, 10 and 11). In action, it soon becomes known to the Allies as the 'Flying Circus' under the command of von Richthofen.

July 27 A British Airco (de Havilland) D.H.4 two-seat bomber reaches the USA for evaluation with a Liberty engine. It arrives at the Dayton-Wright Airplane Company plant at Dayton, Ohio, on August 15. The first American-built example is completed in February 1918.

July 31 The Battle of Ypres begins, with 850 Allied aircraft facing about 600 German aircraft.

August 2 Sqn Cdr E.H. Dunning lands his Sopwith Pup on the deck of HMS *Furious*, which is steaming at 26 knots, thus making the first aeroplane landing on a moving ship.

August 7 Sqn Cdr Dunning tries to repeat the deck landing experiment on board HMS *Furious* but stalls and his aircraft is blown over the side. Although he is killed, Dunning has proved that it is possible to land successfully and the Royal Navy goes on to perfect the concept.

Dunning lands on board HMS _Furious_, August 2 1917.

First flight of the Morane-Saulnier AI parasol monoplane fighter, a superior design for its time with a speed of 209 km/h (130 mph) on the power of its 119kW (160hp) Le Rhône engine.

August 8/9 First enemy night bomber is shot down by fighters over Germany, near Frankfurt/Main.

August 11 Canadian fighter pilot William Avery Bishop, serving with the RFC, is awarded the Victoria Cross for valour while flying over an enemy airfield on June 2.

August 12 Gotha bombers make their last large-scale bombing raid on England during daylight hours, killing or injuring 78 people.

August 13 The American 1st Aero Squadron leaves for France.

August 17 The first French mail carried by air is flown between Paris, Le Mans and St. Nazaire. This starts a regular service.

August 18 The Marine Luchtvaartdienst is formed in the Netherlands.

August 21 German Navy Zeppelin LZ 66 (L 23) is shot down near Jutland by Flt Sub-Lt B.A. Smart, who had flown his Sopwith Pup from a platform on board the cruiser HMS _Yarmouth_.

Two new Fokker F.I (Dr.I) triplane fighters arrive at Courtrai, home of von Richthofen's fighter wing. The F.I was designed by Reinhold Platz.

August 30 Leutnant Werner Voss flies a Fokker F.I (Dr. I) into combat for the first time, shooting down an RFC aircraft.

September The prototype Handley Page O/400 heavy bomber flies for the first time.

September 2/3 Dover receives the first large scale night bombing raid by Gotha aeroplanes on Great Britain.

September 3 The American 1st Aero Squadron arrives in France.

Brig-Gen William L. Kenly becomes the first Chief of Air Service, American Expeditionary Force.

September 5 An Airco (de Havilland) D.H.4 of the RNAS makes an unsuccessful attempt to bring down German Zeppelin LZ 93 (L 44) and has to alight in the

Fokker Dr.Is, August 1917. (*Imperial War Museum*)

North Sea. However, the airship is shot down by anti-aircraft fire over France on October 20.

September 11 Capitaine Georges Marie Ludovic Jules Guynemer dies during a patrol over Poelcapelle, Belgium.

September 17 First raid on England by German Staaken R.VI bombers. These 'R' or 'Giant' bombers could carry 1,000kg bombs – largest bombs used operationally in the First World War.

September 23 Leutnant Werner Voss is killed in action while flying a Fokker Dr I. Flying alone, he meets S.E.5s of No 56 Squadron, RFC, and manages to cause considerable damage to the enemy, finally being shot down by Capt. J.B. McCudden.

September 29 Two Sopwith Camels of the RNAS carry out a unique night bombing raid on the balloon shed near Quiery-la-Motte.

October 2 Three Sopwith Pups carry out a low-level night bombing raid on the airfields at Cruyshautem and Waereghem.

October 8 German Navy Zeppelin LZ 102 (L 57) explodes while entering its shed at Jüterbog, near Berlin.

October 11 The 41st Wing of the RFC is formed to carry out strategic bombing of targets of military importance inside Germany.

October 19 German Navy Zeppelin LZ 50 (L 16) is dismantled, having been wrecked on landing.

October 20 German Navy Zeppelin LZ 85 (L 45) is forced to land in France behind enemy lines and is destroyed by the crew.

German Navy Zeppelin LZ 93 (L 44) is shot down by anti-aircraft fire over St Clement, France.

German Navy Zeppelin LZ 96 (L 49) is forced to land in France and is captured.

German Navy Zeppelin LZ 89 (L 50) goes missing over Mediterranean after losing a gondola.

German Navy Zeppelin LZ 101 (L 55) is wrecked during a forced landing in Germany and is dismantled.

October 21 A Curtiss HS-1 flying-boat test flies the prototype Liberty engine. On August 12 the Secretary of War had announced that the engine had passed its final tests, presumably static tests.

October 28 A Fokker Dr. I triplane flown by Leutnant Heinrich Gontermann breaks-up in the air. This and a later similar accident causes the fighter to be grounded temporarily for examination. Poorly constructed wings are at fault.

October 29 A British-built Airco (de Havilland) D.H.4 is re-engined with an American Liberty engine and test flown for the first time in this configuration.

November 7 The Russian Revolution comes to a climax with the storming of the Winter Palace in Petrograd and the taking of points of communication.

This revolution eventually has the result of releasing massive German forces from the Eastern Front to the Western Front for the Spring offensives. (q.v. December 22, 1917)

November 10   The Bureau of Commissars of Aviation and Aeronautics (BKAV) is set up in Russia just three days after the Bolshevik seizure of power.

November 18   US Navy Tellier flying-boats begin air operations from Le Croisac, France. In total 34 such aircraft are used by the Navy.

November 20   The Battle of Cambrai begins and 289 British aircraft are brought together to support the army and to observe enemy forces and disrupt their communications. (The success of low-level air attacks on ground forces by the RFC, and later by the Germans, had far-reaching effects on the whole concept of aerial warfare).

November 21   The US Navy's N-9 radio-guided flying bomb is demonstrated. (q.v. September 12, 1916).

November 27   Brig-Gen B.D. Foulois becomes Chief of Air Service, American Expeditionary Force, taking over from Brig-Gen William L. Kenly.

November 29   The Air Force (Constitution) Bill receives Royal assent in Britain.

November 30   The prototype British Vickers Vimy heavy bomber flies for the first time.

December   Sopwith Camels of No 44 Squadron, RFC, force down a Gotha bomber, which lands near Folkestone.

December 3   It is announced that the 'American Squadron' or Lafayette Escadrille (now Spa 124 with Spads) will be taken under AEF control from February 1918.

December 7   The United States of America declares war on Austria-Hungary.

December 17   German Navy Oberleutnant Christiansen, flying a Brandenburg W 12 floatplane fighter, shoots down the British non-rigid airship C 27.

December 18   Riesenflugzeugabteilung SO1 drops more than 27,000kg of bombs on the UK without loss through enemy action between now and May 20 1918.

December 22   Russia begins peace negotiations with Germany following the Revolution. Particularly worrying for the Allies is the extra German manpower thus released for the Western Front.

1918

Deutschösterreichische Fliegertruppe (German-Austrian Flying Troop) is formed. Disbanded by Allied Control Commission in 1919.

The Brazilian Army Air Service is formed from the previous Army Balloon Corps.

The Chilean Army Aviation Company is formed.

German fighter pilot Hermann Goering receives the Pour le Mérite.

The Aviation Department, Yugoslav Army, is formed.

January   The German D-Type (fighter) competition at Berlin-Adlershof is won by the Fokker V.11 designed by Reinhold Platz. After some minor modifications it is put into production as the Fokker D.VII.

The first Gotha bomber to be shot down at night over England is destroyed by Sopwith Camels of No 44 Squadron, RFC, at Wickford, Essex.

January 2   The British Air Ministry is established.

Maj-Gen Sir Hugh Trenchard becomes the Chief of the British Air Staff.

January 5   Five German Navy airships are destroyed in an explosion at the Ahlhorn sheds (LZ 87/L 47, LZ 94/L 46, LZ 97/L 51, LZ 105/L 58 and SL 20).

January 18   Maj-Gen Sir Hugh Trenchard hands the command of the Royal Flying Corps in France to Maj-Gen Sir John Salmond.

January 23   The first AEF balloon ascent is made at the Balloon School at Cuperly, France.

February   The British Handley Page O/400 heavy bombers first carry the 1,650lb 'Minor' bomb.

The first combat aircraft to be mass-produced in America (Airco D.H.4s) come off the production lines.

The first operational squadrons of the American Expeditionary Force are formed in France. (Between now and the Armistice American squadrons destroy 781 enemy aircraft).

Lt Stephen W. Thompson becomes the first American pilot to gain an aerial victory while serving with an American squadron (the 103rd Pursuit Squadron, formed from the Lafayette Escadrille on February 18 but still flying with French forces).

February 16/17   Zeppelin Staaken R.VI No 39 bomber becomes the first of the German 'giants' to drop a 1,000kg (2,205lb) bomb on England.

February 18   The first American fighter squadron proper arrives in France as the 95th Aero (Pursuit) Squadron.

March   The Aviation of the 1st Polish Corps is formed from the earlier 1st Polish Aviation Unit.

Ilmailuvoimat, the Finnish air arm, is formed.

A helicopter designed by Dr Ing Theodor von Kármán (see 1944) and Wilhelm Zurovec is completed. It uses an electro-motor to power four rotors, as pioneered by Oberstlt Stephan von Petroczy. Built in Budapest, the PKZ 1 performs four tethered lift-offs, all but one carrying three persons.

March 3   The French-built Astra-Torres AT 1 non-rigid dirigible, the first French Navy airship, is operated by the AEF for the first time.

Germany and Russia conclude peace negotiations.

March 4 The prototype three-seat de Havilland D.H.10 heavy bomber flies for the first time.

The American 94th Aero (Pursuit) Squadron arrives in France.

Edward Vernon Rickenbacker, eventually the highest-scoring US pilot of the First World War, is transferred to the 94th Aero (Pursuit) Squadron (the 'Hat-in-the-Ring' squadron.)

March 5 The first US balloon unit to serve operationally in France with AEF ground forces is the 2nd Balloon Company.

March 10 The German Junkers D.I. (Junkers J9) all-metal single-seat cantilever monoplane fighter is flown as a prototype. Forty-one production aircraft are eventually built.

March 11 The world's first scheduled international airmail service begins, operated between Vienna and Kiev with Hansa-Brandenburg C.I biplanes.

March 14 Aircraft of the 95th Aero (Pursuit) Squadron begin patrol flights on the Western Front.

March 19 The first American observation patrol over enemy lines takes place, by aircraft of the 94th Aero (Pursuit) Squadron.

March 21 The German spring offensives begin under the *Michael* plan, dubbed *Kaiserschlacht* or Emperor's battle. German strength includes 47 infantry attack divisions, thousands of field guns and hundreds of aeroplanes.

March 26 French General Foch becomes the Commander-in-Chief of the Allied Armies fighting on the Western Front.

March 27 The first production aircraft built by the US Naval Aircraft Factory, Philadelphia Navy Yard, makes its first flight. It is a Curtiss H-16 flying-boat.

April RAF Handley Page O/400 heavy bombers make the first of more than 200 cross-Channel flights between Lympne, England, and France, carrying passengers and goods. The service lasts until the following November, by which time many hundreds of people have been carried.

Airco (de Havilland) D.H.4s of No 202 Squadron, RAF, photograph Zeebrugge prior to the raid on the mole.

Fokker D.VII biplane fighters become operational on the Western Front with Jagdgeschwader I. The D.VII proves itself to be the best German fighter of the First World War.

April 1 The RFC and RNAS are amalgamated to form the Royal Air Force.

Bristol F.2B Fighters of No 22 Squadron carry out the first official missions of the RAF (RFC renamed).

April 2 Maj J.T.B. McCudden, RAF, is awarded the Victoria Cross for valour.

The PKZ 2 helicopter designed by Wilhelm Zurovec alone, is flown for the first time. With two contra-rotating rotors driven by three Gnome rotary engines, it thereafter makes tethered flights of up to approximately 50 m (164ft), the longest lasting about one hour.

April 7 Zeppelin LZ 104 (L 59), known as the 'African ship', burns while airborne over the Strait of Otranto off the Italian east coast.

April 11 I Corps Observation Squadron becomes the first American observation unit to fly over enemy lines. (q.v. March 19, 1918)

April 12 The final German Zeppelin raid on England causing casualties among the civilian population is carried out.

April 13 Teniente Luis C. Candelaria, Argentine Army, makes the first crossing of the Andes by air, flying a Morane-Saulnier Parasol monoplane. His route takes him from Zapala, Argentina, to Cunço, Chile.

April 14 The 94th Aero (Pursuit) Squadron becomes the first American fighter unit to see combat. Lts Douglas Campbell and Alan Winslow shoot down two German aeroplanes and the pilots are captured. The American pilots fly French-built Nieuport 28s.

Maj-Gen Sir Hugh Trenchard resigns as Chief of the Air Staff in Britain. His place is taken by Major-Gen Sir Frederick Sykes.

April 15 American fighters make their first combat patrol over enemy lines.

April 21 'Ace of Aces' Rittmeister Manfred Frhr von Richthofen is killed while flying a Fokker Dr I triplane during an engagement with No 209 Squadron, RAF, over Sailly-le-Sec. Capt A. Roy Brown is credited with the victory.

April 22-23 The mole near Zeebrugge, Belgium is attacked by Wing Cdr Fellows flying an Airco (de Havilland) D.H.4.

April 29 Capt Edward Vernon Rickenbacker, subsequently America's top ace of the war, shoots down the first of his 26 victims, an Albatros scout.

May The AEG G.V heavy bomber appears. Several enter commercial service with DLR after the Armistice, each accommodating six passengers.

May 1 Lts A.A. McLeod and A. Jerrard, RAF, are awarded Victoria Crosses for valour.

May 10 German Navy Zeppelin LZ 107 (L 62) explodes while airborne over Heligoland.

May 11 The American Expeditionary Force receives its first US-built D.H.4.

Italian Corpo Aeronautico Militare aircraft are used to fly an air service across the Tyrrhenian Sea. The service lasts until the following month.

May 15 The US Army Signal Corps establishes the first American airmail service between New York and Washington, using Curtiss JNs and Standard J biplanes.

US Army Signal Corps Standard J biplane used to carry mail between New York and Washington, May 15 1918. (*US National Archives*)

May 15   The Packard-Le Père LUSAC-11 fighter flies. It is powered by a Liberty 12 fitted with a turbocharger for its altitude record attempt on February 27, 1920, when Capt Rudolph W. Schroeder attains 10,093m (33,113ft) at Dayton, Ohio, USA.

May 18   The first American bomber squadron, AEF, is formed in France as the 96th Aero Squadron.

May 19   Hauptmann H. Kohl receives the Pour le Mérite, after flying 800 missions.

May 19/20   Night raids on England by Gotha bombers end as losses become too high.

May 20   Overman Act creates the Bureau of Aircraft Production and the Division of Military Aeronautics. The US Army Air Service is formed from these on May 24.

May 24   The All-Russian Air Board is replaced by the new Chief Directorate of the Workers and Peasants Military Air Fleet (GU-RKKVF: Glavoce Upravlenie-Raboche-Krestyanskogo Krasnogo Vozdushnogo Flota).

May 29   Brig-Gen Mason Patrick is made Chief of the US Air Service in France.

June   Oberleutnant Ernst Udet receives the Pour le Mérite.

June 2   Oberleutnant Erich Löwenhardt receives the Pour le Mérite.

June 5   The Independent Force, RAF, is established to operate heavy and light bombers in a strategic offensive role against industrial and military targets inside Germany. Maj-Gen Sir Hugh Trenchard is made Commander of the Force.

June 6   The first Fairey IIIA two-seat naval light bomber makes its maiden flight. This is the first of the famous Fairey III series.

June 12   The first bombing raid by US aircraft on the Western Front is carried out by the 96th Aero Squadron on the railway at Dommany – Baroncourt.

June 19   Maggiore Francesco Baracca, Italy's most successful fighter pilot with 34 victories, is killed during a ground-attack mission at Montello.

June 24   Capt Brian Peck, RAF, starts the first official air-mail service in Canada.

June 25   King George V grants the prefix 'Royal' to the UK's Aeronautical Society.

July 9   Maj James Thomas Byford McCudden, VC, RAF, is killed at Auxi-le-Chateau when the engine of his S.E.5a fails and he crash-lands.

July 10   Leutnant F. Rumey is awarded the Pour le Mérite.

July 15   Gen Ludendorff launches the final major attack of the German spring offensive on Reims. By the 18th it is clear that the spring offensive has failed.

July 19   German Navy Zeppelins LZ 99 (L 54) and LZ 108 (L 60) are destroyed in their sheds at Tonden by aircraft from HMS *Furious*.

July 26 Maj Edward 'Mick' Mannock, Britain's top ace with 73 victories, is killed when the petrol tank of his S.E.5a fighter is hit by German ground fire over the Western Front. (q.v. July 18, 1919)

July 28 The first flight from England to Egypt is started on July 28 by Maj A.S. MacLaren and Brig-Gen A.E. Borton in a Handley Page O/400 bomber. On August 8 they arrive in Egypt.

August German Fokker D.VII biplane fighters gain 565 'kills' over the Western Front in this month alone.

August 1 Flt Sub-Lt Stuart Culley, Royal Navy, achieves the first take-off by aeroplane from a moving barge. The barge is towed behind HMS *Redoubt*. (q.v. August 11, 1918)

August 2 US-built D.H.4s undertake their first patrol over enemy territory in France, an observation flight with the 135th Corps Observation Squadron.

August 5/6 German Navy Zeppelin LZ 112 (L 70) is shot down off the Norfolk coast of England by Maj Egbert Cadbury flying an Airco (de Havilland) D.H.4.

August 7 The Blériot-Spad S.XX fighter flies as a prototype in France. It subsequently sets up post-war speed records.

The first Fokker E.V parasol-wing fighters are received on the Western Front by Jagdgeschwader 1, commanded by Goering. Within a very short time of operational assessment, wing failures result in the withdrawal of the fighter (August 21).

August 9 97 Squadron, RAF, joins the Independent Force to operate Handley Page O/400 heavy bombers.

August 10 Oberleutnant E. Loewenhardt is killed in a mid-air collision with another German pilot, his score standing at 53 victories. (By the end of the war he was ranked third most successful German pilot).

August 11 A patrol of 18 Brandenburg W 29 float-plane fighters attack six British CMBs (Coastal Motor Boats, later MTBs) near Borkum and sink three of them by gunfire. The remaining three CMBs, all damaged, escape to Holland where their crews are interned.

German Navy Zeppelin LZ 100 (L 53) is shot down by Flt Sub-Lt Stuart Culley, who has taken off in his Sopwith Camel from a towed barge in the North Sea.

August 12 The US Post Office takes over air mail services from the Army. The New York to Washington service is flown with Standard R.4s.

An Airco (de Havilland) D.H.4 of No 217 Squadron, RAF, helps sink a German U-boat in the North Sea.

August 17 The Martin MB-1 (or more correctly the GMB) flies. It becomes a standard bomber and observation aircraft with the USAAS.

August 21 The Nieuport-Delage NiD 29 single-seat fighter prototype flies for the first time. It becomes one of the most widely operated aircraft of the 1920s, flown in Belgium, France, Italy and Japan.

August 31 Airco (de Havilland) D.H.9As of No 110 Squadron arrive in France.

September 5 The Royal Canadian Naval Air Service is founded. It lasts just three months.

September 12-15 The largest number of aeroplanes brought together for a single operation is assembled for the assault on the Saint Mihiel Salient during the Battle of Bapaume. Under the command of Brig-Gen William 'Billy' Mitchell, 1,483 aeroplanes of all types support American and French forces.

September 14/15 Forty RAF Handley Page O/400 heavy bombers launch an attack on German targets. In the same month O/400s begin dropping the new 1,650lb bomb.

September 25 Capt Edward V. Rickenbacker is awarded the US Congressional Medal of Honor.

September 26 Frenchman Capitaine René Paul Fonck shoots down four German Fokker D.VIIs, an Albatros D.V and a two-seater.

September 28 Leutnant F. Büchner is awarded the Pour le Mérite.

2nd Lt Frank Luke Jr is killed after destroying three balloons (while officially grounded for misconduct). Having been wounded, he landed his aircraft behind enemy lines and had a shoot-out with German troops. (His score of 21 victories made him the second-ranking American ace of the war.)

September 29 Frank Luke is awarded posthumously the US Congressional Medal of Honor.

October Sopwith Cuckoo torpedo-bombers go to sea on board the carrier HMS *Argus*.

October 4 The first Navy-Curtiss NC flying-boat makes its maiden flight as an anti-submarine aircraft. (q.v. May 8, 1919)

October 5 Roland Garros is killed while flying a Spad fighter at Vouziers.

October 6 2nd Lt Erwin R. Bleckley and 1st Lt Harold E. Goettler are awarded posthumously US Congressional Medals of Honor after an heroic supply-dropping mission at Binarville cost them their lives.

October 12 Pilots of the 185th Aero (Pursuit) Squadron undertake the first US night fighter operations in France.

October 15 The 1st Aviation Unit of the Polish Forces is formed.

October 24 The Fokker E.V arrives at the Western Front as the strengthened D.VIII. It is an immediate success, its good rate of climb and manoeuvrability complementing a maximum speed of 204 km/h (127 mph).

October 26 Maj-Gen Sir Hugh Trenchard becomes Commander-in-Chief of the Inter-Allied Independent Air Force.

Smith, Borton and Salmond arrive in India, December 12 1918.

October 27 Maj William G. Barker wins the Victoria Cross when he flies his Sopwith Snipe through five formations of German fighters during a single patrol, shooting down four aircraft. He is wounded three times but manages to land behind British lines.

October 29 The Czechoslovak Army Air Force is formed.

October 30 Peace between the Allies and Turkey comes after the agreement to an Armistice.

November Canadian Air Force is formed.

The international airmail service from Vienna to Kiev is discontinued. (q.v. March 11, 1918)

November 1 More than 100 Fokker D.VIII monoplane fighters are operational with German aviation service and naval units.

November 6 British airship R 31 makes its last flight before being grounded as a result of its rotting wooden framework. (Total flying time of the R 31 was about nine hours.)

November 8 Capt F.M.F. West is awarded the Victoria Cross for valour while flying an Armstrong Whitworth F.K.8 light bomber on August 10, 1918. (He was the second F.K.8 pilot to win the VC, the other being McLeod.)

November 10 Dr Robert H. Goddard demonstrates rockets at the Aberdeen Proving Ground, Maryland, USA.

November 11 The Armistice ends the First World War at the eleventh hour of the eleventh day of the eleventh month. The RAF finishes the war with the largest air force, comprising well over 22,000 aeroplanes, while the best-equipped air force is generally believed to be the French.

November 25 The Italian airline Posta Aerea Transadriatica begins regular mail flights from Venice. The service is short lived.

November 29 – December 12 Capt Ross M. Smith, Brig-Gen A.E. Borton, Maj-Gen W. Salmond and two other crew members start the first flight from Egypt to India on November 29, flying a Handley Page O/400 from Heliopolis bound for Karachi. They reach Karachi on December 12.

November 30 Capt A.W. Beauchamp-Proctor and Maj Barker, RAF, are awarded Victoria Crosses.

December 1 The Central Aero and Hydrodynamics Institute (TsAGI) is established in Moscow. It is the first establishment of this kind in the world, and becomes the most important aeronautical research centre in the Soviet Union.

December 4-22 Four Curtiss JN-4 'Jennies' complete the first US Army coast-to-coast crossing of the USA, from San Diego to Jacksonville.

December 16 No 18 Squadron, RAF, begins air mail flights to the British Army of Occupation in Germany. The flights end in August of the following year.

1918 – 1919

December 13, 1918 – January 16, 1919 On December 13, 1918, Sqn Ldr A. MacLaren, Lt R. Halley and others begin the first flight from England to India in a

Handley Page V/1500 heavy bomber. They arrive in Delhi on January 16, 1919.

Canadian Naval Air Service is formed.

1919

The Uruguayan Aéronautica Militar is formed.

The Royal Siamese Aeronautical Service is formed from the Royal Siamese Flying Corps.

The Chinese Army Air Arm becomes the Chinese Aviation Service.

The Swiss Militär-Flugwesen is formed.

The Chilean Naval Aviation Service is formed.

An air unit of the Guatemalan Army is formed.

The Peruvian Army Aviation Service is formed.

The Romanian Divisia l-a Aeriana is formed.

Mme la Baronne de Laroche is killed in a flying accident. (q.v. March 8, 1910)

The Argentine Marquis de Pescara begins constructing helicopters with cyclic-pitch control.

January 8 The German Air Ministry restores civil flying. This beats the British Air Navigation Regulations by several months.

A military air mail service is started in Switzerland by the Militär-Flugwesen, flying Haefeli DH-3 between Zürich and Berne. Passenger services follow.

January 10 Regular passenger and mail services are started between London and Paris by No 2 (Communications) Squadron, RAF. The RAF service lasts until September, mainly for the benefit of the Peace Conference at Versailles. The aircraft used are Airco (de Havilland) D.H.4As, modified D.H.4s with enclosed accommodation aft of the pilot for two passengers.

January 11-14 Winston Churchill is appointed Secretary of State for Air. Maj-Gen Sir Hugh Trenchard becomes the Chief of the Air Staff and Maj-Gen Sir Frederick Sykes is appointed Controller-General of Civil Aviation in Britain.

February An express parcel air service between Folkestone and Ghent is started by Aircraft Transport and Travel Ltd., to carry food and clothing to Belgium. The flying is carried out by RAF pilots in Airco (de Havilland) D.H.9s.

Modified Airco (de Havilland) D.H.4A used as a passenger and mail carrier, January 10 1919.

Deutsche Luft Reederei AEG N.1, February 5 1919.

February 5 Deutsche Luft-Reederei (DLR) begins the first sustained daily passenger airline service, flying modified ex-military AEG and DFW biplanes between Berlin and Weimar, Germany.

February 8 The first airline passengers (military) to be carried from Paris to London are flown by Farman F60 Goliath from Toussus-le-Noble to Kenley.

February 12 The Department of Civil Aviation is formed in Britain.

February 21 The prototype Thomas Morse MB-3 biplane fighter makes its first flight. The MB-3 was the first US-designed fighter to enter large-scale production.

March Italian Caproni aeroplanes are used to inaugurate a regular international air service between Padova (then Padua) and Vienna.

The prototype de Havilland D.H.16 makes its first flight. It is a four-passenger biplane, the first purely commercial de Havilland airliner. (q.v. May 1919).

March 1 The German airline DLR extends its air network to Hamburg.

An Army air mail service is begun between Folkestone and Cologne.

March 3 William Boeing and Edward Hubbard use the Boeing Model CL-4S to carry out the first US international air mail service, between Seattle, Washington and Victoria, British Columbia, Canada.

March 10 Brig-Gen William 'Billy' Mitchell becomes the US Director of Military Aeronautics.

March 22 The first regular international passenger service is opened between Paris and Brussels by Lignes Aériennes Farman, using Farman F60 Goliath biplanes.

April The Japanese Army Aviation Department is formed.

April 6 Customs examination of airline passengers begins at Brussels.

April 13 The prototype Vickers Vimy Commercial 10-passenger airliner makes its maiden flight.

April 18 CMA (Compagnie des Messageries Aériennes) inaugurates a mail and cargo service between Paris and Lille. The service is daily using ex-military Breguet 14s. Brussels and London are added to the growing network in August.

April 19 Leslie Leroy Irvin makes the first recorded free-fall jump from an aeroplane, before deploying his parachute.

April 23 The North Sea Aerial Navigation Company is formed as a domestic airline using unwanted military Blackburn R.T.1 Kangaroo torpedo-bombers. Seven passengers are carried by each of three Kangaroos, flying between Leeds and Hounslow. A cargo service to Amsterdam is later provided to carry textiles and other goods, but this is started and closed down in 1920.

May The prototype de Havilland D.H.16 four-passenger airliner enters service with Aircraft Transport

Above North Sea Aerial Navigation Company Blackburn R.T.1 Kangaroo, April 23 1919.
Below de Havilland D.H.16 operated by Aircraft Transport and Travel Ltd, May 1919.

Above **Hawker and Grieve prepare for take-off in their Sopwith Atlantic, May 18 1919.**
Below **Navy-Curtiss NC-4, May 31 1919.**

Lloyd Luftverkehr Sablatnig starts operating with a Sablatnig P.III, June 1919.

and Travel Ltd. It flies to Amsterdam in July for demonstration at the Dutch First Air Traffic Exhibition.

Two Italian ex-military SCA M-class semi-rigid airships are used to inaugurate a passenger and mail service between Rome and Naples. The network is later extended.

May 1 Civil aviation is once again allowed in Britain following publication of the Air Navigation Regulations.

May 5 The Swiss air mail service begins carrying civil mail in addition to military.

May 8 Three US Navy NC flying-boats set out from Rockaway, New York, in an attempt to make the first air crossing of the Atlantic, under the leadership of Cdr John H. Towers. NC-1 and NC-3 fail in their attempt and alight near the Azores. (q.v. May 31, 1919)

May 15 The US Post Office inaugurates the first section of a transcontinental airmail service between Chicago and Cleveland. (q.v. February 22, 1921)

May 18 Harry Hawker and Lieut Cmdr K.F. Mac-kenzie-Grieve attempt a non-stop transatlantic flight between Newfoundland and the UK. They alight on the following day and are picked up by a Danish vessel. They are awarded £5,000 by the *Daily Mail* newspaper for the attempt.

May 24 The Avro Civil Aviation Service begins the first domestic airline service in Britain. It offers daily flights linking Manchester, Southport and Blackpool. The service lasts four months.

May 31 Navy-Curtiss flying-boat NC-4, commanded by Lt Cdr A.C. Read, completes the first transatlantic crossing by air, landing at Plymouth, England. The journey, made in hops, covers stops in Chatham (Massachusetts), Halifax (Nova Scotia), Trepassy Bay (Newfoundland), Horta and Ponta Delgada (the Azores), Lisbon (Portugal) and Ferrol del Caudillo (Spain). Total flying time is 57 hours 16 minutes. (q.v. May 8, 1919)

June The German airline Lloyd Luftverkehr Sablatnig is founded as a domestic operator.

June 7 The British airline Daimler Air Hire is established. It later becomes known as Daimler Airway.

June 14 Handley Page Transport is established. Its first airline operation is between Cricklewood and Bournemouth, England.

The French Nieuport-Delage 29 biplane fighter attains an altitude of more than 9,100m (29,850ft) and is ordered into production. Eventually 25 French escadrilles fly the type, while a large number of others serve in Belgium, Italy and Japan.

June 14/15 Capt John Alcock and Lt Arthur Whitten Brown make the first non-stop crossing of the Atlantic in a Vickers Vimy bomber, flying from St. John's, New-

Above Junkers F13, as operated by Deutsche Luft-Hansa from 1926, June 25 1919.

Left Alcock and Brown, June 14/15 1919.

Left Zeppelins L.42 and L.63 wrecked at Nordholz, June 23 1919. (*Imperial War Museum*)

---

foundland, to Clifden, County Galway, Ireland. Total flying time is 16 hours 27 minutes.

June 23   German Navy Zeppelins LZ 46 (L 14), LZ 79 (L 41), LZ 91 (L 42), LZ 103 (L 56), LZ 111 (L 65) and LZ 110 (L 63) are wrecked by their crews at Nordholz to prevent them being handed over to the Allies, as to be ordered under the Versailles Peace Treaty.

June 25   The world's first purpose-built all-metal commercial aircraft flies as the German Junkers F 13. 322 are eventually built.

June 28   The Versailles Peace Treaty is signed, forbidding the Germans from having an air force or producing military aircraft. (Among many other terms included was the handing over of all Fokker D.VII fighters to the Allies. German aircraft manufacturers got round the manufacturing clause of the treaty by setting up factories abroad.)

July   Compagnie des Transports Aéronautiques du Sud-Ouest is formed as a charter operator flying to points around the Bay of Biscay.

July 2-6   British airship R 34 makes the first airship crossing of the Atlantic, flying from East Fortune, Scotland, to New York.

July 9-13   R 34 leaves Mineola, New York, for Norfolk, England, and arrives five days later, having made the first two-way crossing of the Atlantic.

July 14   An Italian Fiat B.R. light bomber makes the first non-stop flight between Rome and Paris. (q.v. December 23, 1924)

July 15   Aircraft Transport and Travel Ltd undertakes an experimental airline flight to Le Bourget (q.v. August 25, 1919).

July 18   Britain's top ranking ace of the First World War, Maj Edward 'Mick' Mannock, is posthumously awarded the Victoria Cross. (q.v. July 26, 1918)

August 7/8   Capt Ernest Hoy, flying a Curtiss JN-4 Jenny, makes the first aeroplane flight across the Canadian Rocky Mountains, from Vancouver to Calgary.

August 24   Delag airship *Bodensee* makes the first of its regular flights from Friedrichshafen to Berlin.

August 25   A de Havilland D.H.16 belonging to Aircraft Transport and Travel Ltd begins the world's first scheduled daily international airline service proper, flying from Hounslow, England, to Le Bourget, France.

Handley Page Transport makes a Press flight from Hounslow to Le Bourget, using an O/7 ten-passenger airliner. Regular services begin on September 2.

August 26   Handley Page Transport carries the first two women passengers to fly on an airline service between England and France.

September   The London to Paris services by No 2 (Communications) Squadron, RAF, are discontinued after a total of 749 flights.

September 1   The French aircraft manufacturer Forges et Ateliers de Construction Latécoère begins a regular airline service to Casablanca, Morocco. The airline becomes known as Lignes Aériennes Latécoère. Later, the airline adopts the name Compagnie Générale d'Enterprises Aéronautiques. Latécoère also pioneers South American services from 1925.

69

September 2 Handley Page Transport begins a regular London-Paris airline service.

September 19 Compagnie des Messageries Aériennes (CMA) begins its Paris to London passenger service with Breguet 14s.

September 28 Supermarine Aviation Company inaugurates a flying-boat service to Le Havre.

September 29 The Polskie Wojska Lotnicze (Polish Air Force) is formed.

September 30 The British Aerial Transport Company (BAT) inaugurates a short-lived domestic airline service between London and Birmingham, flying Koolhoven F.K.26 four-passenger biplanes (first flown April 1919). A London-Amsterdam service is also flown for a short time.

October The prototype of the Fokker F.II high-wing monoplane airliner appears.

The prototype Vickers Viking four-passenger amphibian makes its maiden flight. (q.v. December 18, 1919)

October 7 KLM (Koninklijke Luchtvaart Maatschappij voor Nederland an Kolonien/Royal Dutch Airlines) is formed.

October 8-31 The first Army air service Transcontinental Reliability and Endurance Test is held in the USA.

October 11 Handley Page Transport offers the first meals on board airliners, at a cost of 3 shillings per basket, on its London-Brussels service.

October 13 The League of Nations sets up the Paris Convention to regulate international flying.

The shipping firm S. Instone and Company begin ferrying staff and light cargo by air between Cardiff (Wales), London and Paris. (q.v. February 1920)

October 17 The Comando de Aviación Naval Argentina is formed.

November The Blériot-Spad 27 two-passenger commercial biplane flies for the first time. It is used by CMA.

November 1 The US airline West Indies Airways begins services between Key West, Florida, and Havana, Cuba. It later merges with Aeromarine Airways to form Aeromarine West Indies Airways.

November 11 An airline service between Berlin and Königsberg (now Kaliningrad), is started by Albatros Werke.

November 12 Australian brothers Capt Ross Smith and Lt Keith Smith set off from Hounslow, England, in a Vickers Vimy bomber in an attempt to be the first men to fly from England to Australia. (q.v. December 10, 1919)

November 14 The American Railway Express Company hires a Handley Page V/1500 to carry 454kg (1,000lb) of parcels and other goods from Mitchell Field, New York, to Chicago. Mechanical problems force an early termination of the flight.

November 16 Capt H.N. Wrigley and Lt A.W. Murphy become the first men to fly across Australia when they fly a B.E.2e from Melbourne to join Ross and Keith Smith. They land at Darwin on December 12 after a flying time of 46 hours.

December 1 Delag's airship service between Friedrichshafen and Berlin is suspended on the orders of Allied Control Commission after more than 100 flights, carrying 2,400 passengers, have been made.

December 2 The prototype Handley Page W.8 biplane airliner makes its maiden flight. It is among the first purpose-built British airliners to appear after the First World War and proves highly successful.

December 5 Aerovias Nacionales de Colombia SA (Avianca) is formed. A Colombian airline, it has (in 1982) the longest continuous record of scheduled services.

December 10 Ross and Keith Smith land their Vickers Vimy in Darwin, having made the first flight from England to Australia, a distance of 18,170km (11,290 miles).

December 18 Sir John Alcock is killed in a flying accident at Rouen, France, while flying the Vickers Viking amphibian to the Paris Air Show.

December 27 Boeing's first commercial aircraft and first flying-boat of its own design makes its maiden flight as the B-1.

1920

The Cuerpo de Aviadores Militares is formed as the air arm of Ecuador.

The Finnish air arm becomes the Ilmavoimat.

The Australian Flying Corps becomes the Australian Air Corps.

The Dayton-Wright RB Racer appears as the first aeroplane with a practical form of retractable landing gear. Built for the 1920 Gordon Bennett Aviation Cup Race, it has a maximum speed of 320 km/h (200 mph).

The first glider competition is held at Rhön, Germany, organised by the Aero Technical Association of Dresden.

January 20 The Fédération Aéronautique Internationale announces that it is prepared to accept new official world records. However, speed records will require four runs (in both directions) over a 1km course, an average then being taken. The effect of wind speed is thus cancelled.

January 24 – March 31 Cmndt Vuillemin, Aéronautique Militaire, crosses the Sahara by aeroplane.

February S. Instone and Company begin commercial airline services to Paris. The air organisation becomes the Instone Air Line the following year. (q.v. May 15, 1920)

February 1 Suid Afrikaanse Lugmag is formed as the South African air arm from the squadron attached to the Royal Flying Corps during the First World War.

February 4 Lt-Col Pierre van Ryneveld and Sqn Ldr Christopher Q. Brand take off from Brooklands in a

Winner of the 1920 Schneider Trophy contest, and only competitor, was the Italian Savoia S.12 flying boat, piloted by Lt Luigi Bologna at Venice. The same city held the 1921 contest, also won by the Italians. (*Stato Maggiore Aeronautica*)

Vickers Vimy bomber in an attempt to make the first flight from England to South Africa. (q.v. March 6, 1920 and March 17, 1920)

February 5 The RAF's Cranwell cadet college is established.

February 7 Frenchman Sadi Lecointe sets the first post-war world speed record, achieving 275.22 km/h (171.01 mph) in a Nieuport-Delage 29.

March 5 The first freight/passenger de Havilland D.H.18 biplane airliner is acquired by Aircraft Transport and Travel Ltd. Instone Air Line and Daimler Hire Ltd share the other five. (q.v. April 7, 1922).

March 6 van Ryneveld and Brand (q.v. February 4, 1920) crash their second Vimy bomber at Bulawayo, Southern Rhodesia, and have to wait until a D.H.9 is provided for the rest of the journey. (see below)

March 17 van Ryneveld and Brand set off in a D.H.9 to complete their England-to-South Africa flight, arriving at Wynberg Aerodrome, Cape Town, on March 20.

March 29 Croydon Airport is first used as London's air terminal.

Grands Express Aériens (CGEA) introduces the Farman F.60 Goliath on its Le Bourget-Croydon service. The Goliath dominates European aviation for a decade.

April 17 The Venezuelan Military Air Service is formed.

April 23 Compagnie Franco-Roumaine de Navigation Aérienne (CFRNA) is established in France. The Potez IX four-passenger biplane becomes its main aircraft. (q.v. October 1920)

May 15 The Instone Air Line is formed in Britain to operate the London-Paris route established by the shipping firm S. Instone and Company.

May 17 KLM begins an Amsterdam-London airline service in conjunction with Aircraft Transport and Travel Ltd. AT & T inaugurates the London to Amsterdam route using a de Havilland D.H.16.

May 25 The Belgian airline SNETA (Syndicat National pour l'Étude des Transports Aériens) begins airline services to England. It becomes best known for its operations to the Belgian Congo. (q.v. July 1, 1920)

June 4 Army Re-Organisation Act creates the US Army Air Service.

July The Farman F.50 is introduced on the Paris-London service of Grands Express Aériens (CGEA). Originating as a bomber, it had equipped French escadrilles F.110 and F.114 in 1918. After the Armistice two were converted into makeshift airliners for five passengers.

July 1 A regular Paris to Geneva, Switzerland, airline service is established by Aéro Transport.

SNETA begins air services between Léopoldville and N'Gombe, Belgian Congo.

August The prototype Fairey IIID makes its first flight. In production form it becomes a general-purpose biplane with the RAF, Fleet Air Arm and others.

October A Paris-Prague air service is started by the Compagnie Franco-Roumaine de Navigation Aérienne. It soon extends to Warsaw, Budapest and elsewhere, reaching Constantinople by Autumn 1922.

October 14 The Hubbard Air Service begins regular air mail services between Seattle and Victoria, using a Boeing B-1 flying-boat.

November 1 Aeromarine West Indies Airways is given the first contract for foreign mail by the US Post Office.

November 16 Qantas (Queensland and Northern Territory Aerial Service) is registered.

November 24 The prototype Dornier Delphin five/six-passenger commercial flying-boat makes its first flight. Later versions of the Delphin carry up to 13 passengers.

D.H.16 in Aircraft Transport and Travel Ltd livery at Schipol Aerodrome, May 17 1920. (*KLM*)

November 25 The first Pulitzer Trophy Race is won by Captain Corliss C. Moseley, USAAS, flying a Verville-Packard 600. Flown over a triangular course from Mitchell Field, Long Island, New York, competing aircraft had to have a landing speed of less than 121 km/h (75 mph).

December 12 The prototype Blériot-Spad 33 four/five-passenger airliner flies for the first time. One of the most successful early French commercial aircraft, it is first operated on the regular Paris-London services of CMA in 1921. The type is developed throughout the 1920s, ending with the Type 126.

December 14 The first fatal accident on a British scheduled commercial service takes place when a Handley Page O/400 crashes in fog at Cricklewood soon after taking off. Two crew members and two of the six passengers are killed.

December 15 Aircraft Transport and Travel Ltd (AT & T) makes it last commercial airline flight.

1921

Junkers Flugzeugwerke AG forms its own airline branch as the Junkers Luftverkehr. Similarly, Edmund Rumpler Flugzeug-Werke GmbH forms Rumpler Luftverkehr. Eventually, Junkers takes control of the Rumpler airline.

The German airline Aero-Union is formed to administer the operations of Deutsche Luft-Reederei (DLR) and Danziger Luft Reederei.

January R 34 is seriously damaged when it strikes a hill in fog. It is returned to Howden, where groundcrew cause further damage. Finally it is caught by gusting winds and rises and then plunges to the ground, causing its total destruction.

The first internal Soviet airline service is flown by demilitarised *Ilya Mourometz* bombers between Sarapul and Yekaterinburg. The second internal airline service between Moscow and Kharkov is inaugurated later the same year, also flown by demilitarised *Ilya Mourometz* bombers.

February 18 C.C. Eversole, US air mail pilot, makes a free-fall parachute jump from a disabled D.H.4.

February 21-24 Lt William Coney completes the first solo flight from San Diego, California, to Jacksonville, Florida. He completes the flight in a flying time of 22½ hours.

February 22 American transcontinental airmail services begin between San Francisco and Mineola, New York. The route, flown in 14 sections in American-built

Short N.3 Cromarty, April 19 1921.

de Havilland D.H.4Ms, takes a day and a half. The first flight is made by pilot Jack Knight. (q.v. July 1, 1924).

March 19 British government subsidy allows the British airlines Handley Page Transport and Instone Air Line to continue their London to Paris commercial services in the face of French competition.

March 31 The Australian Air Force is formed from the Air Corps.

Croydon Airport is officially inaugurated.

April 14 The Fokker F.III five-passenger high-wing monoplane airliner is introduced into service by KLM.

April 19 The first Short-designed and built flying-boat flies as the N.3 Cromarty.

May The US Army's first production armoured aeroplane flies for the first time as the Boeing GA-1 triplane. Carrying eight 0.30in machine-guns and a 37mm Baldwin cannon, plus ten 25lb fragmentation bombs, in addition to very heavy armour plating, it manages only 169 km/h (105 mph).

June 8 Pressurised cabin experiments begin at Wright Field, USA, using a D.H.4 biplane.

D.H.9As of Nos 30 and 47 Squadrons, RAF, begin a regular Cairo-Baghdad desert air mail service.

July 21 US Army MB-2 biplane bombers, under the command of Brig-Gen William 'Billy' Mitchell, sink the anchored and unmanned ex-German battleship *Ostfriesland* in a demonstration of air power against naval vessels. Other ex-German and surplus American warships are also destroyed.

July 30 Francois Durafour, flying a Caudron, lands on and takes off from Mont Blanc.

August 1 The first Vickers Vernon troop-carrying biplane is delivered to the RAF. The Vernon is the first purpose-designed troop carrier.

August 10 The Bureau of Aeronautics, US Navy, is formed.

August 13 The Australian Air Force becomes the Royal Australian Air Force.

August 24 The British dirigible R 38 breaks up while airborne during flight trials, the wreckage ending in the river Humber. Forty-four of the 49 people on board lose their lives, including 16 Americans, the dirigible having been sold to America.

September 13 German Wolf Hirth makes a glider flight of 21 minutes, bettering the previous best set in 1911.

September 17 The first Air League Challenge Cup race is held, initially for RAF teams.

USS Langley, **March 20 1922.** (*US National Archives*)

September 23 The anchored battleship USS *Alabama* is sunk during aeroplane bombing trials in the USA, just one of three unwanted US Navy vessels sunk during further USAAS demonstrations by Brig-Gen William Mitchell.

October 5 Maj-Gen Mason Patrick becomes the Chief of Air Services, USAAS.

October 15 The Spanish airline Compania Española de Trafico Aereo begins services. It is the founding company of the present day Iberia, formed on July 7, 1940.

November The French airline Aéronavale begins services to North Africa.

November 12 Aviation fuel in a container is carried from one aeroplane to another in flight by Wesley May, who climbs from wing to wing.

December 1 The US Navy's dirigible Goodyear-Goodrich C 7 flies for the first time. One of 16 C-class dirigibles ordered, mostly for anti-submarine patrol, it uses helium gas. Some C-class dirigibles are taken over by the US Army.

December 5 West Australian Airways inaugurates the first regular and scheduled airline service in Australia.

1922

The Brazilian Naval Air Service is formed.

The Irish Air Corps is formed.

The French Lioré et Olivier 13 four-passenger flying-boat appears. The Latécoère airline becomes the major user.

The Polish airline Aero Lloyd Warschau is formed by the shipping organisation Nord Deutscher Lloyd, as just one of the company's airline interests. Lloyd Luftdienst becomes a holding company for all Lloyd airlines.

First flight of the ANT-1 light sports monoplane, the first aircraft designed by Andrei N. Tupolev.

February 9 Formation is announced of the Royal Air Force Reserve.

March 13 Portuguese pilots Capt Gago Coutinho and Capt Sacadura Cabral set off from Lisbon on the first flight over the South Atlantic, flying a Fairey IIIC. On June 16 they arrive in Brazil flying their third aeroplane, Fairey IIID *Santa Cruz*, the earlier two planes having been wrecked en route.

March 20 USS *Langley*, the US Navy's first aircraft carrier, is commissioned.

March 26 The first 8-passenger de Havilland D.H.34 makes its maiden flight. Eleven are eventually built, serving initially with Daimler Hire Ltd and Instone Air Line Ltd. These afford new standards of luxury for air passengers. (q.v. April 2, 1922)

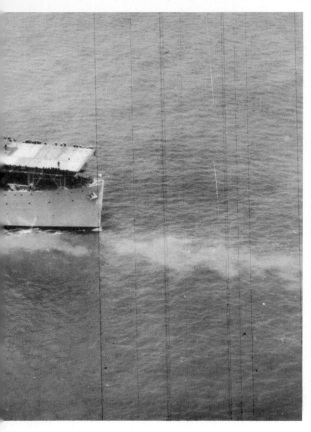

March 31 British government subsidies for commercial flying are suspended after a year.

April The Colombian Army Air Arm is formed.

Shortly after signature of the Rapallo Treaty between Germany and the Soviet Union, preparations are made to establish a clandestine flying training centre at Lipetsk. Between 1924 and August 1933, when the centre is closed down, over 450 German military flying personnel are trained there.

April 2 The British airline Daimler Hire starts London to Paris services using large-capacity de Havilland D.H.34s.

April 7 The first mid-air collision between passenger-carrying airliners on scheduled services takes place over Thieuloy-Saint-Antoine, France, when a Daimler Hire de Havilland D.H.18 and a Grands Express Aériens Farman Goliath collide. The seven passengers and crew are killed.

May The prototype Bréguet 19 bomber and reconnaissance biplane flies. In production form it becomes one of the most widely operated military aircraft of the 'interwar' period.

May 1 The Soviet airline Deutsche-Russische Luftverkehrs AG (Deruluft) begins domestic operations. Passenger services proper begin several months later.

May 11 Maj-Gen Sir Sefton Brancker becomes the Director of Civil Aviation.

May 15 Instone Air Line starts commercial services from London to Brussels using D.H.34s.

June 1 The Swiss airline Ad Astra begins an international service connecting Zürich and Geneva with Nuremberg, Germany.

June 16 Henry A. Berliner demonstrates a helicopter of his own design at College Park, Maryland.

August 12 The fifth Schneider Trophy contest is held at Naples. The Italians need to win this contest to hold the trophy for good, having won the two previous contests. It is won by Briton Henry Biard in the Supermarine Sea Lion II at an average speed of 234.48 km/h (145.7 mph).

August 18 German glider pilot Martens in *Vampyr* makes the first glider flight of more than one hour duration.

August 22 The prototype Vickers Victoria troop transport makes its maiden flight.

September 4 Lt James H. Doolittle flies coast-to-coast across America in a day, piloting his D.H.4 from Pablo Beach, Florida, to Rockwell Field, California. Flying time is 21 hours 19 minutes.

September 8/9 Capt F.L. Barnard wins the first Kings Cup Air Race, piloting a de Havilland D.H.4A over the course from Croydon, England, to Glasgow, Scotland, and back in a flying time of 6 hours 32 minutes.

September 20 Sadi Lecointe sets up the first world speed record of over 200 mph at Villesauvage, France, flying a Nieuport-Delage 29 and achieving 330.75 km/h (205.23 mph).

September 27 Naval Aircraft Radio Laboratory technicians at Anacostia demonstrate radar signatures for the first time. (q.v. 1904)

October 1 The RAF begins its air control operations in Iraq, with the object of keeping the peace and enforcing law and order.

British government subsidies for commercial airline operations are reintroduced.

October 9 Daimler begins its London to Amsterdam service.

October 13 The Curtiss R-6 racing biplane flies for the first time. The R-6 comes first and second in the 1922 US Pulitzer Trophy race, and in the hands of William 'Billy' Mitchell achieves a world speed record of 358.836 km/h (222.970 mph) on October 18.

October 17 Lt V.C. Griffin, flying a Vought VE-7SF fighter, makes the first take-off from an American aircraft carrier. (q.v. March 20, 1922)

October 20 Lt H.R. Harris, US Army Air Service, makes the first parachute escape from a crippled aeroplane in America, jumping from a Loening monoplane.

An early Sabena airliner was this SABCA S-2, registered in 1926, May 23 1923 and December 1926.

October 23 A reversible-pitch propeller is shown by the American Propeller Company.

October 26 Lt Cdr G. DeChevalier, US Navy, flying an Aeromarine 39-B, makes the first landing on USS *Langley*.

November 2 Qantas starts a scheduled service between Charleville and Cloncurry, Queensland.

November 6 The prototype Dornier DoJ Wal flying-boat makes its maiden flight.

November 11 A first flight is achieved by Etienne Oehmichen in his No 2 multi-rotor helicopter in France. On April 14, 1924 he sets a distance in a straight line helicopter record of 360m (1,181ft), bettered on April 17 by a flight of 525m (1,722ft). Oehmichen also gains a time over a 1 km closed-circuit helicopter record, of 7 minutes 40 seconds.

November 18 The prototype French Dewoitine D 1 parasol-wing fighter is flown. D 1s are subsequently operated by the French Navy from the aircraft carrier *Béarn* and by the air forces of Italy (licence-built), Yugoslavia and Switzerland.

November 19 The Hungarian airline Magyar Légi-forgalmi (Malert) is established. Budapest and Vienna are linked by a regular service from mid-1923. The airline can be viewed as the founder of the current Malev, formed in 1946.

November 24 The prototype Vickers Virginia heavy bomber for the RAF makes its first flight.

November 28 The prototype Fairey Flycatcher biplane fighter makes its maiden flight. The production Flycatcher becomes the first FAA fighter to be specially strengthened for catapulting so that it can be launched from warships without carrier-type decks.

December Two de Havilland D.H.16s operated by the de Havilland Aeroplane Hire service fly consignments of an Ulster edition of *The Times* from Sealand to Aldergrove.

December 27 The *Hosho*, the first Japanese purpose-built aircraft carrier, is commissioned. (It survives the Second World War and is decommissioned after the war.)

December 31 A Dornier Komet of Deutsche Luft-Reederei becomes the first German aeroplane to fly to England since the Armistice, landing at Lympne.

1923
The Salvadorean Army Aviation Service is formed.

The Army Air Arm is formed in Nicaragua.

The highly successful Czech general purpose biplane, the Aero A 11, appears. A total of 440 is eventually built. In 1925 A 11s set several duration records (q.v. September 13, 1925), and an Ab 11 is flown in 1926 on a 15,000 km (9,320 mile) intercontinental flight.

American designer Turnbull demonstrates the first variable-pitch aeroplane propeller.

January The French airline Air Union is formed following the merger of CMA and Grands Express Aériens (CGEA).

January 1 The Hungarian airline Aero Express is established to operate a route between Budapest and Vienna. This service, and those of OLAG (q.v. May 31, 1923), Junkers Luftverkehr and Ad Astra, are eventually known under the consortium name of Transeuropa Union.

January 9 The C 4 Autogiro, designed by Don Juan de la Cierva, makes its first flight, marking the beginning of widespread interest in gyroplanes.

February The first take-off and landing of a Japanese fighter on a Japanese aircraft carrier (*Hosho*) are performed by Briton Capt Jordan flying a Mitsubishi IMF1.

February 1 The Danish Army Flying Corps is formed.

March Dobrolet, the original Soviet state airline, is founded. Operations begin with assistance from the Air Force. (q.v. 1929)

March 5 Russian-born Igor Sikorsky forms the Sikorsky Aero Engineering Corporation in the USA.

March 23 The Italian Regia Aeronautica is formed.

April 10 Daimler Airway inaugurates its London – Berlin airline services.

April 29 The prototype Boeing PW-9 biplane fighter takes off for the first time. On September 19, 1924 production examples are ordered for the USAAS.

May 2-3 Lt O.G. Kelly and Lt J.A. Macready, US Army Air Service, make the first non-stop crossing of America by aeroplane, flying a Fokker T-2 from Roosevelt Field, Long Island, to Rockwell Field, California, in a flying time of 26 hours 50 minutes.

May 7 The prototype Armstrong Whitworth Siskin III fighter biplane makes its maiden flight. The production Siskin III becomes only the second newly-designed and built fighter to enter RAF service since the end of the First World War.

May 14 The first prototype Curtiss PW-8 biplane fighter is received by the USAAS.

May 23 Sabena is formed in Belgium to develop routes within Europe and succeed the pioneer airline SNETA in the Belgian Congo.

May 31 The Austrian airline Österreichische Luftverkehrs AG begins services between Vienna and Munich, Germany.

Smith and Richter demonstrate in-flight refuelling over Rockwell Field, California, by remaining airborne for over 37 hours, August 27/28 1923. (*USAF*)

USS *Shenandoah*, September 4 1923. (*Smithsonian Institution*)

June TC 1, the first of the US Army's advanced training non-rigid dirigibles to replace earlier C and D types, is destroyed by fire. It had been launched in 1922.

The first Supermarine Sea Eagle commercial amphibious flying boat is flown. Three join the British Marine Air Navigation Co Ltd. On August 14 one Sea Eagle (G-EBFK) makes the first flight by a commercial aircraft to Germany. Among the passengers is Sir Sefton Brancker.

June 14 The New Zealand Permanent Air Force is formed.

June 23 Flt Lt W.H. Longton, RAF, wins the first Grosvenor Challenge Cup for British aircraft of under 112kW (150hp), in a Sopwith Gnu.

June 27 Capt L.H. Smith and Lt J.P. Richter, US Army Air Service, successfully demonstrate in-flight refuelling in a de Havilland D.H.4B.

July The original JAL (Japanese Air Lines) is established as a domestic operator.

July 19 Československé Statni Aerolinie (ČSA) is formed.

July 30 The de Havilland D.H.50 four-seat transport biplane makes its first flight. In early August it wins the reliability trial at the International Aeronautical Exhibition at Gothenberg, flown by Alan Cobham.

August 14 British Marine Air Navigation Company inaugurates a flying-boat airline service to the Channel Islands and France.

August 21 Ground-mounted electric beacons are first used in the USA to illuminate flight direction.

August 22 The Barling XNBL-1 triplane bomber flies. The largest aeroplane in the world, it proves to be under-powered and remains a prototype.

August 23 First flight of the Polikarpov I-1 (Il-400) cantilever low-wing monoplane fighter, powered by an American Liberty engine. Despite some stability problems the I-1 becomes the first Soviet fighter built in series production.

August 27/28 Smith and Richter remain airborne in their D.H.4B for 37 hours 16 minutes, being refuelled 15 times by a D.H.4B tanker.

September 4 The first flight of the US Navy's rigid airship ZR-1 *Shenandoah*, the Navy's first helium-filled airship, takes place over Lakehurst, New Jersey.

September 9 The first flight is made of a Curtiss R2C-1. US Navy pilots achieve first and second places in the 1923 Pulitzer Trophy race in R2C-1s, and on November 4 one sets a new world speed record of 429.96 km/h (267.16 mph).

September 28 America gains first and second places in the Schneider Trophy contest with Curtiss CR-3 biplanes. The winner's average speed is 285.6 km/h (177.38 mph). America also wins the next contest, held in 1925.

October The Gloster Grebe biplane fighter enters service with the RAF. It is the first new fighter accepted by the RAF since the end of the First World War.

October 2 The prototype de Havilland D.H.53 Humming Bird flies for the first time. The company's first lightplane, it was designed and built as a small single seater powered by a 750 cc Douglas converted motorcycle engine and produced to compete in the *Daily Mail* Lympne Motor Glider Competitions (q.v. October 8, 1923). Other Humming Birds follow, powered by various engines, two being used by the RAF for parasite experiments with the R 33 airship (q.v. October 15, 1925).

October 8 The Lympne (Kent, England) Motor Glider Competitions begin. The main prizes are awarded to the pilots of the English Electric Wren and the ANEC monoplane, both of which manage to fly 140.8km (87.5 miles) on one gallon of fuel.

October 28 ČSA begins scheduled services from Prague to Uzhgorod.

November General Ludendorff and Adolf Hitler declare the establishment of a revolutionary government in Germany. Hitler is subsequently detained.

November 1 The Finnish airline Aero O/Y is established. It begins operations on March 24 the following year. It later joins with Aktiebolaget Aerotransport (q.v. June 1924) on a service between Helsinki and Stockholm. It later becomes Finnair.

December 12 The Italian airline Aero Expresso Italiana is established, although not beginning its services until 1926. It is the first Italian airline founded that eventually operates regular, scheduled and sustained services.

1924

The Soviet Red Air Fleet is renamed Voenno – Vozdushniye Sily (VVS).

The Fuerza Aérea Mexicana is formed from the Aviation Corps.

The Air Office of the Imperial Iranian Army is formed.

Imperial Ethiopian Aviation is formed.

The Soviet naval aviation – Voenno-Vozdushniye Sily – Voenno Morskovo Flota (VVS-VMF) is formed.

KLM introduces the Fokker F.VII eight-passenger monoplane airliner into service. Five are used on regular services in Holland, Poland and Switzerland.

The Peruvian Naval Air Service is formed.

The new German airline Deutscher Aero Lloyd is formed from the previous rival organisations Lloyd Luftdienst and Aero-Union.

King Amanullah forms the Afghan Military Air Arm.

ČSA introduces the Aero A-10 five-passenger biplane airliner on its Prague-Bratislava service. The airline introduces the two-passenger A-22 in 1925, followed by the six-passenger A-23 in 1927, five-passenger A-35 monoplane and A-38 biplane in 1929-30.

The prototype Latécoère 17 four-passenger and mail parasol-wing monoplane appears. It is flown by Lignes Aériennes Latécoère. The Laté 25 (more than 50 built) and Laté 26 passenger/mail transport (more than 60 built) follow for use by several airlines.

The Macchi M.24 appears in military and commercial form, the latter accommodating six passengers. A civil M.24 flies from Varese across the Alps to Amsterdam. Copenhagen, Stockholm, Leningrad and back in 1925.

Huff Daland Dusters is formed as the world's first crop-dusting company. In 1929 Delta Air Service is formed when passenger services are inaugurated.

January 23 Lord Thompson takes up the appointment of Secretary of State for Air.

March 24 Aero O/Y begins its first scheduled passenger service between Helsinki and Tallinn, using a Junkers F 13.

March 31 Imperial Airways, the first British national airline company, is formed from Handley Page Transport, Daimler Airway, Instone Air Lines and the British Marine Air Navigation Company.

April The Fleet Air Arm of the RAF is formed in the UK.

April 1 The Royal Canadian Air Force is formed from the Canadian Air Force.

April 6 Four Douglas DWCs (Douglas World Cruisers) under the command of Maj F. Martin, US Army Air Service, leave Seattle, Washington, in an attempt to circumnavigate the world. (q.v. April 30, 1924 and September 28, 1924)

April 28 Imperial Airways inaugurates its London-Paris service.

April 30 Douglas World Cruiser *Seattle* (see above) crashes into a mountain in Alaska and the crew, including Maj Martin, return to their base. DWC *Boston* later alights in the Atlantic close to the Faroe Islands, leaving two DWCs to continue the flight.

May The prototype Fokker CV general-purpose military biplane is flown in Holland.

May 3 Imperial Airways inaugurates its London to Cologne service, via Brussels.

May 19 Wg Cdr Goble and Fl Off McIntyre, RAAF, return to base after flying around Australia in a Fairey IIID. The flying time is 90 hours.

Douglas World Cruisers *Chicago* **and** *New Orleans*,
September 28 1924.

May 26 First flight of the ANT-2 high-wing monoplane designed by Andrei N. Tupolev as the first Soviet
all-metal aircraft. Its construction is based on German
Junkers designs, but with some original modifications.

June The Swedish airline Aktiebolaget Aerotransport
is established.

June 17 Imperial Airways inaugurates its services to
Switzerland.

June 23 The prototype Focke-Wulf A 16 four-passenger monoplane makes its maiden flight. Apart from
entering airline service, it is important as Focke-Wulf's
first product. Twenty-two are built over three years.

July 1 Regular daily US transcontinental airmail
flights from San Francisco to New York begin, with
sections flown at night. (q.v. February 22, 1921)

August The Cuerpo de Aviación (air force) is formed
in Bolivia.

The first flight is made of the prototype Savoia-
Marchetti S.55 twin-hull flying-boat. Originally for
military use as a torpedo-bomber, a commercial version

is later produced as the S.55C. Aero Expresso Italiana
(founded in December 1923) uses the S.55C to inaugurate its Brindisi-Constantinople route on August 1,
1926. A Brindisi-Rhodes route is added in 1930. (q.v.
January 6, 1931).

September 1 The British Air Ministry announces
that it intends to help form light aeroplane flying clubs in
the UK.

September 28 Douglas World Cruisers *Chicago* and
New Orleans arrive back in Seattle, USA, having flown
around the world in an actual flying time of 371 hours 11
minutes. Countries visited include Japan, China (Hong
Kong), Indo-China, Siam, Malaya, Burma, India,
Persia, Mesopotamia, Turkey, Romania, Hungary,
Austria, France, England, Iceland and Greenland.

October 11 Maj Zanni, Argentine Servicio Aeronautico de Ejercito, ends his round-the-world attempt in
Tokyo, having started from Amsterdam on July 26. His
aircraft is a Fokker C.IV.

October 12 ZR 3 (LZ 126) *Los Angeles*, the dirigible
built under reparations in Germany for the US Navy,
leaves Friedrichshaven for Lakehurst, USA. It arrives
there 81 flying hours later.

November 4 During the annual aerial review at
Centocelle aerodrome, Rome, Italy, the new Fiat C.R.1

Alan Cobham (second from left) and Sir Sefton
Brancker (centre) pose for the crowds with their
de Havilland D.H.50, March 18 1925. (*Sport and General*)

single-seat biplane fighter is demonstrated. The C.R.1
becomes the first new Italian-designed fighter to be
adopted by the Regia Aeronautica.

November 7 Lord Thompson is succeeded by Sir
Samuel Hoare as the Secretary of State for Air in the
UK. (q.v. June 8, 1929)

November 20 – March 18 1925 Alan Cobham, A.
Elliott and Sir Sefton Brancker complete a return flight
between London and Rangoon. The aeroplane used is
the second de Havilland D.H.50 built.

December 13 1st Lt Clyde Finter, flying a Sperry
Messenger, attempts to hook on to the US Army TC-3
non-rigid dirigible. This fails and he makes an emergency landing.

December 15 A Sperry Messenger biplane successfully hooks on to the US Army airship TC-3.

December 23 An Italian Fiat B.R.1 light bomber
establishes a world record by carrying a 1,500kg payload
to an altitude of 5,553m (18,220ft).

1925

French naval aviation becomes Aéronautique Maritime
and then Aéronautique Navale.

The French Potez 25 general-purpose and reconnaissance biplane appears. Eventually some 4,000 are built
in 87 variants.

The Aéronautique Militaire is formed in Belgium.

January 1 CIDNA (Compagnie Internationale de
Navigation Aérienne) is formed as a new French airline
company.

January 3 The prototype Fairey Fox two-seat day
bomber flies for the first time.

February The prototype Gloster Gamecock biplane
fighter is flown for the first time. Production Gamecocks
become the RAF's last biplane fighters of wooden
construction.

February 3-4 Capt Ludovic Arrachart and Capt
Henri Lemaître set a distance in a straight line aeroplane
record in a Bréguet 19, flying 3,166km (1,967 miles).

February 22 The first flight takes place of the
prototype de Havilland D.H.60 Moth, a small two-seat
biplane that eventually revolutionises private and club
flying.

March 1 Ryan Airlines starts regular US domestic
services between Los Angeles and San Diego. Increased
demand forces the replacement of the Standard J with
the one and only Douglas Cloudster, built originally for
an attempted non-stop flight across the USA.

March 10 The first Supermarine Southampton re-
connaissance-bombing flying-boat for the RAF makes its
maiden flight.

March 12 The prototype Fokker F.VIIa flies as an
eight passenger or cargo-carrying airliner. The F.VIIb is
similar but with a greater wing area.

April 13 Henry Ford starts the first regular US
aeroplane freight service, with flights between Detroit,
Michigan and Chicago.

de Havilland D.H.60 Moth with wings folded, February 22 1925.

April 15   The Ukrainian airline Ukvozdukhput begins services from Kharkov to Kiev.

May 1   The Japanese Army Air Corps is formed.

May 10   The first flight takes place of the prototype Armstrong Whitworth Atlas. The Atlas becomes the RAF's first purpose-designed army co-operation aircraft.

May 15   AB Aerotransport introduces the Junkers G 23 nine-passenger monoplane airliner on its Malmö-Hamburg-Amsterdam route. The G 23 becomes one of Europe's most important airliners. (q.v. July 24, 1926)

May 29   The prototype de Havilland D.H.60 Moth is flown by Alan Cobham from London to Zürich and back in a single day.

July 6   The first Douglas mailplane flies as the DAM-1.

July 7   The original Boeing Model 40 mailplane flies, having been designed to a US Post Office Department specification, as had the Douglas Mailplane or DAM-1 (see above).

July 13   Western Air Express is formed as an American airline operator.

July 21   The first de Havilland D.H.60 Moth lightplane destined for a flying club is delivered to the Lancashire Aero Club at Woodford.

July 29   The Blériot 155 17-passenger biplane airliner flies for the first time. Air Union operates two between Paris and London from May 1926.

August 5   Lloyd Aereo Boliviano SA begins services between Cochabamba to Sucre.

September 3   US Navy airship *Shenandoah* breaks into two in a squall over Caldwell, Ohio, and 14 men are killed.
September 4   The prototype Fokker F.VIIa-3m three-engined monoplane airliner flies for the first time. It becomes one of the most widely known airliners in the world.

September 13   An Aero A 11 sets a Czech duration record of 13¼ hours.

October 15   A de Havilland Humming Bird (q.v. October 2, 1923) is released from the R 33 airship while at an altitude of 1,160m (3,800ft). Other successful releases follow.

October 27 – November 19   Three RAF D.H.9s complete a return flight between Cairo, Egypt and Kano, Nigeria.

November 16   Alan Cobham, A. Elliott and B. Emmott start their London to Cape Town and return flight in a de Havilland D.H.50. Cape Town is reached on February 17, 1926, and Croydon, England, on March 13, 1926.

November 24   The prototype Tupolev TB-1 (ANT-4) twin-engined monoplane bomber flies, having been designed by V.M. Petlyakov. Production aircraft enter service as the first Soviet heavy bombers in 1929.

Erhard Milch, an executive of the newly-formed
Deutsche Luft-Hansa, welcomes the press from the
cockpit of an Udet Kondor.

1926

The Junkers G 31 12/15-passenger low-wing monoplane
airliner appears. Deutsche Luft-Hansa receives its first
aircraft in 1928, being introduced on the Berlin to
Amsterdam and London services in March.

The Soviet Scientific Test Aerodrome (NOA) at Kho-
dinki, near Moscow, is renamed Air Force Scientific Test
Institute (NII-VVS), over the years becoming the Soviet
equivalent of the combined RAE Farnborough and
A & AEE Boscombe Down in the UK.

January 6 Deutsche Luft-Hansa is formed by the
merger of Deutscher Aero Lloyd and Junkers Luftverkehr.

January 22 – February 10 The first east-west aero-
plane crossing of the South Atlantic is made by
Commandante Franco in a Dornier Wal flying-boat.
The flight is in stages.

March 1 – June 2 The RAF's first official long-
distance formation flight is carried out. Four Fairey
IIIDs are led by Wg Cdr C.W.H. Pulford from Cairo to
Cape Town, back to Cairo and then to Lee-on-Solent,
England, a distance of 22,530km (14,000 miles).

March 8 Dr Robert H. Goddard statically tests a
rocket at the Clark University. This has an oxygen
pressure-feed system for the propellants.

March 16 Dr Robert H. Goddard launches the first
successful liquid-fuelled rocket from a farm at Auburn,
Massachusetts. It flies for just 2½ seconds, travelling 56m
(184ft) at a speed of about 97km/h (60mph).

The first Armstrong Whitworth Argosy biplane airliner
flies for the first time. Eventually the seven built have a
major effect on civil air transport.

March 19 The prototype Fairey IIIF fleet spotter,
light bomber and general-purpose biplane is flown. In
production form it is widely operated by the RAF and
Fleet Air Arm.

April 1 The Italian airline Società Italiana Servizi
Aerei begins a Trieste-Venice-Pavia-Turin service using
Cant 10 flying-boats. Cant 10s are acquired at about the
same time as the smaller Cant 7s.

April 6 Deutsche Luft-Hansa begins commercial
operations flying between Berlin, Halle, Erfurt, Stuttgart
and Zurich. The aircraft used is a Dornier Komet III.

Varney Speed Lines begins the first US commercial air
mail flights, between Pasco and Elko. The aircraft used
are Swallow biplanes. In 1937 Varney is renamed
Continental Air Lines.

Above **Fokker F.VIIA-3m** *Josephine Ford* **on exhibition, May 9 1926.**
Below **Norge, May 11-14 1926.**

April 17 Airmail flights by Western Air Express begin, operating between Los Angeles and Salt Lake City. Eventually becomes Western Airlines.

May 3 Deutsche Luft-Hansa extends its European services to take in Stockholm.

May 9 Lt Cdr Richard E. Byrd, US Navy, and Floyd Bennett make the first aeroplane flight over the North Pole in Fokker F.VIIA-3m *Josephine Ford*.

May 11-14 Norwegian Roald Amundsen leads an expedition which makes the first airship flight over the North Pole, the airship *Norge* flying from Spitzbergen to Teller, Alaska. Other crew members include the American Lincoln Ellsworth and the Italian Umberto Nobile.

May 23 Western Air Express begins the first sustained scheduled passenger services in the USA, flying between Salt Lake City and Los Angeles. It had inaugurated its mail services on April 17.

June 11 The prototype Ford 4-AT Tri-motor flies for the first time. It is an eleven-passenger airliner.

Armstrong Whitworth Argosy *City of Glasgow*, **June 16 1926.** (*Charles E. Brown*)

June 16 Imperial Airways starts using Argosy biplanes on its London to Paris service and for the first time the route becomes fully self-supporting.

June 30 – October 1 Alan Cobham completes the first England to Australia and return flight in a de Havilland D.H.50, finally landing on the Thames near the British Houses of Parliament.

July 1 A Blackburn Dart makes the first night landing on an aircraft carrier, HMS *Furious*.

The Kungliga Svenska Flygvapnet is formed as the Swedish air arm.

July 2 The US Army Air Service becomes the US Army Air Corps.

July 24 – September 26 Two Junkers G 24 airliners leave Berlin to fly to Peking and back, arriving back in Berlin on September 26. The G 24 is basically a re-engined G 23, becoming the major production version.

July 28 A US Navy submarine deploys and recovers a seaplane during experiments.

August Air Union, a French airline, receives its first Lioré et Olivier 21 18-passenger biplane airliner.

September The US Navy receives the first of its new Martin T3M torpedo-bomber biplanes.

The two Junkers G 24s back in Germany after the Peking flight, September 26 1926.

September 16 The new French heavy bomber, the Lioré et Olivier 20, sets a world distance record while carrying a 2,000kg payload.

September 30 The prototype de Havilland D.H.66 Hercules 14-passenger biplane airliner flies for the first time. Production aircraft are used initially on Imperial Airways' Cairo-Karachi route.

The prototype Dornier Do R Super-Wal 21-passenger flying-boat makes its maiden flight.

October 21 Two Gloster Grebe fighters are released while airborne from the airship R 33.

October 27 The Blériot 165 16-passenger biplane airliner flies for the first time. Two are used on Air Union's Paris-London service.

November 3 The prototype Boeing F2B-1 single-seat biplane fighter for the US Navy flies for the first time.

November 15 – January 8, 1927 T. Neville Stack and B.S. Leete fly modified single-seat de Havilland D.H.60 Moth lightplanes from Croydon, England, to Karachi, India, a distance of about 8,850km (5,500 miles).

December Sabena begins flying a single example of the Belgian SABCA S-2 four-passenger high-wing monoplane airliner.

December 20 – January, 1927 An Imperial Airways Hercules airliner makes a proving flight for the proposed England-India air service.

1927
The Potez 29 five/six-passenger biplane airliner appears. An Army ambulance-liaison version is also produced.

January 7 Imperial Airways begins a Basra-Cairo air service. Cairo is then linked to Port Said, where ships continue to Marseille. In 1929 the route is extended to allow a full London, England, to Karachi, India, service.

January 15 Boeing wins the US Post Office's San Francisco-Chicago mail route and forms Boeing Air Transport to do the flying.

March The first flight is made by the prototype Westland Wapiti two-seat general-purpose biplane. The production Wapiti becomes a standard RAF aeroplane of the 1930s.

March 2 The prototype Boeing F3B-1 naval fighter makes its maiden flight.

March 14 Pan American Airways is formed as a subsidiary of AVCO.

VARIG is founded as an airline in Brazil, May 7 1927.

March 21 Deutsche Luft-Hansa extends its European routes from Berlin, to take in Prague and Vienna.

March 27 Charles Lindbergh's entry for the Raymond Orteig prize is accepted. (q.v. May 20-21, 1927)

March 30 – May 22 Four RAF Fairey IIIDs make a return flight between Cairo and Cape Town.

April 13 A Deutsche Luft-Hansa Rohrbach Roland I crosses the Alps.

April 28 The Ryan NYP, an improved version of the M-1 for Charles Lindbergh, is flown for the first time.

May 1 Imperial Airways starts the first luxury air service, introducing the 'Silver Wing' service providing lunch on its London to Paris Argosy route.

May 2 Deruluft extends its Moscow to Königsberg service to take in Berlin.

May 7 The airline Viacao Aerea Rio-Gradense SA (VARIG) is formed in Brazil.

May 8 Charles Eugène Jules Marie Nungesser takes off for an attempted east-west crossing of the Atlantic in a Levasseur PL8. He dies in the attempt. Nungesser is

remembered as the third highest-scoring French fighter pilot of the First World War.

May 17 The prototype Bristol Bulldog single-seat biplane fighter flies for the first time.

May 20 Flt Lt C.R. Carr and Flt Lt L.E.M. Gillman take off in an attempt to fly a modified Hawker Horsley non-stop to India. They are forced to land in the Persian Gulf after completing 5,505km (3,420 miles). This flight nevertheless represents a new world long-distance record, which lasts for less than a day.

May 20-21 Capt Charles Lindbergh, flying the Ryan NYP monoplane *Spirit of St Louis*, makes the first non-stop solo crossing of the Atlantic from Long Island, New York, to Paris, France. Flying time is 33 hours 39 minutes and the distance covered is 5,778km (3,590 miles).

May 27 *Béarn*, the first French aircraft carrier, is completed after nearly seven years of construction.

June 4-6 Clarence D. Chamberlin and Charles A. Levine fly the Wright-Bellanca W.B.2 *Columbia* from New York, USA, to Eisleben, Germany. This sets a new world record for distance in a straight line of 6,294km (3,911 miles).

June 5 The Society for Space Flight (VfR) is founded in Germany. Its originators and first members include Prof Hermann Oberth, Max Valier, Rudolf Nebel, Winkler, Willy Ley and the young Wernher von Braun.

Above **VARIG Dornier Wal flying-boat.**
Below **Lindbergh (third from right) poses with the** *Spirit of St Louis,* **May 20 1927.**

June 28/29   Lt Albert Hegenberger and Lt L. Maitland fly an Atlantic Fokker monoplane (Army C-2) nonstop from Oakland, California, to Honolulu, Hawaii.

July 17   Five USMC DH-4s dive bomb hostile forces that surround the Marine Corps garrison at Ocotal, Nicaragua.

July 29   The first flight takes place of the Cierva C.6D, the first two-seat autogyro.

July 30   Spaniard Don Juan de la Cierva becomes the first passenger to fly in a rotating-wing aircraft, when he is carried aloft in his Cierva C.6D.

August   The first Keystone bombers are delivered to the USAAC as single-engined LB-1s. These begin the replacement of Martin bombers with Keystone types.

September 1-28   Lt R.R. Bentley, SAAF, flies a de Havilland D.H.60X Moth lightplane named *Dorys* from London, England, to Cape Town, South Africa.

September 7   Cessna Aircraft Company is incorporated, having been founded by Clyde V. Cessna.

September 12   Canadian Transcontinental Airways begins the first commercial airmail service in Canada.

September 15   Pitcairn Aviation Inc is formed. (q.v. July 10, 1929)

October 14-15   Capt Dieudonné Costes and Lt Cdr Joseph le Brix make the first non-stop aeroplane crossing of the South Atlantic in a Bréguet 19 named *Nungesser-Coli*, flying from Saint-Louis, Senegal, to Port Natal, Brazil.

October 19   Pan American Airways begins its first international route between Key West, Florida, and Havana, Cuba, with a Fairchild seaplane. Regular operations begin just over a week later using a Fokker F.VIIa-3m (eventually five were operated).

November 16 and December 14   The US Navy's second and third aircraft carriers are commissioned as USS *Saratoga* and USS *Lexington* respectively. *Lexington* is sunk in 1942 by Japanese forces. *Saratoga* is destroyed in a 1946 atomic bomb test.

December 1   Sindicato Condor Ltda is formed in Brazil by the Kondor Syndicat of Berlin. Eventually becomes Serviços Aéreos Cruzeiro do Sul SA.

1928

Potez 32 five-passenger/mail high-wing monoplane airliners enter service with CIDNA in France.

The Türk Hava Kuvvetleri is formed from the Turkish Army Air Service.

The Junkers F 24 appears as a single-engined conversion of the G 24. Deutsche Luft-Hansa operates nine of the eleven produced.

Pan American Airways begins its international services using Fairchild seaplane *La Nina* as a mailplane, October 19 1927.

USS *Lexington*, December 1927. (*US National Archives*)

The Austrian Kommando der Luftstreitkräfte is formed.

Aeroposta Argentina begins airline services. In 1947 it merges with other airlines to form Aerolineas Argentinas.

Max Valier publicly demonstrates rocket propulsion in Germany, thereafter receiving financial support for his experiments from Fritz von Opel.

January 7 First flight of the Polikarpov U-2 training biplane. Ordered into production in 1930, this simple aircraft is built in very large numbers until 1945. During the Second World War the U-2 gains fame as a 'night harassment bomber', and is re-designated Po-2 in July 1944. It remains in service until 1962.

January 27 The dirigible *Los Angeles* moors at sea to USS *Saratoga*.

February 7 Sqn Ldr H.J.L. 'Bert' Hinkler leaves Croydon in an Avro Avian in an attempt to make the first solo flight from England to Australia. (q.v. February 22, 1928).

February 12 Lady Heath leaves Cape Town in an Avro Avian III in an attempt to make the first solo flight by a woman from South Africa to England. (q.v. May 17, 1928).

February 15 The first flight is made of a Short Calcutta flying-boat, heralding the close association between Short and Imperial Airways that was to last out the 1930s.

February 22 Bert Hinkler arrives in Darwin, Australia, having flown more than 17,700km (11,000 miles). His route has taken him to Italy, Malta, Libya, India, Burma and Singapore.

February 26 The Messerschmitt M.20 seven-passenger high-wing monoplane airliner flies for the first time. Deutsche Luft-Hansa operates 14 from 1929. The eight-passenger M.24 and ten-passenger M.28 follow.

March 1 Aéropostale inaugurates a mail service from France to Buenos Aires, Argentina.

March 9 – April 30 Lady Bailey, flying a de Havilland Moth, completes a flight from London to Cape Town. She makes the return flight between September 21, 1928 and January 16, 1929.

March 30 Maj Mario di Bernardi, Italian Air Force, sets the first world speed record of over 500 km/h and first over 300 mph in a Macchi M.52*bis* floatplane, achieving 512.69 km/h (318.57 mph).

April CMA (Compania Mexicana de Aviacion) inaugurates scheduled airline services in Mexico.

April 12/13 Junkers W33 *Bremen*, flown by Hermann Köhl, the Irish Capt J. Fitzmaurice and Baron von Hünefeld, makes the first east-west crossing of the North Atlantic between Baldonnel, Ireland, and Greenly Island, Labrador.

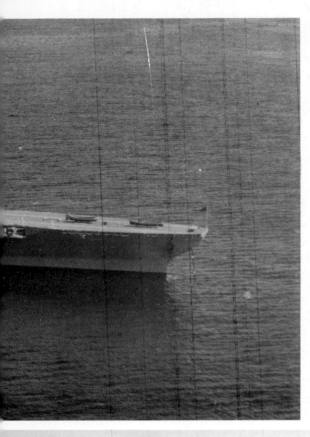

April 15-21 A Lockheed Vega flown by Capt G.H. Wilkins and Lieut Carl B. Eielson, makes the first west-east crossing of the Arctic.

May The first flight takes place of the prototype French Lioré et Olivier 25.

Luft-Hansa introduces the Junkers G31 into service. Food and drinks are served during flights.

May 1 Jacques Schneider, the founder of the Schneider Trophy contests for seaplanes, dies.

May 15 The Australian Inland Mission and Qantas help inaugurate the Australian Flying Doctor service, founded by Rev J. Flynn. The first aircraft is a modified de Havilland D.H.50 named *Victory*.

May 16 The US airline Transcontinental Air Transport is established.

May 17 Lady Heath arrives in Croydon, England, after her epic solo flight from South Africa. (q.v. February 12, 1928).

May 23 The Italian airship *Italia* sets off for a flight over the North Pole, under the command of Gen Umberto Nobile, but crashes on the return flight. Amundsen (q.v. May 11, 1926) is killed while trying to rescue Nobile (who survives).

Köhl, Fitzmaurice and Baron von Hünefeld pose in front of the Junkers W33 Bremen, April 12/13 1928.

May 29 Pan American Airways is awarded the first of six (of a total of seven) foreign airmail contracts from the US government, the first operating over the established Key West-Havana route on September 15, 1928.

May 31 – June 9 Capt Charles Kingsford Smith and C.T.P. Ulm fly Fokker F.VIIB-3m *Southern Cross* from Oakland Field, San Francisco, to Honolulu, Suva (Fiji) and Brisbane (Australia) to complete a trans-Pacific flight. Actual flying time is 83 hours 38 minutes.

June The prototype Hawker Hart two-seat light bomber for the RAF flies for the first time.

June 11 The sailplane Ente (Duck), powered by two Sander solid-fuel rocket motors, becomes the first rocket-powered aeroplane to fly, at Wasserkuppe Mountain, Germany. It flies about 1.2km (0.75 mile) in the hands of pilot Friedrich Stamer.

June 20 Braniff Airlines is formed, operating initially a route between Oklahoma City and Tulsa. The airline becomes Braniff Airways on November 3, 1930, and eventually Braniff International.

June 25 The prototype of the Boeing F4B and P-12 naval and army fighter biplane makes it maiden flight.

July 3-5 The first over 7,000 km distance in a straight line record is set by an Italian Savoia-Marchetti S.64

Italia, **May 23 1928**. (*Stato Maggiore Aeronautica*)

three-seat monoplane, flown by Capt Arturo Ferrarin and Maggiore Carlo Del Prete.

August The British newspaper *Daily Mail* buys a modified de Havilland D.H.61 for use as a flying newspaper office. It is fitted with a desk for a typist, a dark-room for a photographer and a motorcycle for a reporter.

September 15 Compania de Aviacion Faucett SA is formed in Peru as a domestic operator.

September 18 German airship LZ 127 *Graf Zeppelin* is launched.

Don Juan de La Cierva flies his C8L Mark II Autogiro from Croydon to Le Bourget, making the first cross-Channel flight by a rotary-wing aircraft.

October 11 German passenger airship LZ 127 *Graf Zeppelin* crosses the North Atlantic from Friedrichshafen to Lakehurst, New Jersey, USA. The journey takes about 71 hours.

October 22 CAMS 53 four-passenger/mail biplane flying-boats are introduced by Aéropostale on its Marseilles, France, to Algiers, Algeria, service.

October 29 – November 1 The LZ 127 *Graf Zeppelin* flies 6,384.50 km (3,967.137 miles). This remains (in 1982) the longest distance ever covered by a dirigible in a straight line.

HANGAR № 3

URSS-300

November   Air Union takes delivery of its first Breguet 280T eight-passenger biplane airliner. It is used on its 'Golden Ray' meal service across the English Channel, which had been inaugurated in July 1927.

November 14   The first Fairey Long-Range Monoplane makes its maiden flight.

December 19   Harold Pitcairn flies the first American autogyro in Philadelphia. (The Pitcairn experiments are subsequently overshadowed by the Kellett autogyros, which became the US Army's first rotary-wing aircraft).

December 20   Australian Hubert Wilkins and Carl Ben Eielson fly over the Antarctic in a Lockheed Vega. Earlier, between April 15 and 20, 1928, they had made the first trans-Arctic flight from Point Barrow to Spitsbergen.

The prototype Polish PWS.5 two-seat observation and liaison biplane flies for the first time.

December 23 – February 25, 1929   Eight RAF Vickers Victoria transport aircraft and a Handley Page Hinaidi evacuate 586 people and 10,975kg (24,193lb) of baggage from Kabul, Afghanistan, during tribal disturbances.

1929

January   The Italian General Umberto Nobile accepts an offer to design airships in the Soviet Union.

The Cuerpo de Aéronautica Militar is formed in Guatemala.

A modified Soviet TB-1 heavy bomber named *Strana Sovietov* (Soviet Land) flies from Moscow to New York, covering a total distance of 21,243 km (13,200 miles).

TB-1 flown from Moscow to the United States, January 1929. (*William T. Larkins*)

American Edward Albert Link sells the initial model of the world's first electrical-mechanical flight simulator, later known as the Link Trainer.

Dobrolet merges with the Ukrainian airline Ukvozdukhput to become Dobroflot. Reorganised as Aeroflot in 1932.

The Latécoère 28 eight-passenger monoplane appears. It is widely operated by Aéropostale from 1930 on routes to Africa and South America.

The French airline CIDNA introduces the five/seven-passenger Bernard 190T high-wing monoplane on its European network.

Professor Hermann J. Oberth completes a liquid-propellant rocket while living temporarily in Berlin. During the Second World War he works on the A-4 (V2) at the secret Peenemünde establishment, and from the 1950s helps with the US rocket programme.

The prototype Gloster Gauntlet flies. In production form it becomes the RAF's last open-cockpit fighter.

January 1   Polskie Linie Lotnicze – LOT is formed by the Polish government.

January 30   Inter-Island Airways is formed. It begins airline operations on November 11. Later becomes Hawaiian Airlines.

February   United Aircraft and Transport Corporation is formed from a merger of all Boeing's aviation operations with those of Pratt & Whitney, the Standard Steel Propeller Company and others.

March 5   Linea Aeropostal Santiago-Arica is formed. Later becomes Linea Aerea Nacional de Chile.

March 30 Imperial Airways inaugurates a commercial passenger service from Croydon, England, to Karachi, India, via Switzerland, Italy and Egypt. Sections of the journey, which takes seven days, are flown in Armstrong Whitworth Argosy, Short Calcutta and de Havilland Hercules aircraft.

April 24-26 Sqn Ldr A.G. Jones-Williams and Flt Lt N.H. Jenkins complete the first non-stop flight from England to India in a Fairey Long-Range Monoplane. The distance covered is 6,647 km (4,130 miles).

May 16-17 *Graf Zeppelin* has to abandon its planned flight to the USA, after developing engine problems.

May 20 The Peruvian Army and Naval air services are unified into the Cuerpo de Aeronautica del Perú.

June 8 Lord Thompson again becomes Secretary of State for Air. (q.v. October 5, 1930).

July 3 Lt A.W. Gordon, US Navy, successfully hooks on to the airship *Los Angeles* in a modified Vought VO-1 observation biplane during 'parasite' experiments.

July 7 Transcontinental Air Transport inaugurates a two-day transcontinental service. This is not a through journey as part of the distance is covered by train.

July 10 Eastern Air Transport Inc is formed from Pitcairn Aviation Inc.

July 17 Dr Robert H. Goddard successfully fires a rocket carrying a camera.

July 22 A Heinkel He 12 postal seaplane is used in attempts to speed up transatlantic mail services, flying from the German ship *Bremen* while 400 km (250 miles) from New York.

July 25 The Dornier Do X, the largest flying-boat built before the Second World War, makes its maiden flight.

Original engine configuration of the first Junkers G 38, November 6 1929.

August 1 The LZ 127 *Graf Zeppelin* leaves Friedrichshafen for Lakehurst New Jersey, USA. (Count von Zeppelin considered this the start of the round-the-world flight, making Germany the starting and finishing point. However, by arriving back at Friedrichshafen on September 4, this was slower than the Lakehurst to Lakehurst section of the flight). (q.v. August 8-29 1929)

August 8-29 The LZ 127 *Graf Zeppelin* becomes the first airship to circumnavigate the world, flying from, and returning to, Lakehurst, New Jersey, USA, via Germany, Japan and Los Angeles. The journey of over 35,200 km (21,873 miles) takes 21 days 5 hours and 31 minutes. (q.v. October 11, 1928)

September 24 Lt James H. Doolittle undertakes successfully the first blind-flight take off, level flight and landing, at Mitchell Field, Long Island, NY.

September 25 The Polish PZL P-1 single-seat fighter prototype flies featuring the Pulawski wing (gull type).

September 27-29 A Bréguet 19 'Super Bidon' named *Point d'Intérrogation* is flown by Capt Dieudonne Costes and Maurice Bellonte from Le Bourget to Manchuria. The flight sets up a new world distance record of 7,905 km (4,912 miles). (q.v. September 1-2, 1930).

September 30 Fritz von Opel pilots the Opel-Hatry Rak-1 rocket-powered glider near Frankfurt, Germany. It flies for more than 1.8 km (1.1 mile) and reaches a speed of 160 km/h (100 mph).

October 8 Compania Nacional Cubana de Aviación Curtiss is formed.

October 18 Launch of the French submarine cruiser *Sourcouf* which carries a seaplane with folded wings in a watertight container on deck. The only operational European submarine designed to carry an aircraft, *Sourcouf* is accidentally rammed in February 1942 in the Gulf of Mexico.

October 21 The Dornier Do X takes off with ten crew, 150 passengers and nine stowaways. (q.v. July 25, 1929)

Douglas Y1B-7, 1930.

November 6 The first of two remarkable Junkers G 38 monoplane airliners, at that time the world's largest landplane, flies for the first time. Each has passenger accommodation for 34 in main fuselage cabins, in the fuselage nose and in wing-root cabins.

November 28-29 Cdr Byrd, Bernt Balchen, Ashley McKinley and Harold June crew the Ford 4-AT Trimotor *Floyd Bennett* during the first flight over the South Pole. (q.v. May 9, 1926).

December The Hellenic Combat Air Force is formed.

1930

The service test Douglas Y1B-7 flies, becoming the USAAC's first monoplane bomber.

The Jugoslovensko Ratno Vazduhoplovstvo is formed as the air arm of Yugoslavia.

Deutsche Luft-Hansa expands its routes throughout 1928 and thereafter, becoming Europe's fastest growing airline. By the early 1930s its European routes cover a very large network within the geographical boundaries of London (England), Oslo (Norway), Budapest (Hungary) and Barcelona (Spain). Prior to the Second World War it handles more passengers than any other European operator.

January 25 American Airways is established, becoming American Airlines on May 13, 1934.

March 21 The Chilean Army and Navy air arms combine as the Fuerza Aérea Chilena.

April 10-19 C. Barnard, R. Little and the Duchess of Bedford fly from London to Cape Town in a Fokker. They start the return flight two days later.

Boeing Model 200 *Monomail*, May 6 1930.

Ellen Church (third from left), the world's first stewardess, May 15 1930.

April 29 The prototype Polikarpov I-5 single-seat biplane fighter flies. A few production I-5s are still in use when Germany invades the Soviet Union during the Second World War.

May 4 First flight of the German rocket-powered Espenlaub/Sohldenhoff E.15 tailless glider near Bremerhaven.

May 5-24 Amy Johnson becomes the first woman to fly solo from England to Australia when she pilots her de Havilland D.H.60G Gipsy Moth *Jason* from Croydon to Darwin. The *Daily Mail* newspaper awards her a prize of £10,000 for the flight.

May 6 Boeing's famous Model 200 *Monomail* flies for the first time. This introduces cantilever low wings, a retractable landing gear and other modern features and is used as a mail/cargo aeroplane with a payload of 1,043 kg (2,300 lb).

May 15 Registered nurse Ellen Church becomes the world's first airline stewardess, making her first flight with Boeing Air Transport, between San Francisco, California and Cheyenne, Wyoming, USA, in a Boeing Model 80.

May 17 German rocket pioneer Max Valier is killed while testing a liquid-fuelled rocket unit.

May 18 LZ 127 *Graf Zeppelin* makes its first crossing of the South Atlantic.

June 4 Lt Apollo Soucek sets a new world seaplane altitude record in a Wright F3W-1 Apache single-seat experimental fighter, attaining 13,157m (43,166ft) at Anacostia.

June 12 The prototype Handley Page H.P.38 Heyford bomber flies for the first time. It enters RAF service in 1933 in production form, becoming the RAF's last biplane heavy bomber.

July 1 ČSA begins international operations.

July 16 Transcontinental and Western Air (TWA) is formed from Transcontinental Air Transport and Western Air Express.

July 29 The British dirigible R 100 sets out on its first passenger-carrying flight between Cardington, England, and Montreal, Canada. The flight takes 78 hours 51 minutes.

August Wolfgang von Gronau, flying a Dornier Wal, makes the first east-west crossing of the Atlantic by flying-boat.

August 6 The bodies of Salomon August André, Nils Strindberg and Knut Fraenkel are found on White Island. (q.v. July 11, 1897).

August 13-16 R 100 makes the return flight from Canada in 56½ hours. This is also its last commercial flight (q.v. July 29, 1930)

September 1-2 The first east-west crossing of the North Atlantic is achieved by Capt Dieudonné Costes (see October 14-15, 1927) and Bellonte in a Bréguet 19 named *Point d'Interrogation*. They fly from Paris, France, to New York in 37 hours 18 minutes.

September 19   Eurasia Aviation Corporation is founded as an airline operator by German-Chinese interests.

September 24   The first Short Rangoon patrol flying-boat for the RAF is flown.

September 27   The world's first rocket launching drome is founded at Berlin-Reinickendorf.

October   The Polish PZL P-7 single-seat fighter appears. When P-7a fighters equip all of Poland's fighter squadrons (by autumn, 1933), the Polish Air Force becomes the first in the world with only all-metal monoplane fighters in front-line service.

October 4   British airship R 101 sets off from Cardington, England, to fly to Egypt and India, having received a temporary Certificate of Airworthiness.

October 5   The R 101 makes two unexpected dives over Beauvais, near Paris, the second causing it to strike the ground. Only six of the 54 persons on board survive the impact and subsequent fire. The dead include Lord Thompson, Secretary of State for Air, and Major-General Sir Sefton Brancker, Director of Civil Aviation.

October 13   The prototype Junkers Ju 52 single-engined transport aircraft makes its first flight.

October 19 – November 25   RAF Fairey IIIDs make a return flight between Khartoum and West Africa.

October 25   Transcontinental and Western Air inaugurates the first passenger service across the US continent, from New York to Los Angeles.

November 2   A Dornier Do X begins a flight in stages from Friedrichshafen to New York. Damage caused to the wing in Lisbon and to the hull in the Canary Islands, means that the journey is not completed until August 27, 1931. The pilot is Capt Christiansen, a former seaplane fighter ace.

Polish Air Force PZL P-7a fighters fill the sky, October 1930. (*J.B. Cynk*)

The giant Dornier Do X flying-boat.

Prototype Grumman FF-1 fighter, April 2 1931.

November 3 Braniff Air Lines becomes independent of the Universal Aviation Corporation, having first formed in 1928.

November 14 The prototype Handley Page H.P.42 flies as a luxury long-range biplane airliner for Imperial Airways.

November 25 The prototype Fairey Hendon makes its maiden flight. It is the first British heavy bomber with cantilever monoplane wings and in production form becomes the RAF's first monoplane heavy bomber (except for experimental aircraft like the Beardmore Inflexible).

December 2 The Airship Guarantee Company that built the R100 airship ceases trading.

December 22 The first Soviet Tupolev four-engined heavy bomber, the TB-3, makes its first flight as the ANT-6 prototype. At that time it is the largest landplane in the world.

1931

Arado produces one of two biplane fighters for the emerging German Luftwaffe, as the Ar.65.

The Latécoère 300 passenger/mail flying-boat appears.

The Royal Iraqi Air Force is formed.

First trials of the Soviet 67mm recoilless guns mounted on the experimental TsKB-7 fighter and a modified I-4.

The Rocket Propulsion Study Group (GIRD) is founded in Moscow. One of its leading scientists is Fridrikh Tsander, a rocket expert of Latvian origin.

German Wolf Hirth makes the first thermal flight over a city, piloting a sailplane over New York.

January 6 Twelve Savoia-Marchetti S-55 flying boats, under the command of Gen Italo Balbo, complete the first formation flight across the South Atlantic, flying from Portuguese Guinea to Natal, Brazil.

February 26 – March 1 A Blériot 110 two-seat monoplane sets a new distance in a closed circuit record at 8,822.325 km (5,481.928 miles), flown by Lucien Bossoutrot and Maurice Rossi.

February 28 Imperial Airways inaugurates the first commercial service from England to Central Africa, carrying passengers from Croydon to Khartoum (the Sudan) via Greece, Crete and Egypt, and airmail on to Lake Victoria.

March 3 The prototype Fairey Gordon makes its maiden flight. Production Gordons become standard RAF general-purpose and bombing aircraft, serving at home and in the Middle East. Others are sold to Brazil.

March 21 The famous Polish aircraft designer Zygmunt Pulawski is killed while flying the PZL P.12 amphibian.

March 25 The first production Hawker Fury I biplane fighter flies.

March 26 Swissair is formed from Ad Astra Aero AG and Basler Luftverkehr.

April The prototype Ju 52/3m (three engined) transport aircraft makes its first flight.

April 1-9 C.W. Scott makes a solo flight in a de Havilland Moth light plane from Lympne, England, to Darwin, Australia.

Restored Lockheed Vega *Winnie Mae*, **June 23 1931.**

April 2   Grumman receives a US Navy contract which leads to the development of the FF-1 fighter, the first US Navy fighter with an enclosed cockpit and retractable landing gear.

April 13   The Boeing Model 215 cantilever monoplane bomber flies for the first time as the XB-901. It later becomes the YB-9.

April 15   The world's first airmail by rocket is flown near Osnabrück in Germany.

May 26   The prototype Consolidated P2Y patrol flying-boat for the US Navy makes its maiden flight.

May 27   A full-scale wind tunnel is first used at the NACA's Langley Field Laboratory.

June 23 – July 1   Wiley Post and Harold Gatty fly Lockheed Vega *Winnie Mae* around the world in a record time of 8 days 15 hours 51 minutes. (q.v. July 15-22, 1933)

July 1   United Air Lines is formed as a holding company for Boeing Air Transport, National Air Transport, Pacific Air Transport and Varney Air Lines.

July 28 – August 6   Amy Johnson flies from England to Tokyo in under nine days in a de Havilland D.H.80A Puss Moth.

July 22 – September 1   Sir Alan Cobham and a crew of five make a return flight between Rochester, England, and the Belgian Congo in a Short Valetta. The round trip covers 19,800km (12,300 miles).

July 23   A non-stop flight from New York, USA, to Istanbul, Turkey, is made by Russell N. Boardman and John Polando in a Bellanca. Five days later they set a world distance record in a Wright J6, covering 8,065km (5,011 miles).

August   The prototype Polish PZL P-11 gull-wing fighter flies. P-11s enter service in 1934.

The prototype PWS 24T four-passenger monoplane airliner appears.

The first Airspeed aircraft flies as the AS.1 Tern glider.

August 18   Professor Auguste Piccard and Kipfer perform the first stratosphere flight in a balloon, reaching an altitude of 15,781 m (51,775 ft)

August 24   The AS-1 Tern establishes the first distance record for sailplanes in Britain.

September 13   Britain wins the Schneider Trophy outright, having won three competitions in a row, the last with the Supermarine S.6B flown by Flt Lt J.N. Boothman.

September 18   Japan attacks China and starts hostilities which last for the remainder of the decade.

September 20   The prototype Hawker Nimrod naval fighter makes its maiden flight. A production Nimrod I flies on October 14.

September 25   USS *Akron* is flown for the first time. (q.v. October 27, 1931 and April 4, 1933)

September 28   The US Navy receives the first of its Martin BM torpedo-bombers.

September 29   Flt Lt G.H. Stainforth sets a new world speed record and the first over 400mph by flying the Supermarine S.6B at 654.9km/h (406.94 mph) at Ryde, Isle of Wight.

Supermarine S.6B, September 13 1931.

October 3-5 Americans Clyde Pangborn and Hugh Herndon make the first non-stop flight from Japan to America in a Bellanca aeroplane.

October 21 Official flight evaluation of the French Latécoère 290 torpedo bomber begins at St-Raphaël. It has been developed from the Laté 28 commercial aircraft.

USS *Akron*, **October 27 1931.**

October 26 The prototype de Havilland D.H.82A Tiger Moth flies for the first time. It becomes one of the classic aircraft of all time, with large numbers of production aircraft being built as military and civil trainers.

October 27 A Curtiss F9C Sparrowhawk parasite fighter hooks on to the airship *Los Angeles*.

USS *Akron*, the first of two purpose-built aircraft carrier airships for the US Navy, is commissioned. *Akron* carries Sparrowhawk parasite fighters.

October 27-28 Sqn Ldr O.R. Gayford and Flt Lt D.L.G. Bett fly a Fairey Long-Range Monoplane from Cranwell, England, to Abu Sueir, Egypt, a distance of 4,600km (2,857 miles).

Handley Page HP 42W *Helena* **at Croydon airport, January 20 1932.**

October – December 7 Bert Hinkler makes the first solo flight from New York to London in a light aircraft, flying a de Havilland Puss Moth.

November 3 USS *Akron* lifts off with 207 persons on board, a new record.

November 19 The Sikorsky S-40 amphibious flying-boat enters service with Pan American Airways.

December 3 First flight of the Soviet *Zveno-1* ('Link-1') carrier/fighter combination proposed by V.S. Vakhmistrov. This first combination consists of a TB-1 heavy bomber with two I-4 fighters attached on its wing surfaces. Both fighters successfully leave their 'carrier' in flight and return to base. Later, more advanced experiments lead to the final *Zveno* combination that is used operationally during the early stages of the German assault on the Soviet Union. (q.v. August 1, 1941)

1932

In 1932 Walter H. Beech and his wife Olive Ann found the Beech Aircraft Company. The Company's first product is the Model 17 'Staggerwing', which flies on November 4, 1932.

January 20 Imperial Airways extends its weekly mail service from England to Central Africa to take in Cape Town. The first stage is flown by Handley Page HP 42W *Helena*, covering Croydon, England, to Paris, France. The first return flight, which had many mishaps, began on January 27.

February The Chief Directorate of the Civil Air Fleet (GU-GVF) is formed in the Soviet Union.

February 2 The International Disarmament Conference which begins at Geneva proves a fruitless attempt to ensure world peace.

February 14 Flying a Lockheed Vega with diesel power plant, at Floyd Bennett Field, New York, R. Nichols sets a new world altitude record for diesel-powered aircraft of 6,074m (19,928ft).

March 23-26 Frenchmen Lucien Bossoutrot and Maurice Rossi set a world distance record in a closed circuit, flying the Blériot 110 F-ALCC *Joseph le Brix* for 10,601.48 km (6,587.442 miles) at Oran, Algeria.

March 24-28 J.A. Mollison makes a solo flight in the D.H. Puss Moth G-ABKG from Lympne, Kent to Cape Town, South Africa in 4 days 17 hr 30 min.

April 19-28 C.W.A. Scott flies solo in the D.H.60M Gipsy Moth VH-UQA (originally G-ACOA) from Lympne, Kent to Darwin, Australia, for his second record attempt, in 8 days 20 hr 47 min.

Amelia Earhart with her Lockheed Vega at Londonderry, Northern Ireland, May 21 1932. (*Aer Lingus*)

April 27 Imperial Airway's London-Cape Town passenger service is opened for traffic in both directions.

May 9 A first blind solo flight entirely on instruments, with no check pilot on board the aircraft, is made at Dayton, Ohio, by Capt A.F. Hegenberger, flying a Consolidated NY-2 trainer. A feat which wins him the Collier Trophy.

May 20-21 Flying a Lockheed Vega monoplane, American Amelia Earhart becomes the first woman to make a solo flight across the North Atlantic, from Harbor Grace, Newfoundland to Londonderry, Northern Ireland.

May 24 The giant Dornier Do X flying-boat returns to Friedrichshafen, Germany, after a journey to New York and back that had taken about 19 months. It had left New York on May 19.

June 6 First flight of an Armstrong Whitworth Atalanta for Imperial Airways.

June 18 The prototype of the Dewoitine D 500 makes its first flight, and is to become eventually the first cantilever low-wing monoplane fighter to serve with the French Armée de l'Air.

July 21 A Dornier Wal, with von Gronau and crew, begins a round the world flight, the first to be made in a flying-boat and completed in 111 days.

July 25 The Soviet Union signs non-aggression pacts with Estonia, Finland, Latvia and Poland.

July 29 Amy Johnson and Jim Mollison marry.

August 13 First flight of the startling Grenville Brothers Gee Bee R-1 Super Sportster at Springfield, Massachusetts, USA.

August 14-23 In America, Frances Mersalis and Louise Thaden establish a women's flight-refuelled endurance record of 8 days 4 hr 5 min.

August 18 Auguste Piccard and Max Cosyns ascend from Dübendorf, Switzerland, to set a new balloon height record of 16,201m (53,153ft).

August 18-19 Taking off in the D.H.80A Puss Moth *The Hearts Content* (G-ABXY), from the beach of Portmarnock Strand, north of Dublin, J.A. Mollison records the first east-west solo flight across the North Atlantic to land at Pennfield Ridge, New Brunswick 31 hr 20 min later.

August 25 Amelia Earhart, flying a Lockheed Vega, becomes the first woman to achieve a non-stop trans-continental flight across the United States, from Los Angeles, California, to Newark, New Jersey.

September 3 In winning the National Air Race at Cleveland, Ohio, in a Granville Gee Bee monoplane, Maj J.H. Doolittle sets a new world speed record of 476.828 km/h (296.287 mph).

September 7 Taking part in an International Balloon Race held at Basle, Switzerland, US Navy Lts T. Settle and W. Bushnell not only win the event, but in landing at Vilna, Poland, establish a new balloon world distance record of 1,550km (963.12 miles).

September 16 Cyril F. Uwins, flying the Vickers Type 210 Vespa Mk.VII (G-ABIL), establishes a new world altitude record of 13,404m (43,976ft) over Filton, near Bristol, Somerset.

September 25 Capt Lewis A. Yancey sets a new world altitude record for autogyros at Boston, Massachusetts, of 6,553 m (21,500 ft). The aircraft is a Pitcairn PCA-2.

October 15 Tata Sons Ltd begin a Karachi-Madras mail service to connect with the Imperial Airways London-Karachi route. The first mail is carried by J.R.D. Tata from Karachi to Bombay, and by Nevill Vintcent from Bombay to Madras in a D.H.Puss Moth (VT-ADN), marking the beginning of Indian air transport.

November 14-18 Amy Johnson (Mrs J.A. Mollison) flies solo in the DH.80A Puss Moth *Desert Cloud* (G-ACAB) from Lympne, Kent to Cape Town, South Africa in a new record time of 4 days 6 hr 54 min.

Mollison's de Havilland D.H.80A Puss Moth *The Hearts Content*, **August 18 1932.**

November 19 In the United States a national monument to Orville and Wilbur Wright is dedicated at Kitty Hawk, North Carolina.

December 11-18 On her return flight from Cape Town, South Africa, Amy Johnson lands in the *Desert Cloud* at Croydon, Surrey on December 18, having established a new South Africa-England record time of 7 days 7 hr 5 min.

1933
January 2
Orville Wright is awarded the first Honorary Fellowship of the US Institute of Aeronautical Sciences.

January 30 Late in 1932 President von Hindenburg had offered the Chancellorship of Germany to Adolf Hitler. He had declined because Hindenburg would not grant him full power, but after two months of political crisis he now accepts.

February 6 The Fairey Long-Range Monoplane Mk.II (K1991), crewed by Sqdn Ldr O.R. Gayford and Flt Lt G.E. Nicholetts, takes off from RAF Cranwell. Landing at Walvis Bay, South Africa, on February 8, they have established a new nonstop world long distance record of 8,544.37km (5,309.24 miles).

February 6-9 J.A. Mollison takes off from Lympne, Kent, again in the Puss Moth *The Hearts Content*, with Port Natal, Brazil, as his target for a new UK-South America record. When he lands at Natal on February 9 he has become the first pilot to achieve an England-South America solo flight, the first to fly the South Atlantic solo east-west, and the first to have made solo flights across both the North and South Atlantic.

Above **Boeing Model 247D flown by United Air Lines.**
Below **Westland P.V.3 approaches Mount Everest, April 3 1933.**

February 8 The first flight is recorded of the Boeing Model 247, representing an important step towards the modern airliner. It is of all-metal construction, has a cantilever low-set monoplane wing, retractable landing gear, twin-engine power plant with controllable pitch propellers, and carries up to 10 passengers and 181kg (400lb) of mail.

March 30 Boeing's new airliner, the Model 247, enters service with United Air Lines.

April 1 Formation of the Indian Air Force, Bharatiya Vayu Sena.

April 3 Two biplanes built by the Westland Aircraft Company of Yeovil, Somerset, become the first to fly over the 8,848m (29,028ft) peak of Mount Everest. These are the P.V.3 (G-ACAZ), with Sqdn Ldr the Marquis of Douglas and Clydesdale and L.V.S. Blacker, and the P.V.6 (G-ACBR) with Flt Lt D.F. McIntyre and S.R. Bonnet.

April 4 The US Navy dirigible USS *Akron* crashes into the sea off the New Jersey coast during a violent storm, killing 73 personnel. Among them is Rear Adm William A. Moffett, Chief of the US Navy's Bureau of Aeronautics.

April 21 Less than three weeks after the loss of the USS *Akron* a new dirigible for the navy, the USS *Macon*, makes its first flight. It, too, was destined to end its useful life in the sea.

May 27 In an atmosphere of growing international tension, heightened by Japan's invasion of Manchuria in 1931 and the rumblings of new power in Germany, Japan withdraws from the League of Nations.

June 6 A Dornier Do 8-t Wal crosses the South Atlantic with one stop only at a refuelling ship.

June 21 Formation of Indian Trans-Continental Airways, established to operate a trans-India route in conjunction with Imperial Airways.

June 22 First flight of the Soviet Tupolev ANT-25 monoplane. Also known as RD (for Distance Record), it is specifically designed to gain the world distance record for the Soviet Union.

June 23 The new dirigible USS *Macon* is commissioned by the US Navy. One of its tasks is to take over a role carried out formerly by the USS *Akron*, as 'mothership' for the Curtiss Sparrowhawk parasite fighters.

Three Curtiss F9C Sparrowhawk parasite fighters, photographed while serving with the airship USS *Macon*, June 23 1933. (*US Navy*)

Douglas DC-1, July 1 1933.

July 1 Unable to acquire Boeing Model 247s until the requirements of competing United Air Lines had been met, Transcontinental & Western Air requests the Douglas Aircraft Company to develop a worthy competitor. The resulting Douglas DC-1 records its first flight on this date, from Clover Field, Santa Monica.

July 1-15 Under the command of the Italian Gen Italo Balbo, 24 Savoia-Marchetti S-55X flying-boats fly from Italy to Chicago, Illinois, to take part in the Century of Progress Exposition. In the process, they record the first formation flight across the North Atlantic.

July 15-22 Flying the Lockheed Vega *Winnie Mae*, American Wiley Post records the first round the world solo flight. His 25,099km (15,596 mile) route is from and to Floyd Bennett Field, New York, via Berlin, Moscow, Irkutsk, and Alaska.

July 22-24 Flying the D.H.84 Dragon *Seafarer* (G-ACCV), Amy and Jim Mollison make an east-west crossing of the North Atlantic from Pendine Sands, Wales. Their objective was to reach New York, but low on fuel and attempting to land at Bridgeport, Connecticut, the *Seafarer* overturned and was wrecked. Fortunately, neither of Britain's record-breaking pilots is seriously injured.

August 5-7 French air force pilots Lt Maurice Rossi and Paul Codes establish a new world distance record of 9,104km (5,657 miles), flying the Blériot Zapata from New York, USA to Rayak, Syria.

August 17 The Soviet Union flight tests its first rocket, the GIRD-IX with semi-liquid fuel.

August 30 Air France (Compagnie Nationale Air France) becomes established, following acquisitions that had combined Air Orient, Air Union, Compagnie Aéropostale, and some smaller airlines.

September 7-8 Six Consolidated P2Y-1 flying-boats, under the overall command of Lt Cdr H.E. Holland, fly non-stop from Norfolk, Virginia, to Coco Solo, Canal Zone, setting a formation flight distance record of 3,314km (2,059 miles).

September 28 At Villacoublay, France, G. Lemoine flies a Potez 50 to a new world altitude record of 13,661m (44,820ft).

October 4-11 Sir Charles Kingsford Smith, flying the Percival Gull Four *Miss Southern Cross* (G-ACJV), takes off from Lympne, Kent on a solo flight to Australia. Landing at Wyndham, Western Australia on October 11, he has established a new record time of 7 days 4 hr 44 min over the England-Australia route.

October 12 Crewed by C.T.P. Ulm, P.G. Taylor, G.U. Allen and J. Edwards, the Avro Ten *Faith in Australia* (VH-UXX) takes off from Fairey's Great West Aerodrome, Hayes, Middlesex en route to Australia. Landing at Derby, Western Australia on October 19, the flight from England is made in a record 115 hrs flying time.

October 14 Germany withdraws from the League of Nations. This move, coupled with Japan's similar action earlier in the year, marks the dissolution of attempts to achieve agreement on world disarmament.

October 24 In the British House of Commons, Winston Churchill gives an early warning of things to come, stating that Germany was well on the way to becoming the most heavily armed nation in the world.

October 31 Australia's Queensland and Northern Territory Air Service (Q.A.N.T.A.S.) announce that it has completed its first 3.2 million km (2.0 million miles) of route flying.

November 4 The Brazilian airline VASP (Viacao Aerea Sao Paulo SA) is established.

November 20-21 Ascending from Akron, Ohio, Lt Cdr T.G.W. Settle and Maj C.L. Fordney of the United States Marine Corps establish a balloon altitude record of 18,665m (61,237ft).

December 1 The first daily air service in India is started by Indian National Airways, which inaugurates a passenger, freight and mail service between Calcutta and Dacca.

December 31 The prototype of the Polikarpov 1-16 (TsKB-12) is flown for the first time. When the type entered service with Soviet squadrons in the autumn of 1934, it had the distinction of being the first monoplane fighter in the world to have a fully enclosed cockpit and fully retractable landing gear.

1934

On the instigation of Army Commander Tukhachevski, a Rocket Scientific Research Institute (RNII) is founded in the Soviet Union.

Flight trials take place in the Soviet Union of the PI-1 (DG-52) fighter fitted with two 75mm APK-4 recoilless cannon, the first military aircraft so armed.

January 10-11 Under the command of Lt Cdr K.McGinnis, six Consolidated P2Y-1 flying-boats make a nonstop formation flight from San Francisco, California to Pearl Harbor, Hawaiian Islands. This establishes a new world straight line distance record of 3,861km (2,399 miles) under the FAI's C-2 seaplane Class.

January 18 Qantas Empire Airways is registered, and thereafter known as Qantas. The new company combines the interests of Q.A.N.T.A.S. and Imperial Airways, with each company holding 50% of the capital, and is formed to operate the Singapore-Brisbane section of the England-Australia air route.

January 26 Germany concludes a non-aggression treaty with Poland. It also stipulates that Germany would respect existing Polish territorial rights for a period of 10 years.

February 1 South African Airways is founded, beginning operations with aircraft and staff that it took over from South Africa's Union Airways (Pty) Ltd, which had been established during 1929.

February 3 Start of the first scheduled transocean airmail service between Europe and South America by the German airline Deutsche Luft-Hansa, flown from Stuttgart to Buenos Aires via Seville, Bathurst and Natal.

February 19 Following a number of complaints from small airline companies in the US, who believed that major airlines were being given preferential treatment in the allocation of US airmail contracts, President Roosevelt cancels all existing contracts with effect from midnight February 19. Simultaneously, the US Army

Air Corps is given the task of flying the US domestic airmail.

February 25 American airwoman Laura Ingalls begins a solo flight around South America, a distance of some 27,359km (17,000 miles). This is completed successfully on April 25.

March An ANT-4 (TB-1) piloted by A.V. Lyapidevsky makes the first landing on ice in the Arctic while saving the crew of the Soviet ship *Chelyuskin*.

April 11 Flying a modified Caproni 113 at Rome, Italy, Cdr R. Donati establishes a new world altitude record of 14,433m (47,352ft).

April 16 The Brazilian airline VASP begins its first scheduled services.

US airline Northwest Airways, which had been founded in 1926, adopts its current name of Northwest Orient Airlines.

April 17 Originating from Pitcairn Aviation Inc. and renamed Eastern Air Transport during 1929, this large US airline adopts its current title of Eastern Air Lines.

The de Havilland D.H.89 Dragon Six (named later as the Dragon Rapide), makes its first flight from the company's Stag Lane airfield, Edgware, Middlesex, piloted by Hubert Broad.

A first flight is made by the Fairey TSR.2, the Swordfish prototype.

May 8-23 New Zealand airwoman Jean Batten takes off from Lympne, Kent in a third attempt to establish a new England-Australia solo flight record. Flying a de Havilland D.H.60M Moth (G-AARB), she lands at Darwin, in Australia's Northern Territory, on May 23. Her time for the flight, 14 days 22 hr 30 min, beats the record set by Amy Johnson in 1930 by more than four days.

May 13 US airmail pilot Jack Frye sets a new US coast-to-coast record, carrying mail from Los Angeles, California, to Newark, New Jersey, in a flight time of 11 hr 31 min.

Formation date of American Airlines Inc, as a direct successor of American Airways Inc which had been incorporated during 1930.

May 16 Initial revenue use by Imperial Airways of the then giant four-engined Short Type L.17 biplane landplane. The first of two, named *Scylla* (G-ACJJ), is used to carry passengers and airmail on the airline's London-Paris route.

May 28 Capt Maurice Rossi and Lt Paul Codes of the French air force land at Brooklyn, New York, after a 38 hr 27 min flight from Paris, France. This had been an attempt to beat the world distance record they set in 1933, but the long transatlantic flight against strong head winds forced them to abandon their attempt.

Sir Alan Cobham's Airspeed Courier being refuelled in the air by a Handley Page W.10 tanker, during an attempt to fly from England to India non-stop using flight refuelling. Leaving Portsmouth Airport on September 22, 1934, it made a forced landing in Malta due to mechanical failure.

May 29 Britain's first regular domestic airmail service is inaugurated by Highland Airways, with a de Havilland Dragon (G-ACCE), between Inverness and Kirkwall.

June 1 The US Army Air Corps ceases to be responsible for the carriage of US domestic airmail. During its short period of responsibility, flown during a period of extremely bad weather, the service had carried some 347 tons of mail and flown about 2.6 million km (1.6 million miles).

June 18 The Boeing Airplane Company begins the design of its Model 299, a four-engined bomber aircraft which it develops as a private venture to meet a US Army requirement. It eventually becomes known worldwide as the B-17 Flying Fortress.

July 19 – August 20 Under the overall command of Lt Col H.H.Arnold, a flight of ten USAAC Martin B-10 bombers fly from Bolling Field to Fairbanks, Alaska, and return. The outward journey is made in 25 hr 30 min, and the return in 26 hr.

July 20 In the House of Commons, a government proposal for a modest expansion of the Royal Air Force, by some eight squadrons a year over the ensuing five years, is censured by the Labour party with Liberal support, Clement Attlee declaring 'there was no need for an increase in air armaments'.

July 28 A balloon flown as a combined US Air Corps/National Geographic Society effort, carrying Maj

W.E.Kepner and Capts A.W. Stevens and O.A. Anderson, attains an altitude of 18,475m (60,613ft).

August 8-9 L.G. Reid and J.R. Ayling, flying the de Havilland Dragon *Trail of the Caribou* (G-ACJM), record the first nonstop flight from Canada to England. Taking off from Wasaga Beach, Ontario, they land at Heston Airport, Middlesex 30 hr 50 min later.

September 1 In America, Col Roscoe Turner sets a new US coast-to-coast record flight time of 10 hr 2 min.

Formation date of the Mexican airline Aeromexico, which begins initial operations later that month.

September 12 First flight of the Gloster SS.37 prototype (K5200). Ten months later it is ordered into production as the Gladiator and is the last biplane fighter to serve with the RAF.

September 24 The first international airliner to serve with Qantas, a de Havilland D.H. 86, leaves Croydon, Surrey on delivery to Brisbane, Queensland where it arrives on October 13.

September 28 Luft-Hansa carries its 1,000,000th passenger.

October 7 First flight of the Tupolev-Arkhangelsky SB-1 (ANT-40.1) tactical bomber. It is of very advanced conception at the time it is ordered into production six months before completion of the prototypes. In developed form as the SB-2, it is first operational in Spain (where named 'Katyusha') and forms the mainstay of the Soviet tactical bomber force in 1941. From 1938 it is also licence-built in Czechoslovakia as the B.71.

October 9 For his achievement in completing the world's first solo round-the-world flight, Wiley Post is awarded the Gold Medal of the Fédération Aéronautique Internationale.

October 20 The MacRobertson England-Australia air race starts, flown from Mildenhall, Suffolk to Flemington Racecourse, Melbourne. Prize money of £15,000 is given by Sir MacPherson Robertson, as part of the centenary celebrations of the foundation of the State of Victoria. Winner is the D.H. 88 Comet *Grosvenor House* (G-ACSS), flown by Charles W.A. Scott and Tom Campbell Black, in a time of 70 hr 54 min 18 sec.

October 22 – November 4 Flying a Lockheed Altair, Sir Charles Kingsford Smith and Capt P.G. Taylor accomplish the first flight from Australia to the United States. Take-off is from Brisbane, Queensland with the route via Fiji and Hawaii to Oakland, California.

October 23 Flying the Macchi MC. 72 seaplane, the design of which had been initiated by Italy for participation in the Schneider Trophy Contest of 1931, Francesco Agello establishes a new world speed record, and a record in its own FAI sub-class C-2. This speed of 709.209 km/h (440.683 mph) has since been bettered many times as a world speed record, but in 1982 the piston-engined seaplane record was still unbeaten.

November 1 The first issue of Bradshaw's International Air Guide is published.

November 8 Capt E.V. Rickenbacker, with Capt Charles W. France and Silas Morehouse as crew, establishes a new US coast-to-coast record for a commercial transport aircraft. They record a time of 12 hr 3 min 50 sec for the flight from Los Angeles, California to Newark, New Jersey.

November 24 The UK Air Ministry give notice that pilots holding B (commercial) licences must attain an acceptable standard of blind flying experience by April 1, 1935 in order to retain their licences.

December 5 A clash of Ethiopian and Italian forces, in a disputed zone of the Italian Somaliland border, brings a first rift in the six-year-old Treaty of Friendship between these two nations.

December 8 Inauguration date of a regular weekly airmail service between England and Australia. The London-Karachi sector is the responsibility of Imperial Airways, which also shares with Indian Trans-Continental Airways the route between Karachi and Singapore. Qantas flies the sector from Singapore to Brisbane.

December 19 Following a refusal by the UK and USA to allow a parity of naval power to Japan, the latter nation denounces the Washington and London Naval Treaties and gives notice of withdrawal.

December 20 The UK government gives first details of its proposed (for 1937) Empire Air Mail Programme. This plans that all letters from the UK for delivery over Empire air routes would be carried without any special surcharge.

December 31 Airwoman Helen Richey becomes the first woman in the US to pilot an airmail transport aircraft on regular schedule. Her first scheduled flight, flown on this date, is with a Ford Tri-Motor from Washington, D.C. to Detroit, Michigan.

1935

January 11-12 Taking off from Wheeler Field, a USAAC base on the Hawaiian island of Oahu, Amelia Earhart flies solo in a Lockheed Vega to Oakland, California in 18 hr 15 min. In completing this journey, Amelia Earhart becomes the first person to accomplish a flight over the route.

January 15 Maj J.H. Doolittle, flying a commercial transport carrying two passengers establishes a new US coast-to-coast transport aircraft record from Los Angeles, California to Newark, New Jersey of 11 hr 59 min.

January 29 Harry Richman, flying a Sikorsky S-39 amphibian from Miami, Florida, establishes a new world height record in the FAI Class C-2 of 5,682m (18,642ft).

February 3 The death is announced of Prof Hugo Junkers, the pioneer of all-metal aircraft construction.

February 12 The US Navy dirigible USS *Macon* crashes into the sea off the California coast, fortunately with the loss of only two of her crew.

February 22 Flying a transport aircraft over the same coast-to-coast route as Maj J.H. Doolittle (q.v. Jan. 15),

Bristol Type 142 *Britain First* **in military markings, April 12 1935.**

American Airline pilot Leland S. Andrews sets a new record time of 11 hr 34 min.

February 24 First flight of the Heinkel He 111a prototype, ostensibly a twin-engined transport, but intended as a bomber for the still-secret Luftwaffe.

March 1 General Headquarters Air Force, a new formation within the US Army Air Corps, is established with Brig Gen Frank M. Andrews commanding. This is seen by the proponents of air power as a first move towards an autonomous US air force.

March 9 It is announced in Germany that the Luftwaffe, a new national air force, has been established.

March 16 Blaming the failure of other nations to disarm, Germany repudiates the disarmament clauses of the Versailles Treaty and announces a massive rearmament programme.

March 24 To meet an Air Ministry requirement for a twin-engined coastal patrol landplane, Avro offers a military version of its Type 652 which had been developed for Imperial Airways. The prototype of the Type 652A military version (K4771) flies for the first time on this date, becoming known later as the Avro Anson.

March 28 In the USA, Dr Robert Goddard achieves the first successful launch of his gyroscopically controlled rocket. It is stated to have gained a height of 1,463m (4,800ft) and speed of 885 km/h (550 mph).

First flight of Consolidated Aircraft Corporation's XP3Y-1 patrol bomber amphibian prototype, to be developed later as the PBY Catalina. (q.v. May 19, 1936)

April 1 Swissair inaugurates its first regular service to the UK, between Zürich and Croydon, Surrey via Basle, operated with Douglas DC-2 transports.

April 12 First flight of the Bristol Type 142, a six-passenger twin-engined monoplane which has been designed as an executive aircraft for *Daily Mail* owner, Lord Rothermere. Its outstanding performance results in him presenting it to the nation (named *Britain First*), leading to development of the Bristol Blenheim bomber/fighter.

April 13 Imperial Airways, in conjunction with Qantas (q.v. April 17) opens the London-Brisbane route to passengers. The first through passengers (two) are carried on the service that leaves London on April 20.

April 16-17 A Pan American Clipper flying-boat makes the airline's first proving flight from Alameda, California to Honolulu, Hawaii. This is the first stage in creating a transpacific route from the USA to the Philippines.

April 17 The Australia-England air service for the carriage of passengers is inaugurated with the departure of the first aircraft from Brisbane, Queensland.

May 2 Following the announcement of German rearmament, and as a result of the failure of French initiative to create an eastern European pact that would have included Germany, Poland and the Soviet Union, France concludes a separate alliance with the Soviet Union.

May 16 Following the conclusion of its alliance with France (above), the Soviet Union comes to a similar alliance with Czechoslovakia. This does nothing to improve relations between Germany and the Soviet Union, the former believing that the Soviets sought to acquire bases in Czechoslovakia from which air attacks could be launched against Germany.

May 18 What is then the world's worst air disaster involving a heavier-than-air craft occurs when the Soviet ANT-20 *Maxim Gorky* is destroyed after collision with another aircraft, near Tushino, killing 56 persons.

May 22 Proposals to increase the strength of the Royal Air Force by 1,500 aircraft are put before the British Parliament. Following the disclosure of German re-armament plans (q.v. March 16), the announcement is received without undue controversy.

May 28 First flight of the Messerschmitt Bf 109V1 prototype, powered by a Rolls-Royce Kestrel engine and piloted by Hans D. Knoetzsch at Augsburg; Haunstetten. It is the first of more than 33,000 Bf 109s built during the subsequent years, one of the most famous and longest-serving piston-engined fighters of all.

June 1 The Austrian air arm, which had a history stemming from 1892, becomes named Fliegertruppen des Österreichischen Bundesheeres. It is renamed as the Austrian Army Air Force (Österreichische Heeres-fliegerkräfte) during 1955.

June 26 The first flight is recorded of the Bréguet-Dorand Gyroplane Laboratoire helicopter in France. This has counter-rotating co-axial two-blade metal rotors to offset the effects of torque, and such features as cyclic pitch control for lateral and longitudinal move-ment, and collective pitch for vertical movement.

July 23 A first report on radio direction finding, later to become named as radar, is made to Britain's Air Defence Research Committee.

July 28 The Boeing Airplane Company's private-venture Model 299 prototype makes a successful first flight with Boeing's test pilot Leslie R. Tower at the controls.

August 8 First flight of the Morane-Saulnier MS.405 prototype. Ordered into production as the MS.406 in 1937, it is numerically the most important French fighter in autumn 1939.

September 17 First flight of the Junkers Ju 87 prototype powered by a Rolls-Royce Kestrel engine. Soon to be known and dreaded as the Stuka, it is the only dive bomber to make a real impact on history.

September 19 Konstantin Tsiolkovski, the early Rus-sian rocket pioneer dies.

September 30 Allied British Airways is registered in the UK, a new company formed by a merger of Hillman's Airways, Spartan Air Lines and United Airways. In retrospect the name British Airways seems more commercial, and is adopted instead on October 29, 1935.

October 3 Without any prior warning and without an official declaration of war, Italy invades Abyssinia (now Ethiopia), making early use of aircraft and artillery for close support.

October 30 The Boeing Model 299 (q.v. July 28), which is undergoing official tests with the USAAC at Wright Field, crashes on take-off. Boeing feared this might have grave consequences for the company's survival, but subsequent investigation showed that the attempt to take-off had been made with locked control surfaces, thus exonerating the aircraft and its design.

November 4-11 The Parnall Heck (G-ACTC), which had been built by Westland aircraft, is used by Flg Off David Llewellyn and Jill Wyndham to establish a new Cape Town-England record. The route from Cape Town to Lympne, Kent is flown in 6 days 12 hr 17 min.

November 8 The Hawker Hurricane prototype, Sydney Camm's single-seat monoplane fighter designed to the British Air Ministry Specification F.36/34, flies for the first time piloted by the company's test pilot P.W.S. Bulman. This eight-gun fighter (in its Mk I configur-ation) is remembered especially in British aviation history for its vital role in the Battle of Britain.

November 11 With assistance from the National Geographic Society, Capts A.W. Stevens and O.A. Anderson establish a new balloon world altitude record of 22,066m (72,395ft) following launch from Rapid City, South Dakota.

November 11-13 Jean Batten, flying the Percival Gull Six *Jean* (G-APDR) takes off from Lympne, Kent in an attempt to establish a record time for the England-South America route. Landing at Natal, Brazil after an over-ocean flight in a heavy storm, she sets a time for the route of 2 days 13 hr 15 min, almost a day less than the previous record gained by Jim Mollison (q.v. Feb 6, 1933).

Martin M.130 *China Clipper*, **November 22 1935.**

November 22 Pan American inaugurates its first scheduled transpacific airmail service, flown by the Martin M.130 flying-boat *China Clipper* with Capt Edwin C Musick and crew. Its route is from San Francisco's Alameda Airport to Manila, Philippines via Honolulu, and the islands of Wake and Guam.

December 17 A popular date for first flights in the USA, recalling that made by the Wright brothers at Kitty Hawk in 1903, is the date chosen in 1935 for the first flight of the Douglas Sleeper Transport (DST). Better known later under the designations C-47, DC-3, or the name Dakota, many remain in service in 1982, 47 years after that first flight.

December 27 The year closes with a peaceful use of military air power; the USAAC drops bombs at Hilo, Hawaii to divert the lava flow of Mauna Loa away from the local waterworks.

1936
Early in the year, the Special Purpose Air Arm (AON), an independent strategic force, is formed in the Soviet Union. Subsequently reorganised as Supreme Command's Long Range Bomber Arm (DBA-GK) in 1940, it is renamed Long-Range Air Arm (ADD) in March, 1942.

February The Soviet I-16UTI two-seat fighter trainer passes its State Acceptance tests. Also known as the UTI-4, it is the first such two-seat modification of an operational single-seat fighter to assist conversion training.

February 17 First operation by Ansett Airways Pty Ltd., which had been established earlier in the month.

This company adopts its current title of Ansett Airlines of Australia Ltd in June 1969.

February 19 Ex-Brig Gen William ('Billy') Mitchell, the USAAC's advocate of air power, dies in New York.

March First flight test of a liquid-fuel rocket motor developed by Wernher von Braun fitted into an He 112. The aircraft explodes but the pilot, Erich Warsitz, is thrown clear.

March 3 The UK government issues a White Paper on rearmament. Among its detailed proposals is one to increase the number of RAF first-line aircraft for home defence from 1,500 to 1,750.

March 4 First flight of the German Zeppelin Company's LZ 129 *Hindenburg*, the world's largest rigid airship with a length of 245m (803.8ft) and maximum diameter of 41m (134.5ft). This airship, and its sister ship the LZ 130 *Graf Zeppelin II*, are the world's last two rigid airships to be built.

March 5 First flight of the Supermarine Type 300 Spitfire prototype (K5054), incorporating eight-gun armament and with power provided by a Rolls-Royce Merlin piston-engine. Designed by R.J. Mitchell, it benefited from his experience in the design and development of the Supermarine seaplanes that won the Schneider Trophy outright for Britain in 1931.

March 7 A first demonstration of new military ambitions in Europe is seen, following Hitler's renunciation of the Locarno Treaty pacts of 1925, with German reoccupation of the Rhineland.

March 10 First flight of the Fairey Battle light bomber prototype (K4303). Obsolescent in 1939, it was nevertheless built and used in substantial numbers. The first

The prototype Supermarine Spitfire (foreground) is displayed in public at Eastleigh in 1936 alongside a Supermarine Walrus I amphibian, the prototype Vickers Wellesley and the prototype Vickers Wellington.

two VCs awarded to the RAF during the Second World War were gained by Battle aircrews.

March 14 Imperial Airways inaugurates a weekly London-Hong Kong air service which, reportedly, is used initially for the carriage of mail.

March 17 First flight of the Armstrong Whitworth A.W.38 prototype (K4586), later named Whitley which, together with the Hampden and Wellington, forms the mainstay of RAF Bomber Command in the early years of the Second World War.

In the first case of its kind to be brought before a British court, a passenger found smoking in the cabin of a Handley Page Heracles during an Imperial Airways Paris-London flight is fined £10 at Croydon Police Court.

April First flight of the Fieseler Fi 156 Storch (Stork) prototype (D-IKVN) light army co-operation monoplane. Fitted with extensive high-lift devices and stalky landing gear, it is the first true STOL aircraft to be built. It serves subsequently in many roles throughout the Second World War and afterwards.

The German Research Institute for Rocket Flight is established.

April 15 The young German engineer H.J. Pabst von Ohain and Dipl Ing Max Hahn begin development work on a turbojet aircraft engine at the Heinkel plant at Marienehe.

May 4-7 Flying a Percival Gull Six (G-ADZO), Amy Mollison takes off from Gravesend, Kent, in an attempt to establish a new England-South Africa record. Following the shorter West Coast route, she lands at Wingfield Aerodrome, Cape Town on 7 May, setting a new time of 3 days 6 hr 26 min and beating the existing record by just over 11 hrs.

May 5 Following what had been virtually a campaign of terror, in which the Italian Air Force had used modern weapons, including poison gas, against a primitive people armed with almost medieval weapons, Italian forces capture Addis Ababa, marking the collapse of Ethiopian resistance.

May 6 The frequency of the London-Brisbane service, operated jointly by Imperial Airways, Indian Trans-Continental Airways and Qantas, is increased to twice weekly.

May 6-14 First crossings of the North Atlantic by Germany's new Zeppelin, the LZ 129 *Hindenburg*. The outward journey, from Friedrichshafen to Lakehurst, New Jersey, is completed in 61 hr 50 min, the return flight in 49 hr 3 min.

May 9 Following the collapse of Abyssinian resistance, and the flight of Emperor Haile Selassie, Italy annexes the country. Together with Eritrea and Italian Somaliland, this is to form Italy's East African Empire, the King of Italy assuming the title Emperor of Ethiopia.

May 10-15 Endeavouring to set a new time for the return flight from South Africa to England, Amy Mollison takes off from Wingfield. Flying over the orthodox route, she lands at Croydon, Surrey, after taking 4 days 16 hr 17 min, to gain both the outward and return records.

May 12 First flight of the Messerschmitt Bf 110V-1 twin-engined strategic fighter prototype, from Augsburg-Haunstetten airfield. Regarded as a Zerstörer (destroyer) of enemy fighters, it is soon discovered during the Battle of Britain that Göring's much vaunted Zerstörergeschwader could not operate in daylight unless themselves escorted by highly manoeuvrable fighters. Nevertheless, the Bf 110 proved an effective nightfighter

May 19 First flight of the Consolidated XPBY-1 amphibian, a development of the XP3Y-1 (q.v. March 28, 1935), the first of the many Catalinas. A very successful design, it is later also manufactured under licence in the Soviet Union as the GST.

May 22 Aer Lingus Teoranta is established in Dublin, Eire, as a private company.

May 27 Using a de Havilland DH.84 Dragon, Aer Lingus begins its first daily service, between Dublin and

Bristol, Somerset. The route is operated in conjunction with the UK registered Blackpool and West Coast Air Services.

June 6 The Socony-Vacuum Oil Company at Paulsboro, New Jersey, initiates the production of 100 octane aviation fuel using a catalytic cracking process.

June 15 A first flight is made by the Vickers Type 271 bomber prototype (K4049). To become better known as the Wellington, its design incorporates the geodetic construction developed by designer B.N.Wallis, enabling it to retain structural integrity despite heavy punishment from enemy weapons.

First flight of the Westland Lysander prototype (K6127), flown by the company's test pilot Harald Penrose from RAF Boscombe Down, Wilts. This is a two-seat aircraft of unusual high-wing configuration, designed especially to meet the requirements of the army co-operation squadrons of the RAF.

June 25 The Bristol Blenheim I light bomber prototype (K7033), developed from the Type 142 *Britain First* (q.v. Apr 12, 1935), makes its first flight.

June 26 Piloted by Ewald Rohlfs, the Focke Wulf Fw 61 twin rotor helicopter prototype makes its first flight of about half a minute duration. Development over the ensuing twelve months is to establish this aircraft as the world's first completely successful helicopter.

July 1 Australian National Airways is incorporated, merging Adelaide Airways, Airlines of Australia, Holy-

man's Airways, and West Australian Airways. It is this operator that first introduces the Douglas DC-3 into Australian airline service during late 1937.

July 3　First flight at Rochester, Kent of the first of the Short S.23 'C-class' flying-boats for Imperial Airways, piloted by John Parker and flown almost unintentionally for 14 minutes. This is G-ADHL, which was named subsequently as *Canopus*.

July 18　Simultaneous revolt by 12 military garrisons in Spain, and of five in Spanish Morocco, mark the beginning of the Spanish Civil War.

July 20　Twenty Ju 52/3m g3e bomber-transports arrive in Seville and begin transporting Nationalist troops from Morocco. It is the first large-scale airlift operation in the world; a total of 7,350 troops with artillery and other equipment are carried to Spain in about six weeks, followed by two more airlift operations the following month.

July 30　Speaking in the UK House of Lords, Viscount Swinton announces the formation of a Royal Air Force Volunteer Reserve. Volunteers are to be recruited for a minimum of five years, receiving flying training at weekends and during an annual 15-day camp. The RAFVR is expanded subsequently to cover every branch of activity of the Royal Air Force.

Short C-class flying-boat *Canopus*, July 3 1936.

A formation of Junkers Ju 52/3m g3e bomber-transports in 1936.

August 3 The diminutive French Pou du Ciel (Flying Flea) was designed by Henri Mignet as virtually the first aircraft intended for amateur construction. With several examples having been built and flown, an International Flying Flea Challenge Trophy Race is flown at Ramsgate, Kent on this date. First prize goes to a French-built 'Pou', flown by Edouard Bret.

August 7 The first six Heinkel He 51 fighters with their pilots and ground crew arrive in Cadiz, Spain as the initial consignment of German military assistance promised to General Franco.

August 14 Flying a Potez 50 at Villacoublay, France, G. Detre establishes a new world altitude record of 14,843m (48,698ft).

August 24 The airline DETA (Direccao de Exploracao dos Transportes Aéreos) is established in Mozambique. Its current title Linhas Aéreas de Moçambique was adopted during 1975, but continues to be known popularly by its well-known and diminutive name of DETA.

September 4-5 South Africa's Mrs Beryl Markham, flying the Percival Vega Gull *The Messenger* (VP-KCC), takes off from Abingdon, Berkshire to achieve the first east-west solo transatlantic crossing by a woman pilot. She force-lands due to fuel shortage at Baleine Cove, Cape Breton Island, after a flight of 21 hr 35 min.

September 10 Deutsche Luft Hansa inaugurates a flying-boat service between Horta, Azores and Bermuda. The route is extended to New York in October

September 28 Sqdn Ldr S.R.Swain, flying the Bristol Type 138 from Farnborough, Hampshire establishes a new world altitude record of 15,223m (49,944ft).

September 29 – October 1 The Schlesinger Air Race (UK-South Africa), held in conjunction with the Empire Exhibition in Johannesburg, is won by Charles W.A. Scott and Giles Guthrie. Their Percival Vega Gull G-AEKE is the only aircraft to complete the course, in a time of 2 days 4 hr 56 min.

October 5-16 Flying her Percival Gull Six *Jean* (G-ADPR), Jean Batten leaves Lympne, Kent in an attempt to establish a new England-Australia solo record. She arrives Darwin, Northern Territory on October 11 in a time of 5 days 21 hr 3 min, beating the previous record by more than a day. From Darwin she flies to Sydney, NSW, then across the Tasman Sea to Auckland, New Zealand on October 16. Hers was then the fastest solo crossing of the Tasman Sea, and she had set a new solo UK-New Zealand record of 11 days 1 hr 25 min.

October 13 The first Soviet I-15 fighters arrive at Cartagena, Spain. Subsequent Soviet help to the Republicans totals over 1,400 military aircraft, paid for by Spanish gold reserves.

October 15 First flight of the Nakajima Ki-27 prototype, the first low-wing monoplane fighter with an enclosed cockpit to enter service with the Japanese Army Air Force.

October 19 The Swiss Air Force, established originally in 1914, adopts the name Schweizerische Flugwaffe, Kommando der Flieger-und Flieger-abwehrtruppen (Swiss Air Force & Anti-Aircraft Command).

October 21 Pan American inaugurates its scheduled weekly passenger service from San Francisco, California to Manila, Philippines.

October 29-30 Taking off from Harbour Grace, Newfoundland, and flying the rebuilt Bellanca 28-70 monoplane *The Dorothy* (NR190M), J.A. Mollison sets a new transatlantic west-east solo record by landing at Croydon, Surrey 13 hr 17 min later.

October 30 The Imperial Airways' C class flying-boat *Canopus* (G-ADHL) records the first scheduled flight of the type, on the airline's trans-Mediterranean Alexandria-Brindisi route.

November The German Legion Condor is formed in Spain, in response to the increasing number of Soviet aircraft on the Republican side. It begins operating on November 15.

November 4 First operational use of Soviet fighters on the Republican side in Spain: I-15 biplanes flown by Soviet pilots.

November 6 Intensive air bombardment of Spain's capital city, Madrid, fails to dislodge Republican troops holding the city against siege forces.

December 21 First flight of the Junkers Ju 88V-1 prototype (D-AQEN) at Dessau. Designed as a high-speed bomber, it is to see extensive service with the Luftwaffe throughout the Second World War, being used in a wide variety of roles.

December 27 First flight of the ANT-42 (functional designation TB-7) prototype. After prolonged trials it is redesigned in 1938 and becomes operational in 1940 as the Pe-8, the only modern four-engined Soviet heavy bomber to see service during the Second World War.

1937

January 12 Imperial Airways' C class flying-boat *Centaurus* (G-ADUT) makes the airline's first all-air trans-Mediterranean service, Alexandria-Southampton, on the final leg of the India-UK route.

January 16 First flight of the Lioré et Olivier LeO 45 prototype, destined to be the only really modern medium bomber in French Armée de'l Air service at the time of the German attack in 1940.

February 7 British Airways, which had been operating from Gatwick Airport since the previous May, transfers its activities to Croydon Airport, Surrey.

February 9 First flight of the Blackburn Type B-24 prototype (K5178) is made at Brough, Yorkshire. To become known as the Skua, it is the first monoplane to enter service with the Fleet Air Arm, and its first dive-bomber of British construction.

February 18 A nonstop flight of 3,576km (2,222 miles), from Southampton, Hampshire to Alexandria, Egypt is made by the C class flying-boat *Caledonia* (G-ADHM) of Imperial Airways.

March 5 Airmail-carrying Allegheny Airlines is formed, becoming known as All American Airways when it becomes a passenger carrier in March 1949. The name is changed to Allegheny Airlines in 1953, but adopts its current name of US Air during October 1979.

A flying-boat base at Hythe, Hampshire, on Southampton Water, is opened by Imperial Airways as the terminal for its Empire services.

March 13 Italy announces a four-year expansion programme for its air force.

March 30 The crew of a Pan American Sikorsky S-42B flying-boat completes an 11,265km (7,000 mile) survey flight from Pago Pago, American Samoa to Auckland, New Zealand.

April 1 The New Zealand Permanent Air Force, which had been founded during June 1923, adopts its current title of the Royal New Zealand Air Force.

April 5 Lockheed 10 Electras are introduced on the London-Paris route of British Airways.

April 6-9 The second prototype of the Mitsubishi Type 97 (Ki-15) is acquired by the proprietors of Japan's Asahi Shimbun newspaper to be used in a Japan-England record attempt. Named *Kamikaze* (Divine Wind) and registered J-BAAI, it is flown by Masaaki Iinuma with his navigator/mechanic Kenji Tsukagoshi from Tashikawa, arriving at Croydon, Surrey on April 9.

They secured the record in an FAI-accredited flying time of 51 hr 17 min 23 sec for the 15,356km (9,542 mile) route.

April 10 Trans-Canada Air Lines (TCA) is formed, its first scheduled services being inaugurated on September 1, 1937. The current name of Air Canada was adopted in 1964.

April 12 Frank Whittle (later Sir Frank) bench tests successfully for the first time the world's first gas-turbine engine designed specifically for aircraft propulsion.

April 19 The first letter to encircle the world by commercial airmail services is despatched from New York. Routed via San Francisco, Hong Kong, Penang, Amsterdam and Brazil, it is returned to New York on May 25, 1937.

April 26 Guernica, the seat of Spain's Basque government, is bombed by co-operating Luftwaffe aircraft with heavy loss of life.

April 28 A Pan American Clipper arrives at Hong Kong, marking the end of the first complete crossing of the Pacific Ocean by a commercial aircraft.

April 30 The battleship *España*, being operated as the major component of the Spanish Nationalist fleet, is sunk in an air attack by Republican aircraft.

May 2 The Handley Page HP 45 *Heracles* (G-AAXC) records the 40,000th crossing of the English Channel by Imperial Airways aircraft.

LZ 129 *Hindenburg* explodes into a ball of fire at Lakehurst, New Jersey, May 6 1937. (*US National Archives*)

May 6 The pride of German air transport, the Zeppelin LZ 129 *Hindenburg*, is destroyed by fire in an accident at Lakehurst, New Jersey. This disaster brings an end to the development of commercial passenger carrying airships.

May 7 First flight is made by the Lockheed XC-35 high-altitude research aircraft, introducing the world's first completely successful pressurised cabin.

May 8 At Montecelio, Italy a new world altitude record of 15,655m (51,362ft) is established by Lt Col M.Pezzi flying a Caproni 161.

May 28 Spanish Republican SB bombers with Soviet crews bomb the German armoured ship *Deutschland* while at anchor off Ibiza.

May 31 In retaliation for the attack on the armoured ship *Deutschland*, aircraft of the German Condor Legion in Spain make a heavy raid on the coastal town of Almeria, which also comes under shellfire from the German warships *Admiral Scheer* and *Leipzig*.

June 2 The C class 'boat *Canopus* (G-ADHL) of Imperial Airways inaugurates the airline's first through flying-boat service from Southampton to Durban, South Africa.

June 3 Iceland's Flugfelag Akureyrar is formed with a single aircraft. Operations end in late 1939 when this floatplane sinks, but are resumed under the new and still current name Icelandair during 1940.

June 9 Using Junkers Ju 52/3m aircraft, South African Airways inaugurates a Johannesburg-Lusaka service.

June 11 Reginald J. Mitchell, the British Supermarine Aircraft Company's brilliant designer, dies at the age of 42 unaware of the vital part that his Spitfire fighter is to play in aviation history.

June 16 Pan American and Imperial Airways inaugurates a co-operative Bermuda-New York service.

June 18-20 The Soviet ANT-25 (RD) monoplane crewed by V.P. Chkalov, G.F. Baidukov and A.V. Belyakov, makes a non-stop flight from Moscow via the North Pole to the USA, a distance of 9,130km (5,573 miles).

June 29 Imperial Airways' C class flying-boat *Centurion* (G-ADVE) departs Southampton to inaugurate the UK's Empire Air Mail Programme.

June 30 The Bristol .Type 138, flown by Flt Lt M.J.Adam from Farnborough, Hampshire climbs to a height of 16,440m (53,937ft) to recapture the world altitude record for Britain.

July *Projekt X*, the development of a rocket-powered research aircraft designed by Dr Alexander Lippisch at DFS, is initiated by the German Air Ministry. It becomes the DFS 194. (q.v. August, 1940)

July 1 The name Continental Airlines is given to the former Varney Air Transport, itself derived from Varney Speed Lines of 1926.

July 5 Pan American and Imperial Airways begin making survey flights over the North Atlantic using, respectively, the Sikorsky S-42 *Clipper III* and the Short C class *Caledonia*.

July 7 Following a night clash with Chinese troops at Lukouchiao, near Peiping, Japan initiates a full-scale invasion of China. This date is regarded by some military historians as the beginning of the Second World War.

July 8 National Airline System, founded in the USA during 1934, becomes incorporated with its still current title of National Airlines.

July 12-14 Flying an ANT-25 (RD-2), Col M.M. Gromov, Cmdt A.B. Yumashev, and Ing S.A. Danilin establish for the Soviet Union a new world distance record. The flight from Moscow via the North Pole to San Jacinto, Colombia covers a distance of 10,148km (6,306 miles).

July 15 First flight of the Hamburger Flugzeugbau Ha 138 flying-boat prototype. After prolonged trials it is accepted for production as the Blohm und Voss Bv 138 and serves throughout the Second World War.

July 27 A first flight is made by the Focke-Wulf Fw 200V-1 Condor prototype. Designed as a 26-seat passenger aircraft for service with Deutsche Luft Hansa, it is to be adopted by the Luftwaffe for long-range anti-shipping patrols over the North Atlantic during the early years of the Second World War.

July 29 First flight of the Lockheed Model 14 prototype (X-17382), later named as the Super Electra civil transport. (q.v. December 10, 1938)

July 30 The British Fleet Air Arm is transferred from Royal Air Force to Admiralty command, but the RAF retains control of all shore-based naval aircraft.

August 9 A London-Berlin night airmail service is inaugurated as a co-operative effort by British Airways and Deutsche Luft Hansa.

August 11 First flight of the Boulton Paul Defiant prototype (K8310), the first two-seat fighter to be used in RAF squadron service with a power-operated four-gun turret.

August 15 Deutsche Luft Hansa initiates North Atlantic trials, between the Azores and New York. This involves the use of seaplane depot ships, which can retrieve and catapault-launch specially-designed Blohm und Voss Ha 139 four-engined seaplanes. Trials are inaugurated with Ha 139V-2 *Nordmeer* (D-AMIE), which lands at Long Island, New York.

August 23 The first completely automatic landing by a heavier-than-air craft is made at Wright Field, Ohio being accomplished without assistance from a pilot on the aircraft or by radio control from the ground.

August 24 A Luft Hansa Junkers Ju 52/3, crewed by Flugkapitän Untucht, Freiher von Gablenz and mechanic Kirchoff, leaves Kabul on a trial flight to China, they arrive back on September 27.

Hanna Reitsch pilots Focke-Wulf Fw 61V-2, October 25 1937.

September 1 Trans-Canada Air Lines (TCA), which is known currently as Air Canada, inaugurates its first scheduled services.

October 15 A first flight is made by the Boeing Model 294 (XB-15) heavy bomber prototype. Only the single example is built, but it plays an important contribution to development of the B-29 Superfortress.

October 16 First flight of the Short S.25 prototype (K4774), which in production form is to become well known as the Sunderland flying boat.

October 18 Jean Batten, flying the Percival Gull Six *Jean* (G-ADPR), establishes a new solo record flight time from Darwin, Australia to Lympne, Kent of 5 days 18 hr 15 min.

October 25 Hanna Reitsch flying the Focke-Wulf Fw61 establishes a world distance record for helicopters of 108.974 km (67.71 miles).

November 5 Adolf Hitler reveals his Lebensraum (literally living space, or expansion) plans at a secret meeting with his military leaders. To provide this space he plans to take, by force of arms if necessary, Austria, Czechoslovakia, Poland and the Soviet Union.

November 14-20 Flying the de Havilland DH.88 Comet G-ACSS, then renamed *The Burberry*, Flg Off A.E. Clouston and Mrs Betty Kirby-Green establish a record UK/South Africa out and return flight. Total time, Croydon, Surrey to Cape Town and back to Croydon is 5 days 17 hr 28 min, beating the existing record by nearly 4 days.

December 3-27 Capt J.W. Burgess is in command of Imperial Airways' first flying-boat survey flight from the UK to Australia and New Zealand, flown in the Short C class *Centaurus* (G-ADUT).

December 22 The Mozambique airline DETA inaugurates its first scheduled operations.

December 23 The Pan American flying-boat *Samoa Clipper* inaugurates the airline's US-New Zealand airmail and freight service.

December 24 First flight of the Macchi C.200 Saetta (Lightning) prototype. Designed by Dr Mario Castoldi, it is the first monoplane fighter with a fully enclosed cockpit and retractable landing gear to enter service with the Italian air force.

1938

Bristol Aeroplane Company starts series production of the 490kW (665hp) Perseus radial engine developed by Roy Fedden as the world's first sleeve-valve aero engine.

Arkhip M. Lyulka, together with I.F. Kozlov and P.S. Shevchenko, begins work on the first Soviet turbojet engine, the VRD-1. Progress is interrupted by the German invasion in summer 1941, but later continues to modified design leading to the VRD-3 (TR-1). (q.v. December, 1944).

January First flight of the Aichi D3A carrier-borne dive bomber. Known under the Allied SW Pacific reporting name of 'Val' it is the first Japanese all-metal

low-wing monoplane dive bomber and plays an important role in the Japanese surprise attack on Pearl Harbor in December, 1941.

January 20   Under the direction of Sir Alan Cobham, Imperial Airways carries out a first flight refuelling test of a C class flying-boat. The tanker aircraft is the Armstrong Whitworth A.W.23 bomber/transport prototype, loaned by the Air Ministry to Flight Refuelling Ltd and registered G-AFRX.

February 6   First separation in flight of the *Mercury* upper component, from the *Maia* lower component of the Short-Mayo composite aircraft. This represents one approach to the problem of long-range flight.

February 10   Flown by Sqd Ldr J.W. Gillan, commanding officer of the RAF's No 111 Squadron, the new Hawker Hurricane makes headline news. This results from a night flight made between Edinburgh, Scotland and Northolt, Middlesex at an average speed of 657 km/h (408 mph), achieved with assistance from a strong following wind.

February 23   The Empire Air Mail Programme is extended to India, Burma, Ceylon and Malaya, the initial flight being made from Imperial Airways' Hythe terminal on Southampton Water.

March 15-26   The DH.88 Comet G-ACSS, now renamed *Australian Anniversary*, takes off from Gravesend, Kent on a new record attempt. Flown by Arthur Clouston and Victor Ricketts it completes a 42,648km (26,500 miles) UK-New Zealand and return flight in 10 days 21 hr, establishing not only a new record for the route but many new point-to-point records.

March 18   The first Short S.23 C class flying-boat for service with Qantas, VH-ABB *Coolangatta*, leaves Southampton, Hampshire on its delivery flight to Australia.

March 27-29   Catapult-launched from Start Point, Devon, Luft Hansa's Dornier Do 18F D-ANHR is flown by Capt H.W. von Engle to Caravellas, Brazil. This nonstop flight of 8,392km (5,215 miles), completed in 43 hr 5 min, establishes a new world distance record for seaplanes.

Short-Mayo composite, comprising the Short S.20 *Mercury* on top of the Short S.21 *Maia*, February 6 1938.

April 16-22   The last of the pre-war Australia-UK solo lightplane flight records is established by H.F. Broadbent. Taking off from Sydney, NSW in the Percival Vega Gull G-AFEH, he lands at Lympne, Kent having covered 15,469km (9,612 miles) in 5 days 4 hr 21 min.

April 20   Air Cmdre A.H. Harris leads the first British purchasing mission to the USA, seeking suitable aircraft of American manufacture for use by the RAF.

April 21   The UK government announces an expansion of the 'shadow factory' scheme, under which new factories would be built at government expense. When completed they would be managed by approved aircraft manufacturers.

June   The Heinkel HeS 3B turbojet, designed by Pabst von Ohain, is test-flown attached beneath an He 118 – the first 'flying test bed' for a jet engine.

June 9   The Nicaraguan air force, first established as an army air arm in 1923, becomes an independent service with the name Fuerza Aérea de la Guardia Nacional.

This became renamed as the Fuerza Aérea Guardia de Nicaragua in 1947.

It is announced in the UK parliament that as a result of evaluation by the purchasing commission sent to the US, the government has decided to buy 200 aircraft each from Lockheed and North American. These are duly to enter service as the Hudson and Harvard respectively.

June 25   Deutsche Luft Hansa introduces the Focke-Wulf 200 Condor on its Berlin-London route, the inaugural service being flown by *Westfalen* (D-AETA).

July 5   Qantas inaugurates the use of its new C class flying-boats on the Australia-UK route. Initial service from Rose Bay, Sydney, is made by Capt P. Lynch Blosse and crew flying VH-ABF *Cooee*.

July 10   Howard Hughes and crew, flying a Lockheed 14, takes off on a round the world flight. The route – New York, Paris, Moscow, Omsk, Yakutsk, Fairbanks and Minneapolis to New York – is completed in 3 days 19 hr 8 min.

July 11   Germany's long-established Bayerische Flugzeugwerke AG becomes Messerschmitt AG. Following this change existing aircraft with Bf designations (e.g. Bf 109) retain their original designation in all German documents.

July 11 – August 10   Severe fighting breaks out between Japanese and Soviet forces, disputing territory at the frontiers of Korea, Manchuria, and Siberia. Later known as the 'Lake Khasan incident', it is the first occasion the Soviet Air Force uses large numbers of fighters and bombers against the Japanese.

July 21-22   *Mercury* (G-ADHJ), the upper component of the Short-Mayo composite, records the first commercial crossing of the North Atlantic by a heavier-than-air craft. Flown by Capt D.C.T. Bennett with radio operator A.J. Coster, it was launched from *Maia* near Foynes before flying nonstop to Montreal, Canada in 20 hr 20 min.

July 28   DDL Danish Air Lines use the Focke-Wulf Fw 200 Condor *Dania* (OY-DAM), one of two acquired by the airline, for a special inaugural flight between Copenhagen-London. This is the first flight to the UK made by a Danish airliner.

The UK Empire Air Mail Programme is extended to Australia, New Zealand and a number of Pacific destinations. The inaugural flight is by Imperial Airways' C class flying-boat *Calypso* (G-AEUA).

August   Soviet Air Group in Spain begins its withdrawal, leaving their aircraft to the Spanish Republican crews.

First flight of the Supermarine Sea Otter prototype (K8854), designed as successor to the Walrus ASR amphibian. It becomes the last biplane to serve with the Fleet Air Arm.

August 2   Qantas' C class flying-boat *Carpentaria* (VH-ABA) leaves Sydney, NSW with the first airmail carried from Australia under the Empire Air Mail Programme. However, the first official service is made on August 4 by Imperial Airways' *Camilla* (G-AEUB).

August 10/11 The Fw 200 Condor prototype, re-designated Fw 200S-1 and named *Brandenburg* (D-ACON), is piloted by Dipl Ing Alfred Henke on a non-stop flight from Berlin to New York, returning two days later. Less than three months later, on November 28, the same Fw 200 attempts to fly from Berlin to Tokyo and back but is forced to ditch off Manila on the return flight due to a fuel shortage.

August 22 The United States Civil Aeronautics Act becomes effective, co-ordinating all non-military aviation in the USA under the Civil Aeronautics Authority (CAA).

September 2 The UK Empire Air Mail programme is extended to include Hong Kong.

September 10 All foreign aircraft making flights over Germany are prohibited to stray from specified air corridors established for civil aircraft.

September 14 First flight in Germany of the sister-ship of the ill-fated *Hindenburg*, the Zeppelin LZ 130 *Graf Zeppelin II*.

September 15-28 During this period the British Prime Minister, Neville Chamberlain, flies twice to Germany to mediate with Hitler over a growing German-Czech crisis.

September 23 Because of the German-Czech political crisis, Imperial Airways' Handley Page H.P.45 *Heracles* (G-AAXC) is used to evacuate British residents from Prague to London.

September 24 The mobilisation of all Czechoslovakian forces begins.

September 29 Agreement is reached finally at a Munich conference dominated by Axis representatives. With Britain and France too weak, particularly in terms of air power, Germany is pacified by the 'gift' of the Czech Sudetenland with its approximate 3 million Germans. Neville Chamberlain flies back to Britain claiming 'peace in our time'.

October 2 First flight of the Dewoitine D.520 prototype, the most advanced French fighter to participate in the Second World War.

October 5 Imperial Airways receives the first of a fleet of 12 (two added later) Armstrong Whitworth A.W.27 Ensign transports. The first (G-ADSR) was named *Ensign*.

October 6 Imperial Airways' Short-Mayo *Mercury*, flown by Capt D.C.T. Bennett with First Off I. Harvey, is used to establish a new seaplane world distance record. Released from *Maia* just north of Dundee, Scotland *Mercury* lands at Port Nolloth, Orange River, South Africa on October 8, having flown 9651.9km (5,007.43 miles) nonstop in 41 hr 56 min.

October 11 First flight of the Westland Whirlwind prototype (L6844), the only twin-engined single-seat fighter to serve operationally with the RAF during Second World War.

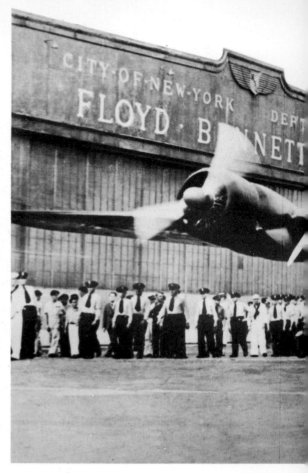

October 14 First flight of the Curtiss XP-40 Warhawk prototype. Almost 14,000 of these single-seat aircraft are built and used in a variety of roles, many serving with the RAF under the names of Tomahawk and Kittyhawk.

October 22 Flying the Caproni 161*bis* at Montecelio, Italy Lt Col M.Pezzi establishes a new world altitude record of 17,083m (56,046ft). This has since proved to be the greatest altitude attained by a piston-engined aircraft.

October 24 Imperial Airways begins operations with the Armstrong Whitworth A.W.27 Ensign (G-ADSR), introducing it on its London-Paris service.

October 26 First flight of the Douglas Model 7B prototype, developed for export to foreign air forces. Production versions are used by the RAF as the Boston day bomber and Havoc night fighter, and it is built in large numbers for the USAAF and also supplied to the Soviet Air Force under the designation A-20.

November 1 RAF Balloon Command is formed, deploying some 1,500 barrage balloons by the outbreak of the Second World War.

November 5-7 Two Vickers Wellesleys of the RAF's Long-range Flight establish a new world distance record. Flown from Ismailia, Egypt to Darwin, Australia, L2638

Focke Wulf Fw 200 Condor prototype in New York, August 11 1938.

captained by Sqdn Ldr R.G. Kellett and L2680 by Flt Lt A.N. Combe land at Darwin on November 7, completing the 11,520km (7158.5 mile) flight in 48 hr.

November 10   The UK Secretary of State for Air, giving details of RAF expansion in the House of Commons, states that fighter strength is to be increased by 30 per cent.

December 6   A Franco-German pact is signed, this serving to guarantee existing frontiers between the two countries.

December 8   *Graf Zeppelin*, the first German aircraft carrier, is launched.

December 10   The first Lockheed Model B14L (N7205), a militarised version of the Model 14 Super Electra which is to serve with the RAF as the Lockheed Hudson, begins flight tests.

December 18   Belgium allocates 600 million Francs for expansion of the nation's air defences.

December 28   During debates on the French air estimates (equivalent to about £60 million) it is stated that it is intended to make a major increase in aircraft production by the introduction of three-shift working.

1939

January   First flight of the Nakajima Ki-43 Hayabusa prototype (c/n 4301), allocated the Allied SW Pacific reporting name of 'Oscar'.

January 4   The German Air Ministry circulates a top-secret discussion paper entitled 'Preliminary technical guidelines for high-speed fighters with turbojet propulsion'.

January 17   The UK Air Ministry announces the formation of an Auxiliary Air Force Reserve.

January 27   First flight of the Lockheed XP-38 prototype is made. Built in large numbers, the unusual twinboom configuration of the P-38 Lightning is to make it one of the best-known of the USAAF's fighter aircraft of the Second World War.

February 5   Flying a specially-modified Percival Mew Gull (G-AEXF), Alex Henshaw establishes a new record time for a UK-South Africa return flight. His total time of 4 days 10 hr 20 min, from Gravesend, Kent, to Wingfield Aerodrome, Cape Town, and return, included 27 hr 19 min on the ground at Cape Town.

February 14   The USAAF's single Boeing XB-15 bomber prototype, which had flown for the first time on October 15, 1937, is used for a mercy mission to Chile.

The huge Boeing XB-15 bomber.

Flown from Langley Field, Virginia, it carries 1,474kg (3,250lb) of medical supplies for earthquake victims in a nonstop flight of 29 hr 53 min.

February 24   The first Boeing Model 314 flying-boat for service with Pan American is handed over officially at Baltimore.

March 9   Announcing the Air Estimates in Parliament, the UK Secretary of State for Air says that the figure of £205 million is the largest in the nation's history.

March 28   Madrid and Valencia surrender to the Nationalists, thus marking the end of the Spanish Civil War.

March 30   Flying the Heinkel He 100V-8 (D-IDGH) at Oranienburg, Germany, Flugkapitän Hans Dieterle establishes a new world speed record of 746.45 kmh (463.82 mph).

March 31   Following Germany's action in Czechoslovakia, Britain and France jointly guarantee aid to Greece, Poland and Romania in the event of German aggression.

April 1   The first flight is made at Kagamigahara, Japan, of the prototype Mitsubishi A6M1 monoplane fighter for the Imperial Japanese Navy. Easily the best-known of the nation's Second World War aircraft, it is later designated Navy Type O Carrier Fighter, becoming nicknamed the Zero. It was allocated subsequently the Allied codename *Zeke*.

April 26   The Heinkel He 100's recently-gained world speed record is broken by another German aircraft. Flown by Flugkapitän Fritz Wendel at Augsburg, Germany, the Messerschmitt Me 209V1 attains an FAI accredited speed of 755.138 km/h (469.22 mph). (q.v. August 16, 1969)

April 26   The UK government announces plans for compulsory military service.

May 7   First flight of the Petlyakov VI-100 prototype, later designated Pe-2 in production form. From mid-1942 onwards, progressively improved variants of the Pe-2 form the backbone of Soviet tactical bombing operations in the Eastern Front. Total Pe-2 production amounts to 11,427 aircraft.

May 14   First flight of the Short Stirling four-engined bomber prototype (L7600), which ends in disaster when the aircraft crashes on landing.

May 20   The first regular scheduled transatlantic airmail service is inaugurated. Pan American's Boeing 314 flying-boat *Yankee Clipper* flies from New York via the Azores, Lisbon and Marseilles to Southampton, which it reaches on May 23.

May 20   First of the large-scale aerial battles between Soviet and Japanese aircraft in Outer Mongolia near Khalkin Gol.

June 1   First flight of the Focke-Wulf Fw 190V-1 (D-OPZE) prototype is made at Bremen, Germany. Designed by Dipl Ing Kurt Tank, it has since become

regarded as the outstanding radial-engined fighter of the Second World War.

In the United States, a plan is inaugurated that uses civilian flying schools to provide primary flight training for USAAC cadets.

June 20   First flight of the He 176 research aircraft powered by one Walter HWK R.I-203 rocket motor at Peenemünde, piloted by Erich Warsitz. It is the first flight of a manned rocket-powered aircraft specifically designed for that purpose.

June 28   Pan American's New York to Southampton flying-boat service is stepped up to a weekly frequency.

July   First operational use of Soviet 82mm RS-82 rocket missiles carried by I-16 and I-153 fighters against the Japanese near Khalkin Gol in Outer Mongolia. In 1941 the same type of missile is also launched from vehicles as the first *Katyusha*.

July 1   The Women's Auxiliary Air Force is founded, intended to allow women to serve in the RAF during wartime.

July 17   First flight of the Bristol Type 156 prototype (R2052), subsequently to enter service as the Beaufighter.

July 25   First flight of the Avro Type 679 twin-engined heavy bomber, later named Manchester. Although not very successful due to its underdeveloped Rolls-Royce Vulture engines, the airframe design proves sound when re-engined with four Merlins as the Lancaster. (q.v. January 9, 1941)

August 5   Imperial Airways inaugurates an experimental weekly transatlantic airmail service over the route Southampton, Foynes, Botwood, Montreal and New York. Operated by Short S.30 C class flying-boats, flight refuelled after take-off by Handley Page Harrow II tankers, the initial service is flown by Capt J.C. Kelly Rogers and crew in *Caribou* (G-AFCV), fuelled after take-off by Harrow tanker G-AFRL.

August 22   Adolf Hitler gives final orders for the invasion of Poland. In Moscow, von Ribbentrop and Molotov sign a 10-year non-aggression pact, the secret clauses of which detail the partition of Poland.

August 27   The world's first flight by a turbojet-powered aircraft is made at Heinkel's Marienehe airfield. The Heinkel He 178, piloted by Flugkapitän Erich Warsitz, is powered by a Heinkel HeS 3b engine designed by Dr Pabst von Ohain.

Heinkel He 178, August 27 1939.

Vought-Sikorsky VS-300 in tethered flight.

August 31 A general mobilisation is ordered in the United Kingdom.

September 1 Preceded by a heavy pre-dawn air bombardment, Germany invades Poland.

Announcing the invasion of Poland in the Reichstag, Hitler says 'I will not war against women and children. I have ordered my air force to restrict itself to attacks on military objectives'.

Formation of the UK Air Transport Auxiliary.

All Royal Air Force reservists are ordered to report for duty, and all RAF squadrons are put at war readiness.

September 2 Ten squadrons of Fairey Battle bombers of the Advanced Air Striking Force are deployed to bases in France.

September 3 Britain and France declare war on Germany.

Within less than an hour of the declaration of war, air raid sirens are sounded in London. This was later found to be a false alarm.

Spain proclaims her neutrality in respect of the war in Europe.

A Blenheim IV aircraft (N6215) of the RAF is the first to cross the German frontier following the declaration of war, photographing German naval units leaving Wilhelmshaven.

September 3/4 RAF Whitley IIIs of Nos.51 and 58 Squadrons drop propaganda leaflets on Bremen, Hamburg and in the Ruhr.

September 4-9 Thirteen RAF squadrons, comprising Blenheim, Hurricane and Lysander aircraft, fly to bases in France as components of the British Expeditionary Force.

September 5 The United States proclaims its neutrality in relation to the conflict in Europe.

September 14 The Vought-Sikorsky VS-300 helicopter, with a single main rotor, makes a first tethered flight in the USA.

September 17 In accordance with agreed clauses of the recently-signed German-Soviet treaty, Soviet forces invade Poland at its eastern border.

September 21 Two Imperial Airways C class flying-boats, which were in Sydney when war was declared, are handed over to the Royal Australian Air Force and converted for military use by Qantas engineers at Rose Bay. Agreement is reached for Imperial Airways to take over two aircraft from Qantas.

October 5 The war in Poland ends with the surrender

of 17,000 Polish troops at Kock; Germany and the Soviet Union divide the defeated nation between them.

October 8 A Lockheed Hudson of the RAF's No.224 Squadron shoots down a German Dornier Do 18 flying-boat. This is the first victory recorded by an American-built aircraft in the Second World War.

October 10 Institution of the Empire Air Training Scheme which, with the participation of Australia, Canada and New Zealand, is to cover the training of air crew in these countries.

October 11 The London-Paris air services, which had been cancelled at the outbreak of war, are resumed jointly by Air France and Imperial Airways with a twice daily frequency.

October 16 In an attack by Luftwaffe aircraft on warships in the Firth of Forth anchorage, the first enemy aircraft to be destroyed over Britain in the Second World War, a Ju88A, is credited to Spitfires of No 603 (City of Edinburgh) Squadron of the Auxiliary Air Force.

October 23 The prototype of the Japanese Mitsubishi G4M bomber is flown for the first time. It is subsequently to be given the Allied codename *Betty*.

October 25 The first flight is made at RAF Bicester, Oxon of the Handley Page H.P.57 four-engined bomber prototype (L7244). Later named the Halifax, it is to form with the Avro Lancaster the mainstay of the RAF's heavy bomber force.

November 4 The United States lifts an arms export embargo initiated at the beginning of the Second World War, allowing Cash and Carry delivery of weapons to the Allies.

November 9 The Spanish Air Force is renamed Ejército del Aire Español, having three earlier titles and a history dating back to 1896. Its current name of Fuerza Aérea Española is adopted during 1980.

November 18 German aircraft drop the first anti-shipping magnetic mines in British coastal waters.

November 19 The Heinkel He 177V-1 heavy bomber prototype makes its first flight from Rostock-Marienehe airfield.

November 20 Forty-one magnetic mines are dropped by the Luftwaffe on the east coast of England. One is recovered intact by the British forces, enabling counter-measures to be devised.

November 21 First flight of the Piaggio P.108B heavy bomber prototype, the only four-engined Italian bomber to see operational service in the Second World War.

November 24 British Overseas Airways Corporation is established under the BOAC Act, merging British Airways and Imperial Airways.

November 25 A first flight is made by Bell's XP-39B prototype, an improved version of the earlier XP-39, which is to be built in large numbers as the P-39 Airacobra. It has a unique power plant installation so far

as USAAF fighters are concerned, the engine being mounted within the aft fuselage.

November 30 The Soviet Air Force makes attacks on Helsinki and Viipuri without declaration of war, followed by invasion of Finnish territory, marking the beginning of the Russo-Finnish War.

December 3 The second Short Stirling prototype (L7605) makes a successful first flight.

December 18 The loss of 12 of 24 RAF Wellingtons making a reconnaissance flight off Wilhelmshaven and the Schillig Roads, brings an end to RAF daylight bomber formations.

December 26 The first Royal Australian Air Force squadron for active service against Germany arrives in the UK.

December 29 The Consolidated XB-24 prototype (39-680) makes its first flight at Lindbergh Field, San Diego, California. It is to be more extensively produced than any other American aircraft of the Second World War, with more than 18,000 B-24 Liberators of all versions built for the USAAF and its Allies.

December 30 First flight of the Soviet TsKB-55 (BSh-2) armoured ground attack aircraft prototype. Its developed form as the Il-2, and later Il-2m 3, it gains renown as the *Shturmovik*. (q.v. October 12, 1940)

1940

January 1 The first flight is recorded of the Yakovlev I-26 (Yak-1) prototype, a design which leads to a valuable and closely related family of Yakovlev fighters to be used by the Soviet air force throughout the Second World War.

January 20 The Brazilian Air Force adopts its current title of Fôrça Aeréa Brasileira, having been founded in 1908 as the Brazilian Army Balloon Corps.

February 1 The Southern Rhodesian government forms the Southern Rhodesian Air Services as a communications squadron of the Rhodesian Air Force.

February 10 It is announced that the UK government has placed contracts valued at £6 million with Canadian aircraft manufacturers.

February 14 A Lockheed Hudson of RAF Coastal Command locates the German prison ship *Altmark* in Norwegian territorial waters.

February 22 Sqdn Ldr Douglas Farquhar of No 602 (City of Glasgow) Squadron, Auxiliary Air Force, takes the first British gun-camera film of the war while attacking and destroying a Heinkel He 111 over Coldingham, Berwickshire.

February 22/23 Luftwaffe He 111s accidently bomb German naval vessels during 'Operation Wikinger'. The destroyers *Leberecht Maas* and *Max Schultz* run into a British minefield and are lost.

February 24 First flight of the Hawker Typhoon prototype (P5212) powered by a Napier Sabre II engine.

February 25 The first unit of the Royal Canadian Air Force arrives in the UK.

February 26 The United States War Department forms the US Air Defense Command, to integrate defences against possible attack from the air.

March 12 Overwhelmed by the sheer weight of the Soviet attack, Finland capitulates to its invaders.

March 25 USAAC contractors are authorised to sell to anti-Axis governments modern types of Army combat aircraft. This is seen as a means of expanding production facilities, to the future benefit of the USAAC should the USA become involved in war.

March 26 A year-end report (for 1939) on the activities of US airlines tells of a 12-month period of operations that had been entirely free from any fatal air accident.

March 30 First flight of the Lavochkin I-22 or LaGG-1 fighter, from which is developed an improved LaGG-3, to be used extensively by the Soviet Air Force during the early stages of the German invasion.

April 5 The first flight is made of the Mikoyan and Gurevich MiG-1 prototype, built in comparatively small production numbers before development of the improved MiG-3. (q.v. August, 1940)

April 9 German forces overrun and conquer Denmark almost without bloodshed.

April 9 German forces invade Norway, with landings on the coast and assaults by parachutists on Oslo and Stavanger.

Vought XF4U-1 prototype, May 29 1940.

April 13 The first anti-shipping mines of the war to be airdropped by the RAF, are released by Handley Page Hampden bombers into Danish coastal waters.

April 14 British forces land at Vaags Fjord, for operations in support of Norwegian resistance at Narvik. Three days later further landings are made at Andalsnes.

April 20 The training begins of air crews under the Empire Air Training Scheme, to be retitled later as the British Commonwealth Air Training Plan.

April 23 The British aircraft carriers HMS *Ark Royal* and HMS *Glorious* are despatched to give support off Andalsnes and Namsos to British, French and Norwegian forces resisting the German invaders in Norway.

April 24 Gloster Gladiators of No 263 Squadron are flown off HMS *Glorious* some 290km (180 miles) from shore, landing on the frozen Lake Lesjaskog near Andalsnes.

April 25 The United States Navy's aircraft carrier USS *Wasp* is commissioned.

April 30 The New Zealand airline Tasman Empire Airways, which had been founded earlier in the month, inaugurates a weekly trans-Tasman air service between Auckland and Sydney. The first flight is operated by the Short C class flying-boat *Aotearoa* (ZK-AMA).

May 7 Aer Lingus operates its first service with a Douglas DC-3 (EI-ACA), on its Dublin-Liverpool route.

May 10 The German invasion of the Low Countries begins, preceded by extensive and effective deployment of paratroops and airborne troops. Belgium's 'impregnable' Fort Eban Emael is easily subjugated by the unexpected use of glider-borne assault troops.

According to Luftwaffe records, their aircraft losses on the first day of the Belgium/Netherlands/France invasion are 304 destroyed and 51 damaged.

In the UK, Prime Minister Neville Chamberlain resigns. A new coalition government is formed, with Winston Churchill as its Prime Minister.

May 13 In the United States, the Sikorsky VS-300 single-rotor helicopter, which uses a small rotor at the tail to overcome the torque effect of the main rotor, makes its first free flight.

May 14 Germany threatens the destruction of all Dutch cities by aerial bombardment in surrender discussions at the Hague. The remainder of the world is shocked by the bombing of the business centre of Rotterdam by the Luftwaffe as these surrender negotiations are in progress. All bomber formations had been recalled when negotiations began but one group failed to receive radio instructions to abort the mission.

May 18 The British battleship HMS *Resolution* is hit but not sunk by a 1,000 kg bomb from a Junkers Ju 88 near Narvik.

May 28 The evacuation of British troops from Dunkirk begins. From British airfields, RAF Fighter Command does its utmost to provide some protection by patrolling the beaches.

May 29 First flight of the Vought XF4U-1 prototype in the US. As the F4U Corsair, more than 12,000 are built to serve with the United States Navy and Marine Corps, and with America's Allies. Most air historians regard it as the best of the carrier-based fighters developed during the Second World War.

June 4 The British evacuation from the Dunkirk beaches is completed. More than 338,000 men are carried to Britain to fight again, this total including some 112,000 Belgians and French.

June 5 German forces regroup and begin the Battle of France. This proves to be an impressive demonstration of air power used in close-support of armour and infantry

June 8 The British 27,560-ton aircraft carrier HMS *Glorious*, returning from operations off Norway with the remnants of Nos 46 and 263 Squadrons aboard, is sunk by the German battleships *Gneisenau* and *Scharnhorst*.

June 10 Italy declares war on the Allies and begins the invasion of Southern France.

With Italian entry into the war, Britain's Empire air routes are severed, although a few services are operated to Khartoum via Bordeaux.

June 11 The Italian air force, the Regia Aeronautica, makes its first attack on Malta.

June 11/12 The RAF reacts to the Italian declaration of war by sending a force of 36 Whitley bombers to attack the Fiat works at Turin.

June 13 Air services between the UK and the Channel Islands are suspended by Air Ministry order.

June 14 Jersey Airways begins to evacuate its staff and equipment to the UK mainland by air, with assistance from the RAF's No.24 (Communications) Squadron.

June 14 German forces enter Paris.

June 17 The imminent collapse of France ends all air routes linking the UK with Africa, Australia, India and the Middle East.

June 17-18 The last serviceable aircraft of the British Expeditionary Force are flown from Nantes, France to RAF Tangmere, Sussex.

June 18-19 Using five of its fleet of six de Havilland DH.86 transports, Jersey Airways evacuates 320 islanders wishing to take refuge in Britain.

June 19 With the severance of UK trans-Mediterranean services, the Horseshoe route is introduced, linking Durban and Australia via Cairo.

June 21 Hitler meets French officials in a railway carriage in Compiegne Forest, where the Armistice of 1918 had been signed, to accept their capitulation. Hostilities between France and Germany end officially four days later.

July 1/2 The RAF drops its first 2,000lb bomb in an attack on the battleship *Scharnhorst* at Kiel.

July 3 Aircraft of the Fleet Air Arm take part in an attack on the French fleet at Oran. This is made in an attempt to ensure that the vessels do not fall into German hands.

July 7 The Spanish airline Iberia is reformed as the national airline, financed originally by the Spanish government and Deutsche Luft Hansa.

July 10 Date regarded generally as the opening phase of the Luftwaffe/RAF confrontation named as the Battle of Britain.

July 14 Air reconnaissance provides evidence of a build up of barges and materials at cross-Channel ports, clearly intended for a German invasion of Britain.

July 16 Bombardier training begins in USAAC schools, initially at Lowry Field, Colorado.

July 26 The first RCAF squadron to be equipped with Canadian-built Hurricanes arrives in Britain.

August First flight of the DFS 194 research aircraft under full rocket power at Peenemünde, piloted by Heini Dittmar.

First flight of the Focke-Achgelis Fa 223 Drache transport helicopter. After prolonged trials small numbers are built and become operational late in 1943. (q.v. also September, 1945)

The Soviet I-200 (MiG-1) fighter, designed by Artyom I. Mikoyan and Mikhail I. Gurevich, successfully passes its State Acceptance tests. Ordered into production, it becomes the first of the famous MiG series of fighters.

Caproni-Campini N-1, August 28 1940.

August 16 Flt Lt J.B. Nicholson RAF wins the only Victoria Cross awarded to a pilot of Fighter Command, by remaining in his blazing Hurricane in order to destroy a German aircraft over Southampton before baling out.

August 17 PO William M.L. Fiske, first regular American pilot to serve with the RAF, dies from wounds received on the previous day.

August 19 First flight of the North American B-25 Mitchell medium bomber prototype, subsequently built in large numbers for service with the US and its Allies.

August 24/25 First German bombs fall on central London.

August 25/26 To maintain the status quo, 43 aircraft of Bomber Command, comprising Hampdens, Wellingtons and Whitleys, make the RAF's first attack of the war on Berlin.

August 28 First flight of the experimental Italian Caproni-Campini N-1 monoplane, powered by a turbine that is driven by a piston engine.

September 2 The United States transfers 50 US First World War destroyers to the UK in exchange for air and naval bases at eight strategic points.

September 6 An invasion alert is given to forces in Britain when air reconnaissance shows that barge and material concentrations in Channel ports has reached a high level.

September 7 The Luftwaffe begins to make heavy bombing attacks on London.

First flight of the Blohm und Voss BV 222 (D-ANTE) six-engined flying-boat. Later named Wiking it becomes one of the largest flying-boats used operationally during the Second World War.

September 17 With the failure of the Luftwaffe to eliminate the RAF, Hitler orders Operation Sea Lion (the invasion of Britain) to be postponed.

September 27 Germany, Italy and Japan conclude a pact, each pledging total aid to the others.

October The Luftwaffe *Gruppe Rowehl* special high-altitude reconnaissance unit is instructed to start photographic mapping of western Russia and the frontier districts.

October 8 It is announced in the UK that the RAF is to form a so-called Eagle Squadron, a Fighter Command unit to consist of volunteer pilots from the USA.

October 12 First flight is recorded of the Ilyushin Il-2 third prototype, this being of similar configuration to the production version. The Il-2 is the first and most famous of the Soviet *Shturmoviki* (ground attack) aircraft, used throughout the Second World War, and built to the tune of more than 36,000.

October 18 It is announced in the House of Commons that, because of Luftwaffe attacks, almost half a million children have been evacuated from London and that thousands are still leaving daily.

October 26   The first flight is made of the North American NA-73 fighter prototype, which had been designed to meet a British requirement for use in Europe. Better known as the P-51 Mustang, more than 15,000 are built, and the extensively-produced P-51D/K versions (almost 8,000) are regarded as classic examples of Second World War fighter aircraft.

November 1   The Hawaiian Air Force is activated at Fort Shafter, Hawaii.

November 10   The first organised transatlantic ferry flights of US-built aircraft begins.

November 11   Italy's Regia Aeronautica makes its one and only major air attack on the UK.

In what is now an historic action, Fairey Swordfish torpedo-bombers of the Fleet Air Arm decimate the Italian Fleet in a night attack on Taranto harbour.

November 14/15   Guided by X-Gerät radio beams, nearly 500 Luftwaffe bombers cause major damage to the city of Coventry, Warwickshire.

November 15   Resulting from the USA's gain of bases by its destroyer deal with the UK, US Navy aircraft begin operations from Bermuda.

November 17   British West Indian Airways Ltd is founded and begins operations with a daily Trinidad-Barbados service. Known in 1982 as BWIA International.

November 25   The first de Havilland DH.98 Mosquito prototype (W4050) makes its first flight at Hatfield. Designed as a bomber aircraft that would be fast enough to dispense with defensive armament, it has a level speed of almost 644 km/h (400 mph). It is to see wide-scale service in a variety of roles.

First flight of the Martin B-26 Marauder prototype (40-1361), a medium-range bomber to be used widely by the USAAF.

November 29   A Lockheed Hudson, on delivery flight from the USA, completes the first transatlantic ferry flight to terminate with a landing at Prestwick.

December   First flight of the Yokosuka D4Y1 Suisei naval dive bomber, allocated subsequently the Allied SW Pacific reporting name 'Judy'.

December 18   The first successful flight is made in Germany by a Henschel Hs 293A radio-controlled bomb.

First flight recorded of the Curtiss XSB2C-1 Helldiver prototype, a carrier-based scout-bomber which is to see service on US Navy carriers in the Pacific theatre.

1941

January   First flight of the Kawanishi H8K1 long-range flying-boat. Considered by many air historians to be one of the outstanding water-based aircraft of the Second World War, it is later allocated the Allied SW Pacific reporting name 'Emily'.

January 9   First flight of the Avro Lancaster prototype (BT308), then known as the Manchester III. It was, in fact, a converted Manchester airframe, but powered by four Rolls-Royce Merlins. The production Lancaster becomes the best-known and most successful of the RAF's wartime heavy bombers.

January 16   Grand Harbour at Malta bombed by Axis aircraft, HMS *Illustrious* being damaged.

January 29   Luftwaffe aircraft airdrop mines into the Suez Canal.

February 25   First flight of the Me 321 Gigant large-capacity glider, designed for the airborne invasion of Britain which was later indefinitely postponed.

Air Defence Force (PVO) is created in the Soviet Union.

February 10   British paratroops, dropped by Whitley Vs of the RAF's No 51 and 78 Squadrons, carry out the first British airborne operation of the Second World War, an unsuccessful attack on a viaduct at Tragino, Campagna, Italy.

February 10/11   The RAF's No 7 Squadron, its first unit to fly four-engined bombers since the First World War, uses Stirlings operationally for the first time in an attack on Rotterdam.

February 24/25   First operational use of the Avro Manchester is made by the RAF in an attack on targets at Brest, France.

February 25   Philippine Air Lines is formed; following the Japanese invasion, it resumed post-war services on February 14, 1946.

March   First flight of the Arado Ar 231 collapsible submarine-borne spotter floatplane. Programme abandoned early in 1942, mainly due to recovery problems, in favour of the more practical Fa 330 rotor kite. (q.v. March, 1942)

March 10/11   First operational use by the RAF of the Handley Page Halifax bomber, deployed against targets at Le Havre, France.

March 11   The Lend-Lease Act is authorised by President Roosevelt, allowing the supply of goods and services to nations that are considered vital to the defence of the USA.

The US airline which had been formed originally during 1925 as Western Air Express, adopts its current title of Western Airlines.

March 27   Infuriated at a coup d'etat by anti-Nazi elements in Yugoslavia, Hitler orders the invasion of that country, and of Greece.

March 28   It is announced in the UK that the RAF's Eagle Squadron, composed of volunteer pilots from the USA, is fully operational.

March 30/31   In the first of many attacks, 109 of the RAF's bomber aircraft are deployed against the German battleships *Gneisenau* and *Scharnhorst* at Brest, France.

Heinkel He 280V-1 flies for the first time, with engine cowlings removed, April 2 1941.

April 1 In an attack on Emden, a Wellington of the RAF's No.149 Squadron drops the first 1,814kg (4,000lb) 'block-buster' bomb to be used operationally.

April 2 First flight of the Heinkel He 280V-1 prototype, the first aircraft to be designed as a jet fighter and also the first with twin-engined turbojet power plant.

April 6 Preceded by air attack, that on Belgrade being particularly heavy, Germany begins the simultaneous invasion of Greece and Yugoslavia.

April 9 An agreement is concluded between the United States and the Danish government in exile, allowing the US to build and operate airfields in Greenland.

April 15 Demonstrating his VS-300 at Stratford, Connecticut, Igor Sikorsky makes an officially recorded flight of 1 hr 5 min 14.5 sec duration.

April 18 First flight of the Messerschmitt Me 262V-1 (PC-UA), powered by a single piston-engine because its intended turbojet engines have not materialised.

April 23 The Greek Army surrenders. British forces are evacuated from eastern Greek ports and transferred to the isle of Crete.

May First Soviet RUS-1 and RUS-2 air defence radar sets are put into service.

First flight of the Nakajima J1N1 Gekko twin-engined fighter. Modified to a night fighting role as the J1N1-S in

1943, it becomes the first Japanese aircraft to carry primitive AI radar and oblique-firing armament.

May 4 First operation on the North Atlantic Return Ferry Service is flown by Capt D.C.T. Bennett, in a Consolidated Liberator I (AM258) from Montreal to Squires Gate, Blackpool.

May 6 First flight of the Republic XP-47B prototype (40-3051), designed by a team under the leadership of Alexander Kartveli. It is to be developed as the excellent Thunderbolt, built to more than 15,000 examples. It becomes one of the three outstanding USAAF fighters of the Second World War.

May 8/9 The Luftwaffe attacks several UK midland towns, claiming that the Rolls-Royce factory has been destroyed. Fortunately for the UK, the attack has been diverted into open country by use of a 'beam bending' technique.

May 10/11 Rudolf Hess, Deputy Führer of Germany, flies to Britain in a Messerschmitt Bf 110 and lands by parachute in Scotland.

May 13-14 First mass flight of bomber aircraft over the Pacific, when the USAAC deploys 21 B-17s from Hamilton Field, California, to Hickham Field, Hawaii.

May 15 The first flight is made at RAF Cranwell of the Gloster E.28/39 experimental jet-powered aircraft (W4041), piloted by P.E.G. Sayer. It is the first flight of a British turbojet-powered aircraft.

May 20 Operation Mercury, the largest airborne assault mounted by the Luftwaffe during the Second World War, lands 22,750 men on the Island of Crete. A successful operation, it results in seizure of the island, but losses of about 5,600 men and some 150 transport aircraft bring an end to Luftwaffe paratroop operations.

May 26 A Catalina of the RAF's No 209 Squadron spots the 50,150-ton German battleship *Bismarck* in the Atlantic. Its steering gear is damaged subsequently in an attack by Swordfish from HMS *Ark Royal*, enabling her to be sunk by British warships.

First flight of the Japanese Kayaba Ka-1 artillery observation autogyro. Converted to an anti-submarine role carrying light bombs, the Ka-1 later becomes the first armed rotary wing aircraft used in action.

June 20 The United States Army Air Force is formed, with Maj Gen H.H. Arnold as its Chief.

June 22 Operation Barbarossa, the German invasion of the Soviet Union, begins with a massive surprise air strike. By nightfall Soviet losses amount to 1,811 aircraft (1,489 destroyed on the ground) for the loss of only 35 Luftwaffe aircraft, but this success is never repeated.

At 0430 hrs Lt Kokorev of the 124th Fighter Rgt, Red Air Force, deliberately rams a Luftwaffe Bf 110 – the first instance of a *taran* (battering ram) attack during this war.

Gloster E.28/39, May 15 1941.

July 8 The RAF makes a daylight attack on Wilhelmshaven using Fortress Is received from the US; this represents the first operational use of the Boeing B-17 Flying Fortress.

July 18 The formation of RAF Ferry Command is announced.

July 21/22 Luftwaffe bombers make their first night attack on Moscow.

August 1 First operational use of Soviet 'parasite' I-16SPB high-speed dive bombers (variant of the standard fighter) carried under the wings of TB-3 heavy bombers. These make a successful attack on Constanza, Romania. (q.v. December 3, 1931)

The United States bans the export of aviation fuel, except to the UK and unoccupied nations resisting the Nazis. This comes as a severe blow to the Japanese, involved in a continuing war with China, and hastens a decision to unite with its Axis partners in war against the Allies.

First flight of the Grumman XTBF-1 Avenger prototype, destined to become the US Navy's standard torpedo-bomber of the Second World War.

August 3 To provide interim air cover for North Atlantic convoys, the UK develops a 'Catafighter' scheme. The first success is gained on this date, when a Sea Hurricane, catapulted from the HMS *Maplin*, destroys a German Focke-Wulf Fw 200 Condor on maritime patrol.

August 7/8 A small number of Soviet Il-4 (DB-3F) bombers of the Soviet Naval Aviation take off from the Estonian islands of Dagö and Saaremaa and raid the Berlin area, which is brightly lit. From then on Berlin is under strict blackout regulations.

August 9-12 In meetings on UK and US warships in Placentia Bay, Newfoundland, Churchill and Roosevelt draft the Atlantic Charter. This pledges their countries to preserve world freedom and, at the conclusion of the war, to improve world conditions.

August 13 First flight of the Me 163A prototype under full rocket power at Peenemünde.

August 18 President Roosevelt announces that Pan American Airways is to ferry US-built warplanes to British forces in the Middle East.

August 27 Following determined attacks by a Lockheed Hudson of the RAF's No 269 Squadron on patrol in the North Atlantic, the German submarine *U-570* surrenders to the Hudson. This is the first U-boat to be captured by the RAF.

September First operational use of Soviet Polikarpov U-2 biplanes as 'night harassment bombers'.

September 7 Hawker Hurricane I fighters of Nos 81 and 134 Squadrons fly off HMS *Argus* to land on a Soviet airfield at Vaenga, near Murmansk, to help bolster the local defences. The aircraft were later handed over to the Soviet air force.

Maj. Gen H. H. Arnold arriving at Hickam Field, Oahu, Hawaii.

September 14 Messerschmitt Me 321 giant assault transport gliders of Staffel [G-S] 1 are first used operationally during the airborne attack on the Saaremaa island in the Baltic, as part of an attempt to capture the fort at Kübarsaare.

September 16 Following an attack of the previous week, the Luftwaffe drops leaflets on Leningrad, threatening its immediate destruction if the city does not surrender.

September 23 Oberleutnant Hans-Ulrich Rudel, flying a Ju 87, succeeds in hitting the 26,170-ton Soviet battleship *Marat* at Kronstadt with a 1,000 kg bomb. The ship is badly damaged and sinks in shallow water. This is almost certainly the greatest single success achieved by a dive bomber pilot in the Second World War.

September 24 BOAC carries out its first operation on the North Atlantic Return Ferry service, using Liberator Is provided by RAF Ferry Command.

USS *West Virginia* and USS *Tennessee* lie crippled and in flames after the Japanese attack on Pearl Harbor, December 7 1941. (*US Navy*)

September 30 At this date, the Luftwaffe claims to have destroyed more than 4,500 Soviet aircraft since the beginning of the invasion.

October First flight of the Heinkel He 111Z, a five-engined heavy glider tug specifically designed to tow the Me 321. It unites two He 111H fuselages by a constant-chord wing section mounting the fifth engine.

October 1 Inter-Island Airways, which had been formed in early 1929, adopts the title of Hawaiian Airlines.

October 2 The third Me 163A rocket-powered proto-type, piloted by Heini Dittmar, achieves a speed of 1,004 km/h (623.85 mph), an unofficial world speed record that remains secret until the end of hostilities.

October 12 BOAC begins a UK-Cairo service, the first flight operated by C class flying-boat *Clare* (G-AFCZ), routed via Lisbon, Gibraltar and Malta.

October 30 A Consolidated B-24 Liberator, with Maj Alva L. Harvey in command, completes a round-the-world flight carrying personnel of the Harriman Mission.

October 31 It is announced that RAF aircraft operating from Malta have destroyed some 76,500 tons of enemy shipping in the Mediterranean.

November 12 The British aircraft carrier HMS *Ark Royal* is sunk by the German submarine *U-81* off Gibraltar.

November 30 First Whitleys to be equipped with ASV Mk II long-range radar are those operated by the RAF's No 502 Squadron. On this date a Whitley VII (Z9190) of the squadron scores Coastal Command's first ASV destruction of an enemy submarine, the *U-206* in the Bay of Biscay.

December First flight of the Kawasaki Ki-61 'Hien' fighter prototype. Allocated the Allied SW Pacific reporting name of 'Tony', it is the only Japanese fighter powered by a liquid-cooled engine to see operational service during the Second World War.

First flight of the Soviet Lavochkin LaG-5 fighter prototype, radial engined development of the LaGG-3. La-5 fighters first became operational near Stalingrad in September, 1942. (q.v. March 30, 1940).

December 1 The US Civil Air Patrol is established, formed to utilise for wartime duties American civil pilots and their aircraft.

December 7 Using carrier-based aircraft, and without any declaration of war, the Japanese attack Pearl Harbor, Hawaii causing extensive damage to the US Pacific Fleet and shore installations.

December 8 Following intensive air attacks on RAF bases in Malaya and Singapore, the Japanese invade northern Malaya.

135

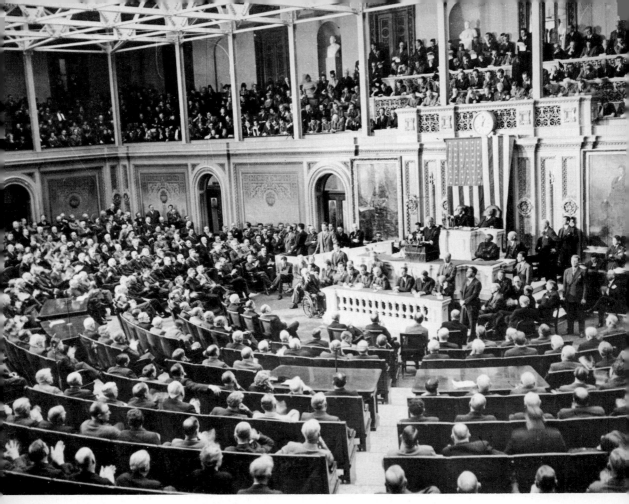

President Roosevelt addresses Congress and delivers his war speech. (*US National Archives*)

The US declares war on Japan, so entering the Second World War.

The UK declares war on Japan.

Lockheed Hudsons are used by the Royal Australian Air Force in their first attacks of the Second World War, made against Japanese forces invading Pacific islands.

December 10 USAAF B-17 Flying Fortress bombers make the first American air offensive of the war, attacking Japanese shipping.

Aircraft from the USS *Enterprise* record the first US victory of the war against a Japanese combat ship, sinking a submarine north of the Hawaiian Islands.

The British battleships HMS *Prince of Wales* and HMS *Repulse* are sunk by Japanese Mitsubishi G3M 'Nell' bombers.

After heavy air attack has wrecked the naval base at Cavite, the Japanese begin their invasion of the Philippines with small amphibious landings at Aparri and Vigan, northern Luzon.

December 11 Germany and Italy declare war on the United States.

The United States declares war on Germany and Italy.

December 18 Lt 'Buzz' Wagner of the USAAF becomes the first American 'ace' of the Second World War, destroying his fifth Japanese aircraft over the Philippines.

December 20 Australian National Airways, operating with Douglas DC-3s, begins to evacuate civilians from New Guinea.

The German Air Ministry initiates the *Amerika-Bomber* programme, to begin the development of bombers with transatlantic capability.

December 21/22 An ASV-equipped Fairey Swordfish of the FAA's No 812 Squadron, sinks the first German U-boat (*U-451*) to be destroyed by an aircraft at night.

December 22 First flight is made by the Fairey Firefly prototype (Z1826), a two-seat carrier-based fighter/reconnaissance aircraft. Production aircraft are to serve mainly with aircraft carriers of the British Pacific Fleet.

December 25 Hong Kong surrenders to the invading Japanese.

December 28 Australian National Airlines begins evacuation of civilians from Rabaul.

1942

January – May   German troops cut off by Soviet forces at Kholm are supplied by air by using DFS 230 and Go 242 cargo gliders, the first large-scale use of air supply to own forces behind enemy lines.

January 1   Following the signature of the United Nations Declaration on this date, the name United Nations is adopted by the coalition of powers fighting the Axis. The name is perpetuated in the United Nations Organisation.

January 14   The first flight is made at Stratford, Connecticut of the Sikorsky XR-4 helicopter prototype (41-18874). (q.v. October 30, 1943 and photograph).

January 28   Two of the earliest North American Mustang Is used by the RAF (AG360 and AG365), are sent to the Air Development Fighting Unit at Duxford. The first operational squadron to receive them is No.26, in February 1942, with the first operational sorties flown over France on 5 May 1942.

January 28   The Headquarters and HQ Squadron of the US Army Eighth Air Force is established at Savannah AAB, Georgia.

January 30   Canadian Pacific Air Lines is founded, being a subsidiary of the Canadian Pacific Railway.

January 30-31   British and Commonwealth troops withdraw from the Malayan mainland into Singapore and destroy the causeway link behind them.

February 1   First US carrier offensive made by the USS *Enterprise* and USS *Yorktown*, their aircraft attacking enemy installations on several of the Marshall and Gilbert Islands.

February 8-9   Following heavy air bombardment, Japanese forces land on Singapore, capturing Tengah airfield.

February 10   The last RAF fighters are withdrawn from Singapore to bases in Sumatra.

February 12   The German warships *Gneisenau*, *Scharnhorst* and *Prinz Eugen*, protected by a strong defensive air cover of fighters, escape through the English Channel.

February 15   Singapore capitulates to the invading Japanese.

February 19   A first practical demonstration of Australia's vulnerability is made clear when Japanese bombers attack shipping in harbour at Port Darwin, Australia.

February 22   The first USAAF Headquarters in Europe is established in the UK, with Brig Gen I.C. Eaker commanding.

Air Marshal Arthur Harris is appointed Commander-in-Chief RAF Bomber Command.

February 27   The UK Army Air Corps is formed, comprising the Glider Pilot Regiment, the Airborne Infantry Units and the Parachute Regiment.

February 27-28   A first British combined operation against Europe, and involving air, land and sea forces, is made against Bruneval in northern France. After overcoming German resistance, components are removed from a *Würzburg* ground radar station, which is then destroyed before the forces withdraw.

March   First flight of the Focke-Achgelis Fa 330 Bachstelze submarine-borne rotor kite. It becomes operational in summer 1942, but is never very popular with the submarine crews due to the delays in submerging when attacked.

First flight of the Me 323 Gigant six-engined large-capacity transport, a powered version of the Me 321 glider.

March 3   The RAF's No.44 Squadron makes the first operational sortie with its new Avro Lancaster bombers, a mine-laying operation in the Heligoland Bight.

March 20   First flight of the Mitsubishi J2M1 Raiden naval fighter prototype, at Kasumigaura. It was allocated subsequently the Allied SW Pacific reporting name of 'Jack'.

March 25   Unsuccessful flight test of the first Me 262 prototype powered by two early BMW 003 turbojets and a central Jumo 210G piston engine.

March 27   The US Navy is given sole command of anti-submarine warfare off the US coastlines, including authority over USAAF coastal patrols.

April 2   The US Tenth Army Air Force makes its first combat operation, heavy bombers attacking shipping off the Andaman Islands.

April 2-9   Japanese carrier based aircraft operating off the coasts of Ceylon and India cause considerable damage to installations at Colombo and Trincomalee. Royal Navy operations to intercept the enemy fleet are disastrous, the aircraft carrier HMS *Hermes*, the cruisers HMS *Cornwall* and HMS *Devonshire*, and the destroyer HMS *Vampire* all being sunk by carrier-based aircraft.

April 6   Carrier-based aircraft from the Japanese formation mentioned above are the first to make air attacks against India.

April 12   Three USAAF B-17s and ten B-25s based in Australia make the first attack against Japanese shipping and installations in the Philippines.

April 18   In a one-way attack on Tokyo, 16 B-25s led by Lt Col J.H. Doolittle are flown off the carrier USS *Hornet* some 400 miles at sea. Having completed the attack, most of the aircraft force-land in China.

April 19   First flight of the Macchi C.205 fighter prototype, arguably the best Italian fighter of the Second World War.

April 20   Malta's air defence is reinforced by 47 Spitfires flown off the USS *Wasp* about 660 miles west of the island.

Lt Col Jimmy Doolittle (fourth from right) with members of his B-25 crew and Chinese friends, pose in China after bailing out of their stricken bomber, April 18 1942. (*USAF*)

Japanese Navy carrier *Shoho* in flames after an attack by US Navy aircraft during the Battle of the Coral Sea, May 7 1942. (*US National Archives*)

April 22 The Assam, Burma, China Ferry Command is established to air-ferry supplies to China over the Himalayas ('Hump route').

April 26 Winston Churchill instructs the UK Petroleum Warfare Department to investigate ways of dispersing fog from emergency airfields.

May 7-8 The Battle of the Coral Sea is fought, by carrier-based aircraft of opposing Japanese and US fleets. It was the first vital naval battle to be fought without a surface ship of either side sighting the enemy fleet. The US Navy loses USS *Lexington* and 69 aircraft. The Japanese lose *Shoho* and 85 aircraft, and *Shokaku* is damaged, which prevents its use during the Battle of Midway.

May 10 The US carrier USS *Ranger*, off the African Gold Coast, flies off 60 USAAF Curtiss P-40s to Accra. They were then flown in stages to join with the US Tenth Army Air Force in India.

May 16 The Canadian airline CP Air (Canadian Pacific Airlines Ltd) is established by the amalgamation of ten small independent air services.

May 26 The first flight is made by the Northrop XP-61 prototype. The USAAF's first purpose-designed radar-equipped night fighter, the P-61 Black Widow enters operational use in the Pacific theatre in 1944.

May 30/31 RAF Bomber Command mounts its first 'thousand bomber' raid against a German target. Deployed against Cologne, 1,046 aircraft are involved, 599 of them being Vickers Wellingtons.

May 31 The RAF uses de Havilland Mosquitoes operationally for the first time in a daylight follow-up attack on Cologne by aircraft of No 105 Squadron.

June 2 – July 4 Successful if costly German assault on Sevastopol, then the strongest fortress in the world, supported by concentrated Luftwaffe bombing raids.

June 3/4 A Vickers Wellington of the RAF's No 172 Squadron is the first to make a night attack on an enemy submarine by using a Leigh light to illuminate its target.

June 3-4 The Battle of Midway is fought, one of the decisive battles of history, in which the Japanese carriers *Akagi*, *Hiryu*, *Kaga* and *Soryu* are destroyed by carrier-based aircraft of the US Navy. The Japanese Navy, deprived of its in-being carrier force, has lost the initiative and, from that moment forward, is compelled to fight on the defensive. The US Navy loses the original USS *Yorktown*.

June 12 Twelve USAAF B-24 Liberators make an unsuccessful strike against the Ploesti oil refineries. It is the AAF's first attack against a strategic target in the Balkans.

June 13 The German A4 (V2) rocket is launched for the first time at Peenemünde, but quickly goes out of control and crashes.

June 18 Maj Gen Carl Spaatz is appointed to command the US Eighth Army Air Force in the UK.

June 26 First flight of the Grumman XF6F-3 Hellcat prototype (02982), a significant Allied shipboard fighter of the Second World War.

July 1 A Boeing B-17 Flying Fortress, the first aircraft to begin equipping the US Eighth Army Air Force in the UK, lands at Prestwick.

July 4 Six crews of the US 15th Bombardment Squadron make the first AAF bomber mission over Europe in the Second World War. Flying RAF Douglas Bostons, they make attacks on four enemy-held airfields in Holland.

July 5 A first flight is made by the Avro York prototype (LV626), a long-range transport development of the Avro Lancaster bomber.

July 11 Making its longest-range daylight raid to date, aircraft of RAF Bomber Command attack shipyards at Danzig, Poland.

July 18 A first jet-powered flight is made by the Messerschmitt Me 262V-3 prototype (PC-UC), fitted with two Junkers 109-004A turbojets, each developing 840kg (1,852lb st). The pilot is Fritz Wendel.

August The German Air Ministry issues to selected German aircraft manufacturers a design request for a single turbojet fighter.

August 7-8 With considerable initial air cover, US Marines begin to make landings on Guadalcanal.

August 15 The RAF's Pathfinder Force is formed, under the command of Air Commodore D.C.T. Bennett.

August 16/17 The first exploratory use of the Pathfinder Force is made in an attack on Emden, Germany.

August 17 The USAAF makes its first Second World War heavy bomber attack against targets in Western Europe. B-17s of the 97th Bombardment Group attack the Rouen-Scotteville marshalling yards in occupied France.

August 19 With large-scale air support, a major Anglo-Canadian amphibious landing is made at Dieppe, France. Although this force suffers heavy losses, lessons are learned that prove valuable in the invasion of Normandy.

August 20 The US Twelfth Army Air Force is activated at Bolling Field, Washington D.C. in preparation for the invasion of North Africa.

August 24 The first Junkers Ju 86P-2 very high altitude pressurised reconnaissance aircraft is intercepted and destroyed. This is achieved by an RAF Spitfire VC from Alexandria, making its interception at about 12,800m (42,000ft) although the pilot had no pressurised protection against operation at that height.

September A Yokosuka E14Y1 ('Glen') light submarine-borne reconnaissance floatplane, launched from the Japanese submarine *I-25*, makes two overflights of the wooded Oregon coast and drops four incendiary bombs. It is the first and only time Japanese fixed-wing aircraft raid the USA during the Second World War.

Bell XP-59A Airacomet (foreground) flying alongside a P-63 Kingcobra, October 1 1942.

September 1   RAF and US Navy Catalinas disperse a 'wolf pack' of German submarines attacking a westbound North Atlantic convoy. One of the submarines is sunk.

September 2   A first flight is made by the Hawker Tempest prototype (HM595), a Mk V built as a conversion of a Hawker Typhoon.

September 12   The first use of para-fragmentation bombs in the Second World War is made by the USAAF's 89th Attack Squadron, during sweeps over Buna airstrip, New Guinea.

September 16   Shortly after the third anniversary of the formation of the UK's Air Transport Auxiliary, it is announced that its pilots had ferried some 100,000 aircraft of 117 different types.

September 21   First flight of the Boeing XB-29 Superfortress prototype (41-2) is made at Seattle, Washington.

September 23   Brig Gen J.H. Doolittle is appointed commander of the USAAF's new Twelfth Air Force.

September 25   A low-level attack on the Gestapo headquarters in Oslo, Norway, is made by Mosquito bombers of the RAF's No 105 Squadron.

September 29   The Eagle Squadrons serving with the RAF are taken over formally by the USAAF's VIIIth Fighter Command and integrated with its 4th Fighter Group.

October 1   The first flight of a Bell XP-59A Airacomet prototype, the first turbojet-powered aircraft to fly in the United States.

October 3   The first fully successful launch of a German A4 (V2) ballistic rocket is made at Peenemünde.

October 7   Formation of the first Luftwaffe night harassment units in direct imitation of the Soviet practice.

October 21   Using B-24 Liberators, the USAAF's India Air Task Force makes its first attack north of the Yellow River, China.

The USAAF's VIIIth Bomber Command flies its first operation, attacking German submarine bases in occupied France.

October 21-22   BOAC makes an experimental flight from Prestwick to Ramenskoye, near Moscow. The nonstop flight of 13 hr 9 min is made in a converted Liberator I.

October 23/24   RAF aircraft make continuous night attacks on Afrika Korps positions and armour, marking the beginning of the third and last battle of Alamein.

October 25   In a first attack on Japanese-occupied Hong Kong, US bomber aircraft cause damage to Kowloon docks.

November 2   The Patuxent River Naval Air Station is established by the US Navy as a test unit for aircraft, equipment and materials.

November 8-11   USAAF aircraft operating from offshore US Navy aircraft carriers contribute air cover for the Allied invasion of North Africa under 'Operation Torch'.

November 9-10   To counter the Allied invasion, large numbers of Luftwaffe fighter and bomber aircraft are flown in to Tunis and troop reinforcements are brought in by air and sea.

November 12   The US Ninth Army Air Force is established in the Middle East.

November 15   First flight of the Heinkel He 219 twin-engined night fighter prototype. Operational from June 1943, it is the Luftwaffe's first operational aircraft with retractable tricycle landing gear and the first in the world with crew ejection seats.

November 19   Start of the Soviet counter offensive north of Stalingrad, supported by four Air Armies. In just three weeks the fate of the German troops in Stalingrad is sealed.

November 25   Start of Luftwaffe supply flights into Stalingrad. Last remaining landing field, at Tatsinskaya, is lost to Soviet tanks on December 24.

November 28   The USAAF's 7th Bomb Group makes a first attack on Bangkok, capital of Japanese-held Thailand, involving a 4,440km (2,760 mile) round trip from Gaya, India.

December   First flight of the Me 264 very long range bomber prototype, dubbed unofficially the *'Amerika Bomber'*.

The prototype Lockheed Model L-49 Constellation in military guise, January 9 1943.

December 4   Making the USAAF's first attack on Italy, B-24 Liberators of the Ninth Air Force bomb Naples.

December 20/21   Japanese bombers make the first night attack on Calcutta, India.

Mosquito bombers of the RAF's No.109 Squadron, equipped with Oboe radar, are used in a night Pathfinder operation for the first time.

December 22   B-24 Liberators of the USAAF's 307th Bombardment Group make the first major air attack on a Japanese air base in the Central Pacific.

December 23   The UK government sets up a committee, under the Chairmanship of Lord Brabazon of Tara, to make recommendations on suitable civil transport aircraft for early post-war development.

December 24   Australian and US forces recapture Buna airstrip, New Guinea.

December 27   First flight of the Kawanishi N1K1-J Shiden naval fighter prototype, allocated the Allied SW Pacific reporting name of 'George'.

1943

January 1   No.6 Group Royal Canadian Air Force, becomes operational as a component of RAF Bomber Command.

January 5   The USAAF's Northwest African Air Forces are activated, with Maj Gen Carl Spaatz in command.

January 9   The first flight is recorded of the first Lockheed Model L-49 Constellation at Burbank, California. Commandeered on the production line for service with the USAAF under the designation C-69, it is still bearing its civil registration NX67900.

A Japanese bomber is hit by a 5-inch shell from USS *Yorktown*, off the island of Kwajalein, April 1943. (*US Navy*)

January 14-23 In a conference at Casablanca, Morocco Churchill, Roosevelt and their Chiefs of Staff reach some important decisions: to step up round-the-clock bombing of targets in Germany, to begin an invasion of Europe's 'soft underbelly' with Sicily as the initial objective, and to defer the cross-Channel invasion until 1944.

January 16 The Brazilian airline Serviços Aéreos Condor is renamed, gaining its present title Serviços Aéreos Cruzeiro do Sul, and known usually as Cruzeiro.

January 27 Attacking Emden and Wilhelmshaven, B-17s of the 1st Bombardment wing, Eighth Air Force, make the USAAF's first heavy-bomber attack on Germany.

January 30 Mosquito bombers of the RAF's No.105 Squadron make the first daylight raid on Berlin.

February 4 BOAC initiates a service with de Havilland Mosquitoes between Leuchars, Scotland and Stockholm, Sweden, for fast delivery of small and urgent items and the transport of agents.

February 11 Air Marshal Sir Arthur Tedder, RAF, is appointed to be Air C-in-C Mediterranean Air Command.

February 13 The first operational use is made of Vought ·F4U Corsairs, aircraft of Marine Fighter Squadron 124 escorting Navy PB4Y Liberators in an attack on Bougainville.

February 15-17 Airdrops of supplies are made to Brig Orde Wingate's Chindits, operating behind Japanese lines at Myene, Burma.

February 17 Mediterranean Air Command is established and incorporates three subordinate commands: Middle East Air Command, Northwest African Air Forces, and RAF Malta Air Command.

March 2-4 Battle of the Bismarck Sea, during which a major Japanese attempt to reinforce Lae is foiled by aircraft of the Southwest Pacific Air Forces. Some 40,000 tons of Japanese shipping is sunk and almost 60 enemy aircraft destroyed.

March 5 A first flight is made by the Gloster Meteor prototype (DG206). The Meteor becomes the first turbojet aircraft to enter service with the RAF, and the only Allied turbojet to see operational service during the Second World War.

March 10 The US Fourteenth Army Air Force is activated, commanded by Maj Gen Claire Chennault.

March 16 First operational trials are carried out on the Eastern Front by the Junkers Ju 87G anti-tank conversion armed with two 37mm Flak guns.

Air Chief Marshal Sir Frederick Bowhill is appointed commander of the RAF's new Transport Command.

April 5 Operation Flax is initiated to make concentrated air attacks on German and Italian transport aircraft shuttling arms and reinforcements from Italy to Tunisia.

April 18 Massacre of German transport aircraft off Cape Bon, Tunisia. Claims of 52 aircraft destroyed are made by British and US fighters.

Admiral Isoroku Yamamoto, Japan's protagonist of naval air power, is killed when the Mitsubishi G4M 'Betty' carrying him and his staff is ambushed and .destroyed over Bougainville. This attack is made by Lockheed P-38G Lightnings of the USAAF's 339th Fighter Squadron, flying 885km (550 miles) from their base to make the interception.

May 11 BOAC begins a service between the UK and Lisbon, operated by Douglas DC-3s.

May 13 Axis troops in North Africa surrender, marking the end of the North African campaign.

The Venezuelan air line Avensa (Aerovias Venezolanas SA) is formed.

May 17/18 Historic attack by the RAF's No.617 Squadron, led by Wg Cdr Guy Gibson, against the Ruhr dams. So-called 'bouncing bomb' mines are used, conceived by Barnes Wallis.

May 23 In a new demonstration of the versatility of the Fairey Swordfish, one operating from the escort carrier HMS *Archer* sinks the German submarine *U-572* by rocket attack.

June The Messerschmitt Me 262A jet-powered fighter is ordered into series production.

June 1 In advance of receiving its Boeing B-29 Superfortresses, the USAAF's 58th Very Heavy Bombardment Wing is activated at Marietta, Georgia. It is created to make strategic attacks on Japanese targets.

June 11 The surrender of the Italian garrison on the island of Pantellaria, midway between Tunisia and Sicily, followed intensive bombing by Allied aircraft. It is the first occasion that a large defended area is conquered by air power alone.

June 14 The RAF announces formation of the 1st Tactical Air Force; formed from the Desert Air Force, it serves in the Mediterranean and Italy. The 2nd and 3rd Tactical Air Forces are also established, in Western Europe and South East Asia respectively.

June 15 The Arado Ar234V-1 Blitz (Lightning), the prototype of the world's first turbojet-powered recce-bomber, makes its first flight.

June 25 In the heaviest of many softening-up attacks made on the island of Sicily, 130 B-17s of the Northwest African Air Force drop more than 300 tons of bombs on Messina.

June 28 First mention is made that air reconnaissance of Peenemünde had revealed large rockets which might be intended for long-range attack.

July 9 Following a month-long bombardment of Axis air bases on Sicily, Sardinia and Italy, the British Eighth Army and US Seventh Army invades Sicily. The amphibious landings are preceded with an assault by paratroops and a large number of troop and cargo-carrying gliders.

July 18 The US Navy airship K-74 is shot down by a German submarine off the Florida coast. It was the only US airship to be destroyed by enemy action during the Second World War.

July 22 The Canadian government's transatlantic service for mail, military personnel and VIPs is inaugurated, being operated by Trans-Canada Air Lines.

July 24/25 The anti-radar device known as 'Window' is used by the RAF for the first time during an attack on Hamburg.

July 27/28 RAF Bomber Command launches a second major attack against Hamburg.

July 30 First flight of the Arado Ar 234A jet reconnaissance bomber prototype.

August 1 Jr Lt Lydia Litvak of the Soviet Union's 73rd Guards Fighter Air Regiment is killed in action, aged 22, having gained a total of 12 victories in aerial combat.

USAAF Mediterranean-based B-24 Liberators make a low-level attack on the Ploesti oil refineries in Romania. This is the USAAF's first low-level attack by heavy bombers against a strongly defended target, and its longest-range bombing mission to date.

August 2/3 RAF Bomber Command makes its fourth major attack on Hamburg within ten days. More than 3,000 bombers are employed in these attacks, but thanks to the use of 'Window' the 87 aircraft which were lost represented 2.6 per cent of the total, rather than the more usual average of about 6 per cent for such operations.

August 13 The Northwest African Air Force attacks Wiener Neustadt, being the first USAAF attack on Austria from Mediterranean bases.

August 17 In daylight attacks against Regensburg and Schweinfurt, the US Eighth Army Air Force loses 59 heavy bombers.

August 17/18 RAF bombers make a heavy attack on the German research establishment at Peenemünde, intended to destroy or delay the design and production of advanced weapons.

First operational use by the Luftwaffe of the Henschel HS 293A-1 rocket-powered remotely-controlled glide bomb, when Dornier Do217E-5s of II/KG 100 carry out an anti-shipping strike against British ships in the Bay of Biscay.

August 27 The British corvette HMS *Egret*, on patrol in the Bay of Biscay, is sunk by an air-launched Henschel Hs 293 radio-controlled bomb.

August 31 First operational use of the Grumman F6F Hellcat by US Navy squadron VF-5, flown off the carrier USS *Yorktown* in an attack by Navy Task Force 15 against Japanese positions on Marcus Island.

September First flight of the DFS 228 rocket-powered high-altitude reconnaissance aircraft prototype in glider form, released from a Do 217K carrier.

September 1 In the USA, Ozark Air Lines is formed to operate intrastate and charter services.

September 3 Peace negotiations between the Allies and Italy are concluded in secret. The armistice became effective on September 8.

September 9 The Italian 46,200-ton battleship *Roma* is sunk by two Ruhrstahl/Kramer Fritz X-1 radio-controlled bombs air-launched by Luftwaffe Dornier Do 217s.

September 12 Benito Mussolini, being held prisoner at an hotel in the Gran Sasso mountains, is rescued by German glider troops and airlifted to safety in a Fieseler Fi 156 Storch.

September 13 In attempts to enable the Allies to break out from the beachhead at Salerno, a reinforcing 1,200 paratroopers of the US 82nd Airborne Division are airdropped.

September 15/16 An RAF Lancaster makes the first operational use of a 12,000lb bomb, this being dropped on the Dortmund-Ems canal in Germany.

September 20 The prototype of the the de Havilland Vampire turbojet-powered single-seat fighter (LZ548) makes its first flight at Hatfield, Hertfordshire.

October 13 Italy, which by its surrender to the Allied forces had also become an ally, declares war on Germany.

The new Italian air force, the Aeronautica Militare Italiana, is formed. It marks also the formation date of Italian naval aviation, the Aviazione per la Marina Militare.

October 14 In a second major attack on ball bearing factories at Schweinfurt, the USAAF loses 60 out of 288 bombers despatched on the mission. Following this attack, the German ball-bearing industry is dispersed.

October 16 The US Ninth Army Air Force is reorganised in the UK, to serve as a tactical arm of the USAAF.

October 26 First flight of the Dornier Do 335 single-seat multi-role fighter prototype (CP+UA), powered by a tractor and a pusher engine.

October 30 In order to evaluate the capability of the helicopter, the US Navy acquires a single Sikorsky YR-4B from the USAAF (46445), redesignating it HNS-1.

October 31 The US Navy scores its first aerial victory by the use of airborne interception radar when an AI-equipped Vought F4U-2 Corsair destroys a Japanese aircraft in New Guinea.

November 2 First operation of the newly-formed US Fifteenth Army Air Force is an attack by 112 heavy bombers on aircraft factories at Wiener Neustadt, Austria.

November 5 Carrier-based aircraft from USS *Princeton* and USS *Saratoga* seriously damage Japanese cruisers and destroyers steaming from Truk through Rabaul.

November 11 Further severe damage is caused to Japanese naval vessels off Rabaul by aircraft from the US Navy carriers *Bunker Hill*, *Essex* and *Independence*.

Aircraft of the US Fifth and Thirteenth Army Air Forces co-operating with US Navy carrier-based aircraft launch a major attack on Rabaul.

November 25 A force of Lockheed P-38s, North American B-25s and P-51s of the US Fourteenth Army Air Force make a first attack on Formosa from bases in China.

November 27 The USAAF's 20th Bomber Command is activated at Smoky Hill Army Air Field, Salina, Kansas.

November 30 The US Navy's giant Martin Mars flying-boat makes a first operational nonstop flight of 7,040km (4,375 miles), from its Patuxent River base to Natal, Brazil.

December 13 Marking the beginning of long-range operations with fighter escort, the USAAF's 8th and 9th Air Forces eventually fly 1,462 daylight sorties.

December 17 Orville Wright, on the 40th anniversary of making his first powered flight, presents the Collier Trophy for outstanding achievement in aviation to his former pupil Gen H.H. ('Hap') Arnold.

December 20 The US Navy's Air Training Command is established at Pensacola, Florida.

Allied aircraft begin intensive bombing attacks on V-1 launching sites that are being prepared in Northern France. It causes the Germans to change over to quick-assembly prefabricated sites.

December 26 Intensive pre-invasion bombing of Cape Gloucester, New Britain is made by the US Fifth Army Air Force.

1944

Dr Ing Theodor von Kárman takes the post of chairman to the Scientific Advisory Board, USAAF. (He initiated the first US Army rocket motor project while holding positions at the California Institute of Technology during 1926-49).

January 1 The United States Strategic Air Forces in Europe (USSAFE) is activated.

January 4 The first high-altitude mine-dropping operation is made by an RAF Halifax bomber off Brest, France.

January 9 First flight of the Lockheed XP-80 Shooting Star prototype (44-83020) is made at Muroc Dry Lake, California. It becomes, in late 1945, the first single-seat turbojet-powered fighter/fighter-bomber to enter service with the USAAF.

January 18 US Navy Catalinas equipped with magnetic anomaly detection (MAD) equipment begin to patrol the Straits of Gibraltar. This is intended to prevent German submarines from getting into the Mediterranean.

January 22 Large-scale Allied landings, protected by massive air support, put some 50,000 Anglo-American troops ashore at Anzio, Italy without opposition.

February 15 Several hundred Allied medium/heavy bombers attack the monastary of Monte Cassino, Italy, ahead of the advancing American 5th Army.

February 16   First flight of the Curtiss XSC-1 Sea-hawk prototype is made. It is to be the last of a long line of scout aircraft to serve with the US Navy.

February 17   A massive air attack is made against German formations endeavouring to push the Allied forces off the Anzio beachhead.

Twelve radar-equipped Grumman TBF-1C Avengers of the US Navy, operating from the USS *Enterprise*, attack Truk by night. This was the first night bombing attack to be made from a US aircraft carrier.

February 18   Mosquito bombers make a daring low-level daylight attack on the German prison at Amiens, France, attempting to liberate patriots awaiting execution for aiding the Allies.

February 29   Aircraft of the US Fifth Army Air Force support the first landing made on the Admiralty Islands, thus completing the isolation of Rabaul.

March 5   Brig Gen Orde Wingate's special force lands at 'Broadway', North Burma, in a night glider operation.

March 6   In its first major attack on Berlin, the USAAF deploys a force of 660 heavy bombers. A total of 69 bombers and eleven escort fighters are lost.

March 10   The Icelandic airline Loftleidir HF is formed, inaugurating its first services on April 7, 1944.

First flight of the Blohm und Voss BV 238 prototype, the world's largest flying-boat flown during the war.

March 25   In landing aboard HMS *Indefatigable*, the pre-prototype of the de Havilland Sea Mosquito (LR359)

becomes the first British twin-engined aircraft to land on the deck of an aircraft carrier.

First operational use by the US 15th Air Force of the VB-I Azon bomb, a general-purpose bomb with a pair of radio-controlled rudders in the tail.

April   The Rolls-Royce Derwent I begins flight tests in a Gloster Meteor flying test bed.

April 4   The US Twentieth Army Air Force is activated in Washington, D.C.

April 15   In order to destroy the mobility of German forces in Europe, all forms of transport are allocated as priority targets for UK and US heavy bomber squadrons.

May 1   Allied aircraft begin a major offensive against the rail transport system of Western Europe.

May 5   The airline Dominicana (Compania Dominicana de Aviación C por A) is founded with assistance from Pan American. Its first scheduled services are flown on July 5, 1944.

May 10   Completion of the Chengtu Project, the construction of bomber and fighter airfields in China. This has been accomplished by some 400,000 Chinese coolies using primitive equipment.

May 11   Operation Strangle terminated. Under this codename the Mediterranean Allied Air Forces dropped some 26,000 tons of bombs on German lines of communication in Italy.

The world's first helicopter production line at Bridgeport, Connecticut, produces Sikorsky R-4Bs. 1944.

Northrop MX-324, July 5 1944.

June 1 The US Navy records a first Atlantic crossing by non-rigid airships, from South Weymouth, Massachusetts to Port Lyautey, Morocco, via Argentina and the Azores.

June 3 A Luftwaffe Junkers Ju 290A transport lands in Greenland to evacuate 26 men of the Bassgeiger weather station, who had been there for ten months.

June 5 Provisional date set for Operation Overlord, the Allied invasion of Europe, but bad weather causes the landings to be postponed.

June 5-6 Despite the fact that the invasion is postponed, Allied aircraft take full opportunity of this period to continue pre-invasion operations against all enemy communications.

June 6 Preceded by airdrops, the D-Day landings on the Normandy coast begin. The biggest amphibious assault in history, it is supported by massive Allied air force operations involving almost 5,000 sorties. By nightfall some five divisions are established ashore.

June 7 The first Allied airstrip to be completed in Normandy following the D-Day landings becomes operational at Asnelles, northeast of Bayeux.

June 10 Allied aircraft begin operating from airstrips and airfields created since the D-Day landings.

June 11 US Navy Task Force 58, comprising seven heavy and eight light aircraft carriers, are assembled and begin to deploy their aircraft in the opening of the campaign to occupy the Mariana Islands.

June 13 The first German V1 'flying bombs' are launched from sites in France against British targets.

June 15 With massive air support from the Task Force

carriers, US forces begin making landings on Saipan, Mariana Islands.

Boeing B-29 Superfortresses of the USAAF's 20th Bomber Command make a first attack on Japan, deployed from their new bases in Chengtu, China.

June 15-16 With growing experience, German launching crews begin to step up the number of V1 flying bombs being despatched against targets in England.

June 24/25 First use by the Luftwaffe of its Mistel composite. The initial variant comprises an upper piloted Messerschmitt Bf 109F-4, mounted above a Ju 88A-4 carrying a warhead containing 1,725kg (3,803lb) of high explosive. In this initial night operation, five composites are deployed against Allied shipping in the Seine Bay.

June 25 Some 2,400 Allied bomber aircraft make a three-hour saturation raid on German positions forward of the American lines at St Lo, France.

July 5 A first powered flight is recorded by the Northrop MX-324, the first American rocket-powered military aircraft.

July 12 The first two operational Gloster Meteors are delivered to the RAF's No 616 Squadron, then based at Culmhead, Somerset.

July 17 The first operational use of napalm incendiary material is made by USAAF P-38 Lightnings during attacks on a fuel depot at Coutances, France.

July 20 First operational use of the Arado Ar 234A turbojet-powered reconnaissance aircraft, flying from Juvincourt, near Reims.

Deployment is completed of a barrage of anti-aircraft guns around England's south coast. They prove to be very effective in countering the German V1 flying bombs, firing shells armed with US-designed proximity fuses.

Arado Ar 234B Blitz, September 1944.

July 27 Gloster Meteors are used operationally for the first time in attacks on V1s. These are unsuccessful because of gun-firing problems.

July 28 First flight of the de Havilland Hornet prototype (RR915). These single-seat long-range fighter/fighter-bombers, which enter service with the RAF after the war, prove to be the fastest twin piston-engined combat aircraft in the world.

July 29 A battle damaged B-29 of the USAAF's 20th Bomber Command lands near Vladivostok and is immediately seized by the Soviet authorities. This B-29 is followed by another three on August 20, November 11 and November 21 1944. These B-29s are carefully dismantled, examined and serve as pattern aircraft for the Tupolev Tu-4 , the first modern Soviet heavy long-range bomber. (q.v. August 3, 1947)

August 2 The First Allied Airborne Army is formed under the command of Lt Gen Lewis H. Brereton, USAAF.

Canadian Air Transport Board established, to be the licensing and regulating body for civil air transport.

August 4 Destroying a V1, by flying alongside it and using the wing of his Gloster Meteor to tip the missile and force it to the ground, Flg Off. Dean of No.616 Sqn scores the Meteor's first combat success.

In a first mission codenamed Aphrodite, radio-controlled B-17s, each packed with 9,072kg (20,000lb) of TNT, are launched against German V2 sites being constructed at Pas de Calais, France.

August 7 The US Navy Carrier Division 11 is commissioned. Comprising the aircraft carriers USS *Ranger* and USS *Saratoga*, it is the first division intended specifically for night operations.

August 8/9 The Mediterranean Air Forces drop arms and supplies to the Polish Home Army in Warsaw, in uprising against the German forces since August 1. This is the first of several such operations.

August 14/15 Mediterranean Allied Air Forces fly more than 4,000 sorties and transport more than 9,000 airborne troops to begin the invasion of southern France, between Cannes and Hyeres. The paratroops are dropped at night and in thick fog.

August 16 Messerschmitt Me 163B-1 Komet rocket-powered interceptor fighters are used operationally for the first time, attacking a formation of USAAF B-17 Flying Fortresses.

First flight of the Ju 287V1 four-jet bomber prototype with forward-swept wings.

August 20 The Falaise pocket is closed on the retreating Germans, pounded mercilessly by Allied aircraft. Many troops escape but leave behind virtually all heavy equipment.

August 28 The USAAF's 78th Fighter Group claims the destruction of a Messerschmitt Me 262, the first jet-powered aircraft to be shot down in air combat.

September First operational use of the Arado Ar 234B *Blitz* in a reconnaissance role.

September 1 The Germans begin to launch their V1 flying bombs against targets in Europe.

September 4 German V1 attacks on Britain from cross-Channel launching sites come to an end.

September 5-6 Start of the German Operation *Zeppelin*, an unsuccessful attempt to assassinate Stalin. The task group is flown from near Riga, Latvia, to a point near Moscow by an Ar 232B transport of KG 200.

September 8 Two German V2 ballistic rockets land in Paris. Later that day the first of these weapons launched against England detonates in Chiswick, West London, killing two people and injuring several others.

Basic specifications for a *Volksjäger* (People's Fighter) are drawn up by the German Air Ministry and issued to seven leading aircraft manufacturers.

September 10 First flight of the Fairchild XC-82 prototype (43-13202), the first US aircraft to be designed from the outset as a military transport.

September 17-26 In an attempt to secure bridges over the rivers Maas, Waal and Lek, Allied paratroops are dropped at Arnhem, Eindhoven and Nijmegen. The desperate stand of the British 1st Airborne Division at Arnhem ranks high in the annals of the British Army. Some 2,200 survivors were evacuated over the Lek on Sept 25/26, leaving some 7,000 dead or prisoners.

October First unpowered test flight of the Yokosuka

MXY-7 Ohka manned rocket-powered suicide weapon, Allied SW Pacific reporting name 'Baka',

October 23 Beginning of the Battle of Leyte Gulf, during which the Japanese introduced the use of Kamikaze attacks by suicide planes, these sinking the USS *St. Lo* and several other vessels. When the battle had ended (October 25) the Japanese had lost three battleships, 10 cruisers and 11 destroyers, marking the end of the Japanese fleet as an effective fighting force.

October 27 Mission flown by the USAAF's 9th Fighter Squadron from Tacloban airstrip marks the first US air operation from the Philippines since 1942.

November 1 A USAAF F-13 (a reconnaissance variant of the B-29 Superfortress) is the first US aircraft to fly over Tokyo since the Doolittle raid of 1942. (q.v. April 18, 1942)

November 3 Start of the Japanese 'Fu-Go Weapon' (balloon bomb) offensive against the USA. (q.v. May 22, 1945)

November 12 The 52,600-ton German battleship *Tirpitz*, anchored in Tromso Fjord, Norway, is sunk by bombs dropped from Avro Lancasters of the RAF's No 9 and 617 Squadrons.

Intelligence summary after the first major bombing attack on Tokyo by Boeing B-29 Superfortresses, November 24 1944. (*USAF*)

A Mitsubishi Zero-Sen fighter is heavily laden with a large bomb in preparation for a Kamikaze attack during the Battle of Leyte Gulf, October 23 1944. (*US Navy*)

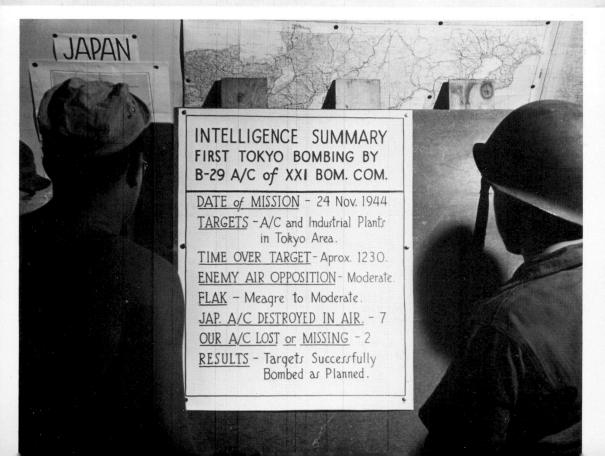

JAPAN

INTELLIGENCE SUMMARY
FIRST TOKYO BOMBING BY
B-29 A/C *of* XXI BOM. COM.

DATE *of* MISSION - 24 Nov. 1944
TARGETS - A/C and Industrial Plants
in Tokyo Area.
TIME OVER TARGET - Aprox. 1230.
ENEMY AIR OPPOSITION - Moderate.
FLAK - Meagre to Moderate.
JAP. A/C DESTROYED IN AIR. - 7
OUR A/C LOST *or* MISSING - 2
RESULTS - Targets Successfully
Bombed as Planned.

Richard Ira Bong in the cockpit of a Lockheed P-38 Lightning fighter. (*USAF*)

November 15   A first flight is made by the Boeing XC-97 Stratofreighter prototype (43-27470).

November 24   First major bombing attack on Tokyo from the Mariana Islands by 88 B-29s of the USAAF's 21st Bomber Command.

December   The TR-1 (VDR-3), the first Soviet turbo-jet engine, reportedly completes its official bench running tests.

December 6   A first flight is made by the Heinkel He 162V-1 Salamander turbojet-powered fighter prototype (200 001) at Vienna-Schwechat.

December 7   The USS *Chourre* is commissioned as the US Navy's first aviation repair ship.

December 14   A first flight is made by the first Short Shetland prototype (DX166), the largest military flying-boat built in the UK.

December 17   The USAAF's 509th Composite Group, assembled to carry out US atom bomb operations, is established in Utah.

Maj. Richard Ira Bong, the USAAF's most successful fighter pilot of the Second World War, scores his 40th and final victory.

December 18   First vertical launch of the German un-manned Bachem Ba 349 Natter, intended for operational use as a manned, vertically-launched rocket-powered interceptor.

1945

January 1   In Operation *Bodenplatte*, the Luftwaffe, in its last major attack, attempts to destroy the maximum

USS *Saratoga* is hit by a Japanese Kamikaze aircraft, February 21 1945. (*US Navy*)

number of Allied aircraft on the ground. About 800 Luftwaffe aircraft are involved in this surprise air strike. A total of 465 Allied aircraft are destroyed or damaged, and more than 220 Luftwaffe aircraft are lost during this operation.

January 4   The Argentine Air Force, which had been established originally during 1912, adopts its current title of Fuerza Aérea Argentina.

January 5   The Yugoslav Air Force, which had originated as the Serbian Military Air Service during 1913, adopts its current name of Jugoslovensko Ratno Vazduhoplovstvo.

January 16   Combined Allied air and ground operations against the German bulge in the Ardennes forces the enemy on the retreat.

February 5   In Australia, Ansett Airways resumes commercial operations.

February 7   A first flight is made by the Consolidated-Vultee XP-81 escort fighter prototype. This has a mixed power plant, comprising a conventionally-mounted turboprop plus a turbojet in the aft fuselage. It is the first turboprop-powered aircraft to fly in the USA.

February 13-15   RAF and USAAF night and day attacks on Dresden, Germany, create a devastating fire storm which virtually destroys the city. The estimates as to the number of dead vary between 35,000 and 220,000.

February 16   After long and heavy bombardment of Japanese guns and positions, USAAF C-47s airdrop more than 2,000 paratroopers over Corregidor.

February 17   The softening-up of Iwo Jima, which is the most strongly defended of all Japanese positions, begins with a combined attack from carrier-based aircraft, naval heavy guns, and US Seventh Air Force B-24 Liberators.

February 19   With massive air and sea support, the US Marines begin landing on Iwo Jima.

February 21   A first flight is made by the Hawker Sea Fury prototype (SR661), which proves to be the last piston-engined fighter to serve in FAA first-line squadrons.

The US Navy aircraft carrier *Saratoga* is hit and badly damaged by Kamikaze attack.

February 22   Some 9,000 Allied aircraft make a concentrated attack on the German transport system.

A Martin B-26 Marauder bomber makes a low-level attack on targets at Nontabaury in Germany, February 22 1945 (*USAF*)

February 23 The Luftwaffe sinks its last ship of the War, the *Henry Bacon* belonging to convoy RA.64.

February 25 First flight is made by the Bell XP-83 prototype, a pressurised turbojet-powered escort fighter developed from the P-59 Airacomet.

February 28 First manned flight test of the vertical take-off Bachem Ba 349 Natter (Viper) rocket-powered target defence interceptor kills the pilot, Oberleutnant Lothar Siebert. Three subsequent manned launches in March are successful, and the Natter is approved for operational use.

March 9 Allied aircraft provide support in operations against German armour attempting to eliminate the Remagen bridgehead, established two days previously.

March 9/10 In a change of tactics, more than 300 Marianas-based B-29 Superfortresses armed with incendiary bombs make a low-altitude night attack on Tokyo.

March 11 Allied air forces make an all-out bombing attack on Essen to cut German rail communications prior to the Rhine crossings.

March 14 First operational use of the 22,000lb 'Grand Slam' bomb, dropped by a Lancaster of No 617 Squadron on the Bielefeld Viaduct, Germany.

March 16 The US Navy claims that in attacks on Japanese bases during the previous month they have destroyed 648 enemy aircraft.

Organised Japanese resistance on Iwo Jima ends. US Marine casualties total 6,891 dead and 18,070 injured, but this small island is to prove a valuable emergency landing field for bomber aircraft attacking the Japanese homeland. By the war's end 2,251 B-29 Superfortresses have found refuge there.

Japanese pilots say farewell as they head for their Yokosuka Ohka suicide aircraft, March 21 1945. (*US Navy*)

March 17 Following the success of the first incendiary attack on Tokyo, 307 B-29s drop 2,300 tons of incendiary weapons on Kobe, Japan.

March 18 First flight of the Douglas XBT2D-1 Skyraider prototype, a single-seat carrier-based dive-bomber/torpedo-bomber, which is the first aircraft of this category to be used by the US Navy. It enters service too late to see operational use during the Second World War.

More than 1,250 bombers plus an escort of some 670 fighters make the USAAF's biggest daylight attack on Berlin.

March 20/21 Luftwaffe aircraft attack Britain. This was the last German attack on the UK by piloted aircraft.

March 21 The first, but unsuccessful, sortie is made by the Japanese Yokosuka Ohka purpose-built suicide aircraft.

March 21-24 The Allied air forces in Europe mount a large-scale attack against the Luftwaffe and its bases. This great strategic effort virtually destroys the Luftwaffe as an effective force.

March 23-24 Allied forces make large-scale crossings of the Rhine, and under Operation Varsity large numbers of Allied airborne forces are used to take advanced positions.

March 27 The last V2 rocket falls on Britain, at Orpington, Kent.

March 31 The British Commonwealth Air Training Plan is terminated officially. It has produced 137,739 trainees, including 54,098 pilots.

April 1 Scoring their first major success, Japanese Ohka suicide aircraft severely damage the battleships USS *West Virginia* and three other vessels. One of them is the British aircraft carrier *Indefatigable*.

April 7 While making a final effort to try and hamper US landings on Okinawa, the 71,000-ton Japanese battleship *Yamato*, a cruiser, and four of eight destroyers are sunk by endless attack from US Navy carrier-based aircraft.

The USAAF is able to begin fighter-escorted B-29 missions against targets on the Japanese homeland.

April 10 The last Luftwaffe wartime sortie over Britain is made by an Arado Ar 234B turbojet-powered reconnaissance aircraft operating from Norway.

In an attack on targets near Berlin, the USAAF loses 19 of its bomber aircraft and eight escort fighters to attacks by Messerschmitt Me 262 turbojet-powered fighters.

April 12 The American destroyer USS *Mannert L. Abele* is sunk by a Japanese Ohka suicide aircraft off Okinawa.

April 19 First flight is made of the de Havilland Sea Hornet prototype (PX212). When the type enters service post-war, it is the first twin-engined single-seat fighter to be operated from aircraft carriers of the Royal Navy.

The International Air Transport Association (IATA) is formed at Havana, Cuba, succeeding the International Air Traffic Association.

April 23 US Navy PB4Y Liberators, of Patrol Bombing Squadron 109, launch two Bat missiles against Japanese shipping in Balikpapan Harbor, Borneo. This is the first known combat use of automatic homing missiles during the Second World War.

April 26 Flying a Fieseler Fi 156 Storch, Hanna Reitsch carries Gen Ritter von Greim from Berlin-Gatow into Berlin. There he is promoted by Hitler to command the Luftwaffe, replacing Hermann Goering.

April 28 Benito Mussolini is captured at Dongo, near Lake Como, and shot by Italian Communist partisans.

April 29 War in Italy comes to an end, with German envoys signing terms of unconditional surrender.

RAF Bomber Command begin to airdrop food and clothing to the Dutch people. Some 6,600 tons are dropped in just over a week.

April 30 Adolf Hitler and Eva Braun commit suicide in the air raid shelter beneath the German Chancellery in Berlin.

May 3 German envoys sent by Admiral Doenitz, Hitler's successor, arrive at Lüneberg to negotiate terms for the surrender of German forces.

May 7 RAF Coastal Command sinks its 196th and last German submarine of the Second World War, the *U-320* west of Bergen by No 210 Sqn.

Documents for the unconditional surrender of all German forces are signed at Gen Eisenhower's Headquarters.

The unconditional surrender of the German forces is ratified in Berlin, and the war in Western Europe ends officially at midnight.

May 22 It is announced in the US that the Japanese have been attempting to attack the continental United States by means of balloons carrying incendiary material. Released in Japan, they were carried by jet streams across the Pacific.

May 26 A de Havilland DH.89 makes the first Jersey/Guernsey Airways landing in the Channel Islands following the German surrender.

May 29 The advance party of the USAAF's 509th Composite Group (the atom bomb team), arrives in the Mariana Islands.

A Japanese incendiary balloon of rubberised silk material crossing the Pacific Ocean towards the United States of America, May 22 1945. (*USAF*)

Above A Sikorsky R-4B about to land on the deck of a ship in the Pacific Ocean, flown by a member of the 6th Aircraft Repair Unit, in May 1945 (*USAF*)
Below Douglas DC-3 in the later markings of the Flying Tiger Line, June 25 1945.

May 31 BOAC and Qantas begin a joint weekly Hurn, Hampshire to Sydney, NSW service with Lancastrian aircraft.

June 11 B-29s of the USAAF's 393rd Very Heavy Bomber Squadron, the only combat aircraft of the 509th Composite Group, land at Tinian, Marianas.

June 14 The first flight of the Avro Tudor I prototype (G-AGPF).

June 17 The USAAF's 21st Bomber Command begins a series of incendiary attacks on all major Japanese towns.

June 22 The prototype Vickers-Armstrongs Viking (G-AGOK) makes its first flight at Wisley, Surrey.

June 25 National Skyway Freight Corporation is established in the USA. First all-cargo airline in the US, it adopts its current title of Flying Tiger Line Inc in early 1946.

July 1 With support from the RAAF, and the USAAF's 5th and 13th Air Forces, the Australian 7th division lands on the southeast coast of Borneo.

July 2 The Japanese begin a major evacuation of the people of Tokyo, due to continuous and devastating air attacks.

July 5 The United States CAB authorises American Overseas Airlines, Pan American and TWA to operate over the North Atlantic.

July 10 The final US Navy aircraft carrier actions of the Second World War begin, the ship-based aircraft attacking targets on the Japanese homeland.

July 11 Transfer is announced of the US Eighth Army Air Force from the UK to the US, en route to the Far East.

July 13/14 The Supreme Headquarters Allied Expeditionary Force (SHAEF) is disbanded at midnight.

July 14 Attacking Japanese-held oilfields at Boela, Ceram Island, USAAF Douglas A-20s from Hollandia make the first use of rocket bombs in the southwest Pacific.

A Consolidated B-24 Liberator of the USAAF's 5th Air Force, strikes Balikpapan in Borneo in support of the Australian landing, July 1 1945. (*USAF*)

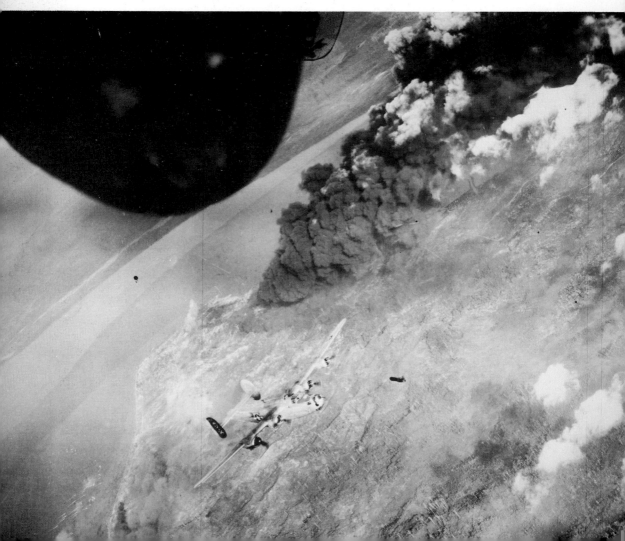

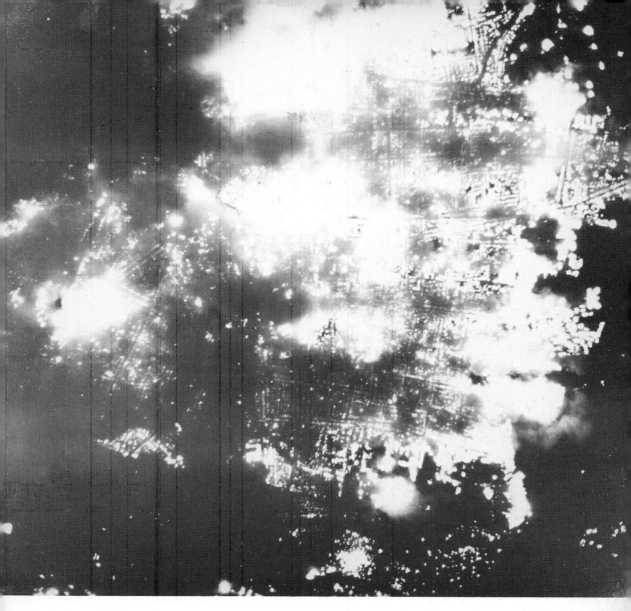

Toyama, Japan, where aluminium was produced, is nearly totally destroyed during the night attacks of August 1 1945 by Boeing B-29s. This was just one of many Japanese cities attacked on August 1. (*USAF*)

July 15 The RAF's 2nd Tactical Air Force is reformed as the British Air Force of Occupation, Germany.

July 16 Maj Gen Curtis LeMay takes command of the USAAF's 20th Air Force.

The world's first experimental atomic bomb is detonated successfully at Alamogardo, New Mexico.

July 20 The 393rd Squadron of the 509th Composite Group begins making practice bombing attacks against Japanese cities, using conventional HE bombs.

July 21 Japanese forces in Burma are decimated by air attack from Mustangs and Spitfires as they attempt to cross the Sittang river.

July 25 Gen Carl Spaatz is instructed that the 509th Composite Group should make its first atom bomb attack on Japan as soon as possible after August 3, 1945.

July 30 The Mediterranean Allied Air Forces are disbanded.

August 1 In the largest operation mounted by B-29 Superfortresses, 851 aircraft are deployed against targets in Japan.

August 2 The operational orders for the atom bomb attack are signed. Hiroshima is named as the primary target, with Kokura or Nagasaki as alternates.

August 3 The Japanese Kyushu J7W Shinden prototype makes its first flight. Intended as a heavily-armed high-performance interceptor for the Navy, it was the only combat aircraft of canard configuration to be the subject of a production contract during the Second World War.

General Douglas MacArthur (left) looks on as General Yoshira Umeza signs the surrender document on board USS *Missouri*, September 2 1945. (*USAF*)

August 6   The B-29 Superfortress *Enola Gay*, captained by Col Paul W. Tibbets Jr, drops the world's first operational atomic bomb over the city of Hiroshima.

August 7   Japan's first turbojet-powered aircraft makes its first flight as the Nakajima J8N1 Kikka Special Attack Fighter prototype.

August 9   Lt Robert H.Gray of the Royal Canadian Navy Volunteer Reserve, the pilot of a Corsair fighter-bomber, is killed attacking a Japanese destroyer. Attached to the Fleet Air Arm, he is posthumously awarded the last Victoria Cross to be won during the Second World War.

The second atomic bomb is dropped over Nagasaki, from the B-29 *Bock's Car* captained by Maj Charles W. Sweeney.

August 14   Flying its last wartime mission, the USAAF's 20th Air Force despatches 754 B-29s and 169 fighters to attack targets in Japan.

August 15   Seven Japanese suicide aircraft make the last Kamikaze attack of the war.

Andrei G. Kochetkov, Head of NII-VVS Fighter Test section, becomes the first Soviet pilot to fly a jet-powered aircraft – a captured Me 262A fighter at Shcholkovo near Moscow.

August 19   Two Mitsubishi G4M *Betty* transports carry the Japanese surrender delegation to Ie Shima.

August 21   All existing contracts under the US Lend-Lease Act are cancelled.

August 27   B-29 Superfortresses airdrop supplies to Allied prisoners of war in the Weihsien camp near Peiping, China.

September   A captured Fa 223 Drache becomes the first helicopter to cross the English Channel, flown by its ex-Luftwaffe aircrew to Brockenhurst, Hampshire.

September 2   Surrounded by the US Pacific Fleet, the Japanese surrender documents are signed aboard the battleship USS *Missouri*, anchored in Tokyo Bay.

September 6   A de Havilland Mosquito photo-reconnaissance aircraft is flown from St Mawgan, Cornwall, to Torbay, Newfoundland in 7 hr 2 min.

Gloster Meteor F.4 *Britannia* **arrives at Herne Bay in preparation for an attempt at the world speed record for aircraft, November 7 1945** (*Central Press Photos*)

September 10 The USS *Midway*, the first of the US Navy's 45,000-ton class carriers, is commissioned at Newport News, Virginia.

September 15 Spitfires lead a formation of some 300 RAF fighters in the first Battle of Britain anniversary fly-past over London.

The Czechoslovak state airline resumes post-war operations under its current title ČSA Czechoslovak Airlines.

September 20 A first flight is made by a Gloster Meteor testbed aircraft, powered by two Rolls-Royce Trent turboprop engines.

September 29 Swissair resumes operations to the UK, making a first post-war flight on its Zürich-London route.

October 4-8 Qantas operates its first post-war flight to Singapore, flown by the C class flying-boat *Coriolanus* (VH-ABG).

October 22 SABENA resumes operations on its Brussels-London route.

The Paris-London route of Air France is re-opened.

October 23 American Overseas Airlines inaugurates post-war transatlantic routes using Douglas DC-4 airliners.

November 6 Flying a mixed power plant Ryan FR-1 Fireball, which has a conventional piston-engine plus a turbojet engine in the aft fuselage, Ensign J.C. West uses the latter engine only to make the first turbojet-powered landing on an aircraft carrier, the USS *Wake Island*.

November 7 Flying a Gloster Meteor F.4, Gp Capt H.J. Wilson establishes a first post-war aircraft world speed record of 975.67km/h (606.25 mph).

November 10 BOAC and South African Airways inaugurate a joint 'Springbok' service between Hurn, Hampshire, and Johannesburg.

November 19 Details are revealed in the UK of various decoy systems used during the war in attempts to divert Luftwaffe bombing attacks from their intended targets.

November 25 Start of negotiations, finalised on December 4, under which the UK government agrees to supply military equipment to the French air force and navy.

November 28 The first Short Sandringham flying-boat, a converted Sunderland, is launched at Rochester, Kent.

November 30 The UK Air Transport Auxiliary is disbanded. During the course of the war its pilots had ferried 307,378 aircraft.

December 2 The first flight is made at Filton of the Bristol Type 170 Freighter prototype (G-AGPV).

December 3 The third prototype of the de Havilland Vampire 1 (LZ551), which had been modified for deck landing trials aboard the HMS *Ocean*, becomes the first pure jet aircraft in the world to operate from an aircraft carrier.

December 4 A Lockheed Constellation of TWA sets a record transatlantic flight time for a commercial aircraft making the first scheduled service from Washington to Paris.

December 7 The New Zealand National Airways Corporation is established.

December 8 A first flight is made by the prototype Bell Model 47 helicopter.

December 26 Ethiopian Airlines is established as the national airline of Ethiopia. Its first scheduled operation is flown on April 8, 1946.

Bell Model 47B-3, the open bubble-type cockpit version of the Model 47B, the first major civil version of the helicopter, March 8 1946.

1946

January 1 Heathrow, which is to become the site of the future London Airport, is handed over from the Air Ministry to the Ministry of Civil Aviation.

The Avro Lancastrian *Starlight* (G-AGWG), of British South American Airways and piloted by Capt D.C.T. Bennett, departs from Heathrow Aerodrome on the first of six proving flights to South America.

The British European Airways Division of BOAC (BEA) is established to take over the UK-Europe services which had been operated by No 110 Wing, 46 Group, RAF Transport Command.

The flying restrictions that had been imposed in the UK at the beginning of the Second World War are rescinded.

East African Airways Corporation is founded.

January 10 A US Army Sikorsky R-5 sets an unofficial helicopter height record of 6,400m (21,000ft) at Stratford, Connecticut.

January 19 A first unpowered flight is made by the Bell X-1 research aircraft, following launch from a Boeing B-29 Superfortress 'motherplane'.

January 26 The USAAF establishes its first experimental guided missile group at Eglin AFB, Florida.

January 29 Iraqi Airways, which had been formed during December 1945, inaugurates its first scheduled service, Baghdad-Basra.

January 31 BOAC resumes its flying-boat services from the UK to Singapore.

February 4 Pan American flies its first scheduled Constellation flight from La Guardia, New York to Hurn, Hampshire in a flight time of 14 hr 9 min.

February 10 A Consolidated Liberator (AM920) completes BOAC's 2,000 transatlantic crossing of the Return Ferry Service.

February 28 The Republic XP-84 Thunderjet prototype makes its first flight from Muroc Dry Lake.

March 4 BEA begins operations with its aircraft in civil markings and its crews in BOAC uniform

March 8 The Bell Model 47 is granted the first commercial helicopter certificate to be awarded by the US CAA.

March 10 After *RMA Berwick* arrives at Baltimore, Maryland, BOAC ends transatlantic operations with Boeing Model 314s.

March 21 The USAAF establishes its Air Defense Command, Strategic Air Command, and Tactical Air Command.

March 26 Braathens SAFE (Braathens South American and Far East Airtransport AS) is founded, beginning operations in February 1947.

April 8 DNL Norwegian Air Lines inaugurates an Oslo-London service with DC-3s.

April 24 First flights of the Yakovlev Yak-15 (one Jumo 004B) and Mikoyan MiG-9 (two BMW 003A) jet fighter prototypes, the first pure jet Soviet aircraft to fly.

One of the most unusual post-war air services begins with inauguration in the US of Winged Cargo Inc, a glider commercial freight service. Freight is carried in a Waco glider, towed by a Douglas DC-3.

May 22 First flight of the de Havilland Canada DHC-1 Chipmunk two-seat elementary trainer at Toronto.

May 31 London's Heathrow Airport (formerly Heathrow Airfield) is opened officially. Its facilities include one runway and several tents for passenger handling.

June 1 A Pan American Constellation lands at London Heathrow on the airline's first scheduled New York-London service.

The Central African Airways Corporation is founded.

June 6 A first flight is recorded by the Aérocentre NC.3020 Belphégor, the first French aircraft designed for stratospheric flight research.

June 7 The first flight is made by the Short Sturgeon prototype (RK787), the FAA's first twin-engined aircraft to be designed specifically for naval use.

June 14 BOAC's last scheduled service is operated from Hurn Airport, Hampshire.

June 22 Two USAAF Lockheed P-80 Shooting Star fighters carry the first US airmail to travel by turbojet-powered aircraft, from Shenectady to Washington D.C. and Chicago, Illinois.

June 26 The USAAF and the US Navy adopt officially the knot and nautical mile as standard aeronautical units for speed and distance respectively.

July 1 BOAC inaugurates a twice-weekly London-New York service operated with the Lockheed Constellation.

Aer Lingus takes over the operation of all scheduled services between Eire and the UK.

In an exercise codenamed Operation Crossroads, a USAAF B-29 drops an atomic bomb over 73 naval vessels anchored at Bikini Atoll in the Pacific Ocean.

July 21 The McDonnell XFH-1 Phantom becomes the first pure turbojet aircraft to operate from a US aircraft carrier, the USS *Franklin D. Roosevelt*.

July 24 Bernard Lynch makes the first recorded manned ejection from an aircraft, a Gloster Meteor on the ground, by means of a Martin-Baker ejection seat. It is reported that ejections were made from German jet aircraft during the Second World War.

July 25 Just over ten years after his death, Brig Gen William ('Billy') Mitchell is posthumously awarded the US Congressional Medal of Honour.

July 27 The first flight is made of the Supermarine Attacker prototype (TS409), then intended for service with the RAF, but no orders materialise. The first naval prototype (TS413) makes its first flight on June 17, 1947.

The first naval prototype of the Supermarine Attacker on board an aircraft carrier, July 27 1946.

July 29   Air India Ltd is established as the successor to Tata Air Lines.

July 30   Sobelair (Société Belge de Transports par Air SA) is formed to operate as a charter company.

July 31   SAS (Scandinavian Airlines System) is formed in a unique post-war collaboration of the national airlines of Denmark, Norway and Sweden.

August 1   British European Airways Corporation is established, primarily to operate over routes in the British Isles and to Europe.

British South American Airways Corporation is established as the successor to British South American Airways Ltd.

August 8   The first prototype of the giant Convair XB-36 bomber (42-13570) makes its first flight.

August 17   Sgt L. Lambert, USAAF, becomes the first person in the US to make a manned test of an ejection seat, from a Northrop P-61 Black Widow flying at 483 km/h (300 mph) at 2,375m (7,800ft).

August 21-23   An Avro Lancaster completes a London-Darwin flight in a time of 45 hr 35 min.

September 1   BEA inaugurates its first scheduled service with the Vickers Viking G-AHOP on the London-Copenhagen route.

September 4   The UK Ministry of Supply orders two de Havilland DH.106 prototypes, later to be named Comet.

September 9   Trans-Australia Airlines inaugurates a scheduled Melbourne-Sydney route operated by Douglas DC-3s.

September 11-12   First post-war meeting of the Fédération Aéronautique Internationale (FAI).

September 12   The first post-war exhibition of the Society of British Aircraft Constructors is held at Radlett, Hertfordshire.

September 15   Australian National Airways inaugurates a transpacific service with Douglas DC-4s, between Sydney, NSW and Vancouver, Canada.

September 16   Alitalia (Aerolinee Italiane Internazional) becomes incorporated in Italy. Initially BEA was a 40 per cent shareholder.

September 19   TAP (Transportes Aéreos Portugueses SARL), which had been formed as a division of the government's Civil Aeronautics Secretariat during 1944, becomes established as an airline and inaugurates its first Lisbon-Madrid service on this date.

September 24   Cathay Pacific Airways, Hong Kong, is incorporated, originally as a small charter airline.

September 27   A de Havilland DH.108 sweptwing research aircraft breaks up in the air over the Thames Estuary killing the pilot, Geoffrey de Havilland Jr.

September 29-October 1   A US Navy Lockheed P2V Neptune crewed by Cdr. T. Davis and E.P. Rankin sets a new nonstop world distance record of 18,081.99km (11,235.6 miles), flying from Perth, Australia, to Columbus, Ohio.

September 30   BOAC begins operations with its Short S.26 G class flying-boats, the initial service operated by *Golden Hind* (G-AFCI) on the UK-Cairo service.

October 1   The Belgian Air Force becomes re-established under its current title Force Aérienne Belge, or Belgische Luchtmacht.

Beginning of the first US experiments of airmail delivery in the Chicago suburbs are made by the US Post Office in conjunction with the USAAF, using Sikorsky helicopters.

October 6   The first nonstop Hawaii-Egypt flight over the North Pole is made in a USAAF Boeing B-29, covering a distance of 17,498km (10,873 miles).

November 1   The US Navy non-rigid airship XM-1 completes a flight of 170 hr 3 min, which is a world record for flight unsustained by any form of refuelling.

November 13   V.J. Schaefer of the General Electric Company produces artificial snow, seeding a cloud with dry-ice pellets from an aircraft flying over Greylock Mountain, Massachusetts.

November 18   Using ex-Luftwaffe Junkers Ju 52/3m transport aircraft, BEA begins a Croydon-Liverpool-Belfast service.

December 9   The first powered flight is made by a Bell X-1 rocket-powered research aircraft.

1947

January 3   The King's Flight of the Royal Air Force is re-established. It is planned to base it at RAF Benson, Oxfordshire.

March 14 Saudia (Saudi Arabian Airlines Corporation), which had been formed by the Saudi Arabian government during 1946, begins scheduled operations.

March 21 The Australian government acquires BOAC's shareholding in Qantas.

April 1 JAT (Jugoslovenski Aerotransport) is established by the Yugoslavian government as the national airline.

April 4 The International Civil Aviation Organisation (ICAO) is established, with headquarters in Montreal, Canada.

April 15 BOAC begins a weekly Constellation service between London and Montreal, this being BOAC's first commercial operation to Canada.

May 1 Malayan Airways inaugurates its first scheduled service, over a route from Singapore to Penang. The airline is known now as the Malaysian Airline System (Sistem Penerbangan Malaysia Berhad), renamed in April 1971 after Singapore has left the Malaysian Federation.

May 7 Alitalia begins scheduled operations.

May 28 British South American Airways begins a series of nonstop flight refuelling trials over a route from London to Bermuda. These are flown by the Avro Lancaster G-AHJV, which is flight-refuelled by an Avro Lancaster tanker over the Azores.

First flight is made by the Douglas D-558-1 Skystreak research aircraft from Muroc Dry Lake, California. The Skystreak is to establish two world speed records, the first on August 20, 1947, flown by Cdr T.F. Caldwell, US Navy, at a speed of 1,030.95 km/h (640.60 mph). The second record is made five days later, by Maj M.E. Carl of the USMC, at a speed of 1,047.33 kmh (650.78 mph).

June 17 Pan American inaugurates a nearly-round-the-world service, flown the long way round from New York to San Francisco.

June 19 A new world speed record of 1,003.60 km/h (623.61 mph) is set by Col Albert Boyd flying a Lockheed P-80R Shooting Star at Muroc Dry Lake, California.

July 2 The first Mikoyan I-310 (Type 'S') jet fighter prototype makes its first flight. This fore-runner of the MiG-15 is believed lost in a flying accident, but a second prototype is more successful. (q.v. December 30, 1947)

July 3 The Philippine Air Force becomes re-established.

July 16 The Saunders-Roe SR.A/1, the world's first turbojet-powered flying-boat, makes its first flight. An experimental fighter, it is the first flying-boat to be flown at a speed in excess of 805 km/h (500 mph).

July 24 First flight of the Ilyushin Il-22, the first Soviet jet powered bomber. The design is unsuccessful and flight tests are terminated soon afterwards.

July 26 President Truman signs the United States Armed Forces Unification Act.

July 27 The Tupolev Tu-12, the first Soviet turbojet-powered bomber to gain production status, makes its first flight.

August 3 First public appearance during the Soviet Aviation Day parade of the Tupolev Tu-4 heavy bomber, a direct Soviet copy of the Boeing B-29 Superfortress. (q.v. July 29, 1944)

August 10 BEA inaugurates a scheduled all-cargo service. This is operated by Douglas DC-3s over a route from London to Prague via Brussels.

Saunders-Roe SR.A/1 turbojet-powered flying-boat fighter, July 16 1947.

**North American XP-86 Sabre fighter prototype,
October 1 1947.**

August 14   Following the partition of India the Royal
Pakistan Air Force is established on this date. It adopts its
present name Pakistan Air Force on March 23, 1956.

September 1-15   Under the title Operation Pakistan,
BOAC and three UK independent airlines carry out
population shuffles following the partition of India.

September 8   CP Air makes its first domestic flight, from
Vancouver to Penticton, but its first international route
is not inaugurated until July 13, 1949.

September 17   Aerlinte Eireann, which was formed in
1947 to operate the international services of Aer Lingus,
receives its first Lockheed Constellations.

September 18   Foundation date of the United States
Air Force, which becomes an independent service within
the new unified US armed services.

September 22   A USAF Douglas C-54 Skymaster
makes a fully-automatic flight from Stephenville, Newfoundland to the UK.

September 24   Formation date of Cyprus Airways,
founded by the government, BEA and private investors.

October 1   Los Angeles Airways inaugurates its first
scheduled helicopter airmail services, operated by
Sikorsky S-51s.

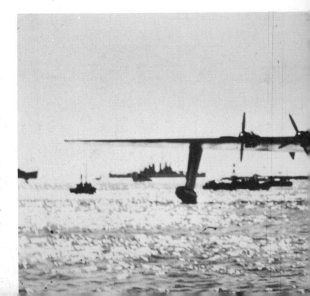

Capt Charles 'Chuck' Yeager climbs into the cockpit of the Bell X-1, October 14 1947.

A first flight is made by the North American XP-86 Sabre prototype (NA-140), which becomes the USAF's first sweptwing fighter.

October 11 The former Trans-Texas Airways begins scheduled operations, adopting its present title of Texas International Airlines during 1968.

October 14 Piloted by Capt Charles Yeager, the Bell X-1 rocket-powered research aircraft becomes the first in the world to exceed the speed of sound in level flight, attaining Mach 1.015 or 1,078 km/h (670 mph) at 12,800m (42,000ft).

October 20 A second population movement, involving some 35,000 people from Pakistan to India, is started by BOAC and seven independent carriers under the codename Operation India.

October 21 The first Northrop YB-49 flying-wing heavy bomber, powered by eight 1,814kg (4,000lb st) Allison J35-A-5 turbojets, makes its first flight.

November 1 BEA operates its last scheduled services from Croydon Airport, Surrey.

November 2 The eight-engined Hughes H-4 Hercules, the largest flying-boat ever built, makes its one and only flight over Los Angeles Harbor, covering a distance of about 1.6km (1 mile).

The giant Hughes H-4 Hercules eight-engined flying-boat at Los Angeles Harbor, November 2 1947.

Boeing XB-47 prototype jet bomber, December 17 1947.

December 1 Qantas operates its first through service from Sydney, NSW to London's Heathrow Airport, flown by the Lockheed Constellation *Charles Kingsford Smith* (VH-EAD).

December 9 Qantas inaugurates unscheduled services with Consolidated Catalina flying-boats between Sydney, NSW and Lord Howe Island.

December 10 Ceylon Airways inaugurates operations with a Douglas DC-3 service between Colombo and Madras via Jaffna.

December 16 Qantas takes over the RAAF's courier service between Australia and Japan, using Avro Lancastrians.

HM King George VI gives his approval for the RAF's Auxiliary Air Force to use the prefix 'Royal'.

December 17 On the 44th anniversary of the Wright brothers first flight, the prototype of the Boeing XB-47 sweptwing jet bomber (46-065) makes its first flight from Boeing Field, Seattle, to Moses Lake AFB.

December 30 First flight of the second Mikoyan Type 'S' fighter prototype powered by an imported Rolls-Royce Nene 2 turbojet. After successfully passing its State Acceptance tests the fighter is assigned the designation MiG-15, its entry into service giving the Soviet Air Force an early performance lead in turbojet-powered fighters.

1948

January 1 Piedmont Airlines becomes established, inaugurating its first revenue flight operations on February 20, 1948.

January 23 The first flight of the de Havilland Australia DHA-3 Drover light commercial transport prototype (VH-DHA) is made at Bankstown, Sydney.

January 29/30 The Avro Tudor 4 *Star Tiger* (G-AHNP) of BSAA is lost inexplicably on a flight from Santa Maria, Azores to Bermuda.

Loading mail onto a BEA Westland Sikorsky S-51 helicopter, June 1 1948.

January 30 The death is announced of Orville Wright, at Dayton, Ohio at the age of 76.

February 2 The original Luxair (Société Luxembourgeoise de Navigation Aérienne SA) flies its first scheduled service.

February 4 The USAF Military Air Transport Service (MATS) is established.

February 15 A first flight is made by the Curtiss XF-87 Blackhawk prototype, a high-altitude all-weather turbojet-powered fighter.

February 18 The Spanish airline Aviaco (Aviación y Comercio SA) is established to operate all-cargo services, but turns to scheduled passenger operations during 1950.

March 8 Air-India, which derived from Tata Airlines, become renamed Air-India International with the inauguration of international services. The word International is dropped from its title on June 8, 1962.

March 23 A new world altitude record of 18,119m (59,445ft) is set by John Cunningham flying a de Havilland Vampire I from Hatfield, Hertfordshire.

March 24 The UK Minister of Civil Aviation states that the Tudor 4 will not be operated over the Azores-Bermuda route pending fuel/range trials.

April 1 Railway passenger traffic between Berlin and West Germany is cancelled by the Soviet military authorities.

April 3 Alitalia operates its first post-war service to the UK with the inauguration of its Rome-London route.

April 5 Growing transatlantic passenger traffic is highlighted by a BOAC announcement that its Lockheed Constellations have made 1,000 North Atlantic crossings.

April 14 The official opening of the Southampton, Hampshire flying-boat terminal by the UK Minister of Aviation shows that, so far as the UK is concerned, the age of the flying-boat has not passed.

April 25 The YP-86A prototype of the North American F-86 Sabre is flown at a speed in excess of Mach 1, making it the first turbojet-powered aircraft to attain such a speed.

May 20 The Israeli air force is in action against Arab forces for the first time.

May 23 The USAF announces the activation of a new wind tunnel at Aberdeen, Maryland, with a test section

RAF Avro York C.1s unload supplies during the Berlin Airlift, June 28 1948.

having a continuous capability of 4,828 km/h (3,000 mph).

May 27 It is announced in the UK that the government had awarded a £100,000 tax-free payment to Air Cdre Frank Whittle for his pioneering work on aircraft turbojet engines.

The Air Force of the Israeli Defence Forces becomes named Chel Ha'Avir, instead of Sherut Avir (Air Service) under which it had been formed during 1947. It adopts its current title of Heyl Ha'Avir during 1951.

June 1 BEA begins the first helicopter public airmail service in the UK, operated by Westland/Sikorsky S-51s from Peterborough, Cambridgeshire to points in East Anglia.

June 8 Air-India International inaugurates a weekly Bombay-London service, the first being flown by Lockheed Constellation *Malabar Princess* (VT-CQP).

June 18/19 All road traffic between Berlin and West Germany is stopped by the Soviet military authorities at midnight.

June 24 Due to so-called 'technical reasons', all rail services between Berlin and West Germany are terminated by the Soviet military authorities.

June 26 A first airlift of supplies into Berlin is organised by the USAF, using C-47s based near Frankfurt, marking the beginning of the Berlin Airlift.

June 28 A first British and international Class G helicopter record is established by Sqdn Ldr Basil H. Arkell, flying the Fairey Gyrodyne G-AIKF at an average speed of 200.06 km/h (124.31 mph).

British air operations in connection with the Berlin Airlift begin.

July 1 Trans-Canada Air Lines begins the unsurcharged carriage of first class mail by air (1oz or under).

July 14 Silver City Airways makes its first car ferry flight between Lympne, Kent and Le Touquet, France. The initial service is operated by the Bristol 170 Freighter G-AGVC.

July 16 First flight of the Vickers Viscount prototype (G-AHRF) is made at Wisley, Surrey. On its entry into service it becomes the world's first turboprop-powered civil transport.

July 20 A first west-east crossing of the North Atlantic by turbojet-powered aircraft is recorded by 16 Lockheed F-80 (formerly P-80) Shooting Star fighters. They complete a flight from Selfridge Field, Michigan to Scotland.

July 23 The USAF's Military Air Transport Service is ordered to establish an Airlift task force for, if necessary, the long-term sustenance of Berlin.

July 25 A Vickers Viking (G-AJPH) which is being used as a testbed aircraft powered by two Rolls-Royce Nene turbojets, is flown London-Paris and return.

August 4 British independent civil operators become involved in the Berlin Airlift.

August 16 First flight of the Northrop XF-89 Scorpion prototype at Edwards AFB, California. When the type enters service during 1950 it becomes the USAF's first all-weather turbojet-powered interceptor.

August 21 Douglas C-54 Skymasters of the USAF's MATS begin operations on the Berlin Airlift.

August 23 A first free flight is made by the McDonnell XF-85 Goblin prototype. It is intended to be used as a parasite escort fighter, carried by the giant Convair B-36, but subsequent analysis shows the concept to be of little worth.

September 1 First flight of the Swedish Saab J-29, which becomes the first European sweptwing jet fighter to enter operational service, in May 1951.

Prototype Vickers Viscount, July 16 1948.

Production Saab J-29s in operational service with the Swedish Air Force.

September 5 The US Navy's *Caroline Mars* flying-boat airlifts a record 28,390kg (62,262lb) of cargo (almost 28 tons), from its Patuxent River base to Cleveland, Ohio.

September 6 The de Havilland DH.108 research aircraft becomes the first British aircraft to exceed the speed of sound, recording more than Mach 1 in a dive.

September 14 Royal Australian Air Force crews join operations on the Berlin Airlift.

September 15 Flying an F-86A Sabre at Muroc Dry Lake, California, Maj R.L. Johnson, USAF, establishes a new world speed record of 1,079.61 km/h (670.84 mph).

September 18 The Consolidated-Vultee XF-92A delta-wing research aircraft makes its first flight. The leader of Germany's wartime delta-wing research programme, Dr Alexander Lippisch, collaborated in its design.

October 15 The RAF and USAF combine their efforts as an Airlift task force.

October 16 South African Air Force crews join operations on the Berlin Airlift.

October 20 First flight of the McDonnell XF-88 Voodoo prototype. Research and development accomplished by the two XF-88 prototypes contribute a great deal to the later successful F-101 which shared the name Voodoo.

November 3 Royal New Zealand Air Force crews join in the continuing Berlin Airlift.

November 15 El Al Israel Airlines is formed, beginning operations from Tel Aviv to Paris and Rome in mid-1949.

November 22 Growing concern about the sale of Rolls-Royce turbojet engines to the Soviet Union leads to questions being raised in the UK Parliament, a deal which had been approved by Stafford Cripps.

November 30 First commercial use of FIDO (fog dispersal system) at Blackbushe, Surrey to allow an urgent take-off by a Vickers Viking in thick fog.

December 8 A USAF Consolidated B-36 completes a 15,128km (9,400 mile) unrefuelled nonstop flight from Fort Worth, Texas to Hawaii and return.

December 17 The 45th anniversary of the first powered flight by the Wright brothers is celebrated by the return to the Smithsonian Institution of the original Wright Kitty Hawk, which had been on display in the United Kingdom for many years.

December 29   The US Defense Secretary announces that work has been initiated on 'an earth satellite vehicle program'.

1949

January 3   The USA introduces a Bill to speed guided missile research.

January 17   The unexplained loss of the Avro Tudor 4 *Star Ariel* (G-AGRE), on a flight between Bermuda and Jamaica, leads to the type being relegated to the freighter role.

February 4   The US CAA authorises the use of GCA (ground-controlled approach) radar as a primary landing aid in bad weather.

February 5   A Lockheed Constellation on domestic service establishes a civil transport coast-to-coast record of 6 hr 18 min, between Los Angeles, California and New York's La Guardia airport.

February 9   The USAF establishes a Department of Space Medicine at its School of Aviation Medicine, Randolph AFB, Texas.

February 14   BEA begins the first UK helicopter night airmail experiments, flown with Westland/Sikorsky S-51s.

McDonnell XF-85 Goblin experimental parasite fighter being released from a modified B-29 during trials in October 1948. (*New York Times*)

February 24   Termination of the Arab-Israeli war is confirmed by the signature of an armistice in Rhodes.

February 26 – March 2   The first non-stop round-the-world flight is made by the USAF's Boeing B-50 Superfortress *Lucky Lady II*, piloted by Capt James Gallagher. The aircraft is flight-refuelled four times during its 94 hr 1 min 37,742km (23,452 mile) flight.

March 4   The US Navy flying-boat *Caroline Mars* carries a record 269 passengers from San Diego, California to Alameda, Idaho.

March 7-8   William P. Odom makes a nonstop flight of 7,977km (4,957 miles) in a Beech Bonanza lightplane, between Hawaii and Teterboro, New Jersey.

March 25   The Bell XH-12 helicopter is flown at a speed of 215.4 km/h (133.9 mph) at Niagara Falls, New York.

March 30   A Bill is authorised in the USA for the establishment of a permanent radar defence network.

April 2   Trans-Australia Airlines takes over from Qantas responsibility for several services, including the Flying Doctor services operated from Charleville and Cloncurry.

April 4   The North Atlantic Treaty Organisation becomes established, following signature of the treaty by 12 nations at Washington. It becomes effective on August 24, 1949.

Martin Mars flying-boat *Marshall Mars*, **May 1949.**

April 16   Peak day of the Berlin Airlift: within 24 hours 1,398 sorties are made, carrying a total of 12,940 tons.

April 21   The French Leduc 0.10 ramjet-powered experimental aircraft makes its first powered flight. This follows launch from a 'motherplane', essential to create sufficient air velocity for the ramjet to operate.

An RAF Sunderland lands on the Yangtse River, taking a doctor and medical supplies to the British frigate HMS *Amethyst* following an attack on it by Chinese Communists.

April 26   Completion of a flight-refuelled world endurance record in the US, made by Bill Barris and Dick Reidel flying the Aeronca Chief lightplane *Sunkist Lady*. During flight, fuel and food is hauled up four times daily from a Geep speeding below. The Chief was kept airborne for 1,008 hr 1 min (one minute over six weeks).

May 1   The Air Arm, Hong Kong Defence Force becomes established with RAF assistance. Its current title of Royal Hong Kong Auxiliary Air Force is adopted during 1970.

May 12   The Soviet Union ends its blockade of Berlin, but the Allied airlift continues until September 30, 1949 (q.v.) in order to build up stocks in the city.

May 13 The English Electric Canberra prototype (VN-799) makes its first flight at Warton, Lancashire. It becomes the first jet bomber to be produced in the UK, and the first to serve with the RAF.

May 14 Aerolineas Argentinas is established to operate domestic and international routes.

May 18 The first New York helicopter station is established at Pier 41 East River.

May 19 The US Navy flying-boat *Marshall Mars*, flying from Alameda, Idaho to San Diego, California, carries a new record total of 301 passengers plus a crew of seven.

May 21 A Sikorsky S-52 helicopter establishes a new helicopter altitude record of 6,468m (21,220ft) over Stratford, Connecticut.

June 3 Pan American introduces Boeing Model 377 Stratocruisers on its North Atlantic services.

June 4 The Lockheed XF-90 prototype makes its first flight. In competition with the McDonnell XF-88 Voodoo it loses out to that aircraft in the form of the developed F-101 Voodoo.

June 6 Trans-Pacific Airlines is formed in Hawaii, adopting its current title of Aloha Airlines on February 11, 1959.

June 26 After one year of the Berlin Airlift, about 1.8 million tons of supplies have been airlifted into the city. Outsize items have included a steam roller and 3.5 ton girders.

July 13 Canadian Pacific Air Lines makes the inaugural flight of its new Vancouver-Sydney transpacific route, flown by Canadair Four *Empress of Sydney* (CF-CPI). It is the airline's first international service.

July 27 The de Havilland DH.106 Comet I prototype (G-ALVG) makes its first flight at Hatfield, Hertfordshire.

July 30 British South American Airways Corporation becomes merged into BOAC.

August 1 An SBAC (Society of British Aircraft Constructors) Challenge Cup race, open to jet-powered aircraft from any nation, is won by Sqdn Ldr T.S. Wade flying the Hawker private-venture P.1040 prototype (VP401). Won at an average speed of 821 km/h (510 mph), one lap was flown at 905.3 km/h (562.5 mph).

August 9 The first use in the US of an ejection seat for an emergency escape from an aircraft is recorded. It is made by Lt J.L. Fruin, US Navy, from a McDonnell F2H-1 Banshee flying in excess of 925 km/h (575 mph) near Walterboro, South Carolina.

September 4 The Avro 707 (VX 784) makes its first flight from Boscombe Down, Wiltshire. This first British delta-wing research aircraft has been built to test the wing configuration of the future Vulcan bomber.

The Bristol Brabazon I prototype (G-AGPW), the largest landplane ever constructed in Britain, makes its first flight.

de Havilland D.H.106 Comet I prototype at Hatfield, **July 27 1949. Note the single large wheels on the main landing gear legs.**

September 12 An Ilyushin Il-12 operated by ĈSA Czechoslovak Airlines lands at Northolt on the airline's Prague-London service. It is the first occasion that an Il-12 had been seen at any London airport.

September 19 First flight is made of the Fairey Gannett prototype (VR546), a carrier-based anti-submarine aircraft. It is the first in the world to be powered by a twin-turbine engine driving contra-rotating propellers via a co-axial shaft.

September 23 The Soviet Union detonates its first atomic bomb, and thus ends the US nuclear monopoly.

September 30 Allied aircraft end the Berlin Airlift. During the 15 months that it had been operated, almost 2.25 million tons of supplies and equipment had been flown into Berlin.

October 17 BEA begins the first night helicopter airmail service in the UK. Flown by Westland/Sikorsky S.51s between Peterborough, Cambridgeshire and Norwich, Norfolk, the service continues until mid-April 1950. (q.v. Feb 14 1949)

South African Airways Lockheed Constellation *Cape Town*, **May 8 1950.**

October 25 During development flying, a de Havilland DH.106 Comet I flies from London Heathrow to Castel Benito, Tripoli and return in the day.

November 7 First flight of the Sikorsky S-55 helicopter prototype at Stratford, Connecticut. It is the first helicopter to have the centre fuselage free from a power plant installation, mounting it instead in the fuselage nose to create increased cabin volume.

November 18 A C-74 Globemaster I of the USAF's MATS lands at Marham, Norfolk, after a nonstop flight from the US. It carries a total of 103 passengers and crew, which is then the largest number of people carried across the North Atlantic in a single flight.

1950
January 23 The USAF Research and Development Command is established.

February 1 The USAF's Continental Air Command is directed to establish a civil Air Raid Warning system.

March 22 The first four of 70 B-29 Superfortresses supplied to the RAF under the US Military Aid Program arrive in Britain. Operated under the name Washington, they first equip No. 149 Squadron at Marham, Norfolk.

April 12 L. Welch makes the first cross-Channel sailplane flight from London to Brussels.

April 16 BEA begins to operate from London's Heathrow Airport, its first service being a Viking flight on the London-Paris route.

April 18 The USAF announces the planned procurement of 1,250 new aircraft at a cost of $1,203 million.

April 24 A DH.106 Comet 1 establishes a new London-Cairo point-to-point record en route to Khartoum and Nairobi for tropical trials.

May 3 The new British aircraft carrier HMS *Ark Royal* is launched by HM Queen Elizabeth.

May 8 South African Airways receives its first Lockheed Constellation ZS-DBR *Cape Town.*

May 9-19 In connection with the British Industries Fair, Westland Helicopters (in conjunction with Rotor Stations Ltd) operates the UK's first scheduled helicopter passenger services. These are flown between London and Birmingham using a Westland/Sikorsky S-51.

May 17 The US airline Transcontinental & Western Air (TWA), which had been established during 1930, changes its name to Trans World Airlines (TWA) to reflect the worldwide operations of the company.

June 1 J. Robinson, in the US, becomes the first sailplane pilot to gain the coveted Diamond C award.

BEA inaugurates the world's first scheduled and sustained helicopter service. This is flown between Liverpool and Cardiff, operated by Westland/Sikorsky S-51s and continues until March 31, 1951.

Frontier Airlines is established. Now one of the largest regional airlines in the USA, the name is adopted following a merger of Arizona Airways and Challenger Airlines.

The USAF is authorised to organise a Ground Observer Corps.

June 19 First flight of the Hawker P.1081 single-seat sweptwing research aircraft (VX279). This is a conversion of the second of the earlier P.1052 prototypes.

June 25 The Korean War begins, with North Korean forces making a dawn crossing of the 38th Parallel borderline into South Korea.

June 27 – 28 The United Nations Security Council calls upon its member nations to assist South Korea in any way possible.

July 3 The first US jet fighter to be involved in air combat is a Grumman F9F-2 Panther of the US Navy. This is flown off the aircraft carrier USS *Valley Forge* to enter action against North Korean forces.

July 24 The first rocket is launched at the Cape Canaveral test range, this being a V2 first stage with a WAC Corporal as its second stage.

July 27 Having regard to the situation in Korea, a large-scale expansion of the USAF is announced.

July 28 The world's first certificate of airworthiness for a turbine powered civil airliner is awarded to the Vickers V630 Viscount.

July 29 The Vickers V630 Viscount G-AHRF is used by BEA to inaugurate the world's first scheduled service to be flown by a turboprop-powered airliner. The type is introduced for a short period on the airline's London-Paris service.

August 3 BEA orders 20 Vickers Type 701 Viscounts, a figure increased later to 26.

August 15 Using the V630 Viscount which has been operating the London-Paris route, BEA provides a London-Edinburgh service for just over a week. This is the first UK domestic service to be flown by a gas-turbine powered airliner.

August 22 It is announced that RAF Sunderlands are involved in 'blockade' operations off the west coast of Korea.

August 25-27 Under the codename Cupola, NATO holds its first large-scale air exercise in Europe.

The use of helicopters for casualty evacuation greatly reduced the death toll during the Korean War. Here a Sikorsky HO5S is loaded with a wounded US Marine.

August 30 Following the lead set by the USAF, and by France on August 6, the UK government announces plans to strengthen its defence forces.

September 22 Col David C. Schilling, USAF, lands at Limestone, Maine after a non-stop flight from the UK in a Republic EF-84E Thunderjet fighter. Two of these aircraft had been converted by Flight Refuelling Ltd for refuelling by their probe and drogue system which is being adopted by Tactical Air Command. It is by using this system for three in-flight refuellings that the Thunderjet records the first non-stop crossing of the North Atlantic by a turbojet-powered fighter aircraft.

September 25 Pan American acquires the assets of American Overseas Airlines.

September 29 At Holloman AFB, New Mexico, Capt Richard V. Wheeler makes a parachute jump from a height of 12,938m (42,449ft).

October 1 The Danish air arm becomes re-established as the Royal Danish Air Force (Kongelige Danske Flyveväbnet).

October 10 Formation of the Royal Ceylon Air Force with British aid. Following formation of the Republic in 1971, this becomes renamed as the Sri Lanka Air Force.

October 20 A parachute drop is made at Suchon, Korea by some 3,000 paratroops of the US 11th Airborne Division.

November 7 Replacing Solent flying-boats with Handley Page Hermes aircraft on its UK-Johannesburg service, BOAC brings to an end the flying-boat services that had been operated by the airline and its predecessors for some 26 years.

November 8 The first victory to be scored in the first all-jet combat is by Lt Russell J. Brown Jr. USAF 51st Fighter-Interceptor Wing, flying a Lockheed F-80C. His victim is a Mikoyan MiG-15 jet fighter of the Chinese People's Republic Air Force.

November 9 In the first encounter between US Navy jet fighters and MiG-15s, Lt Cdr W.T. Amen flying a Grumman F9F-2 Panther becomes the first USN pilot to destroy another jet fighter in combat.

December 9 It is announced that Gloster Meteor 8s are to be acquired by the RAAF. This force eventually uses some 90 of the type in Korea.

December 16 In the USA, President Truman proclaims a state of national emergency. This is essential to allow for action in coping with the war in Korea, and the President also announces plans to double the strength of the armed forces.

December 17 North American F-86A Sabres go into action in Korea with the 4th Fighter-Interceptor Wing.

In their first day of combat operations four MiG-15s are claimed as destroyed.

1951

January 1 Reinforced by some 400,000 Chinese troops, the North Koreans begin a new major advance into South Korea.

February 5 The USA and Canada announce jointly the intention to set up a DEW (distant early-warning) system for North America.

February 21 In flying from Aldergrove, Northern Ireland to Gander, Newfoundland, an English Electric Canberra B.Mk 2 becomes the first jet aircraft to fly the North Atlantic non-stop and unrefuelled. The distance of 3,335km (2,072 miles) is flown in 4 hr 37 min.

February 23 The French Dassault MD.452 Mystère sweptwing jet fighter prototype makes its first flight.

March 6 The USAF gives approval for licence production by The Glenn L. Martin Company of the English Electric Canberra under the designation B-57. It is then the only operational aircraft of non-US design to be accepted for service with the USAF following the end of the Second World War.

March 12 The first flight is made at Boscombe Down, Wiltshire, of the Fairey F.D.1 delta-wing research aircraft.

US Air Force ground crew give a captured Mikoyan-Gurevich MiG-15 fighter a final check before it is flown by US pilots.

Bell X-5 research aircraft with its wings at full sweep, June 20 1951.

March 13 Qantas Catalina *Frigate Bird II* (VH-ASA) begins a survey flight from Rose Bay, Sydney to Valparaiso, Chile, via Easter Island. This is the airline's first flight across the South Pacific.

April 18 An Aerobee research rocket, carrying a monkey in a special capsule for a space biology experiment, is launched from Holloman AFB, New Mexico.

May 18 First flight of the Vickers Valiant prototype (WB210). The type is to become the first of the RAF's V-bombers to enter service.

May 20 Capt James Jabara, an F-86 Sabre pilot of the USAF's 4th Fighter-Interceptor Wing in Korea, becomes the first jet pilot to score five confirmed victories over jet aircraft, destroying his 5th and 6th MiG-15s on this date.

May 25 The Pakistan government orders three Lockheed Super Constellations for the then non-existent Pakistan International Airways.

May 29 The first solo trans-Polar flight is made by American C. Blair, flying a North American P-51 Mustang from Bardufoss, Norway to Fairbanks, Alaska.

June 1 Official opening of BEA's London Airport to Birmingham helicopter service, flown by Westland/Sikorsky S-51s. The first public services are flown on June 4.

June 20 First flight of the first of two Bell X-5 research aircraft. Based on the Messerschmitt P.1101, they are intended to investigate variable wing sweepback.

July 20 The first flight of the first of three Hawker Hunter prototypes (WB188) is made from Boscombe Down, Wiltshire.

August 1 Canada and the US ratify an agreement that is intended to lead to the development and construction of an early warning defence system for the two nations.

August 5 The prototype of the Supermarine Swift single-seat interceptor fighter (WJ960) makes its first flight. It later becomes the first sweptwing jet fighter to enter service with the RAF.

August 15 Two of BEA's DC-3s are given Rolls-Royce Dart turboprop power plant for engine development flying. They are used by BEA on cargo services between Northolt, Middlesex and Hanover, Germany, and the service which starts on this date is the first cargo service to be flown by turboprop-powered aircraft.

August 22 The Supermarine Attacker enters service with the FAA's No 800 Squadron at Ford, Sussex. It is the first jet fighter to be standardised in the FAA's first-line squadrons.

September 20 Greece and Turkey become members of NATO.

The elegant Hawker Hunter prototype, July 20 1951.

The USAF makes a first successful recovery of animals which have been launched into space by a research rocket. The payload of a monkey and 11 mice is recovered with no apparent ill-effects.

September 26 A first flight is made by the de Havilland DH.110 Sea Vixen prototype (WG236).

October 3 Squadron HS-1, the US Navy's first ASW helicopter squadron, is commissioned at Key West, Florida Keys.

November 26 First flight of the first of three Gloster Javelin prototypes (WD804). When the type enters service with the RAF in early 1956 it is the RAF's and the world's first twin-jet delta-winged fighter. It is also the first RAF fighter designed specifically for all-weather operations.

December 5 It is announced that agreement has been reached by 11 airlines to introduce Tourist Class service on the North Atlantic route.

1952

January 3 First flight of the Bristol Type 173 prototype (G-ALBN) at Filton, near Bristol. This is the first twin-rotor twin-engined helicopter to be designed and flown in Britain.

January 5 Pan American inaugurates its first transatlantic all-cargo service, this being operated by Douglas DC-6s.

January 13 The first Lockheed Neptunes allocated to the RAF under the US Military Assistance Program are received at St.Eval, Cornwall. Equivalent to the US Navy's P2V-5, they are designated Neptune MR.1 by the RAF and are used initially to equip No. 217 Squadron.

January 22 The de Havilland Comet 1 gains the first certificate of airworthiness to be awarded to a turbojet-powered airliner.

April 15 First flight of the Boeing YB-52 prototype (49-231), which does not enter service with the USAF until late 1957. A strategic heavy bomber, it is designed to carry nuclear weapons to any target in the world.

May 2 The de Havilland DH.106 Comet 1 (G-ALYP) flies BOAC's inaugural jet service between London-Johannesburg. This is the world's first regular scheduled airline service to be operated by a turbojet-powered aircraft.

June 17 The US Navy takes delivery at Lakehurst, New Jersey, of the world's largest non-rigid airship. Designated ZPN-1, it has an overall length of 98.76m (324ft) and a maximum diameter of 10.67m (35ft).

July 1 The Portuguese Arma da Aeronáutica and Aviacão Maritima are united to form the current Portuguese Air Force – the Fôrça Aérea Portuguesa.

July 3 BOAC begins Comet 1 proving flights on its London-Tokyo route.

July 13-31 Two Sikorsky S-55 helicopters, flown in stages, achieve the first west-east crossing of the North Atlantic by helicopters.

July 19 The USAF announces that for periods of over three days it has successfully flown free balloons at controlled constant altitudes in the stratosphere.

July 29 The first non-stop transpacific flight by a jet aircraft is completed by a North American RB-45, a reconnaissance version of the B-45 Tornado light tactical bomber. This is flown from Elmendorf AFB, Alaska to Yokota AB, Japan.

August 11 BOAC inaugurates a weekly London-Colombo service with Comet 1s.

August 13 The USAF announces that the Boeing B-52 has been ordered into full-scale production.

December 12 A first flight is made by the de Havilland Canada DHC-3 Otter prototype.

December 15 Air France and BEA state the intention to introduce Tourist Class services on the London-Paris route.

December 17 The USAF claims that during the previous twelve months its No. 4 Fighter-Interceptor Wing in Korea, operating with F-86 Sabres, had destroyed 130 MiG-15s.

August 16   The Bristol Britannia prototype (G-ALBO) makes its first flight at Filton, near Bristol.

August 20   The first Saunders-Roe S.R. 45 Princess flying-boat (G-ALUN) is launched at Cowes, Isle of Wight. It flies two days later.

August 30   The Avro Vulcan B.1 prototype (VX770) makes its first flight. This large delta-wing long-range bomber is the second of the RAF's V-bombers.

September 30   A Bell GAM-63 Rascal air-to-surface missile is launched for the first time.

October 3   The first British atomic bomb is detonated over the Monte Bello Islands, off northwestern Australia.

October 14   BOAC introduces Comet 1s on its London-Singapore route, reducing the scheduled time by more than 50 per cent.

October 16   A first flight is made by the French Sud-Ouest SO 4050 Vautour prototype, which has been built in the Vautour N two-seat all-weather fighter configuration.

October 26   A first shadow on the de Havilland Comet's horizon occurs when BOAC's G-ALYZ is damaged severely in a take-off accident at Rome. A similar accident to a Canadian Pacific Comet during March 1953 gives proof that if the nose is held a little too high on take-off the aircraft cannot attain flying speed. Remedial action includes the installation of drooped wing leading-edges.

October 28   First flight of the Douglas XA3D-1 Skywarrior carrier-based attack-bomber prototype. When the A3Ds begin to enter service, in March 1956, they are the heaviest aeroplanes to be used as standardised equipment aboard aircraft carriers.

November 3   The first flight is made by the Saab-32 Lansen two-seat all-weather attack fighter, powered by a Rolls-Royce Avon turbojet. Production aircraft have a Svenska-Flygmotor licence-built version of the Avon with reheat.

November 19   SAS (Scandinavian Airlines System) make the first unscheduled commercial airline flights over the polar regions between Europe and North America. These are flown by Douglas DC-6Bs, but it is not until 1954 that the airline operates scheduled commercial flights over this route.

December 16   The USAF Tactical Air Force Command activates its first helicopter squadron.

December 24   The Handley Page Victor prototype (WB771) makes its first flight. This is the third and last of the long-range medium bombers for the RAF's V-bomber programme.

1953

January 3   BEA takes delivery of the first of its Vickers V.701 Viscount turboprop airliners (G-ALWE).

January 6   Luftag is formed as a German airline, following the closure of Luft Hansa after the end of the

Saunders-Roe Princess, August 20 1952.

Sud-Ouest SO 9000 Trident mixed power research aircraft, March 2 1953.

war. In the following year (1954) it becomes Deutsche Lufthansa.

January 12   The US Navy begins operational flight tests with its first angled-deck carrier, the *USS Antietam* .

February 4-11   After exceptional sea and storm conditions have caused severe flooding in the Netherlands, BEA helicopters become involved in rescue and relief operations.

March 2   The Sud-Ouest SO 9000 Trident mixed power plant research aircraft makes its first flight. This is accomplished on the power of two Turboméca Marboré turbojets mounted at the wingtips. It is not until 1955 that it is flown on the power of the rocket engine mounted in the aft fuselage.

March 20 A first flight is made by the first of the ZP2N-1 production N class non-rigid airships for the US Navy, which are designed for mid-ocean anti-submarine warfare.

March 27 The Royal Netherlands Air Force is established as an independent service, with equal status to the Netherlands Army and Royal Navy.

April 3 BOAC begins to operate a weekly London-Tokyo service with its DH.106 Comet 1s.

April 9 A first flight is made by the Convair F2Y-1 Sea Dart experimental twin-jet delta-wing seaplane fighter. This uses retractable hydro-skis to take off from and land on water.

April 18 BEA begins the world's first sustained passenger service to be operated by turboprop-powered airliners. This is the airline's London-Nicosia route, the first scheduled flight being made by Viscount V.701 *Sir Ernest Shackleton* (G-AMNY).

May 2 On the first anniversary of the inauguration of Comet operations a BOAC Comet 1 (G-ALYV) suffers structural failure and crashes near Calcutta with the loss of 43 lives.

May 4 A new world altitude record is established by W.F. Gibb, flying an English Electric Canberra to a height of 19,406m (63,668ft).

May 15 Pacific Western Airlines, which started operations in 1945 as Central British Columbia Airways, adopts this, its current title, following the acquisition of a number of smaller operators.

May 18 The first flight of the Douglas DC-7 piston-engined transport is made. In its DC-7C long-range version the type is remembered as one of the last of the piston-engined airliners at the peak of their development.

May 19 American airwoman Jacqueline Cochran pilots a Canadian-built version of the North American

Convair GRB-36F acting as 'motherplane' to a Republic GRF-84F Thunderflash strategic reconnaissance aircraft, August 25 1953.

a USAF C-124 Globemaster II which crashes after engine failure on take-off from Tachikawa AFB, Tokyo, killing 129 persons.

July 1 Civil air traffic control in West Germany is handed over by the Western Allies to the Federal German Government.

July 7 The first international helicopter flight into central London is made by a Sikorsky S-55 operated by Sabena. This is flown from the Allée Verte Heliport at Brussels, landing at the South Bank Heliport, Waterloo.

July 13 BEA introduces a helicopter all-cargo service between London Airport and Birmingham, flown by Bristol Type 171s.

July 16 Lt Col W.F. Barnes, USAF, flying a North American F-86D Sabre, sets the world's first 'more-than 700 mph' speed record, the FAI-ratified record being at 1151.64 km/h (715.60 mph).

July 17 Lt Guy Bordelon, flying a piston-engined Vought F4U Corsair, becomes the first US Navy pilot involved in the Korean War to score five confirmed victories.

July 27 After just over three years of fighting, the Korean War terminates with the signature of Armistice terms.

August 1 Indian Airlines is formed from eight private airlines following a government decision to nationalise air transport in India.

August 23 The Martin licence-built B-57 Canberra completes its final tests before entering service with the USAF.

August 25 Following successful tests carried out during May 1953, the USAF announces that the Convair B-36 bomber, in a GRB-36F configuration, is able to launch and retrieve Republic GRF-84F Thunderflash reconnaissance aircraft from an under-fuselage trapeze. About 12 of these bombers are converted to the GRB-36F configuration, enabling them also to launch and control missiles in support of development programmes.

August 27 The first flight of the first production de Havilland Comet 2 (G-AMXA) is made at Hatfield, Hertfordshire.

September 1 The Belgian airline Sabena inaugurates the first scheduled international helicopter services, flown from Brussels to link with Maastricht and Rotterdam in the Netherlands, and Lille in France.

September 7 Flying a Hawker Hunter 3, Sqn Ldr Neville Duke, RAF, establishes a new world speed record off Littlehampton, West Sussex of 1,170.76 km/h (727.48 mph).

F-86 Sabre at a speed of Mach 1.01, becoming the first woman in the world to fly faster than the speed of sound.

May 21 Dan-Air (Dan-Air Services) is founded in the UK, originally as a charter operator. The airline's first scheduled service is inaugurated in June 1955.

May 25 The first North American YF-100A Super Sabre prototype makes its first flight. It has a significant place in world aviation history as the first combat aircraft capable of sustained supersonic performance in level flight.

June 14 A first flight is made by the true Blackburn Beverley prototype (WZ889), powered by Bristol Centaurus 173 engines. It is the first British transport designed specifically to airdrop heavy loads and, when it enters service with the RAF in March 1956, it is then that service's largest aircraft.

June 18 The world's first air disaster involving the death of more than 100 persons occurs. This is suffered by

September 11 The USAF announces that the Sidewinder air-to-air missile has made its first completely successful interception, destroying the Grumman F6F Hellcat drone that was its target.

October 1 Japan Air Lines becomes reorganised and adopts this, its current title.

October 3 Lt Cdr J.B. Verdin, USN, flying a Douglas F4D-1 Skyray at Salton Sea, California sets a new world speed record of 1,211.48 km/h (752.78 mph).

October 12 The US signs an agreement in Athens allowing the US armed forces to make conditional use of Greek air and naval bases.

October 24 A first flight is made by the Convair YF-102A Delta Dagger prototype from Edwards AFB, California. When it enters service in April 1956, initially with the 327th Fighter Interceptor Squadron, it is the USAF's first delta-wing aircraft.

November 29 The Douglas DC-7 enters scheduled airline service in the USA with American Airlines.

December 4 The Uruguayan Air Force, which has been established originally as the Escuela Militar de Aeronautica during 1916, adopts its current title Fuerza Aérea Uruguaya.

December 12 Capt Charles Yeager flies the air-launched Bell X-1A rocket-powered high-speed research aircraft at a speed of Mach 2.435, or approximately 2,655 km/h (1,650 mph), at an altitude of 21,340m (70,000ft).

December 18 The US Navy/Marine Corps XHR2S-1 prototype helicopter (Sikorsky S-56) makes its first flight. Entering service with the US Navy/Marine Corps in 1956 as the HR2S-1, and with the US Army in the same year as the H-37 Mojave, its remains the largest helicopter in use by the US armed forces for some five years.

December 29 ICAO announces that for the first time the world's airlines have carried more than 50 million passengers during the preceding 12 months.

1954

January 1 The US Navy establishes an Air Weapons School at Jacksonville, Florida

January 10 The BOAC Comet 1 G-ALYP, en route from the Far East to London, breaks up in the air. The wreckage falls into the Mediterranean about 16km (10 miles) south of Elba, but none of the 35 persons on board survive.

Immediately the news of the Comet accident is received, BOAC grounds its Comet fleet for the completion of airworthiness checks.

February 25 A first flight is made by the Convair R3Y-1 Tradewind long-range flying-boat transport, which proves to be the only turboprop-powered flying-boat to serve with the US Navy. A prototype XP5Y-1 had flown first on April 18, 1950, but as it did not meet requirements it was adapted instead for transport use.

February 28 A first flight is recorded by the first prototype Lockheed XF-104 Starfighter air superiority fighter. When it enters service in early 1958 its Mach 2 performance and wing span of just under 6.71m (22ft) causes the Press to refer to it as the 'missile with a man in it'.

March 1 The USA control ban on the production of Japanese military aircraft comes to an end.

March 8 The United States and Japan sign a mutual defence agreement, Japan gaining US subsidies of some $100 million.

March 17 BOAC announces that 20 new Comet 4s have been ordered from de Havilland; these will allow the carriage of full payload over the North Atlantic route.

March 20 The de Havilland Sea Venom enters service with No. 890 Squadron which re-formed at Yeovilton, Somerset on this date.

March 23 After inspection reveals no apparent fault in BOAC's Comet fleet they are returned to service.

April 1 An RAF photo-reconnaissance Spitfire makes the last operational sortie of the type while on duty in Malaya.

April 8 BOAC's Comet 1 G-ALYY breaks up and falls into the sea south of Naples with the loss of its passengers and crew. The type is immediately withdrawn from service and subsequent investigation reveals metal fatigue problems adjacent to windows in the pressurised structure, causing an explosive decompression.

May 1 The USAF forms an Early Warning and Control Division, using specially-equipped RC-121C and RC-121D (later EC-121C/D) aircraft for radar surveillance.

May 7 Following prior consultation with France and the UK, the US turn down an application from the Soviet Union to become a member nation of NATO.

May 25 A US Navy ZPG-2 airship flown by Cmdr M.H. Eppes and crew lands at Key West, Florida, after being airborne for just over 200 hours.

June 3 Capital Airlines in America announces an order for three Vickers Viscounts, with options on 37. The option is later converted to a firm order and delivery effected, this being seen by the UK industry as an important break into the US commercial airliner market.

June 7 Pakistan International Airlines (PIA) begins international operations, its services being operated by a fleet of three new Lockheed L.1049C Super Constellations.

July 1 Following Japanese-US agreement on the formation of defence forces for Japan, the three air arms

Two Bristol Britannia prototypes, G-ALBO in background and G-ALRX foreground. G-ALBO first flown on August 16 1952 but G-ALRX was lost on February 4 1954.

Boeing Model 367-80, July 15 1954.

become established officially with US aid. They comprise and are still known as the Japan Air Self-Defence Force (Koku Jiei-tai), Japan Maritime Self-Defence Force (Kaijoh Jiei-tai) and the Japan Ground Self-Defence Force (Rikujye Jiei-tai).

July 15   The Boeing Model 367-80 turbojet-powered prototype of a flight refuelling tanker/transport for the USAF makes its first flight. It is to be built extensively for the USAF as the C-135/KC-135, and to be developed as the Boeing Model 707 civil transport.

August 2   A first free flight, comprising a vertical take-off and landing, is made by the Convair XFY-1 experimental VTOL fighter.

A first free flight is made by the Rolls-Royce test rig that is built to evaluate the potential of jet lift for vertical take-off and the means of controlling such a vehicle in flight. It is dubbed the 'Flying Bedstead' by the Press.

August 3   The second prototype of the Convair XF2Y-1 Sea Dart exceeds a speed of Mach 1 in a shallow dive, thus becoming the first water-based aircraft in the world to exceed the speed of sound.

August 4   A first flight is made by the first English Electric P.I.A. prototype (WG760), later to become known as the Lightning. When production aircraft enter service in December 1959, the Lightning is the RAF's first true supersonic fighter, able to exceed the speed of sound in level flight.

August 26   A height of about 27,430m (90,000ft), then the greatest height attained by a piloted aircraft, is set by the Bell X-1A research aircraft over the Mojave Desert.

September 1   Finnair inaugurates a Helsinki-London service, which it operates with Convair CV-340s.

The USAF Continental Air Defense Command is established, with its headquarters at Colorado Springs, Colorado.

September 29   The first flight of a McDonnell F-101A Voodoo is made at Edwards AFB, California. This supersonic single-seat fighter has been developed for the USAF from the company's XF-88 Voodoo (q.v. October 20, 1948).

October 6   A first flight is made by the Fairey Delta 2 research aircraft, designed to investigate the characteristics of flight and control at transonic and supersonic speeds.

October 17   The Sikorsky XH-39 helicopter sets a new world altitude record for rotary-wing aircraft of 7,468m (24,500ft).

October 23   The Western nations agree to terminate occupation of West Germany and to fully incorporate the German Federal Republic into NATO.

November 1   The USAF retires all of its Boeing B-29 Superfortresses that are serving in a bomber capacity.

November 2   First flight of the Convair XFY-1 experimental fighter is made, during which transitions from vertical to horizontal flight and vice-versa are accomplished (q.v. August 2, 1954).

November 11 Fairey Aviation announces that its Delta 2 research aircraft has exceeded a speed of Mach 1 in a climb.

November 25 Malév (Magyar Légiközlekedesi Vállalat) becomes established as the Hungarian state airline. This follows acquisition by the Hungarian government of the Soviet Union's holding in the original Maszovlet airline, which had been formed with Soviet assistance in March 1946.

December 6 The Curtiss-Wright Corporation in the US announces the development of a new rocket engine. Using liquid fuel, its power can be controlled by a throttle, thus promising more extended range for supersonic vehicles powered by such an engine.

December 20 The US Defense Secretary states that, with the exception of the USAF, the strength of its armed forces is to be reduced. The USAF, however, is to be increased in size.

1955

January 20 An agreement is reached between France, the USA and South Vietnam to reorganise the military forces of this latter country.

February 26 Ejecting from a North American F-100 Super Sabre after the controls had jammed, the com-

pany's test pilot George F. Smith becomes the first man in the world to live after ejection from an aircraft travelling at supersonic speed, in this case Mach 1.05.

March 1 A second USAF Early Warning and Control Wing becomes operational with Lockheed RC-121s, formed at Otis AFB, Falmouth, Massachusetts.

March 2 The Boeing Airplane Company receives its first major production contract for the KC-135 Stratotanker.

March 4 BEA flies its first Heron-operated charter ambulance flight.

March 11 Pakistan International Airlines, which had begun international operations on June 7, 1954, absorbs the fleet and routes of Orient Airways, the latter which had been founded on October 23, 1946.

March 25 The first flight is made by the first of two Ling-Temco-Vought (LTV) XF8U-1 Crusader prototypes. The last fighter designed by the Chance Vought company before becoming a component of the LTV organisation, this carrier-based fighter has an unusual variable-incidence wing.

April 1 Lufthansa, the re-established German airline, flies its first domestic service from Hamburg.

Convair XF2Y-1 Sea Dart with a single hydro-ski fitted.

April 3 A new air traffic control centre for southern England becomes operational at London's Heathrow Airport.

April 15 A Convair CV-340 makes the first post-war landing in the UK by a German-operated civil airliner. This is Lufthansa's D-ACAD on a Hamburg-London proving flight.

April 17 London (Heathrow) Airport Central becomes operational, the first departure made by a BEA Viscount.

April 20 The McDonnell XV-1 experimental con- vertiplane makes its first successful transition from vertical to horizontal flight. This research aircraft combines a three-blade main rotor driven by tipjets, a piston-engine driving a pusher propeller, conventional wings and a twin-boom tail unit.

April 26 The UK Ministry of Transport exempts from registration all sailplanes flown within British airspace.

May 5 The Canadian and US government sign agreements to initiate construction of the DEW line radar early-warning system in Northern Canada.

May 16 Germany's newly-formed Lufthansa begins European international (as opposed to domestic) airline operations.

May 27 The first of two Sud-Est Aviation SE.210 Caravelle prototypes makes its first flight. The Caravelle is the first multi-engined monoplane airliner to preserve a clean wing, uncluttered by engine installations, its two Rolls-Royce Avon turbojets mounted in pods, one on each side of the rear fuselage.

June 2 An agreement is signed under which the US undertakes to provide assistance to the Italian Fiat company in the manufacture and development of three G-91 light jet fighter prototypes. Subject to satisfactory test and evaluation, production aircraft are intended for use by NATO air forces.

June 3-4 Canadian Pacific Air Lines inaugurates a Polar route, linking Sydney, Australia with Amsterdam, Netherlands via Vancouver. The first service is flown by Douglas DC-6B *Empress of Amsterdam* (CF-CUR).

June 7 The Douglas Aircraft Company announces plans to build a new civil transport designated DC-8. It is to become the company's first turbojet-powered airliner.

June 8 Lufthansa begins the operation of scheduled services across the North Atlantic, using a Lockheed L 1049G Super Constellation.

June 9 Lockheed Aircraft Corporation announces an intention to proceed with the development of a new short/medium-range transport under the designation L-188 Electra. Following the company's experience with testing of the C-130 Hercules, turboprop power plant is chosen for the new aircraft.

June 15 The first Tupolev Tu-104 prototype (SSSR-L5400), a turbojet-powered civil transport, makes its maiden flight. The first jet airliner to be flown by Aeroflot, its entry into service from September 1956 completely revolutionises many of the airline's routes.

June 29 The Boeing B-52 Stratofortress enters service with the USAF, initially with the 93rd Bomber Wing at Castle AFB, California.

July 10 The UK government announces measures designed to reduce the annoyance and damage from supersonic 'booms' being caused by aircraft.

July 13 The USAF gives authorisation to The Boeing Airplane Company to proceed with the development and production, in the government-owned plant at Renton, Washington, of a civil transport version of the KC-135 tanker/transport. This new airliner is to become known as the Boeing Model 707.

July 22 A civil aviation agreement is concluded between the governments of the Federal Republic of Germany and the UK.

July 26 Egypt's President Nasser announces that the international company controlling the Suez Canal is to be terminated and the operation of the Canal national- ised. This follows US withdrawal from a plan to help finance construction of the Aswan dam, Nasser intending that revenue from the Canal should finance building of the dam.

July 29 The US President's Press Secretary announces that it is the intention of the US to launch a small earth satellite during the International Geophysical Year (IGY) from July 1957.

July 31 Greek shipowner Aristotle Onassis signs an agreement with the government giving him the rights to acquire the assets of Greek Airlines TAE. The airline which he forms is named Olympic Airways in 1957. Since January 1, 1975, the company has been operated by the Greek government.

August 1 The US begins its first zero-gravity research experiments, using Lockheed T-33 trainers to study the effects of weightlessness.

August 20 Flying a North American F-100C Super Sabre from Edwards AFB, California Col H.A. Hanes sets a new world speed record of 1,323.03 km/h (822.09 mph).

August 23 A first flight is made by the Westland Widgeon prototype (G-ALIK), a five-seat general- purpose helicopter developed from the earlier Dragonfly.

August 29 A new world altitude record of 20,083m (65,889ft) is established in the UK by W.F. Gibb flying an English Electric Canberra.

September 3 The first parachute escape from an aircraft travelling at speed on the ground is made by Sqdn Ldr.J.S. Fifield, RAF. This is made to test a Martin-Baker ejection seat installed in a modified Gloster Meteor 7, which is travelling at about 194 km/h (120 mph) at the moment of ejection.

September 20 The Nord 1500 Griffon, a needle- nosed experimental aircraft to flight test a new airframe design incorporating a combined turbojet-ramjet power plant, records its first flight. This is made on the power of an orthodox turbojet engine.

Westland Widgeon prototype, August 23 1955.

September 21 Skyways Ltd inaugurates a London-Paris coach-air service, passengers being carried by coach from London to Lympne, Kent and from there by DC-3 to Paris. Regular scheduled operations begin nine days later, on September 30.

October 6 The US Department of Defense announces that the Glenn L. Martin Company has been selected to design and build a launch vehicle to place a satellite in Earth orbit.

October 13 Pan American announces orders worth an equivalent of some £96 million, a quite staggering sum for 1955, covering the purchase of 20 Boeing 707s and 25 Douglas DC-8s.

October 16 During the course of experimental flights, Boeing's Model 367-80 flies non-stop from Seattle, Washington to Washington D.C. in 3 hr 58 min and back to Seattle in 4 hr 8 min. These times represent average speeds of 947 km/h (592 mph) and 907 km/h (567 mph) respectively.

October 19 The US Federal Communications Commission authorises the American Telephone and Telegraph Company to work on a computer-controlled defence radar and communications system known as Semi-Automatic Ground Environment (SAGE).

October 22 The Republic YF-105A Thunderchief prototype makes its first flight. This supersonic single-seat fighter-bomber is to prove of great value to the USAF during subsequent operations in Vietnam.

October 25 A first flight is recorded in Sweden by the Saab-35 Draken prototype, a double-delta winged supersonic single-seat fighter.

November 1 A United Air Lines DC-6MB explodes in mid-air and crashes near Longmont, Colorado, killing all 44 occupants. It is established subsequently as one of the most bizarre accidents in aviation history, caused by a bomb introduced onto the aircraft by John G. Graham, intended to destroy the aircraft and his mother who is a passenger. Her death is planned to allow him to claim heavy compensation from large-scale pre-flight insurance.

The first guided missile cruiser, the USS *Boston*, is commissioned by the US Navy.

November 24 The Fokker F.27 Friendship prototype makes its first flight. This short/medium-range turbo-prop-powered airliner remains a current, though much-developed, production aircraft in early 1982.

December 7 The Bristol Aeroplane Company announces the conclusion of an agreement with the Fiat company, covering licence manufacture in Italy of the Orpheus turbojet.

December 10 A first flight is made by the Ryan X-13 VTOL research aircraft. This is accomplished by the installation of temporary landing gear to allow the aircraft to make a conventional take-off.

December 15 The NATO Council approves a co-ordinated air defence and radar system for Western Europe, including the UK.

December 18 The Beech Model 73 Jet Mentor, a turbojet-powered high-performance jet trainer, makes its first flight. This is a private venture development by Beech from their earlier Model 45 Mentor primary trainer.

December 19 An agreement is concluded between Aeroflot and BEA covering the mutual operation of air services between the Soviet Union and the UK.

December 20 The first flight is made of a Douglas DC-7C Seven Seas long-range airliner. It differs from its predecessor by having increased wing span and a slightly 'stretched' fuselage to allow for a maximum 99 tourist class passengers.

December 26 The US aviation industry announces boom conditions following the receipt of orders for new aircraft totalling more than £1,000 million.

December 28 Air France announces that it has placed orders for 24 nationally-built Caravelles, plus 10 Boeing 707s.

1956

January 10 The first US-built rocket engine with a thrust in excess of 181,437kg (400,000lb) is run successfully for the first time at Santa Susana, California.

January 11 The UK Air Ministry announces the formation of a task force to conduct British atomic tests off the Monte Bello Islands in the Indian Ocean.

January 17 The US Department of Defense reveals publicly for the first time the existence of the SAGE defence system (q.v. October 19, 1955).

January 18 The East German government approves the creation of a Defence Ministry and the beginning of re-armament.

February 1 The Air Planning Group of the West German Ministry of Defence initiates a pilot training scheme, marking the first practical steps in the creation of the post-war Luftwaffe.

February 17 A first flight is made by the first production Lockheed F-104A Starfighter, a single-seat air superiority fighter for service with the USAF.

February 18 Finnair inaugurates airline services to Moscow.

Bell X-2 in flight, having been air-launched from its B-50 'motherplane' and with a Sabre chase aircraft in attendance, September 7 1956.

February 20 Formation date in Norway of Scanopter Service, a charter helicopter operator. The company name is changed subsequently to its current title of Helikopter Service A/S.

February 24 The Gloster Javelin all-weather fighter enters service with the RAF's No.46 Squadron at Odiham, Hampshire.

February 27 The Ministry of Transport and Civil Aviation announces that the number of passengers handled by British airports during the preceding 12 months had exceeded 5 million for the first time.

March 1 The Turkish airline known from May 20, 1933 as Turkiye Devlet Hava Yollari (DHY) adopts its current name of THY-Turkish Airlines (Turk Hava Yollari Ao).

March 10 Pushing the world speed record upwards by almost 500 km/h (310 mph) in a single jump, Lt Peter Twiss establishes the world's first over 1,000 mph speed record. This is accomplished flying the Fairey Delta 2 research aircraft off the English coast at Chichester, West Sussex, and gaining a record ratified at 1,821.39 km/h (1,131.76 mph).

March 14 A first successful launch is made from Cape Canaveral of a Chrysler Redstone, or Jupiter-A tactical bombardment missile. This has been developed in the USA by a team headed by Dr Wernher von Braun, the

designer of Germany's V2 (A4) rocket of the Second World War.

April 15 The cargo-carrying airline Sadia SA Transportes Aereos begins scheduled feeder-line services from Sao Paulo. It is currently known as Transbrasil.

April 28 A US Military Assistance Advisory Group begins work in South Vietnam.

May 1 Lufthansa opens its pilot training centre at Bremen.

May 18 The US Press highlights the so-called 'Colonel's Revolt', revealing bitter interservice Army/Air Force rivalry. US Army officers are critical of USAF beliefs that national security must rely primarily upon air power; this is to have later repercussions for the Army.

May 21 A US hydrogen bomb, the first to be released from an aircraft, is detonated over Bikini Atoll in the Pacific.

June 13 The UK completes withdrawal of its troops from Egypt, transferring them to Cyprus, thus ending 74 years of British military presence in Egypt.

June 20 The US Navy commissions its first helicopter assault carrier, the USS *Thetis Bay*.

July 7 The de Havilland Comet 2 enters service with RAF Transport Command at Lyneham, Wiltshire, becoming the world's first turbojet-powered aircraft to see service in a military transport role.

Mongolian Airlines, which had been formed earlier in the year with assistance from Aeroflot, begins the operation of domestic services.

July 24 A first flight is made by the French Dassault Etendard IV prototype which has been built by the company as a private venture. Failing to enter production as a land-based strike fighter, for which it had been intended, it is developed into a successful carrier-based fighter-bomber/reconnaissance aircraft.

July 26 Egypt seizes control of the Suez Canal from the privately owned Suez Canal Corporation.

August 9 The prototype of the Fiat G.91 lightweight fighter makes its first flight, powered by a Bristol Orpheus turbojet engine. It had been designed as a NATO light strike fighter.

August 12 The UK begins the airlift of troops from Britain to bases in the Mediterranean area.

August 23-24 A specially-prepared Hiller H-21 ('Flying Banana') twin-rotor helicopter of the US Army becomes the first rotary-wing aircraft to complete a nonstop transcontinental flight from San Diego, California to Washington D.C.

August 31 The first production example of the Boeing KC-135A tanker/transport for the USAF makes its first flight.

September 2 A Vickers Valiant records the first nonstop transatlantic flight made by one of the RAF's V-bombers, from Lowring, Maine to Marham, Norfolk.

September 6 France begins the transfer of troops from Marseilles to bases in Cyprus.

September 7 The Bell X-2 research aircraft is flown by Capt Iven C. Kincheloe to an altitude of 38,466m (126,200ft).

September 15 The Tupolev Tu-104 turbojet-powered airliner enters service with Aeroflot, initially on its Moscow-Irkutsk route.

The Indian government signs a contract in London covering the purchase of 25 Folland Gnat lightweight fighters, plus licence rights for their production in India.

September 24 Formation date of the post-war German air force, the Luftwaffe der Deutschen Bundesrepublik.

September 27 The Bell X-2 is destroyed in a fatal accident following a flight in which its pilot, Capt Milburn Apt, USAF, had achieved a speed of Mach 3.2, the highest then recorded by a manned aircraft.

October 10 NACA discloses that a speed of Mach 10.4 has been attained by a four-stage research rocket.

October 11 The first atomic bomb to be dropped by a British aircraft is released by a Vickers Valiant of No 49 (Bomber) Squadron over Maralinga, South Australia.

October 11 A first flight is made by the Lockheed L-1649A Starliner prototype, an extra long-range derivative of the Super Constellation.

October 15 The USAF announces contracts valued at $166 million for the supply of Lockheed F-104 Starfighters.

October 24 In secret meetings, an Anglo-French-Israeli agreement is reached to co-ordinate military operations against Egypt. This requires Israel to pose a threat to the security of the Suez Canal, thus precipitating Anglo-French intervention.

The UK government announces that it has given approval to the purchase of 15 Boeing 707s by BOAC.

October 29 Israeli forces begin their planned attack to threaten the Suez Canal, making an airdrop of paratroops at Mitla Pass in the Sinai Peninsula.

October 30 An Anglo-French ultimatum calls upon Egyptian and Israeli troops to cease fighting and allow British and French troops to occupy key points to secure the safety of the Suez Canal.

BEA operates its last scheduled service from Northolt Airport, Middlesex.

October 31 Following rejection by Egypt and Israel of the ultimatum, British and French air forces begin attacks on Egyptian air bases.

The first of 10 Douglas DC-7Cs for service with BOAC arrives at London's Heathrow Airport.

November 5 British and French paratroops are airdropped at Port Fuad and Port Said, Egypt.

November 6 An Anglo-French amphibious landing at Port Said, carried out with air cover, is followed by a midnight cease-fire.

November 8 Ascending from Rapid City, South Dakota Lt Cdr M.L. Lewis, US Navy, and Malcom D.

Convair XB-58 Hustler prototype with underfuselage weapons and fuel pod attached, November 11 1956.

Dassault Mirage III prototype, November 17 1956.

Ross establish a world altitude record for manned balloons of 23,165m (76,000ft).

November 11 A first flight is made at Fort Worth, Texas of the Convair XB-58 Hustler prototype, a four-turbojet delta-wing medium bomber. When the B-58 enters service in early 1960 it is the USAF's first supersonic bomber.

November 12 A Sikorsky S-56 helicopter in service with the US Marine Corps records a speed of 261.8 km/h (162.7 mph).

November 17 A first flight is made by the Dassault Mirage III prototype, a delta-wing high-altitude interceptor/fighter.

November 19 The Royal Moroccan Air Force (Aviation Royale Chérifienne) is formed.

December 4 Giving way to the march of progress, the US Army announces that its Signal Corps has discontinued the use of carrier pigeons.

December 13 In the USAF's altitude research chamber, at its Air Research and Development Command, Dayton, Ohio, Maj Arnold I. Beck attains the equivalent of a flight altitude of 60,585m (198,770ft).

December 26 Convair's F-106A Delta Dart prototype makes its first flight. This supersonic delta-wing all-weather interceptor is to become an important weapon of the USAF.

December 31 A first flight is made by the Bristol Britannia 311 (G-AOVA), the prototype of the long-range 310 series.

1957

January 6 BOAC begins the use of Douglas DC-7Cs on its London-New York services.

January 18 Three of the USAF's Boeing B-52 Stratofortresses, commanded by Maj Gen Archie J. Old Jr, make the world's first round-the-world nonstop flight by turbojet-powered aircraft. This is completed in 45 hr 19 min at an average speed of 859 km/h (534 mph).

January 23 The Nord 1500-02 Griffon II flies for the first time with its mixed ramjet/turbojet power plant.

February 1 BOAC makes its first use of turboprop-powered airliners, introducing the Bristol Britannia on its London-Johannesburg route.

February 19 The Bell X-14, an experimental VTOL aircraft to investigate the potential of direct jet-lift, makes its first hovering flight.

March 15 A US Navy ZPG-2 airship, with Cdr J.R. Hunt and crew, establishes a new unrefuelled endurance record of 264 hr 12 min.

April 2 The Short SC.1 VTOL research aircraft with five Rolls-Royce RB.108 turbojets, four being used for jet-lift, makes its first flight in a conventional take-off mode.

April 4 A first flight is made by the first of three English Electric P.1B prototypes (XA847), upon which is based the production version of the Lightning.

The USAF awards the Rocketdyne Division of North American Aviation a contract to study the potential of ion drive as a power medium for spacecraft.

Following publication of a UK government White Paper on Defence, it is decided that the days of manned aircraft are drawing to a close, soon to be superseded by advanced interception and bombardment missiles. Britain chooses to concentrate upon deterrence by threat of nuclear retaliation.

April 12 The USAF announces that on the previous day the Ryan X-13 VTOL research aircraft had completed a full transition. This involved a vertical take-off followed by conversion to horizontal flight, then the reverse procedure to accomplish a successful tail-sitting landing.

May 15 A Vickers Valiant of the RAF's No 49 (Bomber) Squadron drops the UK's first thermonuclear (hydrogen) bomb over the Pacific, near the area of Christmas Island.

May 16 A first flight is made by the Saunders-Roe S-R.53 experimental mixed power plant interceptor. This relies upon an Armstrong Siddeley Viper turbojet and a de Havilland Spectre rocket motor to give an estimated speed of Mach 2.4, but development is cancelled because of changing British defence policy.

May 17 The Westland Wessex prototype/demonstrator (XL722) makes its first flight. This is a Sikorsky-built S-58 which Westland has re-engined with a Napier Gazelle turboshaft.

May 24 The Canadian airline Nordair begins scheduled operations.

May 30 The USAF discloses development of the Hughes Falcon air-to-air guided missile armed with a nuclear warhead.

June 4 Sabena and Air Charter inaugurate a joint vehicle ferry service between Southend and Ostend.

June 29 During a proving flight, the Bristol Britannia Srs 310 G-AOVA records the first non-stop flight by an airliner from London to Vancouver.

July 31 The North American DEW line early warning system, extending across the arctic areas of Canada, is reported to be fully operational.

August 1 A joint US-Canada North American Air Defense Command (NORAD) is activated informally.

August 13 The first conventional flight by the Boeing Vertol VZ-2A (Model 76) tilt-wing research aircraft.

August 19-20 Ascending from Crosby, Minnesota, Maj David G. Simons, USAF, sets a balloon world altitude record of 30,942m (101,516ft).

Major David G. Simons sits inside his gondola prior to the record balloon ascent, August 19-20 1957.

Ryan X-13 Vertijet, April 12 1957.

Sputnik 1, the first artificial satellite to be put into Earth orbit, October 4 1957.

August 28 In the UK, M. Randrup flying an English Electric Canberra establishes a new world altitude record of 21,430m (70,308ft).

September 1 In the UK an air arm of the British Army becomes established as the Army Air Corps.

September 11 Pan American inaugurates a London-San Francisco service with Douglas DC-7Cs. This is flown via Frobisher Bay, Baffin Island and is to become known as the Polar route.

September 20 The USAF Chief of Staff announces the development of a radar system with the capability to detect ICBMs at a range of 4,830km (3,000 miles).

September 30 Trans World Airlines inaugurates a Los Angeles-London service with Lockheed L-1649A Starliners, flying over the so-called Polar route.

Austrian Airlines (Öesterreichische Luftverkehrs AG) is formed following a merger of Air Austria and Austrian Airways, neither of which had started operations.

October 4 The Soviet Union puts into Earth orbit the world's first artificial satellite. Named Sputnik ('Fellow Traveller') 1, it is launched by a newly-developed ICBM from the USSR's Tyuratam-Baikonur cosmodrome.

October 7 After a break of six years, operation of the London-Prague air route is resumed by BEA and Czechoslovak airlines.

October 16 The USAF achieves its first successful experiment to boost a man-made object to a velocity at which it can escape from the Earth's gravitational pull. This is accomplished by a special Aerobee rocket which, at a height of 87km (54 miles), detonates a shaped charge to boost small metallic pellets to a speed of some 53,100 km/h (33,000 mph).

October 22 Under Operation Far Side a four-stage research rocket is launched from a US balloon flying at some 30,480m (100,000ft) above Eniwetok Atoll. This succeeds in travelling some 4,345km (2,700 miles) into space.

November 6 The first of two prototypes of the Fairey Rotodyne, a combination fixed/rotary-wing VTOL airliner to accommodate 40-48 passengers, makes its first flight at White Waltham, Berkshire.

November 7 Showing American TV audiences a Jupiter nose-cone which has been recovered after launch from Cape Canaveral, President Eisenhower states that the US has solved the missile re-entry problem.

December 6 A first flight is made by the Lockheed L-188 Electra short/medium-range airliner prototype (N1881). This is achieved more than a month ahead of schedule.

December 10 A Directorate of Aeronautics is established by the USAF.

December 12 Maj Adrian Drew, USAF, flying a McDonnell F-101A Voodoo, sets a new world speed record of 1,943.03 km/h (1,207.34 mph).

December 19 BOAC introduces Bristol Britannia Srs 312s on its London-New York route, marking the first transatlantic passenger services to be operated by a turboprop airliner.

December 20 The first production example of the Boeing Model 707-120, the basic domestic version, makes its first flight.

1958

January 14-20 Qantas inaugurates the airline's first scheduled round-the-world route. The first services are flown by the Super Constellations *Southern Aurora* (VH-EAO) eastbound, and *Southern Zephyr* (VH-EAP) westbound.

February 1 Explorer I, the first US satellite to enter Earth orbit, is launched by a Jupiter-C rocket from Cape Canaveral. Travelling in an elliptical orbit, data that it transmits lead to discovery of the Van Allen radiation belts that girdle the Earth.

February 4 The keel of what is to become the world's first nuclear-powered aircraft carrier, the USS *Enterprise*, is laid at Newport News, Virginia.

Fairey Rotodyne, November 6 1957.

February 18 The USAF discloses that an airflow speed of approximately 52,140 km/h (32,400 mph) has been attained briefly in the test section of a wind tunnel at Arnold Research and Development Center, Tullahoma, Tennessee.

March 1 The UK government gives approval for BEA to order 24 de Havilland DH.121s, which are to be built as Hawker Siddeley Tridents.

March 8 US recognition of the vulnerability of large capital ships to enemy air power comes with the retirement of the US Navy's last battleship, the USS *Wisconsin*.

March 17 Vanguard I, the second US satellite to enter Earth orbit, is launched from Cape Canaveral.

The French airline Air Inter, which had been formed at the end of 1954 to specialise in the operation of domestic routes, makes its first revenue flight.

March 27 A USAF Boeing KC-135 tanker completes a nonstop flight from California to New Zealand.

March 31 Austrian Airlines begins its first scheduled operations.

April 1 Economy class services are introduced by carriers operating the North Atlantic routes.

April 9 The two-man crew of a Canberra bomber which explodes over Monyash, Derbyshire make the highest reported emergency escape from an aircraft, 17,070m (56,000ft).

April 10 The Fairey Rotodyne transport aircraft makes its first transition from the helicopter to an autogiro flight mode.

April 18 In the US, Lt Cdr G.C. Watkins, US Navy, establishes a new world altitude record of 23,449m (76,932ft) while flying a Grumman F11F-1 Tiger. This is the last of Grumman's famous 'cat' family to serve with the US Navy.

April 27 The first production de Havilland DH.106 Comet 4 for service with BOAC (G-APDA), makes its first flight at Hatfield, Hertfordshire.

May 2 Lt Cdr G.C. Watkins' two-week old world altitude record is broken by R. Carpentier in France. Flying the Sud-Ouest SO.9050 Trident (F-ZWUM), he attains an altitude of 24,217m (79,452ft).

May 7 Maj H.C. Johnson, flying a Lockheed F-104A Starfighter in the USA, plays his part in keeping the FAI busy by setting a third new world altitude record in less than three weeks, attaining a height of 27,811m (91,243ft).

May 12 The North American Air Defense Command (NORAD), which was activated informally on August 1,

McDonnell F4H-1 Phantom II, May 27 1958.

1957, is established formally with headquarters at Colorado Springs, Colorado.

May 16 The first 'over 2,000 km/h' world speed record is set over southern California by Capt W.W. Irvin USAF. Flying a Lockheed F-104A Starfighter, he attains a speed of 2,259.18 km/h (1,403 mph).

May 20 It is announced from the US Pentagon that a four-division strategic Army Corps has been formed for rapid deployment to any point in the world.

May 24 Formation date in the Netherlands of Martin's Air Charter, primarily to provide charter services. Its current name of Martinair Holland is adopted during 1967.

The Bell X-14 VTOL experimental aircraft makes its first transition from hovering to forward flight.

May 27 A first flight is made by the McDonnell F4H-1 Phantom II carrier-based fighter and tactical strike fighter.

May 30 The first Douglas DC-8 Srs 10, a domestic version of the company's four-jet sweptwing civil transport, makes its first flight.

June 9 London's new Gatwick Airport is opened officially by HM Queen Elizabeth II.

June 15 A first flight is made by the first prototype Westland Westminster (G-APLE), a single-rotor

transport helicopter research aircraft. As flown originally, in the form of a functional flying test rig, almost the entire fuselage structure is left uncovered.

June 20 The Westland-built Wessex prototype (XL727), which derived from the Sikorsky S-58, is flown for the first time.

July 1 Royal Nepal Airlines is formed as a wholly-owned government airline to operate domestic services within Nepal, as well as routes linking Nepal with India.

July 4 Formed by the government of Ghana with assistance from BOAC, Ghana Airways inaugurates its first international operations on July 16, 1958.

July 23 It is announced that the Boeing Vertol VZ-2A (Model 76) tilt-wing research aircraft has made its first successful transition from vertical to horizontal flight and vice versa.

July 30 The last scheduled operation is made by an Elizabethan Class Airspeed Ambassador of BEA (G-AMAF *Lord Howard of Effingham*). In service with this airline the type has flown some 50 million km (31 million miles) and has carried almost 2.5 million passengers.

August 6 The Short SC.1 VTOL research aircraft makes a first tethered vertical flight.

August 7 A de Havilland DH.106 Comet 4 on a proving flight from New York to Hatfield, Hertfordshire completes its flight in 6 hr 27 min.

September 3 The Chilean airline Ladeco (Linea Aérea del Cobre Ltda) is formed to provide domestic services.

September 9 The Lockheed X-7, a pilotless test vehicle for ramjet engines and missile components, achieves a speed of Mach 4 following launch from a Boeing B-50. Recovery is effected after each flight by an automatically-opening parachute.

September 12 A new runway for Hong Kong Airport, extending out into the sea and measuring 2,545m (8,350ft), is opened officially.

September 14 The de Havilland Comet 4 G-APDA makes a proving flight from Hong Kong to Hatfield, Hertfordshire within the day, in a flight time of 16 hr 16 min.

September 24 A first flight is made by the Beijing (Peking) No.1, a twin-engined light transport which is the first aircraft to be designed and built in the Chinese People's Republic.

September 30 UK commercial flying-boat operations come to an end when Aquila Airways withdraws its Southampton-Madeira service.

The US National Advisory Committee for Aeronautics (NACA) issues its final report and then ceases to exist.

October 1 The US National Aeronautics and Space Administration (NASA) is established to absorb the functions of NACA, and to control all US non-military space projects.

President Eisenhower appoints an administrator for the newly-formed Federal Aviation Agency (FAA), which absorbs the former Civil Aeronautics Administration (CAA).

October 4 BOAC inaugurates simultaneous London-New York and New York-London services with the de Havilland Comet 4. These are the first transatlantic passenger services flown by turbojet-powered airliners.

October 11 The USAF makes a second attempt to put a research probe in orbit around the Moon. This is Pioneer 1B which, because its third stage cuts out fractionally too soon, travels about 113,780km (70,700 miles) before falling back toward Earth.

October 26 Pan American inaugurates its first transatlantic services operated by the Boeing 707-121 turbojet-powered airliner.

November 3 The Soviet Union launches its Sputnik 2 satellite, carrying the dog Laika which is destined to die when its oxygen is exhausted.

November 15 Air India begins a weekly cargo service on its Bombay-London route, operated by chartered Douglas DC-4s.

December 12 The balloon *Small World*, commanded by A.B. Elloart, ascends from the Canary Isles in an attempt to traverse the South Atlantic. It lands in the sea on December 15, having travelled some 2,800km

(1,740 miles), and completes its journey on the ocean surface some 20 days later.

December 18 The USAF places in Earth orbit a small communications relay satellite. Carrying a pre-recorded tape, it transmits to the US on the following day President Eisenhower's Christmas message to the nation.

1959

January 2 The Soviet Union launches a scientific probe, named Luna 1, which is intended to impact on the Moon's surface. It misses its target by some 5,955km (3,700 miles), passing the Moon to enter a solar orbit.

January 5 The Fairey Rotodyne sets a 100km closed-circuit speed record for convertiplanes of 307.22 km/h (190.9 mph) at White Waltham, Berkshire.

January 8 The Armstrong Whitworth A.W.650 Argosy (G-AOZZ) records its first flight.

January 20 The first Vickers Vanguard 950 prototype (G-AOYW) makes its first flight from Weybridge, Surrey.

February 1 Operational control of the North American DEW line is transferred from the US Air Force to the Royal Canadian Air Force.

February 11 A US weather balloon climbs to a record height of 44,500m (146,000ft).

February 12 The USAF withdraws its last operational Convair B-36 bomber from service.

February 17 The US Navy launches the weather reporting Vanguard II satellite into Earth orbit.

February 25 The Nord 1500 Griffon, powered by a combined turbojet-ramjet propulsion unit, establishes a 100km closed circuit record. Flown by André Turcat, it records a speed of 1,638.32 km/h (1,018.01 mph).

March 3 The US Pioneer 4 space probe is launched in an attempt to obtain crude pictures of the Moon's surface while making a fly-past at a distance of about 32,200km (20,000 miles). It passes the Moon at almost double this range and travels on into solar orbit.

The US Chief of Naval Operations highlights the danger to US warships posed by a constantly growing Soviet submarine fleet. This is to spur the development of more effective ASW aircraft.

March 5 Lufthansa inaugurates a non-stop cargo service to New York.

March 13 Aviation Cadet E.R. Cook becomes the US Navy's first student pilot to fly solo in a turbojet-powered trainer without prior experience in a propeller-driven aircraft.

April 6 It is announced in the US that seven pilots have been selected from the nation's armed services for training as space vehicle pilots.

Two Hound Dog missiles carried by a Boeing B-52D Stratofortress, April 23 1959.

April 23 The US Hound Dog thermonuclear stand-off missile makes a successful first flight following launch from a Boeing B-52D bomber.

April 24 Cathay Pacific Airways begins services with its first Lockheed Electra (VR-HFO).

May 1 Trans-Australia Airlines initiates operations with its first Fokker F.27 Friendship (VH-TFB) from Melbourne to Sydney via Canberra.

May 15 The last operational flight is made by an RAF Sunderland, marking also the last use of water-based aircraft by the Royal Air Force.

May 19 Aerolineas Argentinas inaugurates Comet 4 services between Buenos Aires and London, which is the first turbojet-powered airliner service to link South America and the UK.

May 28 Two monkeys named Able and Baker are recovered unharmed after a 483km (300 mile) flight in a compartment in the nose-cone of a Jupiter rocket.

June 1 BOAC introduces Comet 4s on its London-Singapore route, the first service from London operated by G-APDE.

June 3 The American satellite Discoverer 3 is launched carrying four mice for a biological experiment.

June 4 Max Conrad lands his Piper Comanche at New York at the termination of a 12,365km (7,683 mile) nonstop flight from Casablanca, Morocco which sets a new lightplane distance record.

June 8 Sudan Airways, which had been formed in early 1946, begins operating a Khartoum-London (Gatwick) weekly 'Blue Nile' service.

The first unpowered free flight of the North American X-15A high-performance research aircraft is made following launch from beneath the wing of its Boeing B-52 'motherplane'.

June 17 A first flight is made by the Dassault Mirage IV-A strategic bomber prototype.

June 28 The Tupolev Tu-114 Rossiya (Russia), having created considerable interest at the Paris Air Show a little before this date, makes a nonstop flight from Moscow to New York in 11 hr 6 min.

July 2 No 892 Squadron becomes the first Royal Navy unit to become operational with de Havilland Sea Vixens.

July 13-23 A London-Paris air race, held throughout this period to mark the 50th anniversary of Louis

Blériot's first crossing of the English Channel (q.v. July 25, 1909), is won by Sqdn Ldr Charles Maughan, RAF. Using a combination of two motor-cycles, a Bristol Sycamore helicopter and a Hawker Hunter T.Mk 7, his city-centre to city-centre time is a remarkable 40 min 44 sec.

July 14   Maj V. Ilyushin of the Soviet Union sets a new world altitude record of 28,852m (94,659ft) flying the Sukhoi T-431.

July 27   Air France introduces the Sud-Aviation Caravelle on its services to the UK, the initial operation flown by Caravelle *Lorraine* (F-BHRB).

July 29   Qantas operates its first jet service from Sydney to San Francisco, with the Boeing 707-138 *City of Canberra* (VH-EBC). This is also the airline's first scheduled transpacific flight by a turbojet-powered airliner.

July 30   A first flight is made by the Northrop N-156C prototype, which exceeds a speed of Mach 1 during this initial flight test. It is to become known internationally as the F-5 Freedom Fighter.

August 7   NASA's Explorer 6 is launched into Earth orbit from Cape Canaveral, and is to return the first TV pictures of the Earth as seen from space.

Sea Vixen F (AW).1s lined up for the commissioning ceremony of No 892 Squadron, July 2 1959.

August 17   A NASA research rocket ignites a sodium flare at an altitude of some 240km (150 miles) in a project to provide information on high altitude wind direction and velocity, and the rate of matter diffusion in the upper atmosphere.

August 24   Thai Airways International is formed by Thai Airways Company with assistance from SAS.

The data capsule of an Atlas-C rocket is recovered successfully after a 8,050km (5,000 mile) flight down range. It provides the first cine films of Earth taken from an altitude of 1,125km (700 miles).

September 4   An unmanned US scientific balloon records an altitude of some 45,720m (150,000ft).

September 5   Qantas operates its first jet service to London, flown by the Boeing 707-138 *City of Melbourne* (VH-EBA) via Fiji, Honolulu, San Francisco and New York.

September 9   Big Joe, which was NASA's test version of the Mercury astronaut capsule, is recovered successfully in the Caribbean Sea after a 2,415km (1,500 mile) flight following launch by an Atlas rocket.

September 12   The Soviet Union's Luna 2 space probe is launched. It becomes the first man-made object to impact on the Moon, between the craters Archimedes, Aristillus and Autolycus.

Aeroflot Ilyushin Il-18 arrives at London Airport, October 14 1959.

September 17 The second example of the North American X-15A research aircraft makes a successful first powered flight following launch from its B-52 'motherplane'.

September 18 The Douglas DC-8 Srs 10 turbojet-powered airliner makes its first entry into US domestic service, flown by Delta Air Lines and United Air Lines.

September 30 A nostalgic day in British civil aviation history is marked by the closure of Croydon Airport, Surrey at 22.30 hrs BST.

October 1 A US Air Force Aerospace Medical Center is activated at Brooks AFB, Texas.

October 4 The Soviet Luna 3 space probe is launched towards the Moon. It is to record the first circumlunar flight, and is the first to photograph the Moon's hidden surface. The photographic images are transmitted over a TV link to Earth.

October 6 The Spanish airline Spantax Air Taxis is formed, but its current title of Spantax S.A. is adopted at a later date.

October 10 The Pan American Boeing 707-321 *Clipper Windward* inaugurates the first round-the-world passenger service by turbojet-powered airliners.

October 14 The Soviet Ilyushin Il-18 turboprop-powered airliner is seen at London's Heathrow Airport for the first time. Il-18s are used on Aeroflot's Moscow-Copenhagen-London route for a short period.

October 28 NASA launches by rocket from Wallops Island an inflatable aluminium-coated plastic sphere.

Released and inflated at a height of 400km (250 miles) the 30m (100ft) diameter sphere is visible over long ranges.

October 31 Flying a Mikoyan Type Ye-66 at Sidorovo, Tyumenskaya, Col G. Mosolov establishes a new world speed record of 2,681.00 km/h (1,665.89 mph).

November 1 BOAC introduces the de Havilland Comet 4 on its London-Sydney route, the first flight made by Comet G-APDL.

November 3 Argentina's Army air arm is formed. This is known currently as Argentine Army Aviation Command (Comando de Aviación del Ejercito).

November 16 Capt Joseph W. Kittinger Jr makes a balloon ascent from White Sands, New Mexico. Having gained an altitude of 23,285m (76,400ft) in an open gondola he parachutes to the ground, recording a free-fall of 19,505m (64,000ft).

December 1 A 12-nation treaty establishes Antarctica as an area of the world accessible only for peaceful purposes.

December 4 NASA tests the Mercury capsule escape system, launching a capsule with a Rhesus monkey aboard, which is recovered alive and quite unharmed.

South African Airways begins an air service between Johannesburg and Durban for 'non-white' passengers.

December 6 A US Navy McDonnell F-4 Phantom II piloted by Cdr L. Flint establishes a new world altitude record of 30,040m (98,556ft).

December 9 At Bloomfield, Connecticut a Kaman H-43B rescue helicopter, crewed by USAF officers Maj William J. Davis and Capt Walter J. Hodgson, sets a helicopter altitude record of 9,097m (29,846ft).

February 20-21 In the course of its delivery flight from Seattle, a Boeing 707 for Air India records the first non-stop London-Bombay flight.

March 2 Lufthansa receives its first Boeing 707 at Hamburg.

March 11 NASA launches its Pioneer 5 satellite into a solar orbit, between the transit paths of Earth and Venus. This confirms the possibility of maintaining communications over very long ranges, in this case some 35 million km (22 million miles).

March 15 The first meeting of a 10-nation disarmament committee. It is discovered, at an early date, that its efforts would be wasted and is broken up in just over three months.

April 1 Tupolev Tu-104s are introduced by ČSA Czechoslovak Airlines on its Prague-London service.

Trans-Canada Air Lines introduces Douglas DC-8 turbojet-powered transports on its transcontinental service from Montreal to Vancouver via Toronto.

NASA's drum-shaped Tiros 1 (Television and Infra-Red Observation Satellite) is launched successfully. It carries two TV cameras which transmit some 22,000 cloud cover pictures before the satellite's batteries are exhausted after 78 days in orbit.

BEA initiates turbojet-powered airliner operations, introducing de Havilland Comet 4Bs on its London-Moscow route.

April 10 BOAC resumes air services through Cairo, operations which had been suspended since the Suez war of 1956.

April 13 The US Navy launches its Transit 1-B navigational satellite into Earth orbit, the first of a series intended to provide an accurate all-weather navigational reference for its missile-launching submarines.

The UK abandons ballistic missile development, deciding that its air deterrent will rely upon the use of its V-bombers armed by the US Skybolt missile.

April 29 First test firing by NASA of all eight Rocketdyne H-1 engines of the Chrysler Saturn 1 first stage produces a combined 589,670kg (1,300,000lb)st.

May 6 At a first public demonstration for the Press, a USAF Minuteman is launched successfully from an underground launch pad (not a silo) at Edwards AFB, California.

May 7 A Lockheed U-2 high-altitude reconnaissance aircraft overflying the Soviet Union, piloted by Gary Powers, is shot down from an altitude of some 19,810m (65,000ft) by a Soviet SAM near Sverdlovsk.

May 11 A US Army Signals Corps balloon ascends to a record night-time altitude of 43,890m (144,000ft) before bursting.

May 12 A USAF Lockheed C-130 Hercules makes a successful parachuted airdrop of a 15,876kg (35,000lb) load (nearly 16 tons).

December 14 The eight-day-old world altitude record of Cdr L. Flint, USN, is broken by a Lockheed F-104C Starfighter piloted by Capt J.B. Jordan to a height of 31,513m (103,389ft).

December 15 A new world speed record of 2,455.74 km/h (1,525.93 mph) is set by Maj J.W. Rogers, USAF, flying a Convair F-106A Delta Dart at Edwards AFB, California.

December 16 China Airlines is established in Taiwan, initially to operate domestic services. International routes are opened up during 1966.

1960

January 1 To make provision for expansion, Fiji Airways is reconstituted, being owned equally by BOAC, Qantas and Tasman Empire Airways.

January 16 NASA announces the successful launch and inflation at high altitude of a 30m (100ft) diameter plastic balloon.

January 21 In a further low altitude test of the Mercury escape system, NASA launches a monkey named Miss Sam. She is recovered unharmed after the escape system is activated almost immediately following launch.

February 9 The USAF activates a National Space Surveillance Control Center at Bedford, Massachussets.

February 13 France explodes an atomic weapon in the Sahara Desert, thus becoming the world's fourth nuclear power.

February 16 The UK government announces a change in its national defence policy. It is decided that instead of a ground-based nuclear deterrent the nation will rely upon ballistic nuclear missiles launched by aircraft or from submarines.

May 14 Air India inaugurates a London-New York service with its Boeing 707-437s, the first service flown by *Annapurna* (VT-DJJ).

May 17 KLM's 40th anniversary of its London-Amsterdam service is marked by Sir Frank Whittle giving his name to the airline's Douglas DC-8 PH-DCC in a ceremony at London Airport, followed by a flight to Amsterdam carrying as passengers Sir Frank, and H. ('Jerry') Shaw who had flown the first service 40 years earlier.

An angry denouncement by Khrushchev of American spying activities over the Soviet Union, resulting from the Gary Powers incident, causes the break-up of a Summit conference in Paris.

May 21 The USAF's last B-25 Mitchell is withdrawn from service at Eglin AFB, Florida.

May 27 BOAC begins the use of Boeing 707-436s on its London-New York route.

June 1 Trans-Canada Air Lines begins North Atlantic turbojet-powered passenger services, introducing the Douglas DC-8 on its Montreal-London route. The first service is flown from London to Montreal by the DC-8 CF-TJC.

June 3 The US Marine Corps carries out successful launch tests of the Martin Bullpup air-to-surface guided missile from a Sikorsky UH-34D helicopter.

June 20 Pakistan International Airlines operates its first international Karachi-London service with a Boeing 707. This is leased from Pan American but operated by an all-Pakistani crew.

June 24 The Avro 748 prototype (G-APZV), later H.S.748, makes its first flight at Woodford, Cheshire.

July 1 British United Airways becomes operational, combining a number of smaller units into this independent airline.

July 15 The first Boeing 707-344 (ZS-CKC) for service with South African Airways lands at Johannesburg on delivery from Seattle.

July 9-28 Following the government granting independence to the Belgian Congo (June 30), Sabena airlifts 25,711 Belgian nationals back to the homeland.

July 20 Continuing its airdrop experiments, the USAF's Air Research and Development Command paradrops a 18,370kg (40,500lb) load from a Lockheed C-130 Hercules.

The Short SC.1 jet-lift VTOL research aircraft makes its first full transitions from vertical to horizontal flight and vice-versa.

August 12 Following successful test launches in which balloons are inflated to a large diameter in space (q.v. October 28, 1959 and January 16, 1960), NASA places into orbit the Echo 1 communications satellite. This is of plastic material coated with an aluminium film, and serves as a test vehicle for the relay of several types of communication signals.

Maj Robert White, USAF, pilots the North American X-15A research aircraft to a height of 41,600m (136,500ft).

August 16 Following the success of his earlier parachute jump (q.v. November 16, 1959), Capt Joseph W. Kittinger Jr, USAF, jumps from a balloon at 31,150m (102,200ft), making a free fall of 25,815m (84,700ft).

August 18 Following ejection of a data capsule from the Discoverer 14 satellite in orbit, this is recovered in mid-air at an altitude of some 2,440m (8,000ft) by a Fairchild C-119 transport using a specially-developed 'snatch' technique.

August 19 The Soviet Union's Sputnik 5 satellite is launched into Earth orbit, carrying two dogs named Belka and Strelka. They are recovered successfully after completing 18 orbits.

September 10 NORAD carries out operation Sky Shield, an air exercise to test the capability and preparedness of the US/Canadian radar and electronics early warning system.

September 15 Tasman Empire Airways carries out its last flying-boat operation with the departure of the Solent *Aranui* (ZK-AMO) from Tahiti to Auckland.

September 17 East African Airways operates its first de Havilland Comet 4 service, from London to Nairobi. The first reciprocal service is made two days later.

September 21 The USAF's Tactical Air Command accepts formally its first Republic F-105 Thunderchief supersonic tactical fighter-bomber in a ceremony at Nellis AFB, Nevada.

October 1 South African Airways introduces Boeing 707-344s on its Johannesburg-London route.

A US BMEWS (Ballistic Missile Early Warning System) radar site becomes operational at Thule, Greenland.

October 16 Marking the end of what had once seemed to be a great success story for the British aviation industry, BOAC operates its last scheduled Comet 4 New York-London service.

October 21
A first tethered flight is made by the Hawker Siddeley P.1127 Kestrel experimental V/STOL tactical fighter.

October 24-31 In a combined US Army/US Air Force exercise codenamed South Wind, the USAF's MATS and TAC test their capability to deploy over 10,000 Strategic Army Command troops to a distant base.

October 27 Air Mali is formed as the national airline of the Republic of Mali, with assistance from Czechoslovakia and the Soviet Union.

October 31 BEA flies its last scheduled Douglas DC-3 service, between London and Birmingham; it is also the last scheduled service operated from London (Heathrow) by a piston-engined aircraft.

November 1   Making its first operation with a turbine-powered aircraft, Air Ceylon introduces a Lockheed Electra on its Amsterdam-Singapore route.

November 4   The USAF discloses for the first time its use of the Boeing C-97 as an airborne tactical command post and communications centre.

November 9   The US Post Office demonstrates the potential of the Echo 1 satellite, using it for the high-speed transmission of a 'speed mail' letter from Washington D.C. to Newark, New Jersey by bouncing microwave signals from its surface.

November 12   Launching Discoverer 17 from Vandenburg AFB, a restartable rocket engine is used for the first time.

November 16   The first flight is recorded of the Canadair Forty Four (CL-44) civil/military freighter prototype. It is the world's first production transport aircraft to introduce a swing-tail configuration to simplify bulk loading.

November 18   On its delivery to Shannon for Irish International Airlines, the Boeing 720-048 completes the New York-Shannon flight in a record 4 hr 57 min.

November 23   NASA's second meteorological satellite Tiros II is launched into a high-altitude orbit.

December 3   Ghana Airways takes delivery of the first two of six Ilyushin Il-18 turboprop-powered transports.

December 6   The prototype of the Sikorsky S-61L non-amphibious civil transport helicopter makes its first flight.

Determined to become completely independent of the USA, President de Gaulle announces plans to establish a French nuclear strike force.

December 7   In continuing tests of data-capsule retrieval from orbiting space vehicles, a mid-air 'snatch' is made of a capsule ejected from Discoverer 17 after completing 48 Earth orbits.

December 8-10   BOAC introduces the Boeing 707-436 on its London-Hong Kong route, flown via New York, San Francisco, Honolulu and Tokyo. Connecting with Comet 4s flown London-Hong Kong via the eastern route, it marks the completion of BOAC's first all-jet round-the-world service.

December 14   Using its first Boeing 720-048, Irish International Airlines inaugurates its first turbojet-powered transatlantic Dublin-New York services via Shannon.

December 17   On the 57th anniversary of the first powered flight, BEA introduces the Vickers Vanguard on its London-Paris route.

December 19   NASA carries out an unmanned test-routine of the Mercury space capsule. Launched from Cape Canaveral by a Redstone booster rocket it attains a height of 217km (135 miles) and range of 378km (235 miles) before its parachute is deployed. It is recovered from the sea within 32 min of splash-down.

December 20   Australia's first commercial heliport is opened officially at Melbourne.

1961
January 31   Extending the last unmanned Mercury experiment, NASA launches a Mercury capsule containing a chimpanzee named Ham. Although subjected to 17g during the launch phase, Ham is recovered successfully after a 676km (420 mile) down range flight, apparently with no ill effects.

February 9   The USAF Chief of Staff transfers responsibility for space surveillance functions from the Air Research and Development Center to the Air Defense Command, marking establishment of the USAF's SPADATS (space detection and tracking system).

February 10   During initial tests of the prototype Rocketdyne F-1 rocket engine, a thrust of just over 680,390kg (1,500,000lb) is developed for a few seconds.

February 21   In the last stage of preparation for NASA'S Mercury programme, John H. Glenn, Virgil I. Grissom and Alan B. Shepard are named to begin final training for early ballistic flights.

February 25   Paul F. Bikle, Director of NASA's Flight Research Center at Edwards AFB, California, pilots a Schweizer 1-23-E sailplane to a height of 14,102m (46,267ft).

March 7   The McDonnell GAM-72A (later AD-20) Quail decoy missile, providing the same image on radar

---

Yuri Gagarin, the first man in space, April 12 1961. (*Soviet Weekly*)

Hawker Siddeley P.1127 Kestrel, March 13 1961.

screens as a Boeing B-52 Stratofortress bomber, is declared operational.

March 13 The Hawker Siddeley P.1127 Kestrel experimental V/STOL tactical fighter makes a first conventional flight.

March 17 The first Northrop T-38 Talon advanced jet trainer is delivered to Randolph AFB, Texas for service with the USAF's Air Training Command.

March 28 Air Afrique (Société Aérienne Africaine Multinationale) is formed as a joint venture involving Air France and several now-independent African states.

March 30 NASA pilot Joe Walker attains a height of 51,695m (169,600ft) in the North American X-15A research aircraft.

April 1 The Venezuelan airline Viasa (Venezolana Internacional de Aviación SA), which had been formed during January 1961, begins scheduled operations.

April 12 The Soviet Union staggers the world by announcing that it has launched the spacecraft Vostok 1 into Earth orbit, carrying Yuri Gagarin, the first man in space. He lands successfully after one orbit of the Earth in a total flight time of 1 hr 48 min.

April 17 A constant-altitude balloon is launched by the USAF's Cambridge Research Center. The balloon remains stable at an altitude of 2,135m (7,000ft) for a period of nine days.

April 21 Maj Robert White, USAF, pilots the North American X-15A during the first test flight at full throttle. A speed of 4,947 km/h (3,074 mph) is attained at 24,080m (79,000ft), before coasting upward to an altitude of 32,034m (105,100ft).

April 24 The Malagasy Air Force (Armée de l'Air Malagache) is established with French assistance. Since 1978 it has received MiG fighters and training assistance from North Korea.

April 26 Seaboard and Western Airlines Inc was formed in 1946 to operate unscheduled specialist transatlantic cargo operations. Continued as such until 1956, when scheduled operations began, and adopts present title of Seaboard World Airlines on above date.

April 27 The New Zealand government acquires Australia's 50 per cent holding in Tasman Empire Airways.

April 28 Col G. Mossolov, flying a Mikoyan Ye-66A, regains the world height record for the Soviet Union at an altitude of 34,714m (118,898ft).

May 5 Alan B. Shepard becomes the USA's first man in space, with a flight time of 15 min 22 sec. Carried in the Mercury ballistic capsule Freedom 7, following launch by a Redstone rocket, this is a sub-orbital trajectory during which a height of 187km (116 miles) and range of 478km (297 miles) is attained.

May 15 NASA discloses that its Ames Research Center has achieved experimentally a simulated free flight speed of 51,500 km/h (32,000 mph).

May 17 First flight tests of the Avro Canada Avrocar (VZ-9V) circular aircraft designed under USAF sponsorship. Project abandoned seven months later due to stability problems.

May 19 The first production Boeing C-135A Stratolifter makes its first flight. This is a long-range military transport developed from the KC-135A tanker/transport.

June 9 The first Boeing C-135A Stratolifter is delivered to MATS, marking the start of a modernisation programme to eliminate its all-propeller fleet of transports.

June 27 The government-owned airline Cubana (Empresa Consolidada Cubana de Aviación) begins operations under this, its current title.

June 28 Air Congo is formed with the assistance of Sabena. The airline is now known as Air Zaire, adopted after the Congolese Republic became renamed Republic of Zaire in October 1971.

June 29 The US Navy's Transit IV satellite is launched, the first known to carry a nuclear power source in the form of a radioisotope-powered battery.

July 1 NORAD begins the operation of SPADATS, designed to catalogue electronically all man-made space objects.

July 10 A Tactical Air Command pilot flies a Republic F-105D Thunderchief for more than 2,410km (1,500 miles) without any external vision. This is a test to ensure that the instrumentation and radar system of the F-105 is adequate for a squadron pilot to make a long-range IFR mission at altitudes between 152 and 305m (500 and 1,000ft).

July 21 The US puts its second man in sub-orbital flight down the Atlantic Missile Range; Virgil Grissom in the Mercury capsule Liberty Bell 7.

August 1 Air Afrique begins scheduled operations, taking over routes in French Africa that have been operated formerly by Air France and UAT.

August 6 The Soviet Union launches its second man into Earth orbit in Vostok 2. Cosmonaut Herman Titov completes 17 Earth orbits before landing after 1 day 1 hr 19 min.

August 8 Under the joint US Army/US Air Force operation Swift Strike, 7,500 paratroops are dropped near Fort Bragg, North Carolina.

September 13 Continuing research into conditions at high altitudes, NASA launches an Argos D-4 rocket to release sodium clouds for the study of atmospheric winds, temperature and density.

The worldwide tracking network which has been set up for the US Mercury programme, is used for the first time to observe the orbit of an unmanned Mercury capsule. Data from this network convinces NASA that the Atlas is capable of putting a manned Mercury capsule into Earth orbit.

The Mercury-Redstone III that takes Alan B. Shepard into space, is readied for flight, May 5 1961. (*NASA*)

September 19   NASA announces that the location of its new Manned Space Center will be near Houston, Texas.

October 3   Qantas begins services to New Zealand with Lockheed Electras, flying from Sydney and Melbourne to Wellington, Auckland and Christchurch.

October 4   Launch of the world's first active communications satellite Courier 1B (USA).

October 7   The Soviet Kamov Ka-22 Vintokryl, a large twin-engined convertiplane, sets a new world speed record for aircraft in this class of 356.3 km/h (221.4 mph).

October 13   The US confirms the provision of military assistance to Yugoslavia, including the supply of substantial numbers of fighter aircraft.

October 14   NORAD operation Sky Shield II, the largest air defence exercise then held in the western hemisphere, involves thousands of NORAD and SAC aircraft, and the grounding of all commercial aircraft for a period of 12 hours.

October 18   A USAF Kaman H-43B Huskie helicopter attains an altitude of 10,010m (32,840ft).

November 6   Following the inauguration of scheduled services on this date, Queenstown-Mount Cook Airways adopts its present title of Mount Cook Airlines.

November 9   In the last high-speed flight made by the X-15A during 1961, Maj Robert White, USAF, attains a speed of 6,587 km/h (4,093 mph) at 30,970m (101,600ft).

November 22   At Edwards AFB, California, Lt Col R.B. Robinson establishes a new world speed record in a McDonnell F4H-1F Phantom II at a speed of 2,585.43 km/h (1,606.51 mph).

November 29   In its last unmanned Mercury capsule test, NASA launches the chimpanzee Enos into Earth orbit.

December 1   Euravia (London) Ltd is formed to operate inclusive-tour flights, but adopts its present title of Britannia Airways during August 1964.

December 11   The first direct military support for South Vietnam is provided by the arrival at Saigon of a US Navy aircraft carrier transporting two US Army helicopter companies.

December 15   NORAD's SAGE system becomes fully operational with the completion of a 21st and final control centre at Sioux City, Iowa.

The USAF graduates its first class of five military space pilots from the Aerospace Research Pilots School.

1962

January 1   Air Madagascar (Société Nationale Malagache de Transports Aériens) is formed. It is founded from Madair, which was itself derived from the original Air Madagascar of 1947.

January 10-11   Major Clyde P. Evely and crew establishes a new world distance record in a Boeing B-52H Stratofortress, flying from Okinawa, Ryukyu Islands to Madrid, Spain, a distance of 20,168.78km (12,532.3 miles). This remains the current absolute world distance record in early 1982.

January 22   The USAF exercise Long Thrust II concludes, during which 5,273 US troops were flown from the US to Germany within seven days.

January 26   NASA's unmanned Ranger 3 space probe is launched to impact on the lunar surface but fails to hit the Moon.

February 5   A US Navy HSS-2 Sikorsky Sea King helicopter records a speed of 338.9 km/h (210.6 mph) during a flight between Milford and New Haven, Connecticut.

February 20   Launched by an Atlas booster, the Mercury capsule Friendship 7 carries America's first astronaut into Earth orbit. Lt Col John H. Glenn, USMC, completes three orbits to record a flight time of 4 hr 55 min 23 sec before splash-down.

February 28   In the first manned test of the steel cocoon-type escape capsule carried by the General Dynamics/Convair B-58A Hustler, WO Edward J. Murray is ejected from the aircraft which is travelling at 909 km/h (565 mph) at 6,100m (20,000ft). After a 26 second free-fall a parachute is deployed automatically, bringing him safely to the ground eight minutes after ejection.

March 21   A bear is used as the 'guinea pig' for a high-speed test of the B-58 escape capsule. The capsule is ejected from a B-58A travelling at 1,400 km/h (870 mph) at 10,670m (35,000ft), landing its occupant safely.

April 26   The first US/UK international satellite launch is made at Cape Canaveral, a Thor-Delta booster putting into orbit the Ariel I containing six UK space experiments.

April 27   In order to provide an increased counter-insurgency capability, the USAF establishes within Tactical Air Command a Special Air Warfare Center at Eglin AFB, Florida.

April 30   Flown by NASA pilot Joe Walker, the North American X-15A attains a new record height of 75,195m (246,700ft).

May 24   NASA's Mercury capsule Aurora 7 is launched into Earth orbit carrying Lt Cdr M. Scott Carpenter, US Navy, on a similar three-orbit mission to that of Friendship 7. Experiencing re-entry problems, he guides the spacecraft manually through re-entry but splashes down some 420km (260 miles) from the target area after a 4 hr 56 min mission. He remains in his liferaft until rescued.

June 8 A further and higher-speed test of the General Dynamics/Convair B-58A Hustler escape system is made. A capsule carrying the chimpanzee 'Zena' is ejected at a speed of 1,706 km/h (1,060 mph), subsequently landing safely.

June 19 A USAF superpressure balloon lands near Iwo Jima after a 19-day flight from Bermuda at a constant height of 20,725m (68,000ft).

June 27 The North American X-15A, flown by NASA pilot Joe Walker, attains its highest recorded speed of 6,693 km/h (4,159 mph).

Flying the Mikoyan Type Ye-166 at Sidorovo, Tyumenskaya, Col G. Mosolov establishes a new world speed record of 2,681.00km/h (1,665.89 mph).

July 7 A first conventional take-off flight is made by the Lockheed XV-4A two-seat VTOL research aircraft.

July 10 The Telstar 1 communications satellite is placed in Earth orbit by a Delta booster from Cape Canaveral. It makes possible the first transatlantic exchanges of TV programmes, proving to 'the man in the street' that he might gain some benefit from the space race.

August 8 In tests carried out to determine the effects of kinetic heating, the second North American X-15A attains a surface temperature of 482°C (900°F) at an altitude of 27,430m (90,000ft) and speed of 4,665 km/h (2,900 mph).

August 11 and 12 Launch dates respectively of the Soviet Union's Vostok 3 (Andrian Nikolayev) and 4 (Pavel Popovich) into Earth orbit. The two spacecraft make a rendezvous in orbit, approaching to within 5km (3 miles) of each other. TV cameras in the spacecraft provide the first TV transmission from a manned vehicle in space.

August 12 After two years in orbit the Echo 1 satellite, basically a balloon of aluminium-coated mylar film, is still operational. By then it has completed more than 9,000 Earth orbits and travelled some 446.3 million km (277.3 million miles).

August 13 Ten USAF pilots terminate a test during which they had spent one month in a simulated spacecraft.

August 27 The US launches the Mariner II interplanetary probe which is intended to scan the surface of Venus and sample its atmosphere.

September 19 A first flight is recorded by the first outsize transport conversion of a Boeing Stratocruiser, the Aero Spacelines B-377PG. Later named Pregnant Guppy, it was converted for Aero Spacelines by the On Mark Engineering Company of Van Nuys, California.

September 29 The Canadian-built and designed Alouette 1 satellite, the first to be built outside of the US or USSR, is launched successfully by a Thor-Agena B booster.

October 3 Cdr Walter M. Schirra, USN, completes a 9 hr 13 min space mission in the Mercury-Atlas 8 Sigma 7.

October 4 Sterling Airways, which had been formed in Denmark earlier in the year for charter and inclusive-tour operations, make its first revenue flight.

October 12 The first tethered flight is made by the Dassault V-001 Balzac jet-lift VTOL research aircraft; its first free flight is made six days later.

October 22 President Kennedy announces that US reconnaissance aircraft have established that offensive missile sites are being erected in Cuba.

October 23 The Soviet Union alerts its armed forces and challenges US rights to be concerned about Cuba.

October 24-29 Lengthy exchanges between Kennedy and Khrushchev ends the 'Cuban missile crisis'. The US pledges that it will not invade Cuba and, in return, the USSR agrees to halt construction of missile bases and remove its missiles.

October 29 The first Douglas DC-8F Jet Trader, a combined cargo/passenger or all-cargo version of the DC-8 transport, makes its first flight.

November 1 The Soviet unmanned Mars 1 interplanetary space probe is launched in an attempt to fly past Mars, but communications are lost en route.

November 2 A first flight is made by the Lockheed Model 186 (XH-51A) research helicopter, incorporating a rigid main rotor.

November 30 The first multi-national co-operative study of the Earth's upper atmosphere begins with the launching of two rockets by NASA. This involves Argentina, Australia, Canada, France and the USA.

A first tethered hovering flight by the Lockheed XV-4A Hummingbird VTOL research aircraft is made (q.v. July 7, 1962).

December 7 The first of two Sud-Aviation SA 3210 Super Frelon prototypes is flown. A heavy-duty helicopter powered by three turboshaft engines, it is developed with assistance from Sikorsky in the US.

December 8 A first flight is made by the Bell Model 206 (OH-4A) prototype, which has been developed to meet US Army requirements for a lightweight observation helicopter (LOH).

December 13-14 Under the designation Project Stargazer, a balloon manned by Capt Joseph A. Kittinger, USAF, carries civilian astronomer William C. White and a specially-mounted telescope to a height of 25,000m (82,000ft). This enables White to make a number of observations under ideal conditions.

December 14 NASA's Mariner II scans the surface of Venus for 35 min as it flies past at a distance of 34,830km (21,642 miles). A surface temperature of 428°C (834°F) is recorded.

December 24 The Nord 262 pressurised light transport prototype (F-WKVR) makes its first flight.

December 31 The US Navy announces that it has discontinued all activities related to lighter-than-air craft, and has disposed of its last airship and equipment.

The US Department of Defense announces that the air-launched ballistic Skybolt missile programme, upon which the UK intended to base its deterrent capability, has been cancelled. The USAF had also planned deployment of Skybolt.

1963

January 7 The USS *Buck*, having completed qualification trials, is the first US warship to become operational with Gyrodyne GH-50C ASW drone helicopters.

The Short Skyvan prototype (G-ASCN) makes its first flight powered by two 291kw (390hp) Continental GTSIO-520 piston engines. It first flies with its intended turboprop power plant on October 2, 1963.

January 17 NASA pilot Joe Walker flies the North American X-15A to a height of 82,600m (271,000ft). He qualifies for 'astronaut's wings' having exceeded a height of 80km (50 miles).

January 28 First flight of the Hiller OH-5A helicopter prototype, the second contender for the US Army's light observation helicopter (LOH) competition.

February 9 The Boeing 727 prototype is flown for the first time, a short/medium-range jet transport. Incorporating three rear-mounted engines and a T-tail it is in other respects similar to the Model 707/720 that had preceded it.

February 27 The Hughes OH-6A prototype, the third of the contenders for the US Army's light observation helicopter (LOH) competition, flies for the first time.

March 1 Trans-Canada Airlines inaugurates a trans-atlantic all-freight service operated by Douglas DC-8F Jet Traders.

April 5 Following the 'Cuban missile crisis', which had highlighted the potential dangers of quick reaction to international tension, a Soviet-US 'hot-line' is established for instant urgent communication between East and West.

April 18 A first conventional flight is made by a Northrop X-21A laminar-flow control system research aircraft. For this programme two Douglas WB-66D weather reconnaissance aircraft have been modified by Northrop, the work including installation of a completely new wing.

April 30 – 12 May American airwoman Betty Miller makes the first transpacific solo flight by a woman. This is accomplished in a four-stop flight from Oakland, California to Brisbane, Australia.

May 1 Jacqueline Cochran, flying a Lockheed TF-104G Starfighter near Edwards AFB, California, sets a 100-km closed-circuit world speed record for women of 1,937.14 km/h (1,203.686 mph).

May 7 The death is announced of Prof Theodore von Kármán, one of the world's foremost space flight pioneers and scientists.

May 15-16 In the longest US space mission to date, Maj L. Gordon Cooper, USAF, orbits the Earth 22 times in Mercury-Atlas 9 Faith 7. Cooper carries out experiments related to the navigation and guidance of spacecraft, is monitored by a TV camera, and makes a manually-controlled re-entry, to record a total mission time of 34 hr 19 min 49 sec.

May 27 A first flight is made by the F-4C version of the McDonnell Phantom II, a two-seat tactical fighter for the USAF.

June 7 Following a merger of Air Liban and Middle East Airlines, the current title Middle East Airlines Air Liban is adopted. The company still uses as its main identity the well known initials MEA.

Jacqueline Cochran in the cockpit of the TF-104G after setting a new women's world speed record, May 1 1963.

June 14-19   The Soviet Union's Vostok 5 spacecraft, carrying Valery Bykovsky, records the longest space mission to date of 119 hr 16 min.

June 16   With the launch of a second spacecraft within two days, the Soviet Union's Vostok 6 carries the first woman into space, cosmonaut Valentina Tereshkova.

July 19   NASA pilot Joe Walker flies the North American X-15A to an unofficial height record of 106,010m (347,800ft).

July 20   United Technology Center's first solid-propellant booster for Titan IIIC produces more than 453,590kg (1 million lb) thrust at its first static test firing.

July 25   A nuclear test ban treaty is finalised after almost three years of discussion: signed subsequently by most nations of the world, it brings an end to tests in the atmosphere.

August 20   The BAC One-Eleven short/medium-range twin-turbofan transport prototype (G-ASHG) makes its first flight.

August 28   The first test in the US Apollo programme is made when a Little Joe II booster, which has been designed for unmanned sub-orbital testing of this vehicle, makes a first test with a dummy Apollo spacecraft.

September 1   The title Interflug (Gesellschaft für Internationalen Flugverkehr mbH) is adopted by the national airline of the German Democratic Republic, instead of its former Deutsche Lufthansa, to avoid confusion with the West German national airline.

September 16   The Royal Malaysian Air Force (Tentara Udara Diraja Malaysia) adopts this title, having had three previous names and a history dating back to September 1940.

October 1   Under the command of Rear Adm James R. Reedy, a ski-equipped Lockheed C-130 Hercules makes a first transpolar nonstop flight from Capetown, South Africa to McMurdo Sound, Antarctica.

UTA (Union de Transports Aériens) is formed, following a merger of Union Aéromaritime de Transports with Transports Aériens Intercontinentaux.

October 17   The United Nations General Assembly confirms earlier unilateral declarations made by the US and USSR that no weapons will be mounted in or used from space.

November 11   The Fleet Air Arm forms its first Small Ship Flight, using Westland Wasp light anti-submarine helicopters for operation from platforms on frigates.

November 20   The USAF accepts formally its first two McDonnell F-4C Phantom II fighters at MacDill AFB, Florida.

November 29   By an executive order President Johnson renames Cape Canaveral as Cape Kennedy, and its space facilities as the John F. Kennedy Space Center.

December 15   Alia (Alia Royal Jordanian Airline) begins operations. Formed in October 1963, it is the successor to Air Jordan.

December 17   A first flight is made by the Lockheed C-141A four-turbofan long-range military transport ordered for service with the USAF's MATS.

December 21   The prototype of the Hawker Siddeley 748MF military transport (G-ARRV) is flown for the first time. This has been ordered for service with the RAF under the name Andover.

1964

January 5   A first flight is made by the Short SC.5/10 four-turboprop heavy transport, ordered for service with RAF Transport Command under the designation Belfast C. Mk 1.

January 29   Saturn I SA-5 is launched successfully, recording the first flight with a live second stage.

February 2   NASA's Ranger 6, launched on 30 January and carrying six TV cameras to send data on the Moon, impacts on the lunar surface without transmitting any pictures.

February 10   The death is announced of Professor Eugene Sänger, the pioneer of space transport.

February 18   France deploys troops to Gabon by air to counter an army coup against the government of President Leon Mba.

February 24   A first flight is made by the Northrop F-5B, a two-seat trainer version of the Northrop F-5A lightweight tactical fighter.

February 29   President Johnson reveals publicly for the first time the existence of the Lockheed A-11 high-altitude reconnaissance aircraft.

April 2   The Soviet Union's Zond 1 space probe is launched, passing within 99,800km (62,000 miles) of Venus on July 19, but by which time communications have been lost.

April 8   The first unmanned Gemini spacecraft is placed in Earth orbit by a Titan II booster.

April 9   A first flight is made by the de Havilland Canada DHC-5 Buffalo, a twin-turboprop STOL utility transport.

April 17   At the end of a 29-day flight in her Cessna 180 *Spirit of Columbus*, US airwoman Jerrie Mock lands at Columbus, Ohio, so becoming the first woman pilot to fly solo round the world.

May 1   A first flight is made by the BAC 221 research aircraft. This had formerly been the Fairey Delta 2, but has been extensively rebuilt with slender ogival delta wings plus new control surfaces, engine intakes and landing gear.

May 7   The BAC Super VC10 civil transport makes its first flight, differing from its VC10 predecessor by having a lengthened fuselage, more powerful engines and greater fuel capacity.

May 11 Piloting a Lockheed F-104G Starfighter, Jacqueline Cochran sets a new world speed record for women over a 15/25km course of 2,300.14 km/h (1,429.246 mph).

May 12 American Joan Merriam, flying a Piper Apache, becomes the second woman to make a solo round-the-world flight, taking 56 days to cover the route which had been planned by Amelia Earhart.

May 25 The Ryan Model 43 (XV-5A) 'fan-in-wing' VTOL research aircraft makes a first conventional take-off.

June 1 After becoming independent in June 1963 Kenya begins the formation of an air force with British assistance. The Kenya Air Force is established officially on this date.

June 6 The UK cross-Channel car ferry operated by Silver City Airways, first founded in mid-1948, carries its one millionth car.

June 26 The Curtiss-Wright Model 200 (X-19A) tilt-rotor research aircraft makes a first hovering flight.

June 28 The North American X-15A No. 2 research aircraft which following an accident has been rebuilt with new large external fuel tanks, makes its first flight under the new designation X-15A-2.

July 16 The Ryan XV-5A 'fan-in-wing' research aircraft makes its first vertical take-off, hovering flight and vertical landing. The first complete transitions from vertical to forward flight and vice versa are made on November 5, 1964.

July 27 The Daniel Guggenheim Medal for 1964 is awarded posthumously to Dr Robert H. Goddard, in recognition of his important contributions to rocket theory and design.

July 28 NASA's unmanned Ranger 7 is launched from Cape Kennedy, subsequently taking 4,316 TV pictures of the lunar surface in the last 13 mins of flight before it impacts on the Moon.

July 31 In the USA A.H. Parker sets the first over 1,000km (1,040km; 646 miles) sailplane distance record, flying a Sisu-1A.

August 2 and 4 US destroyers are attacked by North Vietnamese patrol boats. On both occasions the attackers are repelled or destroyed, primarily by air action.

August 5 In retaliation for the unprovoked attack by the North Vietnamese patrol boats, President Johnson orders carrier-based aircraft to attack North Vietnamese naval bases.

August 7-9 Turkish air attacks on Greek Cypriot positions in Cyprus are terminated by intervention of the United Nations.

August 19 The Hughes Syncom 3 communications satellite is launched into a geostationary Earth orbit. It is used extensively later in the year, providing TV coverage of the 1964 Olympic Games in Tokyo.

September 21 The North American XB-70A Valkyrie prototype makes its first flight. This Mach 3 strategic bomber programme is subsequently abandoned.

September 27 The BAC TSR.2 two-seat all-weather supersonic attack/reconnaissance aircraft prototype (XR219) makes its first flight. It proves to be the only one of the type to fly as the programme is subsequently cancelled.

BAC TSR.2 with landing gear down, September 27 1964.

September 29 The LTV-Hiller-Ryan XC-142A, a four-engined tilt-wing transport research aircraft, makes its first conventional take-off.

October 1 Derby Airways, which has been a UK charter operator since 1948, adopts its current title of British Midland Airways.

October 12 The Soviet Union launches the Voskhod 1 spacecraft into Earth orbit. It is the first to carry a multiple crew, consisting of Vladimir Komarov, Konstantin Feoktistov and Boris Yegorov, who are able to carry out their mission without wearing spacesuits.

October 14 A first flight is made by the Sikorsky CH-53A Sea Stallion prototype, a heavy assault helicopter accommodating up to 38 combat troops which has been developed for the US Marine Corps.

October 16 The People's Republic of China detonates its first atomic bomb, becoming the world's fifth nuclear power.

October 30 NASA pilot Joe Walker makes the first flight with the Bell Lunar Landing Research Vehicle (LLRV). This has a variable-stability system that allows pilots to gain the reactions and sensations of operating in a lunar environment.

November 18 The first of three pre-production Grumman C-2A carrier on-board delivery aircraft for the Navy is flown for the first time.

November 26 Qantas inaugurates its Sydney-London 'Fiesta route', flown via Fiji, Tahiti, Acapulco, Mexico City, the Bahamas and Bermuda.

November 28 The US space probe Mariner 4 is launched. This passes within 8,690km (5,400 miles) of Mars on July 14, 1965, transmitting 21 pictures of the Martian surface.

December 21 The first General Dynamics F-111A variable-geometry (swing-wing) multi-purpose fighter makes its first flight. This is carried out with the wings locked at 26° sweepback but full wing sweep, from 16° to 72.5°, is first accomplished on January 6, 1965.

December 22 President Johnson approves development by Lockheed of the CX-HLS military transport for the US Air Force. This becomes the C-5A Galaxy.

December 22 A first flight is made by the Lockheed SR-71A strategic reconnaissance aircraft.

December 29 The LTV-Hiller-Ryan XC-142A research transport makes its first successful hovering flight.

1965

January 11 The LTV-Hiller-Ryan XC-142A research transport makes its first full transitions from vertical to forward flight and vice versa.

January 26 Brazil's naval air arm, which had been absorbed into the air force in early 1941, is re-established as an independent service. It is known as the Brazilian

Naval Air Force (Fôrça Aeronaval de Marinha do Brasil).

January 27 The potential of geostationary satellites for emergency communications is demonstrated. For the first time a comsat is used as a link between a Pan American Boeing 707 in flight and a remote ground control station.

February 12 The Dassault Mirage III-V single-seat VTOL strike aircraft begins hovering trials.

February 23 A first flight is recorded by the Douglas DC-9 short/medium-range airliner, powered by two rear-mounted turbofan engines.

March 6 A Sikorsky SH-3A Sea King makes the first nonstop helicopter flight across the North American continent. Taking off from the carrier USS *Hornet* at San Diego, California it lands on the carrier USS *Franklin D. Roosevelt* at Jacksonville, Florida having completed a distance of 3,405km (2,116 miles). This establishes a new international straight-line distance record for helicopters.

March 18 The Soviet Union launches Voskhod 2 with cosmonauts Pavel Belyayev and Alexei Leonov. During their mission Leonov makes the first 'spacewalk', tethered to the spacecraft while floating in space for about ten minutes.

March 23 Launched by a Titan II booster, NASA's Gemini 3 spacecraft is placed in Earth orbit. It carries the first US two-man crew, astronauts Virgil Grissom and John Young, on a 4 hr 53 min mission.

March 29 Qantas introduces the Boeing 707-338C on its scheduled 'Kangaroo' route to the UK.

Lockheed YF-12A, May 1 1965.

April 1 Tasman Empire Airways, which had become wholly nationally owned in 1961, adopts the name Air New Zealand.

April 6 The Hughes Early Bird I comsat is launched into geostationary earth orbit. When it becomes operational, on June 28, 1965, it is the world's first commercial satellite for public telephone services.

April 15 The first prototype of the Sud-Aviation SA.330 medium-size transport helicopter (F-ZWWN) makes its first flight. Subsequently named Puma, it becomes one of the three aircraft involved in the Anglo-French (Westland-Aérospatiale) helicopter development programme.

May 1 Flying a Lockheed YF-12A from Edwards AFB, California Col R.L. Stephens establishes a new world speed record of 3,331.507 km/h (2,070.11 mph).

May 7 The Canadair CL-84 Dynavert, a twin-engined tilt-wing V/STOL close-support/transport prototype, achieves its first vertical take-offs and landings.

May 9 The Soviet unmanned spacecraft Luna 5 is launched towards the Moon. It later crashes instead of making an intended automatic soft-landing on the lunar surface.

June 3 The NASA spacecraft Gemini 4 is launched into Earth orbit, carrying astronauts James McDivitt and Edward White. During this mission White makes a 21 min spacewalk, known in US aerospace terminology as an extra-vehicular activity (EVA).

June 12 The prototype of the Britten-Norman BN-2 Islander (G-ATCT) makes its first flight. This twin-engined feeder-line transport marks the beginning of a UK post-war success story.

August 1 The UK Army Air Corps, which had been formed on September 1, 1957, is re-named Army Aviation.

August 21 NASA's Gemini 5 spacecraft, with astronauts Gordon Cooper and Charles Conrad on board, carries out the first exploratory 'long' space mission, lasting 7 days 22 hr 56 min.

September 1-25 During hostilities between India and Pakistan, both sides make fairly extensive use of air power.

September 7 A first flight is made by the prototype Bell Model 209 HueyCobra armed helicopter, which has been developed as a private venture for the US Army from the UH-1B Iroquois.

September 13 The Fédération Aéronautique Internationale homologates its first hot-air balloon record, an altitude of 2,978m (9,780ft) attained by B. Bogan in the US.

September 27 The first of three evaluation LTV A-7A Corsair II single-seat carrier-based attack aircraft makes its first flight. The type is to prove a valuable addition to US Navy carrier-based aircraft operating off Vietnam.

November 15 A first circumnavigation of the world overflying both poles is made by a Boeing 707 of the Flying Tiger Line.

November 16 The Soviet interplanetary space probe

Venera 3 is launched, later becoming the first man-made object to impact on the surface of Venus.

November 26 Using a Diamant launch vehicle, the French Asterix 1 (Matra A1) test satellite is placed in Earth orbit. France thus becomes the first nation, other than the US or USSR, to develop and orbit a satellite by its own efforts.

December 4 NASA's Gemini 7 spacecraft is launched into Earth orbit carrying astronauts Frank Borman and James Lovell. In addition to carrying out a longer-stay mission (13 days 18 hr 35 min), Gemini 7 serves as a rendezvous target for Gemini 6.

December 15 The Gemini 6 spacecraft is launched with astronauts Walter Schirra and Thomas Stafford on board. Manoeuvring to within 1.8m (6ft) of Gemini 7 in orbit, this is the first manoeuvred rendezvous in space.

1966

January 10 A first flight is made by the Bell Model 206A JetRanger, a five-seat turbine-powered general-purpose helicopter.

January 31 The Soviet Union launches the unmanned spacecraft Luna 9, which becomes the first man-made vehicle to soft-land on the lunar surface and transmit panoramic still pictures of the terrain.

February 8 'Freddie' Laker, formerly managing director of British United Airways, announces the formation of his own airline, Laker Airways.

February 23 The Dornier Do 28D Skyservant prototype (D-INTL) makes its first flight, this being a STOL utility transport developed from the Do 28.

February 26 Japan's Nihon University NM-63 Linnet single-seat man-powered aircraft makes a successful first flight.

March 9 President de Gaulle announces that France is to withdraw from military alliance with NATO.

March 12 Sir Sydney Camm dies at the age of 72. One of the really great aircraft designers, he is best known in Britain for the Hawker Hurricane.

March 14 The Douglas DC-8 Super 61 makes its first flight at Long Beach, California. Then the largest airliner to have flown, it has accommodation for a maximum of 251 passengers.

March 16 NASA's Gemini 8 spacecraft, carrying astronauts Neil Armstrong and David Scott, is launched into orbit to carry out docking manoeuvres with an Agena docking target. Although they achieve the first docking of two spacecraft in orbit, this has to be aborted almost immediately because of uncontrollable spinning.

March 17 The Bell X-22A V/STOL tilting-duct research aircraft is flown for the first time, making four vertical flights to a height of about 7.6m (25ft).

April 15 The US FAA announces regulations making the use of weather radar compulsory for all freighter aircraft. In addition, this is to become mandatory by the end of 1967 for all commercial aircraft operating within US airspace.

May 18 British airwoman Sheila Scott takes off from London (Heathrow) Airport in a Piper Comanche 260B in an attempt to make a solo round-the-world flight.

May 30 NASA launches the Surveyor 1 lunar probe which makes the first fully-controlled soft-landing on the Moon on June 2. It transmits 11,150 high-resolution pictures of the lunar surface.

June 3 NASA launches Gemini 9 with Thomas Stafford and Eugene Cernan on board. Cernan performs a 2 hr spacewalk during the 3 day 21 min mission.

June 20 Sheila Scott lands at London (Heathrow) Airport at the conclusion of her solo round-the-world flight. She is not only the first British airwoman to complete such a flight, but she has established a new record for women of 33 days 3 min.

July 1 Demonstrated to the UK Press at Leavesden airfield, a Mitsubishi MU-2B executive transport is the first Japanese aircraft to visit the UK since 1936.

July 12 The Northrop/NASA M2-F2 lifting-body research aircraft makes its first (unpowered) flight after being launched from a Boeing B-52 'motherplane' at 13,715m (45,000ft).

July 18-21 During the Gemini 10 mission (Michael Collins and John Young), a scientific experiment package is retrieved from an orbiting Agena craft. This gives evidence of a capability to rendezvous with and repair/service satellites in Earth orbit.

July 21 United Air Lines announces that it has carried more than 2 million passengers during the previous month (2,007,971 in June).

August 2 Following moves by BEA to acquire US-built aircraft as fleet replacements, the UK Minister of Aviation states that BEA can only buy British aircraft to meet its needs.

August 10 NASA launches the Lunar Orbiter 1 unmanned spacecraft which duly goes into orbit around the Moon and obtains high resolution pictures of potential Apollo landing sites.

August 11 A Tupolev Tu-114 makes the first proving flight over the proposed Moscow-Tokyo route to be operated jointly by Aeroflot and Japan Air Lines.

August 26 The renowned Swiss mountain rescue pilot Hermann Geiger is killed in a flying accident.

August 31 The first of six Hawker Siddeley Harrier development aircraft (XV276) makes its first hovering flight at Dunsfold, Surrey.

September 1 The SBAC's 25th Show is opened at Farnborough. It is the first to allow the inclusion of foreign aircraft, provided they have a proportion of British equipment.

September 12 NASA launches Gemini 11 with Charles Conrad Jr and Richard Gordon Jr on board, to carry out docking tests. The mission lasts 2 days 23 hr 17 mins.

September 15 Reinhold Platz dies at the age of 80. He is best remembered as the designer of several outstanding German aircraft of the First World War.

September 24 In the Soviet Union Marina Solovyeva, flying a Ye-76 (MiG-21) sets a new women's world speed record of 2,044 km/h (1,270 mph).

October 13 Following lengthy technical studies, NASA suggests that liquid methane might prove a suitable fuel for use by SST (supersonic transport) aircraft, offering more than 30 per cent benefit in payload.

October 21 The Yakovlev Yak-40 tri-jet light transport makes its first flight.

November 4 The Hawker Siddeley Trident G-ARPB, fitted with Smiths' Autoland system, makes three test landings at London Heathrow. These are made in conditions of 46m (150ft) visibility when all other operations have been cancelled.

November 11 NASA launches Gemini 12 with James Lovell and Edwin Aldrin on board. Three spacewalks and a docking manoeuvre are performed during the 3 day 22 hr 34 min mission.

November 21 The UK government proposes that the nation's two major aircraft companies, British Aircraft Corporation and Hawker Siddeley, should merge as one.

December 6 After losing its 65th Lockheed F-104G Starfighter in an accident, the Luftwaffe grounds its entire fleet of 770 of these aircraft.

December 11 Pratt & Whitney's JTF17A two-spool turbofan engine, which has been developed as a potential powerplant for America's first SST, produces more than 25,855kg (57,000lb)st during a first test run.

December 23 The first flight of Dassault's Mirage F 1 single-seat fighter prototype is made successfully .

1967
January 2 It is announced in the US that Boeing has been awarded a contract for the design of an SST, and that General Electric is to develop the power plant for it.

January 4 Following modifications that occupied a period of almost a month, the Luftwaffe returns its F-104G Starfighters to operational service.

Hindustan Aeronautics announces that it is assembling MiG-21s from Soviet-built components for delivery to the Indian Air Force.

January 16 Air California, which was formed as a US intrastate airline during 1966, makes its first revenue flight.

January 27 In a tragic accident on the ground, US astronauts Roger Chaffee, Virgil Grissom and Edward White are burnt to death during tests of an Apollo capsule. They had been scheduled to make the first Apollo orbital flight on February 21, 1967.

February 10 The Dornier Do 31E experimental V/STOL transport aircraft makes its first flight.

March 1 France and the Soviet Union sign an agreement in Paris which is intended to lead to the development and marketing of new generation aircraft.

March 8 It is announced by the Federal German Defence Ministry that the Lockheed C-2 ejection seats in the F-104G and TF-104G Starfighters in use with its armed forces are to be replaced by Martin-Baker GQ-7 seats.

March 9 The Royal Aeronautical Society announces that the Kremer prize, which had been offered for a first significant man-powered flight, has been increased to £10,000 and that any nation is eligible to compete.

A first flight is made by the Slingsby T.53 two-seat sailplane which has been developed to meet an Air Ministry requirement for air cadet training. It is the first all-metal sailplane to be designed and built in the UK.

March 10 The Soviet Minister of Aviation states that in order to be aligned with western civil aviation technology and usage the Soviet Union intends to become a member of ICAO.

March 11 A first flight is made by the Bede BD-2, an extensively rebuilt Schweizer 2-32 all-metal sailplane. Provided with special power plant, Jim Bede intends to use it for an attempted non-stop unrefuelled round-the-world flight.

March 13 The receipt of an order from Lufthansa brings the total order book for Concorde SSTs to 72 aircraft from 16 airlines.

March 15 A first flight is made by the Sikorsky HH-53B heavy-lift helicopter which is intended for use by the USAF's Aerospace Rescue and Recovery Service.

March 18 In attempts to prevent oil spillage from reaching nearby coastlines, RAF and Royal Navy aircraft make bomb attacks on the crippled supertanker *Torrey Canyon*.

March 21 The Swedish Defence Minister states that 100 Saab Viggens (83 AJ 37s and 17 Sk 37s) have been ordered for the Royal Swedish Air Force.

March 22 Bases for USAF B-52 bombers are established in Thailand by agreement between the US and Thai governments.

March 29 A first flight is made by the HAL HF-24 Marut supersonic single-seat fighter. Power is provided by a Helwan-developed E-300 turbojet, for which the airframe serves as a flying testbed.

April 6 Trans World Airlines becomes the first of the US airlines to complete the transition to an all-jet fleet.

April 7 The Sud-Aviation SA.321F helicopter flies for the first time. This is a 37-seat civil version of the heavy-duty SA.321 Super Frelon.

The UK Ministry of Civil Aviation orders from West-land Aircraft three Black Arrow satellite launchers. These will allow the UK to start the development of its own space programme.

April 9 A first flight is made by the Boeing Model 737-100 twin-jet short-range transport. This basic version provides accommodation for 80-101 passengers.

April 18 A Tupolev Tu-114 operates the inaugural flight of the joint Aeroflot/JAL Moscow-Tokyo service, landing at Haneda International after a flight of 10 hr 35 min.

April 21 The Sud-Aviation Caravelle 11R mixed passenger/freight transport makes its first flight. This version has been developed to meet a demand for some freight capacity on medium-range routes.

April 23 Launch date of Soyuz 1 in which Soviet cosmonaut Col Vladimir Komarov is killed when the spacecraft crashes during the final stages of landing. He is the first man known to have died in the course of a space flight.

April 27 Totally destroying the Gloster Meteor drone which is its first live target, the UK BAC Rapier tactical anti-aircraft missile completes a highly successful test.

April 28 Queen Juliana of the Netherlands opens the new central terminal complex of Amsterdam's Schiphol Airport.

May 5 UK-3 (Ariel 3), the first all-British satellite, is launched into Earth orbit from the Western Test Range, California.

May 9 The prototype of the Fokker F.28 Fellowship short range transport makes its first flight from Schiphol Airport, Amsterdam.

May 10 The Northrop/NASA M2-F2 lifting-body research aircraft crashes on landing at Rogers Dry Lake, Edwards AFB, California.

May 18 The Dassault Mirage F1 prototype is destroyed in an accident near Marseilles, killing the company's chief test pilot.

May 23 A first flight is made by the Hawker Siddeley Nimrod prototype, a maritime reconnaissance aircraft developed from the Comet 4 airliner.

The Trident G-ARPP operated by BEA completes a week-long cycle of automatic flight, this including 34.5 hrs under automatic control and 27 automatic landings.

June 5 Monarch Airlines is formed in the UK to operate inclusive-tour flights and worldwide charter operations.

The Boeing Company delivers its 1,000th jet airliner, a Model 707-120B for American Airlines.

Outbreak of the '6-day war' between Israel and the Arab states. Pre-emptive air strikes by the Israeli Air Force make the Egyptian, Jordan and Syrian air forces virtually ineffective.

June 8 The first launch of a Petrel rocket is made from the South Uist Range in the Outer Hebrides. This rocket has been developed for the UK Science Research Council for Earth environment studies.

June 10 Following the enforcement of a cease-fire the '6-day war' ends. It is theoretically an Israeli victory, due largely to their skilful deployment of air power.

June 17 The Chinese People's Republic detonates its first thermonuclear weapon.

July 4 As concern has been expressed in the UK over the new phenomenon of sonic booms, the UK Minister of State for Technology states that random Lightning flights will be made over the country to gauge public reaction.

July 7 A Pan American Boeing 707-321B (N419PA) records the first fully-automatic approach and landing by a four-engined turbojet aircraft with passengers on board.

July 9 Trans-Mediterranean Airways inaugurates a twice-weekly London-Tokyo all-cargo service.

August 1 Three farm workers are killed in France when the barn in which they were working collapses as the result of a sonic boom.

QANTAS, which became Qantas Empire Airways in January 1934, adopts its current title of Qantas Airways Ltd.

August 7 Aerolineas Argentinas and Iberia inaugurate jointly the world's longest nonstop air route, between Buenos Aires and Madrid.

August 12 On this date Lt Col Ivan Savkin of the Soviet Union makes his 5,000th parachute descent.

August 17 The US lunar probe Surveyor 3 is launched to the Moon, achieving a soft-landing in the Ocean of Storms. A mechanical scoop, activated from Earth,

Canadair CL-215 about to lift from the water, October 23 1967.

Major Knight and the North American X-15A-2, October 3 1967.

allows soil samples to be taken for photographic transmission to Earth and, in addition, more than 6,000 pictures are taken of the landing site.

September 1   Air Malawi becomes the state airline of the Republic of Malawi, following dissolution of Central African Airways.

Zambia Airways becomes a wholly-owned governments corporation.

September 8   A first flight is made from the dockside at Avonmouth of the Westland Sea King prototype (XV370).

September 15   The Soviet Minister for Aviation states that it is hoped to begin testing of the Tupolev Tu-144 SST during 1968.

October 3   Flown by Maj William Knight, USAF, the North American X-15A-2 attains its highest speed of Mach 6.72 (7,297 km/h; 4,534 mph).

October 10   Lockheed's AH-56A Cheyenne armed helicopter makes its first flight. Incorporating a pusher propeller in its design, it is anticipated that speeds of up to 402 km/h (250 mph) may be achieved as development progresses.

October 20   The first emergency escape using the crew module of a USAF F-111A is made over Texas, the two crew members remaining within it until reaching the ground unhurt.

October 23   The first flight of a new flying-boat is made, the Canadair CL-215. It is intended primarily for use as a fire-fighter and equipped to uplift while taxiing large volumes of water for water-bombing operations.

November 3   The US Defense Secretary states that the USSR has developed a fractional-orbit bombardment system (FOBS) that will allow orbiting satellites to release nuclear weapons against Earth targets.

November 8   Involved in its biggest transport operation since the Berlin Airlift of 1948-49, the RAF uses 50 transport aircraft in the withdrawal of troops from Aden.

November 18   The first flight is made at Istres, France, of the Dassault Mirage G prototype, the first variable-geometry ('swing-wing') aircraft of European design and manufacture to be flown.

November 29   The last public appearance is made by de Havilland Vampires, seen in an aerobatic display at RAF Leeming, Yorkshire.

Australia's Wresat 1 research satelite, the nation's first, is launched into Polar orbit from Woomera using a modified Redstone missile as booster.

December 11   The Aérospatiale-built Concorde 001 prototype is rolled out at Toulouse.

December 16   The Dornier Do 31E experimental V/STOL transport makes its first transition from vertical to horizontal flight. The first transition from horizontal to vertical flight is made on December 21.

Dornier Do 31E in vertical flight, December 16 1967.

December 28   The first production Hawker Siddeley Harrier GR.1 (XV738) makes a 20 min flight at Dunsfold, Surrey.

1968

January 4   The first McDonnell Douglas F-4K Phantom II for service with the Royal Navy is handed over officially at St Louis, Missouri.

January 5   The RAF bids farewell to the Handley Page Hastings which has given 20 years of valuable service. The type's first major task had been in the Berlin Airlift, carrying 55,000 tons of coal into the city in 12 months.

January 10   It is announced in Paris that France has concluded an agreement with the Soviet Union for collaboration in space projects.

January 15   The UK government announces cancellation of its order for 50 General Dynamics F-111K variable-geometry aircraft. These had been intended to serve with the RAF in a strike/reconnaissance role.

January 21   A USAF Boeing B-52 of Strategic Air Command carrying four nuclear weapons crashes on sea ice on its approach to Thule AFB, Greenland.

January 29   It is announced that the highly successful North American X-15 research programme is to terminate at the end of 1968.

The UK Empire Test Pilot's School, which had been based at RAE Farnborough since 1947, is transferred to the A & AEE at Boscombe Down..

February 23 Considered as an important first order of British aircraft for Eastern Europe, BAC announces it has received an order for six BAC One-Elevens for the Romanian State airline Tarom.

March 2 Lockheed's C-5A Galaxy, which has been designed to lift a 45,359kg (100,000lb) payload over a range of 10,783km (6,700 miles) is rolled-out.

The first Dassault Mirage IIIs for service with the Swiss Air Force are delivered to Beuchs airfield, near Lucerne.

March 10 French aviation pioneer René Leduc, who had become well-known for his work on ramjet-powered aircraft, dies at Istres, France.

March 11 The first Short Skyvan 3 (G-ASZI), powered by Garrett TPE331-201 turboprop engines, lands back at Belfast on completion of altitude and high temperature trials.

March 13 The President of the UK Board of Trade states that BEA has ordered 26 Hawker Siddeley Trident 3Bs with options on 10.

March 17 USAF General Dynamics F-111As are used operationally for the first time in Vietnam. Two are lost by the end of the month.

March 18 The UK Minister of State, Mintech, states that talks have been held with Canadian, Dutch, German and Italian ministries to consider British participation in the design and development of a European multi-role combat aircraft (MRCA).

March 28 Col Yuri Gagarin, Soviet cosmonaut and first man in space, is killed when the MiG-15UTI that he is flying crashes near Kirzhatsk, north of Moscow.

March 29 Rolls-Royce announces that it has won the very important contract to supply RB.211 turbofan engines for the new Lockheed L-1011 wide-body transport.

April 1 The Royal Air Force celebrates the 50th anniversary of its foundation.

April 2 A go-ahead is announced for the Anglo-French helicopter programme which has been concluded between Aérospatiale and Westland Aircraft.

April 4 Marshal of the Royal Air Force, Sir Dermot Boyle, launches an appeal for donations to help found an RAF Museum at Hendon.

April 13 Martin-Baker announces that a successful ejection on that date marks the 2,000th life to be saved by the company's escape system.

April 15 The first Boeing 727 to enter service outside of the USA, Air France's F-BOJA, is introduced on to the airline's Paris-London route.

The Soviet Union's unmanned spacecraft Cosmos 212 and 213 dock and undock automatically in Earth orbit.

April 17 The Anglo-French Jaguar E-01 prototype, a two-seat version for service with the French Air Force, is rolled out at Bréguet's Villacoublay works.

April 23 The UK Minister of Technology announces in the House of Commons that Britain has withdrawn from the European ELDO space programme.

April 26 *The Daily Mail*, a long-term sponsor of aviation, announces an Atlantic Air Race for 1969 to commemorate the 50th anniversary of the first non-stop transatlantic flight. Prize money is to total £45,000.

April 29 BAC announces a £100 million plus package arms deal with Libya covering the supply, installation, commissioning and support of a complete Thunderbird/Rapier air defence system.

Three of the Royal Navy's McDonnell Douglas F-4K Phantom IIs fly in to RNAS Yeovilton, Somerset on delivery via the Azores.

May 1 The UK Hot Air Group's inaugural meeting, at the Balloon and Airship Flying Centre, Blackbushe, Hampshire, is opened by an ascent of the hot-air balloon *Bristol Belle* (G-AVTL).

May 5 A Grumman Gulfstream II lands at London (Gatwick) after completing a 5,633km (3,500 mile) flight from Teterboro, New Jersey. It is the first executive jet to make a nonstop transatlantic flight.

May 14 HM King Olav of Norway opens officially a chain of Decca Navigator stations to give high-accuracy navigational coverage of the entire Norwegian coastline.

May 16 Carbon-fibre reinforced plastics turbine compressor blades are exhibited for the first time at a Royal Society Meeting.

BOAC's Super VC 10 G-ASGK, carrying 146 passengers, makes the airline's first fully automatic approach and landing at the completion of a scheduled flight from Chicago and Montreal.

May 21 Genex Airlines is formed in Yugoslavia, but the current title of Aviogenex Air Transport is adopted at a later date.

May 22 A first flight is made by a Spanish-built SF-5B, a two-seat trainer version of the Northrop F-5.

June 8 Dr Barnes Wallis, known to the British public for skip-bombs and to the nation's aviation industry for geodetic airframes and variable-geometry wings, receives a Knighthood at the age of 80.

June 14 In commemoration of the RAF's 50th Anniversary, HM Queen Elizabeth II reviews the Service at RAF Abingdon.

June 17 Roll-out of the first McDonnell Douglas C-9A aeromedical transport for the USAF at Long Beach, California.

June 18 The Lockheed AH-56A Cheyenne armed helicopter, with a rigid rotor and pusher propeller, attains a speed of 378 km/h (235 mph).

General Dynamics F-111C variable-geometry combat aircraft in RAAF markings, September 4 1968 and June 1 1973.

June 20   The Romanian airline Tarom flies its inaugural Bucharest-Frankfurt service with a BAC One-Eleven (YR-BCA).

June 26
Demonstrating the development that is being made in nuclear propulsion, a Phoebus 2A nuclear reactor on test at the Nuclear Rocket Development Station, Jackass Flats, Nevada generates a thrust of 90,718kg (200,000lb) for a 12 min test run.

June 28   Retirement of the Avro Anson from RAF service is marked by a formation fly-past of six 'Annies' at RAF Bovingdon, Hertfordshire.

June 30   The Lockheed C-5A Galaxy makes a successful first flight at Dobbins AFB, Georgia, the largest landplane to be flown.

July 1   The Californian domestic airline Air West begins operations. Following the acquisition of this airline by Hughes Air Corporation in April 1970, the title of Hughes Airwest is adopted.

Australia's army air arm becomes known as the Australian Army Aviation Corps.

July 15   Using Ilyushin Il-62s, Aeroflot inaugurates a Moscow-New York service via Montreal. Simultaneously, Pan American begins a reciprocal service from Kennedy International Airport, via Copenhagen.

July 17   A meeting of representatives from Belgium, Canada, the Federal German Republic, Italy, the Netherlands and UK takes place in Bonn to discuss co-operation to develop an Advanced Combat Aircraft for common military use.

August 5   A special airstrip for STOL operations is brought into use at La Guardia Airport, New York.

August 18   The Soviet Union's Tupolev Tu-154 three-turbofan medium/long-range transport is rolled out.

August 23   The first McDonnell Douglas F-4M Phantom II for service with the RAF is received at No.226 OCU, RAF Coningsby, Lincolnshire.

August 24   France detonates a 2-megaton thermonuclear weapon suspended from a balloon over Mururoa Atoll.

August 28   Robert Morane, the founder of the French Morane-Saulnier aircraft company dies in Paris at the age of 82.

August 31   A first successful test of the Rolls-Royce RB.211 turbofan engine is made at the company's Derby works.

September 4   The Australian Minister of Defence accepts formally the first General Dynamics F-111C for service with the Royal Australian Air Force at Fort

Worth, Texas. However, the type does not then enter service with the RAAF.

September 5 The 3,000th production example of the McDonnell Douglas F-4 Phantom II is delivered to the US Navy.

September 8 The Anglo-French Jaguar E-01 prototype makes a successful first flight from the Centre d'Essais en Vol at Istres, France.

September 24 A first emergency ejection is made successfully from a Luftwaffe F-104G Starfighter equipped with a Martin-Baker GQ-7A seat. (q.v. March 8, 1967)

September 30 The Boeing Model 747 prototype, the world's first wide-body jetliner, is rolled out at Everett, Washington.

The New York City Police, which was the first police force in the world to make regular use of helicopters, celebrates the 20th anniversary of their introduction into daily use.

C.C. Walker, aircraft designer, engineer, and one of the five founders of the de Havilland Company, dies at the age of 91.

October 11-22 The first Apollo test mission is made, lasting for 10 days 20 hr 9 min. This is Apollo 7, launched by a Saturn 1B and carrying astronauts Walter Schirra, Don Eisele and Walter Cunningham.

October 21 The General Electric CF6 turbofan engine, which has been developed to power the McDonnell Douglas DC-10 wide-body jet, begins tests two weeks ahead of schedule.

October 26 The Soviet Union launches Soyuz 3 with Georgi Beregovoi on board. The mission, which lasts 3 days 22 hrs 51 mins, includes a rendezvous with unmanned Soyuz 2.

Tupolev Tu-144 SST, the world's first supersonic transport aircraft to fly, December 31 1968.

October 31 In an effort to assist peace negotiations, President Johnson orders a cessation of all air and naval bombardment of North Vietnam.

November 6 The new No.1 Terminal at London Heathrow is opened for limited operation.

November 12 NASA announces that its Apollo 8 mission, scheduled for December 21, 1968, would put the Apollo spacecraft in orbit around the Moon.

Loftleidir Icelandic Airlines begins a low-fare North Atlantic service via London Gatwick, giving this latter airport its first scheduled transatlantic route.

November 13 A first rocket-powered flight by the Northrop/NASA HL-10 lifting-body research aircraft is made from Edwards AFB, California.

November 19 The only known surviving Hawker Typhoon fighter is handed over at RAF Shawbury for inclusion in the RAF Museum.

November 27 The UK Minister of State, Mintech, states that following the multi-nation meeting at Bonn a feasibility study for an MRCA (multi-role combat aircraft) is being carried out.

December 8 A Bell lunar landing research vehicle crashes and is destroyed at Ellington AFB, but its pilot is able to eject safely.

December 11 Sud-Aviation and Hawker Siddeley announce preliminary details of a smaller and less costly version of the European Airbus, designated A-300B.

December 21-27 The Apollo 8 spacecraft is launched by a Saturn V booster carrying astronauts Frank Borman, James Lovell and William Anders. During its 6 day 3 hr 1 min mission, this spacecraft completes the first manned flight around the Moon (on December 24).

December 31 The prototype of the Soviet Union's Tupolev Tu-144 SST makes a successful first flight, the world's first supersonic transport aircraft to fly.

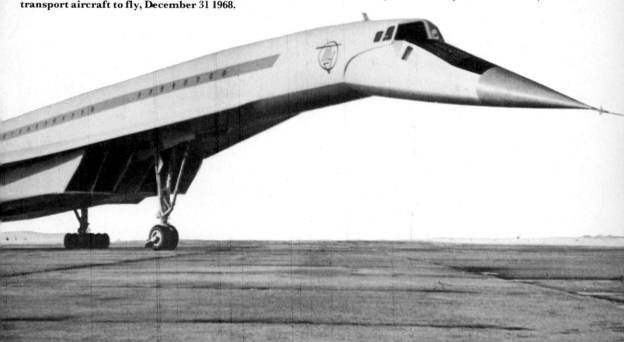

1969

January 7 Almost 10 years after the first flight of the type, Northrop delivers for service with the USAF the 1,000th example of its T-38 Talon supersonic trainer.

January 9 NASA announces that the first Moon landing crew, to be carried by Apollo 11, will comprise Neil A. Armstrong, Lt Col Michael Collins and Col Edwin E. Aldrin.

January 14 BAC announces that it has received an order for 100 Jet Provost Mk 5 basic trainers for supply to the RAF.

No.767 Squadron, the Royal Navy's first McDonnell Douglas F-4K Phantom II training unit, is commissioned at RNAS Yeovilton, Somerset.

January 14 and 15 Launch dates respectively of the Soviet Union's Soyuz 4 and 5 spacecraft. They accomplish the first docking of two manned spacecraft in Earth orbit and the first crew exchange carried out by EVA methods.

February 9 Tacomsat, the largest tactical communications satellite then built, is launched into geostationary Earth orbit. It has been designed to provide a large capacity communication system for the US armed forces.

The Boeing Company achieves a successful first flight of the Model 747 wide-body transport. Dubbed 'jumbo-jet' by the world's Press, it is the first aircraft of this class to be flown.

Mil Mi-12 (V-12), the largest helicopter ever flown, February 12 1969.(*M. Fricke*)

Sud Aviation/BAC Concorde 001 SST prototype, March 2 1969.

226

February 12 Three days after the first flight of the world's largest fixed-wing civil transport, there is an announcement in the Soviet Union to the effect that Russia has developed the world's largest helicopter, the giant Mil Mi-12. This is confirmed early the following month when it is established that on February 12 the helicopter set a number of load-to-height records.

February 26 The death is announced of W.G. Carter, designer of the UK's first turbojet-powered aircraft to be flown, the Gloster/Whittle E.28/39.

March 2 The first Sud-Aviation/BAC Concorde 001 SST prototype makes a completely successful first flight at Toulouse, piloted by Sud's chief test pilot André Turcat.

March 3-13 The US astronauts James McDivitt, David Scott and Russel Schweickart are launched into Earth orbit aboard Apollo 9. During this mission the first in-space tests of the Lunar Module are carried out, and it is the first occasion that a crew-transfer is made between two space vehicles through an internal connection.

March 18 RAF Air Support Command carries out an airlift of troops and equipment to the Caribbean island of Anguilla.

March 19 A weekly return service between Montreal, Canada and Resolution Bay, Cornwallis Island is inaugurated by Nordair. This is the world's first scheduled jet service inside the Arctic circle.

The US Secretary of Defense announces that the US Marine Corps plans to procure an initial batch of 12 Hawker Siddeley Harriers.

Astronaut David Scott performs an EVA (extravehicular activity-spacewalk) on the fourth day of the Apollo 9 mission. (*NASA*)

March 28 BAC announces the formation by BAC, Fiat, Fokker and Messerschmitt-Bölkow of a new aerospace company. This is the international Panavia GmbH, created to develop the multi-role combat aircraft (MRCA).

April 2 Aer Lingus receives delivery at Dublin of Boeing 737-248 *St Albert* (EI-ASA), the first of eight for service with the airline.

April 9 The first UK-built SST prototype, Concorde 002, makes a successful first flight piloted by Brian Trubshaw.

April 10 The Royal Norwegian Air Force receives the first of five Lockheed P-3B Orions, thus becoming the first European air force to operate this ASW aircraft.

It is announced that the UK has withdrawn from participation in the European Airbus programme.

April 17 The No.1 Passenger Terminal at London Heathrow is opened officially by HM Queen Elizabeth II.

April 24 The Hawker Siddeley Harrier T.2 two-seat trainer prototype (XW174) makes its first flight at Dunsfold, Surrey.

April 28 A Hawker Siddeley Harrier GR.1 of the RAF records a first transatlantic crossing by the type, flying from Northolt, Middlesex to Floyd Bennett Field, New York.

April 30 The long-established Bomber Command and Fighter Command of the Royal Air Force are united to form a new RAF Strike Command.

May 11 *The Daily Mail* Transatlantic Air Race ends at midnight. Beginning a week earlier, to allow time for a maximum number of individual efforts, it is won by Lt Cdr Brian Davis, Royal Navy, with a time of 5 hr 11 min 22 sec to get from the top of the Post Office Tower, London to the top of the Empire State Building, New York.

May 18-26 The Apollo 10 spacecraft, carrying astronauts Thomas Stafford, Eugene Cernan and John Young, carries out a Moon-landing rehearsal. While the Apollo 10 travels in lunar orbit, Stafford and Cernan detach the Lunar Module and make two descents to within 14km (8.7 miles) of the Moon's surface. .

May 23 A new Royal Navy anti-submarine squadron is commissioned at RNAS Culdrose. This is No.820 Naval Air Squadron, equipped with Westland Wessex helicopters derived from the Sikorsky S-58.

May 26 The USAF cancels a $900 million contract with Lockheed for the supply of 375 Lockheed AH-56A Cheyenne armed helicopters.

May 29 Following the UK's withdrawal from the European Airbus programme, the French and German governments sign an agreement to initiate joint development of the A300B.

June 5 USAF bombers renew their attacks on North Vietnam, the first since the cease-fire which had been ordered by President Johnson on October 31, 1968.

June 10 The US Department of Defense cancels the Manned Orbiting Laboratory programme (MOL); it would have placed a long-term workshop in Earth orbit.

Lympne Airport, Kent is renamed officially as Ashford Airport.

June 15 An Ilyushin Il-62 long-range airliner is used by Aeroflot to inaugurate a joint service with Pan American, linking Moscow and New York.

June 18 The Australian destroyer HMAS *Hobart* is damaged accidentally off Vietnam by American air-launched Sparrow missiles.

June 19 The death is announced of Siegfried Günter, co-designer of the Heinkel He 111 and designer of the world's first jet-powered aircraft, the Heinkel He 178.

June 20 Westland Aircraft announces the receipt of an order for the supply of 22 Sea King ASW helicopters for service with the German Navy.

June 25 Westward Airways inaugurates a shuttle service between London's Gatwick and Heathrow Airports, operated by a Britten-Norman Islander.

July 16-24 NASA's Apollo 11 is launched to the Moon, carrying astronauts Neil A. Armstrong, Edwin E.A. Aldrin and Michael Collins. On July 21 Neil Armstrong becomes the first man on the Moon after he and Aldrin have descended to the Moon's surface in the Lunar Module Eagle. The mission is completed by a successful splashdown on July 24, the total time being 8 days 3 hr 19 min.

July 21 It is announced in the UK that despite the lack of government support for the European Airbus programme, Hawker Siddeley Aviation is to join France and Germany in the project. The company is to act as design consultants and build the wings under sub-contract.

July 22 An agreement between Fiat and Rolls-Royce is signed in Turin. This covers technical collaboration on the design, development and manufacture of a new series of Viper turbojet engines.

July 23 Aermacchi and BAC sign a memorandum of agreement to initiate detailed study for the development of a basic and an advanced jet trainer.

July 30 NASA's Mariner 6 interplanetary probe transmits 24 pictures of Mars, taken some 3,428km (2,130 miles) from its surface and relayed over a distance of 1.24 million km (0.77 million miles).

August 4 The US Department of Defense places a $461 million contract with Lockheed for development of the S-3A anti-submarine aircraft for the US Navy.

August 8 Handley Page Ltd announces that the company is without financial resources and is to go into voluntary liquidation.

Lift-off of Apollo 11 on its historic Moon mission, July 16 1969. (NASA)

August 16 Flying a modified Grumman F8F-2 Bearcat over a 3km course at restricted altitude, US test pilot Darryl Greenamyer sets a new world speed record for piston-engined aircraft of 769.23 km/h (477.98 mph). This beats by just over 13 km/h (8 mph) the record set by a Messerschmitt Me 209V1 in 1939.

August 18 The first British-assembled SEPECAT Jaguar strike aircraft is rolled out at Warton, Lancashire.

August 19 A Sea King Intensive Flight Trials Unit, the Royal Navy's N.700(S) Squadron, is commissioned at RNAS Culdrose.

September 3 The RAF takes delivery at its Central Flying School, Little Rissington of the first of more than 100 BAC Jet Provost T.5 trainers.

September 4 The UK Ministry of Technology announces that, subject to satisfactory contract negotiations, the Rolls-Royce RB.199 engine has been chosen to power the European MRCA.

September 15 The Cessna Citation (N500CC), the first of a new family of turbofan-powered executive business jets, makes its first flight at Wichita, Kansas.

September 19 It is announced that under a contract valued at $50 million, the Canadian government has ordered 50 Bell CUH-1N helicopters for its armed services.

October 1 Delivery is made to the RAF of the first of 100 Hawker Siddeley Buccaneer multi-role two-seat strike/reconnaissance aircraft.

October 2 The first of 38 Hawker Siddeley Nimrod maritime strike/reconnaissance aircraft is handed over officially to the RAF at Woodford.

October 11, 12 and 13 The respective launch dates of the Soviet Union's Soyuz 6, 7 and 8 spacecraft, which are the first to make a group flight without docking.

October 12 The first SEPECAT Jaguar prototype to be completed in the UK (XW560) makes its first flight, during which it exceeds a speed of Mach 1.

October 13 A joint contract for development of the RB.199 engine is signed by Fiat, MTU of Germany, and Rolls-Royce.

October 20 Finnair becomes the world's first airline to operate aircraft with an inertial guidance system on scheduled passenger services. This dispenses with the requirement for a navigator as a member of the aircrew.

October 24 It is announced in the UK that financially-troubled Handley Page is to receive US backing.

October 29 The US Secretary of Defense states that as an economy measure the USAF's B-58 Hustler, the world's first supersonic strategic bomber, is to be phased out of service.

The last of 170 McDonnell Douglas F-4 Phantom IIs for service with the RAF and Royal Navy is delivered to No 23 MU, RAF Aldergrove.

November 3 The USAF issues Requests for Proposals for a bomber aircraft, to meet its Advanced Manned Strategic Aircraft (AMSA) requirement, under the designation B-1.

November 7 At a meeting of NATO armaments directors in Brussels, the European MRCA is designated officially as a NATO project.

November 7-10 Flying the unorthodox BD-2 (q.v. March 11, 1967), James Bede sets an unrefuelled closed-circuit world distance record for piston-engined aircraft of 14,441.26km (8,973.4 miles). This remains unbroken until late 1981. (q.v. December 5, 1981)

November 8 West Germany's Azur research satellite is launched into orbit by a NASA Scout from the Western Test Range. It is the first West German space satellite.

November 14 The first flight of the naval version of the SEPECAT Jaguar is made at Melun Villaroche airfield.

November 14-24 A second Moon landing is made by the Apollo 12 mission, its all-US Navy crew comprising Charles Conrad, Richard F. Gordon and Alan L. Bean.

November 15 Due to escalating costs, the US Department of Defense reduces the order for Lockheed C-5A Galaxy transports from 155 to 81.

November 17 The first US/Soviet SALT (Strategic Arms Limitation Talks) begin in Helsinki, Finland.

November 22 The first of two Skynet communication satellites, for use by the UK armed forces, is placed in orbit by a Delta rocket from Cape Kennedy.

December 1 The US Federal Air Regulation Pt 36 is introduced, the first legislation to limit aircraft noise at airports.

December 17 The first Lockheed C-5A Galaxy for service with the USAF is handed over officially at Marietta, Georgia.

December 18 Hawker Siddeley Aviation and Beech Aircraft Corporation announce plans to co-operate on the development and marketing of a range of business jets, this including the Hawker Siddeley HS.125.

Aircraft competing in the England-Australia Commemorative Air Race begin taking off from London's Gatwick Airport. Marking the 50th anniversary of the first England-Australia flight, and the bi-centenary of the discovery of Australia, it is won by Capt W.J. Bright and Capt F.L. Buxton in the Britten-Norman BN-2A Islander G-AXUD.

December 19 An agreement is finalised between the US Navy and the UK Ministry of Technology covering the supply of 12 Hawker Siddeley Harriers for the US Marine Corps. A clause allows for the possibility of licence-production by McDonnell Douglas of 100 or more additional aircraft.

December 23 The Secretary of the US Air Force states that the McDonnell Douglas Corporation has been

Pan Am Boeing 747, January 22 1970.

selected as prime contractor for the F-15 air superiority fighter for the USAF.

1970

January 12 The first Boeing Model 747 wide-body transport lands at London Heathrow, a Pan American aircraft on a proving flight from New York.

January 22 Pan American inaugurates its first transatlantic scheduled service with the Boeing 747, introduced on the airline's New York-London route.

January 28 During a survey flight for a proposed Tokyo-London service, a DC-8-62 of Japan Air Lines makes what is believed to be the first trans-Siberian flight by an airliner of a non-Communist country.

January 31 The death is announced at the age of 61 of Mikhail Mil, recognised by the Soviet Union with the award of the Order of Lenin for his contribution to helicopter development.

February 1 Capt Raymond Munro makes the first hot-air balloon crossing of the Irish Sea, from Brittis Bay, Co Wicklow to Ennerdale, Cumberland.

February 11 Japan becomes the fourth nation in the world to launch a domestic satellite using a nationally-built launch rocket, the Ohsumi, boosted by a Lambda 4S carrier rocket.

February 15 Air Chief Marshal Sir Hugh Dowding, who had been AOC-in-C of RAF Fighter Command during the Battle of Britain, dies at the age of 87.

February 16 Hawker Siddeley Harriers of the RAF's No.1 Squadron stage out to RAF Akrotiri, Cyprus making their first overseas proving flight.

February 21 The first of the Sud-Aviation-Westland SA.330 Pumas which have been equipped to RAF requirements, are delivered to the A & AEE at Boscombe Down for testing.

Severely damaged Apollo 13 Service Module photographed from the Lunar Module/Command Module after SM jettisoning, April 11-17 1970 (*NASA*)

February 24 The Royal Navy's aircraft carrier HMS *Ark Royal* is recommissioned. This follows a £30 million refit to allow for the operation of McDonnell Douglas F-4 Phantom IIs and Hawker Siddeley Buccaneers.

March 2 A Boeing B-52 testbed aircraft makes the first flight test of the General Electric CF6-6 turbofan engine which has been developed to power the McDonnell Douglas DC-10.

March 4
Cargolux Airlines International is formed by three airlines to provide specialised charter cargo operations.

March 6 The Rolls-Royce RB.211 three-shaft turbofan engine to power the Lockheed L-1011 TriStar is flown for the first time on a VC10 testbed aircraft.

March 10 The Finnish government announces that preliminary negotiations are under way to acquire Saab-35 Drakens to replace the Folland Gnats in service with its air force.

March 13 The Aero Spacelines Guppy-101 makes its first flight. The 22.30m (73ft 2in) long constant-section portion of the cargo compartment has a maximum width of 5.59m (18ft 4in).

March 19 A first powered flight of the Martin Marietta SV-5P Pilot (X-24A) lifting-body research aircraft is made by Maj Jerauld Gentry following launch from a B-52 'motherplane'.

March 23 Lockheed Aircraft Corporation opens a maintenance base at RAF Seletar, Singapore, to carry out major overhauls of all Singapore Defence Force aircraft.

March 26 The British 'Gee Chain' which provided valuable navigational services during the Second World War is finally closed down.

April 1 Air Jamaica begins scheduled operations. This airline was formed during 1968 to succeed an earlier company of the same name.

April 11-17 NASA's Apollo 13 mission focuses the world's attention when an oxygen tank explodes during the outward flight. The resulting emergency is resolved by brilliant evaluation and improvisation, returning astronauts James Lovell, John Swigert and Fred Haise safely to Earth.

April 13 The UK and USSR sign an agreement allowing BOAC aircraft to overfly Siberia on the airline's London-Tokyo route.

April 17 A Sikorsky CH-53D is used between London and Paris city centres to demonstrate the potential of modern helicopters to provide reliable inter-city services.

April 24 The Chinese People's Republic launches its first satellite into Earth orbit using an indigenous booster rocket. A basic research satellite, it is identified as Chicom 1 by NORAD.

The VFW-Fokker VAK 191B single-seat V/STOL aircraft which is to serve as a systems testbed for the European MRCA is rolled out at Bremen.

April 29 The Royal Danish Air Force receives the first

of 20 Saab 35XD Drakens, a long-range all-weather attack/reconnaissance version.

May 1 The Canadian government announces that it has ordered from Bell Helicopters 74 OH-58A Kiowa light observation helicopters for service with the Canadian Armed Forces.

May 12 NASA announces that McDonnell Douglas and North American Rockwell are the two finalists in negotiations for the development of a re-usable Space Shuttle.

The Sir Alan Cobham Trophy, a new award for presentation annually to the outstanding tanker squadron of RAF Strike Command, is won for the first time by No.57 Squadron.

May 13 BAC announces the receipt of a multi-million pound order to supply refurbished versions of the Canberra for service with the Argentine Air Force.

May 18 The Northrop/NASA HL-10 lifting-body research aircraft begins a series of powered landing tests to evaluate whether the Space Shuttle will require auxiliary power for landing purposes.

May 25 The US government announces that Multiple Individual Re-entry Vehicles (MIRVs), or multiple warheads, have been developed and are available for deployment on the nation's ICBMs.

May 26 It is reported that the Soviet Union's Tupolev Tu-144 SST has flown at Mach 2.02 at a height of 16,155m (53,000ft).

June 1 The first production Lockheed C-5A Galaxy to enter operational service with the USAF is delivered to Military Airlift Command (MAC) at Scott AFB, Charleston, Virginia.

The Soviet Union's Soyuz 9 spacecraft is launched into Earth orbit carrying cosmonauts Andrian Nikolayev and Vitali Sevastyanov. They land successfully after completing what is then the longest space mission, totalling 17 days 16 hr 59 min.

June 3 A licence agreement is completed between Rolls-Royce, Turboméca and Ishikawajima-Harima for Japanese manufacture of the Adour turbofan engine.

June 11 BAC announces the receipt of an order valued at £47 million for a Rapier low-level defence system for Iran.

June 12 Aeroflot inaugurates a direct air service between Moscow and Amman.

June 13 The first eight of 30 Dassault Mirage 3s for service with the Spanish Air Force are delivered at Valencia.

June 16 The Spanish airline Iberia inaugurates a Barcelona-London (Heathrow) cargo service operated by Fokker F.28 Fellowship aircraft.

June 23 The Australian Ministry of Defence states that the government is to arrange the lease of 24 F-4E Phantom IIs from the USA pending finalisation of a decision whether or not to acquire the General Dynamics F-111C.

July 1 The Melbourne International Airport is opened at Tullamarine.

July 2 A first flight is made by the Saab Sk 37 Viggen two-seat trainer prototype from the company's airfield at Linköping.

July 8 The Boeing Company is awarded an initial £16.5 million contract to start development of an Airborne Warning and Control System (AWACS) aircraft.

July 18 The first flight of the Aeritalia (Fiat) G222 general-purpose military transport prototype (1625-0) is made at Torino-Caselle Airport.

July 22 The governments of the UK and German Federal Republic sign a Memorandum of Understanding to launch development of the MRCA.

Sikorsky and Westland Helicopters agree to present the latter company's WG.13 Lynx in the US as Sikorsky's contender for the US Navy's LAMPS (Low-Altitude Multi-Purpose System) requirement.

July 28 The French and UK governments sign an agreement in Paris covering mutual plans for development and production of the SA.341 Gazelle helicopter, and continued development of the WG.13 Lynx.

August 3 The UK government gives approval for the establishment of a second-force national airline.

August 6 Spain and the US sign a renewal of their mutual defence agreement, allowing the US continued use of naval and air bases in Spain. In return Spain is to receive military equipment worth some £153 million.

August 12 West Germany and the Soviet Union conclude a non-agression treaty in Moscow.

August 17 The Soviet Union launches the interplanetary probe Venera 7. The instrument capsule from this probe makes the first confirmed landing on Venus in January 1971, transmitting a weak data signal for 23 min.

August 22 Two Sikorsky HH-53C helicopters complete a non-stop transpacific flight of some 14,484km (9,000 miles), refuelled en route by Hercules tankers.

A first flight is made by the prototype (I-AMKK) of the Aermacchi MB.326K, a single-seat operational trainer and close-support version of the two seat trainer/ground attack MB.326G.

August 29 The first flight of the McDonnell Douglas DC-10 wide body jet (N10DC) is made at Long Beach, California.

September 9 The Rolls-Royce Small Engine Division's Gnome H.1400-2 turboshaft engine is run successfully for the first time.

September 11 A first flight is made by the Britten-Norman 'stretched' three-engined Islander prototype

(G-ATWU), later named Trislander. Within hours of its first flight it is flown to Farnborough, Hampshire for exhibition at the SBAC Show.

September 12 The first two of 72 USAF General-Dynamics F-111Es to be based in the UK arrive at RAF Upper Heyford, Oxfordshire.

The Soviet Union's Luna 16 Moon probe is launched. This remarkable vehicle makes an unmanned automatic soft-landing on the lunar surface and scoops up a sample of surface soil which it stores within the vehicle before taking off and returning to Earth on September 24.

Three commercial transports which had been hijacked by Arab guerrillas are destroyed by dynamite on the desert airstrip known as Dawsons's Field near Amman, Jordan. They comprise a Boeing 707 of Trans World Airlines, a McDonnell Douglas DC-8 of Swissair, and a BAC VC 10 of BOAC.

October 2 The USAF takes formal delivery of its first Bell UH-1N twin-turbine helicopter.

October 9 Due to heavy financial losses Bahama Airways ceases operations.

October 15 The first MiG-21 to be constructed entirely in India is handed over to the Indian Air Force at the Hindustan Aeronautics factory.

October 16 The British third-level airline Westward Airways ceases operations.

October 20 It is announced that British United Airways and Caledonian Airways are to merge at the end of November to form the UK's second-force airline.

October 23 The Argentinian government signs a contract in Buenos Aires covering the supply of 14 Dassault Mirage IIIs for the Argentine Air Force.

October 24 The last flight of the North American X-15 research programme is made by NASA pilot William H. Dana.

October 26 Five NASA representatives meet their Soviet counterparts in Moscow to discuss co-operative space rescue arrangements.

October 29 A first flight is made by the Aérospatiale Caravelle 12 prototype (F-WJAK), a 'stretched' version of the Caravelle Super B.

November 4 The Concorde 001 prototype attains its design cruising speed of Mach 2 for the first time. The UK-built 002 achieves this milestone nine days later.

It is announced in the UK that a new company named Cargo Airships Ltd has been formed to study the use of very large airships for cargo transport.

November 6 The USAF launches a military reconnaissance satellite into a geostationary orbit above the Indian Ocean. It is reported to have sensors able to detect infra-red emissions from rocket plumes.

November 10 The Soviet Union launches the Luna 17 moon probe. This soft-lands on the lunar surface to deploy a Lunokhod rover vehicle on November 17 which

travels more than 9.5km (6 miles) during the ensuing nine months, conducting experiments and transmitting the results to Earth.

November 12 A first flight is made by the Japanese NAMC XC-1, the nation's first military jet transport of indigenous design and manufacture.

A Boeing 747 on test at Edwards AFB takes off at a gross weight of 372,263kg (820,700lb) – just over 366 tons.

November 16 The Australian airline Qantas Airways celebrates the 50th anniversary of its formation.

The first Lockheed L-1011 TriStar wide-body jet airliner (N1011) makes its first flight.

November 30 British Caledonian Airways is formed as the UK's second-force airline by a merger of British United Airways and Caledonian Airways.

December 9 The death is reported of Artem Mikoyan in the Soviet Union, renowned as the originator of the MiG series of fighter aircraft.

December 15 The US Congress declines to provide funding for the licence production by McDonnell Douglas of the Hawker Siddeley Harrier.

December 18 Aérospatiale, Deutsche-Airbus and Fokker-VFW establish Airbus Industrie to be responsible for the A300B programme.

December 21 A first flight is recorded by the prototype of the Grumman F-14A Tomcat carrier-based variable-geometry multi-role fighter for the US Navy.

December 30 Hawker Siddeley signs a contract covering the supply of 30 refurbished Hunters for service with the Swiss Air Force.

1971

January 6 The first AV-8A Harrier for the US Marine Corps is handed over officially at Hawker Siddeley's airfield at Dunsfold, Surrey.

January 8 Bell Helicopter is awarded a $37.5 million contract for the supply of an additional 300 UH-1N utility helicopters for the US Army.

January 14 The first F-4EJ Phantom II for the JASDF is flown at St Louis, Missouri.

January 20 Four members of the RAF's Red Arrows aerobatic team are killed at RAF Kemble, Gloucestershire when two of their Folland Gnats collide during practice of the 'roulette' manoeuvre.

January 21 The TF34 twin-spool turbofan, developed by General Electric to power the Lockheed S-3A, makes its first flight installed in a Boeing B-47 testbed aircraft.

January 22 The national airline of Nigeria, which was known as WAAC (Nigeria) Ltd from 1958, adopts its present title of Nigeria Airways.

January 22 The crew of a US Navy Lockheed P-3C Orion, led by Cdr Donald H. Lilienthal, establish a

Commander Donald H. Lilienthal (front row, second from left) and the crew of the record breaking Lockheed P-3C Orion, January 22 1971.

new world long distance record for aircraft with turboprop engines at just over 11,281km (7,010 miles). On January 27 the same aircraft sets up a speed in a straight line record at 806.10km/hr (500.89mph), also in Class C, Group II.

The first of 40 SA.330E Pumas for service with RAF Air Support Command, under the designation Puma HC.Mk 1, is handed over officially at Westland's Yeovil works.

January 31 The new London Air Traffic Control Centre at West Drayton, Middlesex becomes operational.

January 31 – February 9 NASA's Apollo 14 is launched to make the third US Moon landing, and completed successfully by astronauts Alan Shepard, Stuart Rossa, and Edgar Mitchell.

February 4 Rolls-Royce announces that it is in financial difficulties, due primarily to the cost of developing the RB.211 engine, and that it has no alternative but to request the appointment of a Receiver.

February 5 The UK Air Training Corps celebrates the 30th anniversary of its foundation.

February 18 The Australian Defence Minister announces a $37 million contractual agreement with Bell Helicopters covering the manufacture in Australia of 190 OH-58 Kiowa light observation helicopters.

March 19 The Aeroplane & Armament Experimental Establishment at Boscombe Down, Wilts, celebrates the 50th anniversary of its formation.

March 21 A successful first flight is made by the Westland WG.13 Lynx multi-purpose helicopter prototype (XW835) at Yeovil, Somerset.

March 24 The US Senate decides by a single vote not to provide funding for development of an American SST, bringing cancellation of the Boeing 2707-300 project.

March 29 Air Southwest, which had been formed in Texas on March 15, 1967, adopts its current title of Southwest Airlines.

April 1 A British Caledonian VC10 makes the first scheduled flight on a London-Accra service via Kano and Lagos, a route which has been transferred from BOAC.

April 5 The VFW-Fokker VFW 614 short-haul transport prototype is rolled out at the company's Bremen factory.

April 6 KLM inaugurates a trans-Siberian service with Ilyushin Il-62s leased from Aeroflot.

April 12 The USAF announces the use of a so-called 'daisy cutter' bomb in Vietnam. This is a conventional high-explosive bomb designed to clear jungle areas.

April 14 Trans-Mediterranean Airways, which was formed during 1953 to provide non-scheduled freight services from Beirut, inaugurates the first round-the-world cargo service.

April 15 The US Marine Corps' first Harrier squadron, VMA-513, becomes operational at Beaufort Air Station, South Carolina.

April 19 The Soviet Union launches the Salyut 1 space station into Earth orbit.

April 22 Following an Anglo-French Ministerial meeting, authorisation is given to Aérospatiale and BAC for the construction of four additional Concorde SSTs, making a total of ten.

April 22-24 The Soviet Union's Soyuz 10 spacecraft is launched into orbit, docking with Salyut 1, but no crew board the space station.

April 23 John H. Shafter, US FAA administrator on a visit to the UK, states that Concorde will be allowed to land at US airports.

April 25 The UK's oldest flyable aeroplane, a Blackburn Monoplane built in 1912, reappears after an absence of five years to take part in a Shuttleworth Air

Pageant at Old Warden, Bedfordshire.

BOAC operates its first Boeing 747 flight between London Heathrow and New York.

April 26 The UK government announces that Foulness in Essex has been chosen as the site for a new third London Airport.

May 3 A first fight is made in the UK by the Kestrel experimental sailplane designed and built by Slingsby Sailplanes. This incorporates a carbon fibre main spar.

HMS *Ark Royal* embarks the RAF's No 1 Squadron with its Harriers for sea trials off the Scottish coast.

May 8 The first flight is made by a Dassault Mirage G8 variable-geometry combat aircraft prototype.

May 10 The UK Minister for Aerospace states in the House of Commons that conditional agreement has been reached with Lockheed Aircraft Corporation to help finance Rolls-Royce (1971) Ltd in order to continue development and production of the RB.211 engine.

May 13 Concorde 001 makes its first fully automatic approach and landing at Toulouse.

May 15 Toa Domestic Airlines is formed as the result of a merger of Toa Airways and Japan Domestic Airlines.

May 20 The US House of Representatives Armed Services Committee approves funding for the procurement of 30 more Hawker Siddeley Harriers

The US Supersonic Transport Program is terminated officially by Congress.

May 24 A successful first flight is made by the second Grumman F-14A Tomcat prototype. The first had been lost at the termination of its first flight due to a complete hydraulic failure.

May 25 Boeing and Aeritalia sign an agreement for the joint development of a 100/150-seat jet-powered STOL transport.

May 26 Making its first appearance in the West, the Soviet Union's Tupolev Tu-144 SST files into Le Bourget to take part in the 1971 Paris Air Show.

May 28 The Soviet Union launches the interplanetary space probe Mars 3, which subsequently puts the first data capsule on the Martian surface.

May 30 Launch date of NASA's Mariner 9 interplanetary probe which becomes the first artificial satellite of Mars. It transmits more than 7,000 pictures, many of which provide remarkable detail of the Martian surface.

June 3 The UK government announces that subject to suitable negotiations it is intended to acquire French Exocet long-range surface-to-surface anti-ship missiles for the Royal Navy.

June 6 The Soviet Union puts the Soyuz 11 spacecraft in orbit with cosmonauts Georgi Dobrovolski, Vladislav Volkov and Viktor Patsayev. They dock with Salyut 1 and make a stay of more than three weeks, but all three die during the landing phase of their mission.

June 11-Aug 4   The first flight by a lightplane from equator to equator via the North Pole is made by UK airwoman Sheila Scott flying a Piper Aztec D.

June 18   The Soviet Union announces the death of Alexei Isayev, aged 62, leader of the design teams responsible for many of the nation's successful rocket engines.

June 24   The West German Defence Ministry approves the purchase of 175 single-seat McDonnell Douglas F-4E Phantom IIs to replace the Luftwaffe's Fiat G.91s and Lockheed F-104G Starfighters. The order is changed later to similar two-seat F-4Fs.

July 7   The first Scottish Aviation (formerly Beagle) Bulldog two/three-seat primary trainer for the Royal Swedish Air Force is handed over officially.

July 14   The VFW-Fokker VFW 614 short-haul transport prototype (D-BABA) makes its first flight at Bremen, West Germany.

July 20   First flight of the Mitsubishi XT-2 jet-trainer prototype, the first Japanese supersonic aircraft of indigenous design and manufacture.

July 26   Cam-Air (Cameroon Airlines) is formed by the government, beginning scheduled operations on November 1, 1971.

July 26 – August 7   The US achieves its fourth Moon landing with the Apollo 15 mission. It is distinguished by the first use of the Lunar Roving Vehicle.

August 1   BEA celebrates the 25th anniversary of its establishment, by which time it has carried more than 8.7 million passengers.

August 2   By a single vote margin the US Senate agrees to provide $250 million support for Lockheed Corporations's TriStar programme.

August 4   A first flight is made by the prototype of the Agusta A 109 twin-engined general purpose helicopter.

August 5   The UK Civil Aviation Act 1971 bill is approved, establishing the Civil Aviation Authority (CAA) and British Airways Board.

August 6   The last of the Royal Navy's shore-based FAW.2 Sea Vixen squadrons is disbanded at RNAS Yeovilton, Somerset

The first production Aérospatiale/Westland SA.341 Gazelle makes its first flight at Marignane, France.

August 23   Air Paris inaugurates a Le Havre-Gatwick service using de Havilland Canada DHC-6 Twin Otters.

Britain, France, the US and USSR sign a new agreement concerning access to Berlin.

August 24   Hawker Siddeley receives confirmation of an order for the supply of six Trident 2Es to the Civil Aviation Administration of the People's Republic of China.

September 3   A first flight is made at Sao Jose dos Campos, near Sao Paulo, of the EMBRAER/Aermacchi EMB-326GB Xavante jet trainer, the first jet aircraft to be built by the Brazilian aircraft industry.

September 13   First flight in the USA of the Bede BD-5 Micro, an unusual aircraft designed for construction by homebuilders, the development of which is to have far-reaching consequences.

September 14   It is announced that with final negotiations settled between airlines, bankers, Rolls-Royce and the US government, Lockheed Aircraft Corporation is given a go-ahead for production of the L-1011 TriStar.

September 27   The first bench test of the RB.199 augmented turbofan to power the European MRCA is made successfully at Patchway, Bristol.

September 30   The US and USSR come to a Nuclear Accidents agreement, with each nation advising the other of test accidents or detection of suspicious activity in order to prevent an accidental nuclear war.

A first flight is made by the Hawker Siddeley Shackleton AEW. Mk 3, a specially-developed airborne early warning aircraft for service with the RAF's No 8 Squadron.

October 4   The Soviet Union announces that its Lunokhod 1 lunar roving vehicle has ended its useful life.

October 10   Derived from Misrair, then becoming named United Arab Airlines under President Nasser, Egypt's national airline becomes Egyptair on the above date.

October 11   The Soviet Union's orbiting space laboratory Salyut 1 is destroyed as it re-enters the Earth's atmosphere after its mission had been terminated.

October 20   A new international air terminal is opened at Brasilia Airport, Brazil.

NASA and the Soviet Union agree to exchange space findings of special interest and to co-operate in several other spheres.

October 21   The UK Minister of State for Defence Procurement states that an additional 16 Hawker Siddeley Buccaneers have been ordered for service with the RAF.

October 22   The Britten-Norman company on the Isle of Wight, which has become beset by financial problems, requests the appointment of a Receiver.

October 26   The Receiver appointed to investigate Britten-Norman's financial affairs states that limited production will continue in the hope of selling the company as a going concern.

October 28   The all-British Black Arrow launcher successfully orbits the first UK X.3 Prospero technology satellite at Woomera, Australia.

November 1   British Caledonian inaugurates a London-Paris service with BAC One-Elevens. This is the first occasion that a British carrier has been authorised officially to compete against BEA in Europe.

November 8 The first prototype of the Lockheed-S-3A Viking is rolled out at Burbank, California.

November 9 Air France orders six Airbus A 300Bs with options on a further ten.

November 11 The USSR and West Germany sign an agreement for the establishment of direct air services between their two countries.

November 22 The Australian Minister of Defence accepts officially the first of 75 Bell OH-58A light observation helicopters for service with the Australian Army.

November 23 Carried by an Aero Spacelines Super Guppy operated by Aeromaritime, the first set of A300B wings is delivered from Hawker Siddeley's Chester factory to Toulouse.

Britten-Norman (Bembridge) Ltd is formed to continue the activities of the former company until a sale is negotiated.

December 3 The Pakistan Air Force launches air attacks on all major Indian Air Force bases, but this has been foreseen by India and defence is ready.

December 6 The Spanish government states that the nation's aircraft industry is to participate in the Airbus A300 programme.

December 8 The French government gives approval for joint development by SNECMA and General Electric in America of the CFM 56 two-spool turbofan engine.

December 13 A new Soviet deep space tracking and research ship, the *Kosmonavt Yuri Gagarin*, sails from Odessa on its maiden voyage.

December 16 The Canadian Minister of Defence accepts formally the first of 74 Bell COH-58A light observation helicopters for service with the Canadian Armed Forces.

December 17 A cease-fire in the Indian-Pakistan war is called for and accepted by both sides.

1972

January 4 Bangladesh Biman is formed as the national airline of the state of Bangladesh, known formerly as East Pakistan.

January 5 A US Presidential announcement authorises a $5,500 million 5-year budget for the development of NASA's Space Shuttle.

January 17 The Spanish airline Iberia finalises a contract with The Boeing Company covering the supply of 16 Advanced 727-200s.

January 21 The UK Minister of Aerospace states that the UK government will provide Rolls-Royce (1971) Ltd with an additional £11 million to finance development of the M45H turbofan engine.

A first flight is made by the Lockheed S-3A Viking carrier-based ASW prototype (157992).

January 24 Singapore Airlines is formed following the dissolution of Malaysia-Singapore Airlines.

January 26 Jetstream Aircraft, the company which was formed to continue production of the Jetstream after the collapse of Handley Page, delivers its first production aircraft.

January 30 The French domestic airline Air Inter places the first firm order for the Dassault-Bréguet Mercure short-haul twin-jet airliner.

February 15 BAC, Messerschmitt-Bölkow-Blohm and Saab-Scania announce their intention to collaborate on the design and development of a quiet STOL civil transport.

February 16 French and German Defence Ministers sign a draft agreement to proceed with joint development of the Alpha Jet training aircraft.

February 23 Laker Airways in the UK announces that it has placed an order for two McDonnell Douglas DC-10 wide-body airliners.

February 24 The UK Minister of State for Defence says that the government intends to purchase 25 Jetstreams for service with the RAF.

February 29 All scheduled services are terminated by Channel Airways in the UK.

March 3 NASA launches the Pioneer 10 interplanetary probe intended to fly past Jupiter during 1973.

March 8 The Goodyear non-rigid airship *Europa*, which has been assembled in the UK, makes its first flight from RAE Cardington, Bedfordshire.

March 27 The Soviet Union's interplanetary probe Venera 8 is launched towards Venus. An instrument capsule is landed successfully on the surface of the planet on July 22, 1972, transmitting data for a period of 50 min.

April 1 The British Airways Board combines the activities of BEA and BOAC under the title of British Airways.

The UK Civil Aviation Authority (CAA), the nation's first independent body for regulating civil aviation and providing air traffic control and navigation services, begins its functions.

April 12 The last revenue flight is made by the oldest surviving Vickers Viking (G-AWLF). It is subsequently placed on permanent display at Liverpool's Speke Airport.

April 13 The UK Secretary of State for Trade and Industry says that authority has been given for Aérospatiale and BAC to build an additional 6 Concordes.

April 16-27 NASA's Apollo 16 mission, and the fifth Moon landing, is carried out successfully.

April 25 A Schleicher ASW 12 flown by Hans Gross (Germany) establishes a new world distance record for single-seat sailplanes of 1,460.8km (907.7 miles).

April 26 The first revenue flight of a Lockheed L-1011 TriStar is made by Eastern Airlines on its Miami-New York service.

April 27 The UK Minister of Defence states that about 1,000 tactical aircraft and helicopters operated by the UK armed services are to be equipped with Madge (microwave aircraft digital equipment). This British-designed equipment has won the NATO tactical landing-aid competition.

April 29 A specially-equipped McDonnell Douglas F-4 Phantom II becomes the first aircraft to be flown in the US with a fly-by-wire control system.

May 1 The de Havilland Canada C-8A Buffalo augmentor wing research prototype (N716NA) makes its first flight. This has been developed under a programme sponsored by NASA and the Canadian Department of Industry, Trade and Commerce.

May 2 20th anniversary of the inauguration by BOAC of the world's first jet airliner service, from London to Johannesburg by the Comet 1 G-ALYP.

May 4 The first SEPECAT Jaguar strike trainer to enter military service is flown from Toulouse to the French Air Force base at Mont de Marsan.

May 10 India and the USSR sign a development agreement under which the Soviet Union will launch India's first nationally-designed and built satellite.

The prototype of the Fairchild A-10A, one of the two contenders for the USAF's AX close-support requirement makes its first flight.

May 19 An Indian government spokesman in New Delhi says that Indian security forces have orders to destroy all Pakistani aircraft violating India's airspace.

May 22 BEA receives formal approval from the UK CAA for the use of Smiths Autoland on Trident 3Bs down to ICAO Category 3B weather minima.

Fairchild A-10A prototype on its first flight, May 10 1972.

Northrop A-9A, which eventually lost the USAF's AX programme competition, May 30 1972.

May 23 The Australian Prime Minister announces an order for 20 Nomad light twin-turboprop transports. These are to be built by the Government Aircraft Factories with 11 for use by the Army and the balance for commercial use.

May 24 President Nixon and Premier Kosygin sign an agreement covering a US/USSR Earth orbital mission during 1975.

May 25 The Westland/Aérospatiale Lynx HAS.Mk 2 prototype (XX469), an ASW version for service with the Royal Navy, makes a successful first flight from Yeovil, Somerset.

British Airways places a firm order for five Aérospatiale/BAC Concorde SSTs.

May 26 At a Summit meeting in Moscow, President Nixon and Leonid Brezhnev sign the first SALT agreement.

Cessna Aircraft Corporation announces completion of the company's 100,000th aircraft, the first company in the world to achieve such a production figure.

May 30 The Northrop A-9A, the second contending prototype for the USAF's AX close-support fighter programme, makes its first flight at Edwards AFB, California.

June 1 Easily recognisable from earlier versions by having a third main landing gear unit, the long-range McDonnell Douglas DC-10-30 is rolled out at Long Beach, California.

June 2 A first flight is made by Aérospatiale's SA.360

helicopter prototype, a private-venture development of the Alouette III.

June 19 A large number of international airline pilots stage a one-day strike in protest at what they consider to be insufficient action by governments against hijacking and other forms of airborne crime.

June 21 Jean Boulet flies an Aérospatiale Lama helicopter to a world record height of 12,442m (40,820ft), a record that is unbeaten in early 1982.

June 22 The first of 20 pre-production McDonnell Douglas F-15A fighters is rolled out at St Louis, Missouri.

June 23 The first Northrop F-5E Tiger II is rolled out at the company's Hawthorne, California factory.

July 26 NASA announces that Rockwell International Corporation has been selected to build the Space Shuttle Orbiter, awarding the company an initial $450 million to cover the first two years of development.

July 27 A first flight is made by the first pre-production McDonnell Douglas F-15A fighter (71-0280) from Edwards AFB, California.

July 28 The Italian Minister of Defence announces the award to Aeritalia of a contract valued at £90 million for the production of 44 G222 military transports.

August 1 Delta Air Lines merges with Northeast Airlines, retaining the name Delta Air Lines and forming a combined fleet of almost 200 aircraft.

August 7 The UK Minister for Aerospace says that the European division of British Airways has been authorised to acquire six Lockheed L-1011 TriStars with an option on an additional six.

August 11 The NATO MRCA Management Agency signs the main development contract for the MRCA.

A successful first flight is made by the Northrop F-5E Tiger II at Edwards AFB, California.

August 15 It is reported that Dornier, Hawker Siddeley and VFW-Fokker are to co-operate in the project definition of a quiet short/medium-haul transport.

August 26 The death is announced of Sir Francis Chichester at the age of 70. He is remembered in aviation history for a display of superb navigation in his lightplane crossing of the Tasman Sea.

August 28 HRH Prince William of Gloucester and his passenger are killed in a flying accident at the beginning of a Goodyear Trophy Race in the UK.

September 11 Cyril Uwins, a pioneer test pilot who has tested every Bristol aircraft from the Scout to the Type 170 Freighter, dies at the age of 76

September 22 Receipt by The Boeing Company of an order for 14 Model 727s from Delta Air Lines brings total sales for this aircraft to 1,000. It is the first jetliner to attain such a sales figure.

September 29 The People's Republic of China and Japan sign a peace treaty, ending officially a state of war that had started 35 years earlier.

Air Florida, which had been formed during September 1971 to provide intrastate services, begins its first scheduled operations.

October 1 Malaysian Airline System (Sistem Penerbangan Malaysia Berhad), which had been established as the government-owned national airline during April 1971, begins scheduled operations.

October 14 The 25th anniversary of the world's first supersonic flight, made by Capt Charles ('Chuck') Yeager in the Bell X-1 research aircraft.

October 26 The death is announced of Igor Sikorsky, pioneer aircraft designer renowned in particular for the development of a practical single-rotor helicopter.

October 28 A first flight is made at Toulouse-Blagnac of the first Airbus A300B1 (F-WUAB), piloted by Max Fischl.

November 10 The Secretary of the USAF announces the award of contracts to Boeing and McDonnell Douglas to build prototypes of their proposals for an AMST (Advanced Medium STOL Transport) requirement.

November 12 The first McDonnell Douglas DC-10-10 for service with Laker Airways is delivered to London Gatwick.

November 15 A new passenger-handling complex, together with a hangar to accommodate four Sikorsky S-61N helicopters, is opened at Dyce Airport, Aberdeen. It emphasises the close relationship between helicopters and offshore oil/gas exploration/development.

HM Queen Elizabeth II opens the Royal Air Force Museum at Hendon, north London.

November 30 The West German Minister of Defence states that support for the VFW-Fokker VAK 191B experimental V/STOL fighter programme has been withdrawn.

December 7-19 NASA's successful Apollo 17 mission is the last of the Moon landings. It, like the two that had preceded it, made use of a Lunar Roving Vehicle, and a 75-hour stay on the lunar surface was the longest of the Apollo missions.

December 16 Launch of the West German weather satellite Aeros 1.

December 21 The Swiss Defence agency signs a contract with Hawker Siddeley for the supply of an additional 30 refurbished Hunters for service with the Swiss Air Force.

December 23 The Hertfordshire Pedal Aeronauts (HPA) Toucan man-powered aircraft makes a first flight of 640m (2,100ft) at Radlett. It is the first to have a two-man crew/power unit.

1973

January 7 The world's first hot-air airship (G-BAMK), developed in the UK by Cameron Balloons of Bristol, makes a successful first flight.

January 15 President Nixon orders a halt to air strikes and all other offensive military action against North Vietnam.

January 24 An agreement to end the war in Vietnam is initialled in Paris. It calls for a cease-fire at 23.59 hrs GMT on January 27.

Cameron D-96 prototype hot-air airship on its first flight, January 7 1973.

US Navy Phantom II fighter-bombers from USS *Coral Sea* **drop bombs on North Vietnam a few months before a halt is called to air strikes, January 15 1973.**

February 1   Pan American and Trans World Airlines terminate their optional purchase contracts for the Aérospatiale/BAC Concorde SST.

February 2   The Soviet Novosti Press agency states that the Tupolev Tu-144 SST will enter service on Aeroflot's long-range domestic routes during 1974.

February 21   A Boeing 727 of Libyan Arab Airlines is shot down by two Israeli F-4E Phantom II fighters.

February 23   The death of Air Vice-Marshal A.C. Kermode is announced. He is remembered by untold numbers of RAF and ex-RAF air and ground crew for two books that simplified an understanding of aircraft structures and the way they flew.

The Aérospatiale/BAC Concorde 002 flies non-stop from Toulouse to Iceland and return. This represents a greater distance than the guaranteed entry-into-service range.

February 28   A first flight is made at Long Beach, California by the McDonnell Douglas DC-10-30CF, a version of the company's wide-body jet that can be converted overnight from passenger to full cargo configuration or vice versa.

March 5   Sikorsky Aircraft celebrates the 50th anniversary of the company's formation in the US, originally as Sikorsky Manufacturing Corporation.

March 24 The prototype of the Dassault-Bréguet Falcon 30, a 30-seat commuter airliner, is rolled out at Bordeaux-Merignac.

April 2 The first Lockheed L-1011 TriStar to operate in Britain, Court Line's *Halcyon Days*, makes an inaugural flight to Palma carrying members of the UK Press and 360 fare-paying passengers.

April 6 A new passenger terminal is opened officially at Hanover Airport. It has been designed to cater for an estimated annual traffic of four million passengers by 1976-77.

Four months ahead of schedule, the first example of the Northrop F-5E Tiger II is delivered to the USAF at Williams AFB, Florida.

April 10 A first flight is made by the Boeing T-43A (71-1403), a navigation trainer for the USAF developed from the Model 737-200 civil transport.

April 13 A deep-space tracking antenna with a diameter of 64m (210ft) is commissioned at Tidbinbilla, Australia.

April 18 CAAC, the national airline of the People's Republic of China, inaugurates scheduled services to the Albanian capital of Tirana.

April 19 A Turbo-Union RB.199 reheat turbofan, chosen power plant for the MRCA, is flown for the first time in an Avro Vulcan testbed aircraft operated by Rolls-Royce.

May 1 KLM inaugurates a 12 flights-per-week frequency service between Amsterdam and London Gatwick.

May 2 A new radar station, for use by the London Traffic Control Centre at West Drayton, is commissioned at Burrington, North Devon.

May 3 The second L-1011 TriStar for service with Court Line (*Halcyon Breeze*) is delivered to Luton, Bedfordshire. Its entire 8,850km (5,500 mile) non-stop delivery flight, from take-off at Palmdale to touch-down at Luton is carried out completely under automatic control.

May 8 An Airbus A300B prototype makes the first fully automatic landing of the type at Toulouse.

McDonnell Douglas hands over to the US Navy at Long Beach, California the first two of eight C-9B Skytrain IIs. A fleet logistic transport, like the USAF's C-9A Nightingale, it is based on the DC-9-30.

May 14 The last Saturn V booster is used to launch NASA's Skylab 1 Orbital Workshop into Earth orbit. Air pressure causes damage to a micrometeoroid shield immediately after lift-off.

May 20 Because of an 80km (50 mile) fishing limit dispute with the UK, the government of Iceland bans RAF use of the NATO base at Keflavik.

May 22 The UK Secretary of State for Trade and Industry states that the government has given approval to Short Brothers for development and production of the SD3-30 30-seat transport.

Aero Peru (Empresa de Transporte Aereo del Peru) is formed as the government-owned national airline.

May 23 Sabena, Belgium's national airline, celebrates its 50th anniversary.

May 24 The first of 175 McDonnell Douglas F-4F Phantom IIs for the Luftwaffe, a two-seat version with leading-edge manoeuvring slats, is rolled out at St Louis, Missouri.

May 25 NASA's Skylab 2 is launched into orbit to rendezvous with Skylab 1. Astronauts Charles Conrad, Joseph Kerwin and Paul Weitz are able to effect repairs to Skylab 1 during several EVAs. Total mission time is 28 days 49 min.

May 30 The first production SEPECAT Jaguar GR.Mk 1 for RAF Strike Command is delivered to RAF Lossiemouth, Morayshire.

June 1 Ten years after the order had been placed, and subsequently postponed, the first six of 24 General Dynamics F-111Cs are delivered to the Royal Australian Air Force at Amberley AFB, near Brisbane.

June 3 The 30th Paris Air Show closes on a tragic note with the loss during a flying display of the second pre-production Tupolev Tu-144 SST, killing all six crew members.

June 6 Working groups are set up in Geneva by the US/USSR to supervise agreed measures resulting from SALT meetings.

June 16 The 25th anniversary of the formation of Air-Britain is celebrated by an international balloon meeting at Cirencester Park. An active participant is the 80-year-old French veteran balloonist Charles Dollfus.

June 19 France's first Jaguar squadron is formed at the French Air Force base at St. Dizier.

June 26 The first of 26 Scottish Aviation Jetstream T.Mk.1s for the RAF is handed over officially at the company's Prestwick base. They have been procured for use as multi-engine pilot trainers.

A Pan American Boeing 747 carrying 220 passengers makes a completely uneventful fully-automatic landing at London Heathrow. This is made because storm damage to the flight deck windscreen had completely cut off all forward view.

June 27 The first flight by a NASA Earth-resources survey aircraft is made to investigate moth damage to fir trees in Oregon and Washington.

June 28 The gem of the Strathallan Collection, Hawker Hurricane P3308, is flown for the first time following restoration. This brings to a total of three the known airworthy Hurricanes.

June 29 A Fleet Air Arm Westland/Aérospatiale Lynx HAS.Mk 2 makes the first at-sea deck landing of the type aboard the helicopter support ship RFA *Engadine*.

Martin Marietta X-24B photographed in July 1973, shortly before flight trials began. (*NASA*)

June 30 Concorde 001 is used to carry scientists and equipment across North Africa to allow extended observation of a solar eclipse.

July 1 Wien Air Alaska adopts this name, having been known since April 1968 as Wien Consolidated Airlines following a merger of two earlier companies.

KLM celebrates the 60th anniversary of its formation.

July 18 The SNECMA M53 turbofan is flown for the first time installed on a Caravelle III testbed aircraft.

July 25 Flying the Mikoyan Ye-266 in the Soviet Union, A. Fedotov establishes a new world altitude record of 36,240m (118,898ft).

July 26 A first flight is made by the Sikorsky S-69 Advancing Blade Concept (ABC) research helicopter. The use of two co-axial contra-rotating rigid rotors makes it possible to dispense with an anti-torque tail rotor.

August 1 The first unpowered flight is made by the Martin Marietta X-24B lifting-body research aircraft following launch from its B-52 'motherplane' at a height of 12,190m (40,000ft).

August 14 The Ferranti Company donates a Gloster Meteor NF.14 to the Royal Scottish Museum. Handed over at Turnhouse Airport, Edinburgh, it had been used by Ferranti for airborne radar development.

The USAF ends its bombing attacks on Cambodia, terminating more than nine years of US air combat in Southeast Asia.

August 17 The UK Ministry of Defence announces an order, received via the US, for the supply of eight Hawker Siddeley Harriers for service with the Spanish Navy. They are to be equipped in the US to US Marine Corps AV-8A standard before delivery to Spain.

August 29 Hawker Siddeley announces receipt from the UK government of a £46 million go-ahead investment for development and production of the company's HS 146 project. This is a four-turbofan airliner of 70/102-seat capacity.

August 31 RAF Maintenance Command and No 90 Group are disbanded. Their duties are assumed from September 1 by the newly-formed RAF Support Command with HQ at RAF Andover, Hampshire.

September 3 The Boeing Company announces its intention to proceed 'incrementally' with the development of a lower-weight long-range version of the Model 747. Designated 747 SP (Special Performance), the first order is received from Pan American a week later.

September 12 A first flight is made by the Westland Commando Mk 1 (G-17-1), a tactical military helicopter based on the Sea King airframe.

September 20 In Washington, President Nixon presents the Harmon Trophy, awarded for outstanding contributions to aeronautical science, to the Concorde chief test pilots of Aérospatiale and BAC, André Turcat and Brian Trubshaw respectively.

September 23 The Italian Air Force celebrates the 50th anniversary of its foundation.

September 24 A Memorandum of Understanding is concluded between NASA and ESRO (European Space Research Organisation). As a result, ESRO is given responsibility for design and construction of the Spacelab to be used in conjunction with NASA's Space Shuttle.

September 27-29 The Soviet Union's Soyuz 12 mission carries cosmonauts Vasily Lazarev and Oleg Makarov into Earth orbit. This is the first Soyuz mission since the tragic loss of the Soyuz 11 crew (q.v. June 6,

Skylab III with astronauts Alan Bean, Dr Owen Garriott and Jack Lousma on board, is about to have a flotation collar fitted by divers from USS *New Orleans*. Launched on July 28 1973, the astronauts splashed down on September 25. (*NASA*)

1971), and is the first flight of an improved Soyuz vehicle intended to serve as an Earth-space ferry to the Salyut space workshops.

October 1 The first bench test of the uprated Rolls-Royce RB.211-524 is made successfully at Derby.

The name of Taag-Angola Airlines is adopted by DTA (Divisiao de Exploracao dos Transportes Aereos de Angola) which had been formed originally during 1939.

October 6 A massive air strike by the Egyptian Air Force against Israeli artillery and command positions marks the beginning of the October or Yom Kippur War.

October 6-8 Israeli air counter-attack against Egypt's air and ground forces is frustrated by large-scale use of Soviet-made and effective SAMs. For the first time it is seen that air power is no longer the decisive weapon for control of ground operations that it had been during the Second World War.

October 8 Aircraft operated by El Al begin to fly in supplies for Israel from the US.

October 13 Supplementing El Al's efforts, the USAF despatches seven Lockheed C-5A Galaxy transports with supplies. These arrive in Israel, having travelled via the Azores, on October 14.

October 17 Air France and Alitalia, the last foreign airlines to maintain services to Tel Aviv, cancel their operations until the end of the conflict.

October 21 The death is announced of Sir Alan Cobham at the age of 79. One of the UK's most colourful aviation pioneers, he is remembered by thousands of UK citizens not only for his pioneering and survey flights but for giving them, by means of his 'air circuses', a first taste of air travel.

At Linz, Austria, the Militky MB-E1 (Militky Brditsch-ka Electric 1) becomes the first electrically-powered manned aircraft to fly. A specially modified Brditschka HB-3 sailplane, it has a Bosch electric motor driven by rechargeable batteries.

October 22 The first cease-fire is negotiated in the Yom Kippur war but fighting flares up again on the following day.

October 24 The second cease-fire of the Yom Kippur war is negotiated but only slowly comes into effect.

October 25 Tom Sage of the UK Cameron Balloon company establishes a hot-air balloon duration record of 5 hr 45 min.

October 26 the Dassault-Bréguet/Dornier Alpha Jet trainer prototype makes a successful first flight at Istres.

October 31 British Airways retires the Comet 4B from service after G-ARJL completes a final BEA Airtours service from Le Bourget.

November 1 Air Niugini, which had been formed as the national airline of Papua earlier in the year, begins its first operations.

November 15 A Swissair DC-8-63 in Red Cross markings is used in operations between Cairo and Tel Aviv, providing a shuttle repatriation service for prisoners of the recent war.

November 16-February 8 NASA's Skylab 4 is launched to rendezvous with Skylab 1, carrying astronauts Gerald Carr, Edward Gibson and William Pogue. This is the final Skylab mission and when the astronauts land they have completed a record 84 days 1 hr 15 min in space.

November 21 Sir Roy Fedden, aero-engine designer responsible for the design lead on such well known Bristol engines as the Jupiter, Pegasus, Mercury, Hercules and Centaurus, dies at the age of 88.

November 24 The death is announced of Nikolai Kamov, a pioneer designer of Soviet rotary-wing aircraft, at the age of 71. The Soviet Union has thus lost her two great helicopter pioneers in less than three years.

December 1 At midnight British inclusive tour operators impose a fuel surcharge. This is to offset large rises in fuel costs resulting from moves that followed the Middle East war.

December 5 Sir Robert Watson-Watt, the British radar pioneer, dies at the age of 81.

December 6 Hawker Siddeley announces a follow-on order from the People's Republic of China for an additional 15 Trident 2Es.

The first French-built production Concorde (F-WTSB) makes its first flight at Toulouse.

December 13 The first of two General Dynamics YF-16 prototypes is rolled out at Fort Worth, Texas. They have been designed to meet the requirements of the USAF's Lightweight Fighter (LWF) Prototype Program, and are to be flown in competitive evaluation against two YF-17 prototypes built by Northrop.

December 25 Gabriel Voisin, a pioneer of French aviation, dies at Ozenay, France at the age of 91. With his brother Charles, he had built and flown his first powered aircraft in 1907.

1974

January 1 Sikorsky S-61N helicopters operated by Bristow Helicopters mount a rescue operation, evacuating the 50-man crew of North Sea drilling platform *Transocean 3* shortly before it overturns.

January 4 Teledyne Ryan rolls out two YQM-98A RPV long-endurance reconnaissance prototypes. Built for the USAF's Compass Cope programme, they are designed to take-off from and land on normal runways.

January 6 London's Heathrow Airport is ringed by troops and armoured vehicles after a threat has been made by terrorists to destroy civil airliners during the take-off or landing phase.

January 7 The US Pentagon states that Iran has signed a Letter of Intent to purchase 30 Grumman F-14A Tomcat fighters.

January 16 The Luftwaffe receives delivery of the last of 121 Dornier Do 28D Skyservant utility aircraft.

February 2 A first flight is made by the first General Dynamics YF-16 lightweight fighter prototype (72-01567) at Edwards AFB, California. The same aircraft had made a brief unofficial first flight on January 20, when it lifted off during high-speed taxi tests.

February 15 Westland Helicopters announces the receipt of a production order for 100 Westland/Aérospatiale Lynx multi-role helicopters for service with the French and UK armed services.

February 18 US Army reservist Col Thomas Gatch lifts off from Pennsylvania in an attempt to make a North Atlantic balloon crossing.

February 21 The distinctive balloon of Col Gatch (above), comprising ten small balloons supporting a sealed and pressurised gondola, is reported by a merchant ship some 600 km (1,000 miles) west of the Canary Islands, but is never seen again.

March 1 A first flight is made by the Sikorsky YCH-53E prototype (71-59121), a three-turboshaft development of the Sikorsky S-65A to provide the US

Navy and Marine Corps with a heavy-lift multi-purpose helicopter.

March 3 The world's worst air disaster involving a single aircraft occurs soon after a THY Turkish Airlines McDonnell Douglas DC-10 takes off from Orly Airport. All 346 people on board are killed, and subsequent investigation shows that the failure of a cargo door had caused decompression, resulting in loss of control.

March 4 It is announced by the Soviet Union that Prof Mikhail Tikhonravov, a space pioneer who had contributed a great deal to the design of the original Sputniks, has died at the age of 74.

March 8 Charles de Gaulle Airport at Roissy-en-France, 25km (15.5 miles) from the centre of Paris and Europe's newest international airport, is opened officially by the French Prime Minister.

March 13 The first four of 126 Northrop F-5E Tiger IIs are delivered for service with the South Vietnamese Air Force.

A Lockheed L-1011 Tri-Star airliner, one being operated by Court Lines of the UK, is flown to Moscow for demonstration to Aeroflot.

March 28 The first of 38 McDonnell Douglas F-4E Phantom IIs for service with the Hellenic Air Force is handed over officially at St Louis, Missouri.

April 1 Air Malta, which had been formed as the national airline during March 1973, begins operations with aircraft provided by shareholding Pakistan International Airlines.

April 4 UK telephone links with the People's Republic of China become available on a full time basis, instead of 3 hours each day. This follows the commissioning of a satellite terminal at Peking able to communicate via Intelsat IV.

April 10 A Martin Marietta Titan III-D launches an additional Big Bird reconnaissance satellite into Earth orbit from Vandenberg AFB, California.

April 13 At Kennedy Space Center a Thor-Delta launcher is used to put the first of two Westar domestic comsats into geostationary orbit.

April 15 The test programme for the SSME (Space Shuttle Main Engine), developed for NASA by Rockwell's Rocketdyne Division, begins with a 3.5 second run of a combustion chamber pre-burner.

April 20 The governments of Japan and the People's Republic of China sign formal agreements covering the provision of air services between the two countries.

April 23 Bell Helicopters announces the delivery of the company's 20,000th helicopter. Of this total, some 80 per cent have been delivered since the beginning of 1964.

April 25 The first of 12 Valmet-assembled Saab 35S Drakens is handed over for service with the Finnish Air Force.

April 30 Eastern Airlines, celebrating the 13th anniversary of its launch of shuttle services linking New York and Boston, and New York and Washington, states that more than 34 million passengers have been carried on these routes since their inauguration.

May 22 The 25th anniversary of the first flight of the English Electric Canberra (on May 13, 1949) is celebrated by a Canberra fly-in at RAF Cottesmore. No fewer than 33 different marks of this aircraft are to be seen there.

May 23 Europe's first wide-body jetliner, an Airbus A300B2 of Air France, makes its inaugural revenue flight on the airline's Paris-London route.

May 29 The 40th anniversary of the first official inland airmail service in the UK (q.v. May 29, 1934).

May 31 A United Nations Disengagement Observer Force is established in the Golan Heights to monitor Arab-Israeli observance of the cease-fire.

June 5 A nine-nation consortium, led by ERNO/VFW-Fokker, is awarded the NASA development contract for the Spacelab orbiting laboratory for launch by a Space Shuttle Orbiter.

June 9 The first of Northrop's two YF-17 lightweight fighter prototypes (72-01569) makes its first flight. They are built for the USAF LWF programme and are to be flown in competition against the General Dynamics YF-16s (q.v. February 2, 1974).

June 14 The Hellenic Air Command signs a contract in Athens valued at more than $400 million. This covers the supply of LTV A-7H Corsair IIs and 16 Lockheed C-130 Hercules transports.

June 23 It is announced that during their first month of airline service, the Air France Airbus A300B2s have carried more than 20,000 passengers at an average load factor of 79.3 per cent.

June 30 The first flight is made at Yeovil, Somerset of a Westland Sea King Mk 50 with uprated Rolls-Royce Gnome H1400-1 turboshaft engines, uprated transmission and a six-blade tail rotor. It is the first of ten for service with the Royal Australian Navy.

July 1 The UK Air Attache in India accepts on behalf of the RAF Museum a reconditioned Consolidated B-24 Liberator. This had served with the Indian Air Force, and is presented to the Museum as a gift from the Indian government.

July 6 The Aérospatiale/Westland SA.341 Gazelle enters service with the UK Army, equipping first No.660 Squadron Army Air Corps.

July 13 The first UK National Hang Gliding Championships are held at Steyning Hill, Sussex. Some 80 aircraft and more than 100 pilots take part.

July 16 America's first Moon-landing team, Edwin Aldrin, Neil Armstrong and Michael Collins, are united again at Launch Complex 39, Kennedy Space Center.

Cameron balloon *Gerard A. Heineken*, August 19 1974.

They are there for dedication of the site as a national landmark to commemorate the historic event.

July 20 The death is announced of the US aircraft designer Alexander Kartveli. Well known from the late 1930s, he was particularly renowned for design of the Republic P-47 Thunderbolt, one of the great aircraft of the Second World War.

Turkey invades Cyprus making extensive use of air power, the Turkish Air Force deploying F-100 Super Sabres for air strikes, Douglas C-47s for the airdrop of paratroops, and Bell AB.204 and 205 helicopters to fly in supporting troops.

July 26 RAF transport aircraft, including the Belfast, Britannia, Comet, Hercules and VC10, ferry out from Cyprus more than 7,500 tourists.

August 12 The Hawker Siddeley Hawk two-seat advanced trainer is rolled out at the company's airfield at Dunsfold, Surrey.

August 14 The Panavia 200 MRCA prototype (D-9591) makes its first flight at Manching, West Germany piloted by BAC's Paul Millet.

August 15 The Court Line Group in the UK announces that it is going into voluntary liquidation.

August 17 As a result of Court Line's collapse, British Airways, British Caledonian Airways, Dan-Air, and Laker Airways begin an airlift for some 49,000 tourists stranded overseas.

August 19 The Cameron balloon *Gerard A. Heineken* is flown for the first time at Bristol, Somerset. Then the world's largest hot-air balloon, with a volume of 14,158m (500,000 cu ft), its two-tier basket could accommodate a total of 12 passengers.

August 21 The first flight of the Hawker Siddeley Hawk (XX154) is made by the company's chief test pilot Duncan Simpson at Dunsfold, Surrey.

August 22 The first flight of the Short SD3-30 prototype (G-BSBH) is made at the company's airfield at Queen's Island, Belfast.

August 26 The death is announced of Charles Lindbergh, probably the best known pilot in aviation history. His solo west-east crossing of the North Atlantic 47 years earlier had captured the imagination and interest of the world.

August 30 Launch of the first Dutch satellite ANS.

August 31 The Apollo command module for the 1975 US/USSR space flight is delivered to Kennedy Space Center by Lockheed C-5A Galaxy.

September 11 A first flight is made by the Bell Model 206L Long Ranger prototype (N206L), a turbine-powered general-purpose light helicopter.

September 23 Following a five-week evaluation of the Northrop F-5E Tiger II by the Swiss Air Force, it is reported that the Swiss Government will probably buy between 60 and 80.

September 25 A first flight is made by the Northrop F-5F Tiger II, a two-seat trainer version of the F-5E which can be used also in a combat role.

September 29 Japan Air Lines flies a special service from Tokyo to Peking with one of its Douglas DC-8-62s to mark the beginning of air services between the two countries.

September 30 The first of eight Boeing Vertol CH-147 Chinook twin-rotor medium transport helicopters for service with the Canadian Armed Forces is delivered to the US Army. Under a military sales agreement these would then be redelivered to Canada.

October 17 A first flight is made at Stratford, Connecticut of the first of three Sikorsky YUH-60A prototypes (21650). This is a utility transport helicopter that has been designed to meet the US Army's UTTAS (Utility Tactical Transport Aircraft System) requirement, to be flown in evaluation against Boeing Vertol YUH-61A contenders.

October 18 Hawker Siddeley announces that work on development of the HS 146 short-range transport is to end because of reduced sales prospects caused by worldwide economic problems.

October 23 The Royal Australian Navy's first Sea King Mk 50 flight is formed at RNAS Culdrose. Aircrew and maintenance personnel to operate the helicopters in Australia are trained at Culdrose.

October 26 The first Rockwell International B-1 strategic variable-geometry supersonic bomber prototype (71-40158) is rolled out at Palmdale, California.

October 28 The first of two prototypes of the Dassault Super Etendard carrier-based fighter, which is derived from the standard Etendard IV-M, makes its first flight at Istres.

November 1 Royal Brunei Airlines is formed as the government-owned national airline of Brunei.

November 7 Kuwait signs a contract with McDonnell Douglas for the supply of 36 A-4M Skyhawk IIs at a cost of $250 million.

November 14 Formation date of the Papua New Guinea Defence Force, Air Transport Squadron, which is established in advance of gaining independence from Australia on September 16, 1975.

November 15 Launch of the first Spanish satellite INTASAT.

November 17 The death is announced of Air Marshal Sir Ralph Sorley, aged 76. He is remembered in UK aviation history for his influence on the development of multi-gun fighter aircraft such as the Hawker Hurricane.

November 28 Belize Airways is formed as the national airline of Belize (formerly British Honduras).

November 29 A first flight is made by the first of Boeing Vertol's YUH-61A prototypes (21656), for evaluation against the Sikorsky YUH-60A (q.v. October 17, 1974).

December 2-8 The Soviet Union places Soyuz 16 into Earth orbit for a final rehearsal of the ASTP (Apollo-Soyuz Test Project) planned for 1975.

December 5 The UK Secretary of State for Industry states that a firm contract has been finalised between the government and Rolls-Royce for development of the RB.211-524 to power the long-range Lockheed TriStar.

December 9 The UK Secretary of State for Industry states that the Hawker Siddeley HS.146 project has not been cancelled: it is in 'cold storage' and can be revived when circumstances permit.

The Defence and Interior Minister of Kuwait states that the order for McDonnell Douglas A-4 Skyhawks has been confirmed, and that it is intended to procure also Mirage F1s and related two-seat trainers, plus Gazelle and Puma helicopters.

December 16 Bell Helicopters receives a $54.25 million contract from the US Army for the conversion of AH-1G HueyCobras to an AH-1Q anti-armour standard, equipped to carry and launch eight TOW anti-tank missiles.

December 18 Symphonie A, Europe's first communications satellite, is launched into geostationary orbit by a Delta vehicle from Cape Kennedy.

December 19 Short Brothers & Harland announces a contract for six SD3-30 transports which has been received from the US commuter airline Air New England.

December 23 A first flight is made by the first Rockwell International B-1 prototype (71-40158) at Palmdale, California.

December 26 The first Airbus A300B4 (F-WLGA), the long-range development of Europe's wide-body jetliner, makes its first flight.

1975

January 12 British Airways inaugurates a shuttle service between London Heathrow and Glasgow. Operated with Hawker Siddeley Trident 1s, this is the first no-booking guaranteed-seat shuttle service in Europe.

January 14 It is announced in Washington that the USAF has selected the General Dynamics YF-16 as the winner of its LWF (lightweight fighter) programme.

January 21 Following two terrorist attacks at Orly Airport, Paris the French Minister of the Interior states that special new security measures will be introduced to prevent any repetition.

January 30 Highlighting one area of aviation's contribution to humanity, a UK announcement states that during 1974 RAF SAR helicopters were called out 1,018 times and rescued 319 people.

February 1 During a 16-day period that ended on this date, all eight world time-to-height records are captured by the McDonnell Douglas F-15 Eagle in a programme named 'Streak Eagle'. The final record set a time of 3 min 27.8 sec from standstill on a runway to a height of 30,000m (98,425ft).

February 6 Air Chief Marshal Sir Keith Park dies at Auckland, New Zealand. He was AOC No.11 Group Fighter Command during the Battle of Britain, responsible for the defence of London and the Home Counties.

March 7 A first flight in the Soviet Union of the first of three prototype Yakovlev Yak-42 three-turbofan short-range transports.

March 24 During a defence discussion in the House of Commons it is revealed that Hawker Siddeley is to be contracted for project definition of an airborne early warning (AEW) version of the Nimrod.

March 27 A first flight is made by the first of two de Havilland Canada DHC-7 Dash 7 pre-production aircraft (C-GNBX-X), a 50-passenger short/medium-range quiet STOL transport.

March 31 The first flight is made by a specially-modified de Havilland Canada XC-8A Buffalo STOL military transport which, under joint Canadian/US funding, has been provided with an air cushion landing

Launch of Soyuz 19, July 15 1975. (*NASA*)

system (ACLS). It is to be used in a programme to determine the suitability of an ACLS for operation from surfaces which could include swamps, water, ice and snow.

April 1   The Republic of Singapore Air Force is formed, acquiring the Bloodhound SAM units from the British when their armed forces are withdrawn in 1976.

May 30   European Space Agency (ESA) is founded.

June 3   A first flight is made by the first prototype Mitsubishi FS-T2-KAI, a single-seat supersonic close-support fighter developed from the T-2 jet trainer. Required to replace the JASDF's F-86F Sabres, it becomes designated F-1 when it enters service.

June 8   The Soviet Union's Venera 9 interplanetary probe is launched towards Venus. This very successful probe later becomes the first artificial satellite of Venus, and the data capsule which it ejects makes a successful landing on the planet's surface, its 53 min transmission including TV pictures.

June 22   A new world speed record for women is established in the Soviet Union by Svetlana Savitskaya, flying a Mikoyan Ye-133 at a speed of 2,683.44 km/h (1,667.42 mph).

July 15-24   Combined US/USSR space mission during which the Soviet Union's *Soyuz 19* spacecraft and the US Apollo ASTP (Apollo-Soyuz Test Project) dock together in Earth orbit for crew exchanges and combined experiments.

July 21   A first flight is made by the Israel Aircraft Industries IAI 1124 (4X-CJA), a longer-range turbofan-powered version of the IAI 1123 Westwind.

August 20   NASA's interplanetary probe Viking 1 is launched. It subsequently places a landing module on Mars which transmits the first pictures of the planet's surface.

August 26   The first prototype of the McDonnell Douglas YC-15 (01875) STOL transport, designed to meet the requirements of the USAF's AMST programme, makes its first flight.

September 1   The fourth production Aérospatiale/BAC Concorde becomes the first aircraft to make two return transatlantic flights (London-Gander-London) or four transatlantic crossings in a single day.

September 30   A first flight is made by the first of two Hughes Model 77 (YAH-64) prototypes (22248). The YAH-64 is designed to meet the US Army's Armed Attack Helicopter (AAH) requirement, and for fly-off evaluation against the Bell YAH-63 (below).

October 1   The first of Bell's competing prototypes (22246) for the US Army's AAH programme, the Model 409 (YAH-63), makes its first flight.

November 17   The Soviet Union launches the unmanned Soyuz 20 to conduct experiments in the resupply of Salyut space stations.

November 28   After becoming a subsidiary of Evergreen Helicopters Inc, Johnson International Airlines adopts the name Evergreen International Airlines.

December 6   Carrying airmail between Moscow and Alma Ata, the Soviet Union's Tupolev Tu-144 SST makes the first airmail flight by a supersonic airliner.

1976

January 21   The world's first passenger services by a supersonic airliner are made, with Concorde SSTs of British Airways and Air France taking off simultaneously for Bahrain and Rio de Janeiro.

March 24   A first flight is made by the first General Dynamics' YF-16 prototype following conversion as a control configured vehicle (CCV) testbed aircraft

(72-01567). The CCV is shown to be able to point its nose in any direction without changing its flight path, or to rise, descend or move sideways without changing its nose direction, providing development potential for improved weapon delivery accuracy.

May 19 In a ceremony at Toulouse-Colomiers the Armée de l'Air accepts delivery of its 100th SEPECAT Jaguar.

May 24 Air France and British Airways begin transatlantic Concorde passenger services, from Paris and London respectively, to Washington's Dulles International Airport.

May 26 A first flight is made by the Dassault Mirage F1-B, a two-seat trainer version of Dassault's F1 multimission fighter.

June 22 The Soviet Union launches into Earth orbit the unmanned Salyut 5 space station.

July 1 Clive Canning arrives in the UK after a solo flight from Australia in a homebuilt Thorp T-18 Tiger. This is the first Australia-England flight made in an aircraft of amateur construction.

July 3 It is reported that in an Israeli commando assault on Entebbe airport on this date the Israelis destroy four MiG-17s and seven MiG-21s.

July 6 The Soviet Union launches Soyuz 21 to dock with Salyut 5 in orbit. Cosmonauts Boris Volynov and Vitali Zholobov carry out a 49 day 5 hr 24 min space mission.

July 8 The Swiss Air Force receives delivery of its 160th and last Hawker Hunter at Emmen airbase.

July 20 A first public demonstration of the IAI Kfir-C2 is given at the Israeli Air Force Hatzerim air base. It is seen to have been given fixed foreplanes to improve dog-fight capability.

July 21 The Canadian government announces the finalisation of a contract with Lockheed Aircraft Corporation for the supply of 18 long-range ASW and maritime patrol aircraft, a developed version of the Lockheed Model 85 Orion designated CP-140 Aurora.

July 22 The US State Department grants a licence allowing Pratt & Whitney to start co-operative development of the JT10D high by-pass ratio turbofan with Fiat, MTU and Rolls-Royce.

The Royal Navy retires its last piston-engined helicopter when the Whirlwind HAS.MK 7 XN299 is withdrawn from service at Old Sarum, Wiltshire.

July 28 Flying a Lockheed SR-71A strategic reconnaissance aircraft, Capt E.W. Joersz and Maj G.T. Morgan Jr, USAF, establish a new world speed record of 3,529.56 km/h (2,193.17 mph). In early 1982 this straight course speed is still the absolute world record for air-breathing aircraft.

July 29 It is stated in the House of Commons that the government is making funds available to BAC and Hawker Siddeley to support development of the One-Eleven and HS.146 respectively.

The governments of West Germany, Italy and the UK sign a Memorandum of Understanding covering the production of 809 Panavia Tornado multi-role combat aircraft.

August 9 A first flight is made by the first Boeing YC-14 prototype (01873) for evaluation under the USAF's AMST programme.

October 12 The first of two Sikorsky Model 72 RSRA prototypes (NASA 545) makes its first flight. Developed under contract to NASA and the US Army they are intended for long-term use to develop and test a wide range of rotor and integrated propulsion systems.

November 1 Cargo Air Lines, formed in Israel to provide freight charter services, begin operations.

November 7 A first flight is made by the Dassault-Bréguet Mystère-Falcon 50 prototype (F-WAMD), a three-turbofan executive transport developed from the Mystère-Falcon 20.

November 16 The US Department of Defense approves the sale of 110 LTV A-7 Corsair II aircraft for service with the Pakistan Air Force. This sale is later blocked by the Carter administration.

December 1 The US supplemental carrier Trans International Airlines acquires Saturn Airways. A combined operating name of Transamerica Airlines is adopted during 1979.

December 2 A first flight is made by the Boeing 747-123 (NASA 905) following modification by Boeing to a Space Shuttle carrier configuration.

December 9 The 008 Escuadrilla of the Arma Aéreade la Armada Española, Spain's AV-8A/TAV-8A Matador (Harrier) squadron, becomes operational at Rota, Cadiz.

December 22 A first fully automatic landing by an Airbus A300 in commercial service is made by an A300B2 of Air Inter in a bad weather landing at Orly Airport.

December 22 The prototype of the Soviet Union's Ilyushin Il-86 wide-body jetliner (CCCP-86000) makes its first flight from the old Moscow Central Airport of Khodinka, piloted by Hero of the Soviet Union A. Kuznetsov.

December 23 The Sikorsky S-70(UH-60A) is declared winner of the US Army's UTTAS competition. The Army plans to procure 1,105 by 1985 to serve as its primary combat assault helicopter.

1977

January 5 Despite considerable opposition from US manufacturers, the US Coast Guard is authorised to complete a contract with Dassault-Bréguet covering the supply of 41 Mystère-Falcon 20Gs for use in a number of medium-range surveillance missions. The designation HU-25A Guardian is allocated subsequently by the US Coast Guard.

Bell XV-15 (702) tilt-rotor research aircraft on its test rig.

January 8 The first bench test of the General Electric F404 advanced technology augmented turbofan is completed successfully. It has been chosen to power the McDonnell Douglas F-18 NACF (Navy Air Combat Fighter).

January 21 Bell makes the first tie-down test of the Model 301 (XV-15) tilt-rotor research aircraft.

January 22 Following the collapse of East African Airways Corporation, Kenya Airways is established as an independent airline.

January 31 A first flight is made by the Cessna Citation II (N550CC) at Wichita, Kansas. This is a larger-capacity version of the earlier Citation I which it is intended to complement rather than replace.

February 16 The first flight of a CFM International CFM56 two-shaft turbofan engine is made, installed in the first McDonnell Douglas YC-15 as part of the AMST development programme.

February 17 Beech Aircraft Corporation completes production flight testing of its 10,000th Model 35 Bonanza.

February 18 The first flight of the Boeing Space Shuttle carrier, with the Space Shuttle *Enterprise* mounted above it, is made successfully at NASA's Dryden Flight Research Center. In this test, and the five that are planned to follow, the *Enterprise* is unmanned.

March 11 Air Tanzania is formed to operate services which had terminated with the collapse of East African Airways Corporation.

March 16 The first new production Bell AH-1S TOW-firing HueyCobra is handed over officially to the US Army at Fort Worth, Texas.

March 24 The first operational Boeing E-3A AWACS aircraft is delivered to the USAF's 552nd Airborne Warning and Control Wing at Tinker AFB, Oklahoma.

The Lockheed YC-141B StarLifter prototype (66-0186), a lengthened-fuselage (7.11m; 23ft 4in) conversion of a C-141A, is flown for the first time.

March 27 The world's greatest air tragedy (579 people killed) occurs when two Boeing 747s collide on the runway at Santa Cruz Airport, Tenerife.

March 31 The UK Secretary of State for Defence states that full-scale development of an AEW version of the Hawker Siddeley Nimrod is to go ahead.

April 1 British Airways introduces shuttle operations on its London-Belfast route.

April 5 Delivery of a Beechcraft T-44A advanced trainer to Corpus Christi NAS marks service entry of the type, a militarised version of the Beech King Air.

April 6 A first flight is recorded by the Britten-Norman BN-2A-41 Turbo Islander prototype (G-BDPR), a turboprop-powered version of the standard Islander.

May 3 The first of two Bell XV-15 tilt-rotor research aircraft (702) makes its first hovering flight.

May 19 The Soviet Union's Cosmos 909 satellite is launched to serve as the target for a space interceptor satellite.

June 1 Air Gabon, the national airline of the Republic of Gabon, inaugurates international operations.

June 9 An agreement is signed between Piper Aircraft Corporation and Poland's Pezetel Foreign Trade Enterprise covering the assembly of some 400 Piper Seneca IIs over a period of five years.

June 10 A Britten-Norman Islander with two Dowty Rotol ducted propulsor units (G-FANS) makes its first flight at Shoreham Aerodrome, Sussex.

June 10 In a special ceremony at Myrtle Beach AFB, South Carolina the USAF Tactical Air Command recognises the introduction into operational service of the Fairchild Republic A-10A close-support aircraft. Initial deliveries of A-10As to the 356th Tactical Fighter Squadron at Myrtle Beach AFB have been made during March 1977.

June 13 President Carter approves the US CABs recommendation that Laker Airways should be allowed to operate a Skytrain service between London and New York for a one year trial period.

June 16 The death is announced of Professor Wernher von Braun.

June 17 The Soviet Union's Cosmos 918 satellite is launched and intercepts the Cosmos 909 target (q.v. May 19).

June 30 President Carter announces cancellation of the Rockwell International B-1 supersonic strategic bomber programme: the US was to rely instead on the cruise missile for strategic attack.

July 28 The US Congress blocks the proposed sale of seven Boeing E3-A AWACS aircraft to Iran.

August 13 The US Space Shuttle *Enterprise* makes its first free gliding flight following launch from the Shuttle Carrier aircraft at a height of 6,950m (22,800ft).

August 20 The UK's pre-production Concorde 01 makes its last flight to Duxford, Cambridge for inclusion in the Duxford Aviation Society/Imperial War Museum collection of historic aircraft.

NASA launches the unmanned spacecraft Voyager 2, which flies past Jupiter in July 1979 then continues via Saturn. Having passed Saturn it is scheduled to reach Uranus in 1986.

August 23 Gossamer Condor, designed under the leadership of Dr Paul MacCready in the US and piloted by racing cyclist Bryan Allen, wins the £50,000 Kremer Prize for the first 1.6km (1 mile) figure-of-eight flight by a man-powered aircraft.

August 31 In the Soviet Union Alexander Fedotov, flying the Mikoyan Ye-266M, establishes a new world altitude record for air-breathing aircraft of 37,650m (123,524ft). This remains unbeaten in early 1982.

September 16 The first Mitsubishi F-1 close-support fighter for service with the JASDF is handed over officially at the company's Komaki factory.

September 26 Six years after making initial proposals, Laker Airways inaugurates its London-New York Skytrain service. Almost immediately six scheduled airlines introduce low-cost transatlantic fares.

September 30 Lockheed Aircraft Corporation adopts the name Lockheed Corporation to reflect the corporation's wider range of activities.

October 23 British Caledonian Airways inaugurates a daily nonstop service between London and Houston, Texas.

November 5 Transmeridian Air Cargo inaugurates a regular cargo service between the UK and Australia.

November 12 The last Douglas Dakotas are retired by the Royal New Zealand Air Force 34 years after the type first entered service.

November 22 After seemingly endless delays Air France and British Airways inaugurate Concorde services to New York.

November 23 Launch of the first European weather satellite Meteosat.

December 4 British Airways in conjunction with Singapore Airlines begin Concorde services from Bahrain to Singapore.

December 13 Eastern Airlines in the US inaugurate services with Airbus A300B4s leased from the manufacturers. This is to prove a significant event for Airbus Industrie.

December 22 A first flight of the Soviet Union's Antonov An-72 prototype (CCCP-1974), a new twin-turboprop STOL transport of unusual power plant layout.

December 29 Hawker Siddeley Aviation finalises a contract covering the supply of 50 Hawk trainers for the Finnish Air Force.

1978

January 1 The assets and business of British Aircraft Corporation, Hawker Siddeley Aviation, Hawker Siddeley Dynamics and Scottish Aviation are transferred to British Aerospace. The latter corporation had been established by UK government Act on April 29, 1977 and became technically the owner of the companies named above although they have continued to trade under their original titles until this date.

January 10 The Soviet Union's Soyuz 27 is launched to dock with Salyut 6/Soyuz 26 in Earth orbit, its cosmonauts carrying mail and supplies to record the first mail delivery in space.

January 20 The Soviet Union's unmanned space ferry Progress 1 is launched, carrying supplies to and docking automatically with Salyut 6.

January 26 The Royal Navy's first Westland/Aérospatiale Lynx squadron, No 702 Naval Air Squadron, is commissioned at RNAS Yeovilton, Somerset.

January 31 The UK Ministry of Defence contracts with Boeing Vertol for the supply of 30 CH-47 Chinook twin-rotor medium transport helicopters for service with the RAF.

February 10 The first of 6 Lockheed C-130H Hercules transports for service with the Sudan Air Force is delivered to Khartoum.

February 27 Westland Helicopters and Rolls-Royce sign contracts in Cairo covering production of the Westland/Aérospatiale Lynx and Rolls-Royce Gem in Egypt. This is the first stage toward the planned development of an Arab British Helicopter Co (ABHC).

March 2 Vladimir Remek is carried as a crew member aboard Soyuz 28, thus becoming the first Czechoslovakian to take part in a space mission.

March 10 A first flight is made at Istres of the first Dassault Mirage 2000 prototype, a single-seat interceptor and air superiority fighter that was selected in 1975 as the primary combat aircraft for service with the French Air Force from the mid-1980s.

March 22 British Aerospace Corporation seeks UK government approval to continue development of the HS.146.

April 4 A contract is signed by British Aerospace in Jakarta covering the supply of eight Hawk trainers for the Indonesian Air Force.

Air France introduces the Airbus A300 on its Paris-Moscow route.

April 5 Aeroflot inaugurates international services with its Ilyushin Il-76T freighters on the Moscow-Sofia route.

April 6 Following experimental operations made with Airbus A300s leased from the company (q.v. December 13, 1977), Eastern Airlines in the USA places an order for 25 A300B4s plus nine options.

April 9 A first flight is made by the Dornier Do 28 D-5 Turbo Skyservant prototype (D-IBUF), powered by two Avco Lycoming LTP 101 turboprop engines.

April 10 A first flight is made by the second example of the Sikorsky S-72 RSRA research aircraft. This differs by being a compound helicopter with auxiliary turbofan engines and wide span wings.

April 18 The Vickers Viscount becomes the first turbine-engined airliner to complete 25 years of regular commercial service.

April 19 ICAO delegates meeting in Montreal vote in favour of the US-developed Time Reference Scanning Beam microwave landing system, selecting it for introduction as the standard international landing system by 1995.

May 9 David Cook flying a Revell VJ-23 powered hang-glider records the first crossing of the English Channel by such an aircraft.

May 20 McDonnell Douglas delivers its 5,000th F-4 Phantom II 20 years after the first flight of the prototype.

May 21 Some four years later than planned, largely because of action by protesters, Tokyo's new Narita International Airport becomes operational.

June 6 It is reported that Aeroflot's Tu-144 services between Moscow and Alma Ata have been suspended because of excessive fuel consumption.

June 8 The USAF announces the award of the first £407.5 million contract to Lockheed Corporation for the conversion of its 277 strong fleet of C-141A StarLifters to 'stretched' C-141B standard.

June 9 British Caledonian in conjunction with British Airways Helicopters inaugurates a Heathrow-Gatwick helilink operated by a Sikorsky S-61N .

June 15 British Aerospace finalises an agreement with Grupul Aeronautic Bucuresti covering the manufacture in Romania of approximately 80 BAe One-Eleven transports.

June 27 The Soviet Union launches Soyuz 30 to dock with Salyut 6. In an operation similar to that of the Soyuz 28 mission, Miroslaw Giermaszewski becomes the first Pole to take part in a space mission.

June 28 The first Dassault-Bréguet Super Etendard is handed over officially to the Aéronavale at Bordeaux-Merignac.

July 1 Following the formation of a new airline by the governments of the Yemen Arab Republic and Saudi Arabia, the former Yemen Airways Corporation becomes renamed Yemen Airways on this date.

July 7 Airbus Industrie announces that it intends to proceed with development of the Airbus A300-10 (formerly A300B10).

July 11 The UK government gives approval for full-scale development of the BAe 146 (formerly HS.146).

July 14 Having received an order from United Air Lines for 30 examples of its proposed Model 767-200 wide-body medium-range transport, the Boeing Company announces that it will enter full-scale development and production.

July 28 During a US-Korea Security Conference in San Diego, the US government states that it is willing to supply the General Dynamics F-16 to the Republic of Korea Air Force.

August 12-17 A balloon duration record of 137 hr 5 min 50 sec, a record distance of 5,001.22km (3,107.62 miles), and the first transatlantic crossing by a gas balloon is recorded by *Double Eagle II* , crewed by Ben L. Abruzzo, Maxie L. Anderson and Larry M. Newman.

August 14 The Boeing Company and Aeritalia sign a contract under which the Italian company becomes a risk-sharing partner in development and production of the Model 767.

August 20 A first flight is made by the British Aerospace Sea Harrier FRS.Mk 1 (XZ450) from the company's airfield at Dunsfold, Surrey.

August 26 The Soviet Union launches Soyuz 31, crewed by Valeri Bykovsky and the East German Sigmund Jahn. They return to earth in Soyuz 29, having previously docked with the Salyut 6 space station.

August 31 The UK government states that following a British Aerospace proposal the government has acquired a 20 per cent interest in the Airbus Industrie A310 development programme.

September 13 A first flight is made by the Aérospatiale AS 332 Super Puma prototype (F-WZJA), a twin-turbine multi-role civil/military helicopter.

September 15 Prof Willy Messerschmitt dies, designer of the famous Bf 109 fighter and other aircraft.

September 28 The first of 26 Westland/Aérospatiale Lynx Mk 2 (FN) for service with Aéronavale is handed over officially at Merignac.

October 2 Aeroflot begins route-proving trials with the Ilyushin Il-86 on its Moscow-Mineralnye Vody route.

October 3 The RAF's No 13 Squadron is redeployed to the UK from Malta as part of the withdrawal of UK forces from the island.

October 29 British Airways introduces three-class services on its UK-USA services comprising First, Club and Discount.

October 30 It is announced in New Delhi that the Indian Air Force has decided to procure substantial numbers of the SEPECAT Jaguar International. It is planned to acquire an initial 40 from SEPECAT, with licence production of 130-150 in India.

November 8 A first flight is made by the Canadair CL-600 Challenger prototype (C-GCGR-X), a new twin-turbofan business, cargo and commuter transport derived from the LearStar 600 designed by William Lear.

November 9 The McDonnell Douglas YAV-8B Advanced Harrier prototype (158394) makes its first flight, a development of the British Aerospace Harrier to give increased weapons payload/combat radius.

November 18 A first flight is made by the McDonnell Douglas F/A-18 Hornet prototype (160775), a single-seat carrier based fighter developed jointly by McDonnell

Douglas and Northrop from the latter company's YF-17 prototype that had taken part in the USAF's LWF programme.

November 20 The USAF authorises McDonnell Douglas to begin production of the KC-10A Extender, a military tanker/transport developed from the company's DC-10 wide-body transport.

December 19 Britons David Williams and Fred To fly Solar One, the world's first solar-powered aircraft.

1979

January 1 Boeing E-3A Sentry AWACS aircraft of the USAF's 552nd Airborne Warning and Control Wing begin to assume a role in US air defence.

January 6 The first General Dynamics F-16A single-seat lightweight air combat fighter is handed over officially to the USAF's 388th Tactical Fighter Wing at Hill AFB, Utah.

January 12 Braniff International inaugurates scheduled subsonic Concorde services between Washington and Dallas/Fort Worth.

January 24 Pilatus Aircraft of Switzerland finalises the take-over of the assets of Britten-Norman (Bembridge) Ltd.,the resulting British subsidiary established by Pilatus being known as Pilatus Britten-Norman Ltd.

January 29 The Northrop RF-5E prototype, a specialised reconnaissance version of the F-5E, makes its first flight at Edwards AFB, California.

February 3 An unusual first flight is recorded at RAE Cardington, Bedfordshire by the Aerospace Developments AD 500 non-rigid airship (G-BECE). This has an overall length of 50m (164ft).

February 5 It is confirmed in the US and Iran that the Iranian government has cancelled orders for US arms valued at some £3,500 million.

February 27 Production of the McDonnell Douglas A-4 Skyhawk ends after 26 years with the delivery of the 2,960th and last (an A-4M) to the USMC's Marine Attack Squadron VMA-331.

March 2 British Airways signs a formal contract with The Boeing Company covering the supply of 19 Model 757s, a short/medium-range transport based on the fuselage of the Model 727.

March 9 The Dassault Super Mirage 4000 prototype makes its first flight, a single-seat multi-role combat aircraft incorporating a delta wing, canard foreplanes and a fly-by-wire active control system.

March 10 The USAF flies two Boeing E-3A Sentry AWACS to Riyadh to monitor hostilities between North and South Yemen.

March 14 Swissair signs a contract for the supply of 10 Airbus Industrie A310s plus options on an additional 10.

March 22 The first flight is recorded of the first Lockheed CP-140 Aurora (N64996), a long-range mari-

The first production Panavia Tornado is rolled out, June 5 1979.

time patrol aircraft for service with the Canadian Armed Forces.

March 23 Following finalisation of an additional contract from Eastern Airlines for 21 Model 757s, Boeing orders the aircraft into full-scale production.

April 15 A first flight is made by the Dassault Mirage 50 prototype, a multi-mission fighter retaining the basic airframe of the Mirage III/5 series but incorporating the higher-rated SNECMA Atar 9K-50 turbojet.

April 20 The 16th and last production Concorde makes its first flight.

May 1 The USAF awards a £413 million contract to Fairchild Republic for the production of additional A-10As which, by then, have acquired the name Thunderbolt II.

May 4 Air Europe, which was formed during August 1978, inaugurates operations with a Gatwick-Palma inclusive-tour service operated by Boeing 737-200.

May 11 The Boeing Vertol YCH-47D, a modernised CH-47A Chinook, makes its first flight. Subject to satisfactory development Boeing Vertol hopes to obtain a contract to update the US Army's 361 Chinooks to this new standard.

May 25 A serious accident on take-off from Chicago Airport, involving the physical loss of an engine and its pylon from the wing of a McDonnell Douglas DC-10, brings grounding of the type in the US.

June 1 Sixteen Egyptian Air Force pilots arrive in the USA for training on F-4E Phantom IIs, resulting from an agreement to supply 35 of these aircraft to Egypt from USA stocks.

June 5 The Chrysalis man-powered biplane built at the Massachusetts Institute of Technology makes its first flight. When dismantled in September 1979, 345 flights have been made by 44 different pilots.

The first production Panavia Tornado is rolled out in a ceremony at BAe's Warton aerodrome.

June 6 Following the DC-10 accident at Chicago Airport the FAA withdraws the Type Certificate temporarily, causing worldwide grounding of the type.

June 12 The Gossamer Albatross, designed and built under the leadership of Dr Paul MacCready, wins the £100,000 Kremer Prize for a first crossing of the English Channel by a man-powered aircraft.

June 17 The 20th anniversary of the first flight of the Dassault Mirage IV, and at which time 47 are still in service with the Armée de l'Air.

June 27 Combat debut of the McDonnell Douglas F-15 Eagle: serving with the Israeli Air Force, these aircraft destroy five MiG-21s of the Syrian Air Force.

July 11 The US Skylab space station re-enters Earth's atmosphere and breaks up, pieces falling on Australia and in the Indian Ocean.

July 13 The McDonnell Douglas DC-10 is cleared for flight and its Type Certificate restored.

BAe Sea Harriers of No 800 Squadron, Royal Navy.

July 19 The first two examples of the SEPECAT Jaguar for the Indian Air Force are handed over.

July 20 The UK Secretary of State for Trade states that the government intends to offer a substantial minority shareholding in British Airways to private investors.

July 23 The UK Secretary of Trade for Industry states that the government plans to sell about half of the shares of British Aerospace to public investors.

July 24 A Boeing KC-135A tanker with winglets installed at the wingtips makes its first flight. Developed under a joint NASA/USAF programme, it is intended to evaluate the potential fuel savings of drag-reducing winglets.

The second Bell XV-15 tilt-rotor research aircraft (N703NA) makes the type's first full inflight transition from hovering to conventional forward flight.

August 15 A first test firing of a British Aerospace Sky Flash air-to-air missile is made from a Phantom FGR.Mk 2, completely destroying its Meteor U.Mk 10 drone target travelling at 740 km/h (460 mph) and at much lower altitude.

August 23 The first British Aerospace Nimrod MR.Mk 2 (XV236) is handed over to RAF Strike Command at RAF Kinloss.

September 3 The first of 10 uprated Westland/ Aérospatiale Lynx Mk 27 ASW helicopters are handed over to the Netherlands Marineluchtvaartdienst by Aérospatiale at Marignane, where they are to be equipped with Alcatel dunking sonar.

September 19 The Royal Navy's first Sea Harrier squadron, No 700A, is commissioned at RNAS Yeovilton, Somerset. No 700A later becomes the shore-based

No 899 HQ Squadron. Front line Sea Harrier units become Nos 800, 801 and 802 Squadrons.

September 28 With disbanding of US Navy Squadron RVAH-7, the North American Rockwell RA-5C Vigilante is withdrawn from operational service.

October 18 A first flight is made by the McDonnell Douglas DC-9 Super 81 (N980DC), an increased wing-span/lengthened fuselage version of the DC-9-50 to provide increased capacity on short/medium-range routes.

November 15 The ninth British Aerospace Hawk for the RAF's Red Arrows aerobatic team is handed over at BAe's Bitteswell Aerodrome.

November 16 A first flight is made by the first production example of the Lockheed L-1011-500 TriStar, which introduces extended wingtips to reduce drag, and active controls for automatic correction of any wing gust loads.

December 4 The USAF's Military Airlift Command accepts its first C-141B StarLifter at Marietta, Georgia.

December 11 The first Lockheed Hercules C.Mk 3 for the RAF is handed over at Marietta, Georgia. This virtually represents a prototype conversion to provide 40 per cent increase in freight volume and 29 more in RAF service are to be converted to the same standard by Marshall of Cambridge in the UK.

December 14 The unusual Edgley EA-7 Optica prototype (G-BGMW) makes its first flight in the UK, a three-seat slow-flying observation aircraft with ducted-fan propulsion.

December 21 The NASA/Ames AD-1 oblique-wing research aircraft (N805NA) makes a first flight: after take off with the wing in a conventional position, it is designed so that the wing can be slewed to a maximum angle of 60° in flight to investigate potential drag reduction/fuel economies.

Three of the Sikorsky RH-53 Sea Stallion helicopters on board USS *Nimitz* prior to Operation Evening Light. (*US Navy*)

1980

March 10 The first of four Airbus A300B4-200s for Pakistan International Airlines (AP-BAX) is handed over.

March 28 Gates Learjet announces that it has delivered its 1,000th Learjet.

April 18 Air Zimbabwe adopts its present title, having been known temporarily as Air Zimbabwe Rhodesia during independence negotiations. It had been formed originally as Air Rhodesia in September 1967.

April 24 An attempt to rescue American hostages held in Iran is initiated as 'Operation Evening Light'. Sikorsky RH-53 Sea Stallion helicopters from USS *Nimitz* are among aircraft used, but the rescue fails as accidents at a desert landing area bring an end to the mission.

May 15 LTU (Luftransport-Unternehmen) introduces the Lockheed L-1011-500 TriStar on its long-range scheduled route Dusseldorf-Los Angeles.

May 20 de Havilland Canada announces that it has received Letters of Intent for 55 of its new 32/36-passenger DHC-8 Dash 8 quiet short-haul transports.

May 29 Westland Helicopters announces the receipt of orders for 32 Lynx helicopters, including 14 for Aéronavale and 10 for the Royal Navy.

June 1 The Dutch Fokker Company adopts the title Fokker BV following termination of the merged activities of VFW-Fokker.

Braniff International ends its Concorde leasing from Air France and British Airways, said to be due to increased fuel costs which have almost doubled since the leasing arrangement began.

June 4 The first of two McDonnell Douglas F-15Js for service with the JASDF makes its first flight at St Louis, Missouri.

June 5 The Soviet Union's first manned Soyuz T capsule, incorporating an automatic docking system, is launched into Earth orbit.

British Airways Helicopters initiates the use of Sikorsky S-76 helicopters on its services to North Sea offshore gas/oil platforms.

June 6 The first of 8 British Aerospace Hawk T.Mk 53s for the Indonesian Air Force is handed over officially at the company's Dunsfold, Surrey airfield.

June 19 Sikorsky delivers its 136th and last S-61 commercial helicopter.

June 20 Beech Aircraft flies its Beechcraft Commuter C 99 (N4199C), marking the company's return to the commuter airline market.

July 2 Aérospatiale signs a contract with the government of the People's Republic of China covering the assembly in China of 50 AS 365N Dauphin 2s.

July 12 The first McDonnell Douglas KC-10A Extender tanker/transport (79-0433) makes its first flight.

July 17 Cathay Pacific Airways inaugurates a Hong Kong-London route operated by Boeing 747s.

July 18 The Indian Space Research Organisation (ISRO) successfully launches into Earth orbit the Rohini RS-1 test satellite, designed primarily to evaluate the efficiency of the launch vehicle.

July 21 In a ceremony at Hill AFB, Utah the USAF names the General Dynamics F-16 officially as the Fighting Falcon.

July 25 The Bellanca Aircraft Corporation of Alexandria, Minnesota which has a long association with general aviation aircraft in the US, files a petition of bankruptcy.

August 1-8 The EAA's 28th Convention at Oshkosh, Wisconsin sets new records with a quarter million first day visitors and 6,000 visiting aircraft.

August 1 The 50th anniversary of the opening of the original Gatwick Airport, Surrey.

August 7 It is announced that Scotland's Strathallan Aircraft Collection will close permanently at the end of the summer season and that most of its aircraft will have to be sold.

The MacCready Gossamer Penguin makes its first straight (no turns) solar-powered flight of about 3km (2 miles) piloted by Janice Brown.

August 8 The death is announced of Jacqueline Cochran, world-famous American businesswoman/pilot. The first woman to fly an aircraft in excess of the speed of sound, she at one time held more than 200 US aviation records.

August 14 The first re-winged Lockheed C-5A is flown. Having suffered wing structural fatigue, all 77 of the USAF's in-service C-5As are scheduled to be similarly modified.

August 19 A first flight is made by the Boeing Vertol Model 234 Commercial Chinook, a development of the military CH-47 which in a long-range version will seat a maximum of 44 passengers.

September 13 RAF Coltishall, Norfolk stages a public air show to commemorate the 40th anniversary of the Battle of Britain. Coltishall is not only the home of the RAF's Battle of Britain Flight, but is the only RAF Battle of Britain fighter station that is still operational.

September 19 Fighting breaks out between the nations of Iran and Iraq, with extensive use of air power being made.

September 22 The Royal Navy's last conventional aircraft carrier, HMS *Ark Royal*, sails from Plymouth en route to the scrapyard.

September 25 A first flight is made by a Cameron hot-air airship of new design, the Cameron D-38 (G-BGEP).

October 2 A Westland Sea King helicopter is used in the rescue of 22 crew and passengers from the Swedish freighter *Finneagle* on fire at sea. The operation is carried out in 129 km/h (80 mph) winds with very high sea conditions, and with a crew of four and a doctor a total of 27 persons is carried by the Sea King on its return flight to Kirkwall, Orkney Islands.

October 3 A Boeing 747 begins a series of testbed flights with the Pratt & Whitney JT9D-7R4D chosen to power the new Boeing 767.

October 11 Soviet cosmonauts Valeri Ryumin and Leonid Popov land successfully in Soyuz 37 after spending 185 days in space on board the Salyut 6 orbiting laboratory. During that period they have received visits and supplies from three manned spacecraft, and supplies and equipment from three unmanned Progress cargo spacecraft.

October 11-15 The Goodyear airship *Europa* is used for pollution-monitoring in the Gulf of Genoa as part of a Mediterranean Pollution Monitoring Research Programme.

October 20 The first production British Aerospace Sky Flash air-to-air missile for Flygvapnet is handed over to the Swedish Defence Material Administration. Skyflash has been chosen as the primary weapon of the Saab AJ 37 Viggen.

October 26 All UK-Spain services operated by British Airways are transferred from London Heathrow to London Gatwick.

October 29 In a private-venture development of the F-16 as a tactical fighter for export, General Dynamics begins flight testing an F-16/79 with a General Electric J79-GE-119 power plant.

November 1 With load factors running at only about 40 per cent, British Airways terminates its Concorde services to Bahrain and Singapore.

November 5 A Bell 212 helicopter is used to save the lives of 12 people trapped on the upper floor of a blazing building at Kuala Lumpur, Malaysia.

November 6 A first battery-powered flight test is made at Shafter, California of the Solar Challenger designed under the leadership of Dr Paul MacCready.

November 9 The last revenue flight of a de Havilland Comet 4C (G-BDIW) is made from London Gatwick, a special flight for air enthusiasts and recalling the first flight more than 30 years earlier.

November 11 NASA's Voyager 1 spacecraft flies past Saturn's largest moon, Titan, at a distance of about 4,500km (2,796 miles). It subsequently passes below Saturn's rings before travelling on out of the solar system.

November 12 Delta Air Lines of Atlanta, Georgia places the largest ever order for a single jetliner type: 60 examples of the Boeing Model 757.

November 14 Raoul Hafner dies at the age of 75, his place in aviation history assured by his important contribution to the development of rotary-wing aircraft.

November 18-21 British airwoman Judith Chisholm, flying a Cessna Turbo Centurion, establishes a new 3 days 13 hr woman's solo flight record between England and Australia.

November 20 The MacCready Solar Challenger makes its first short-duration test flight solely on solar power.

November 24 Fokker celebrates the 25th anniversary of the first flight of an F.27 Friendship medium-range airliner. It remains a current production aircraft in early 1982 with more than 600 in use worldwide.

December 2 The first of 33 Boeing Vertol Chinook HC.Mk 1 medium-lift helicopters for service with the RAF is handed over officially at Odiham, Hampshire.

MacCready Solar Challenger, November 20 1980.
(*Martyn Cowley*)

December 3 Judith Chisholm (q.v. November 18) lands at London Heathrow after completing her solo round-the-world flight in 15 days 22 min 30 sec and thus virtually halving the previous time set by Sheila Scott.

December 4 The first of 212 Messerschmitt-Bölkow-Blohm BO 105 PAH-1 anti-tank helicopters for service with the West German Army is handed over officially at Celle.

The first successful burn of the cluster of three Space Shuttle main engines, lasting 9 min 51 sec, is carried out by NASA. The test is performed at 102 per cent of rated thrust.

December 5 Piloted by Janice Brown, Dr Paul MacCready's Solar Challenger records a flight of one hour 32 min solely under solar power.

December 6 The MacCready Solar Challenger is flown for a distance of 29km (18 miles) between Tucson and Phoenix, Arizona, the flight being terminated by a heavy rainstorm.

December 9 The 500th Boeing 747 is rolled out at Everett, Washington, this being for service with SAS (OY-KHB).

December 10 An Airbus A300 makes its first flight with the SFENA/Smiths/Bodenseewerk Category III digital all-weather automatic landing system.

December 12 A first flight is made by a Dassault-Bréguet/Dornier Alpha Jet A1 (98 + 33) equipped with an experimental TST (Transsonik Tragflügel) transonic supercritical wing of Dornier design.

December 15 After more than three years of negotiations a basic agreement is reached for the merger of Messerschmitt-Bölkow-Blohm (MBB) and Vereinigte Flugtechnische Werke (VFW) in West Germany.

December 16 British Aerospace Dynamics announces the finalisation of a £200 million contract with Switzerland covering the supply of a Rapier/Blindfire defence system.

The first two of the 50 British Aerospace Hawk trainers for service with the Finnish Air Force are handed over officially at the company's Dunsfold, Surrey airfield.

Saudi Arabian Airlines announces that it has ordered 11 Airbus A300B4-600s, this being the initial order for the B4-600 variant.

December 17 Pacific Southwest Airlines introduces the McDonnell Douglas DC-9 Super 80 into airline service, initially on its San Francisco-Los Angeles route.

December 18 The first of 18 Boeing E-3A Sentry AWACS for service with NATO is flown from Renton to Seattle for equipment installation.

December 19 General Dynamics begins a 100-hour flight test programme of the F-16/101 at Edwards AFB, California. This is a standard F-16A re-engined with the General Electric F-101DFE (derivative fighter engine) for evaluation of this power plant in a fighter aircraft.

December 31 Teledyne Continental in the USA and Rolls-Royce in the UK terminate the licensing agreement under which several types of Continental engines have been manufactured by Rolls-Royce since 1961. Teledyne Continental is to continue to provide technical support for all UK-built engines.

1981

January 1 In accordance with UK government plans to return British Aerospace to private ownership, British Aerospace Ltd is vested with all assets, liabilities and obligations of the nationalised corporation. It is then re-registered as British Aerospace Public Limited Company.

January 5 The first formal course begins at the Tri-National Tornado Training Establishment (TTTE), RAF Cottesmore. This is to train the pilot and navigator instructors who will serve with TTTE.

Sir James Martin, well-known in aviation history as the designer and manufacturer of Martin-Baker ejection seats, dies at the age of 87.

January 6 Laker Airways collects the first of its 10 Airbus A300s (G-BIMA) from Toulouse.

January 15 Operating in a 129 km/h (80 mph) blizzard, Bell 212s of Bristow Helicopters, a Sikorsky S-61N of British Airways Helicopters and Westland Sea Kings of the Royal Norwegian Air Force combine efforts to rescue nine men from a sinking vessel some 185 km (115 miles) north-east of the Shetlands.

January 18 A Bell Model 222 light commercial helicopter delivered to Omniflight Helicopters is the company's 25,000th production helicopter.

Fifth anniversary of the joint inauguration of Concorde supersonic passenger services by Air France and British Airways.

January 26 Pan American flies its last service with the Boeing Model 707-320C: Model 707s have been operated by the airline for just over 22 years.

The Soviet Union's Progress 12 unmanned cargo spacecraft docks with and refuels automatically Salyut 6 in Earth orbit. Two days later Progress 12 is used to raise the space station's orbit.

January 28 Pan American begins a regular twice-weekly New York-Peking (Beijing) service.

January 29 The Royal Navy's No 815 Squadron, the Lynx HQ squadron, is formed at RNAS Yeovilton, Somerset.

The Tri-National Tornado Training Establishment is opened officially at RAF Cottesmore.

January 30 British Airways make a record 96 automatic landings at London Heathrow on a day when fog has virtually closed the airport to other airlines, with an RVR of 125-150m (410-492ft) throughout the day.

February 1 Donald W. Douglas, founder of the Douglas Aircraft Company, dies at the age of 88.

February 7 The Australian regional carrier Northern Airlines terminates operations after recording a loss of A$1.2 million in six months.

February 8 British Airways Helicopters receives the first of six Boeing Vertol Model 234 Commercial Chinooks at Gatwick, Surrey.

February 12 US balloonists Max Anderson and Don Ida lift off from Luxor, Egypt in the helium-filled balloon *Jules Verne*. Their round-the-world flight attempt is aborted two days later after travelling some 4,667km (2,900 miles) to a point east of New Delhi.

February 13 The USAF signs a $284 million follow-on contract for an additional six McDonnell Douglas KC-10A Extender tanker/cargo aircraft.

February 18 The death of John K. Northrop, founder of the Northrop Corporation, marks the loss of two famous US company founders in a single month.

February 20 Delivery is made of the first of 20 Aeritalia G222T twin-turboprop general purpose transports for the Libyan Arab Republic Air Force.

February 26 A new variable-angle ski jump (7-15°) becomes operational at RNAS Yeovilton, Somerset.

March 11 British Caledonian Helicopters opens new facilities at Aberdeen Airport to allow expansion of its operations to offshore gas/oil platforms.

March 14 Following some two years of restoration work, a Supermarine Spitfire Mk 16 built in 1945 flies for the first time for almost 24 years.

March 17 The first of the McDonnell Douglas KC-10A Extender tanker/cargo aircraft for service with the USAF's Strategic Air Command is delivered to Barksdale AFB, Louisiana.

March 26 The Boeing Company announces that a go-ahead has been given for full-scale development and production of a new larger capacity/more fuel efficient Model 737-300.

March 28 A first flight is made by the Dornier 228-100 prototype (D-IFNS), a new 15-passenger light turboprop-powered transport.

Air France flies its last service with the Aérospatiale (Sud-Aviation) Caravelle, almost 22 years after the type first entered service.

March 29 British Airways operates its last service with the BAC (Vickers) VC10. The comparatively small fleet of these aircraft (12 VC10s and 17 Super VC10s) has carried some 13 million passengers without accident.

April 1 Pan American resumes a New York-Paris service after a break of six years, resulting from a 1975 route-exchange agreement.

April 3 Juan Trippe, the founder of Pan American World Airways and a pioneer of air transport, dies at the age of 81.

April 9 A first flight is made by the first Transall C-160 Second Series transport aircraft. It differs from earlier production aircraft by having a reinforced wing, optional increased fuel capacity and advanced avionics.

April 12 UK hot-air balloon manufacturer Thunder-Colt Balloons records the first flight of its new A.S.80 hot-air airship.

NASA's Space Shuttle *Columbia* on mission STS-1 is launched successfully from Cape Canaveral under the power of its own rocket engines and two jettisonable boosters, crewed by John Young and Robert Crippen. It makes 37 orbits and the flight lasts for 2 days 6h 21 mins.

April 14 After 37 orbits of the Earth, *Columbia* makes a controlled re-entry into the atmosphere before completing a near-perfect unpowered landing on the dry bed of Rogers Lake at Edwards AFB, California.

April 17 Beech Aircraft Corporation delivers the 3,000th example of its King Air range.

April 30 The Indonesian Air Force orders three Boeing Model 737-200s for use primarily in a maritime surveillance role. These are to be equipped with side-looking multi-mission radar.

May 8 The first of two prototypes of the Dassault-Bréguet Atlantic NG (Nouvelle Génération) maritime patrol aircraft is flown at Toulouse-Blagnac.

Columbia **lifts off on its first test mission, April 12 1981. (***NASA***)**

Astronauts John Young and Robert Crippen leave *Columbia* **after a highly successful landing on Rogers Dry Lake Runway 23.** (*NASA*)

May 9 A Boeing Model 747 testbed aircraft begins flying with the Rolls-Royce RB.211-535C turbofan, which has been selected as power plant for initial versions of the new Boeing Model 757.

May 20 The first of three British Aerospace 146 development aircraft is rolled out at Hatfield, Hertfordshire.

Hughes Helicopters of Culver City, California announces that it is beginning construction of a prototype NOTAR (no tail-rotor) helicopter, which will rely upon pressure air circulation control to offset main rotor torque.

June 1 A first flight is made by the Short Brothers 360 prototype (G-ROOM), a new 36-seat twin-turboprop commuter transport.

June 5 Flying a specially-prepared Rutan Long-EZ lightplane, Richard G. Rutan sets a world straight line distance record in the FAI class C-1-b. The distance of 7,344.56 km (4,563.7 miles) is ratified subsequently by the FAI.

June 6 Air France announces the conclusion of a preliminary contract with Airbus Industrie for the supply of 25 A320s with options on an additional 25

June 7 Eight Israeli Air Force F-16s, escorted by F-15s, attack the Osirak nuclear reactor near Baghdad, Iraq. As a result the US imposes a temporary embargo on the supply of further F-16s to Israel.

June 15 The Pakistan Foreign Minister states that the US administration has agreed to supply General Dynamics F-16s to the Pakistan Air Force.

June 19 Launch of the French Meteostat 2 weather satellite with Ariana LO 3 rocket booster from Kouron, French Guyana.

June 25 The UK Defence Secretary announces that the government intends to procure 60 McDonnell Douglas AV-8Bs for service with the RAF under the designation Harrier GR.Mk 5.

June 26 The first production Grumman/General Dynamics EF-111A (66-049) makes its first flight. This is a specially-developed ECM tactical jamming aircraft for service with the USAF.

July 1 British Airways Helicopters introduces the first of its Boeing Vertol Model 234s into commercial service, operating contract flights to North Sea offshore gas/oil platforms.

July 2 The Swiss government signs a letter of agreement with Northrop for the supply of an additional 32 F-5Es and six two-seat F-5Fs.

Above **Roll-out of the BAe 146, May 20 1981.**
Below **The Goodyear airship** *Europa* **is used to transmit fine aerial pictures of the Royal Wedding in Britain, July 1981.** (*Thames Television*)

July 3 Aeroflot inaugurates its first international service with the Ilyushin Il-86 on the airline's Moscow-East Berlin route.

July 7 The MacCready Solar Challenger makes the first crossing of the English Channel by a solar-powered aircraft. The 5 hr 23 min 290km (180 mile) flight from Cergy Pontaire, near Paris to Manston Airfield, Kent is piloted by Steve Ptacek.

July 14 The first flight in a short evaluation programme is made by a Grumman F-14 Tomcat powered by two General Electric F101-DFE advanced augmented turbofan engines.

July 15 The first Lockheed TR-1A single-seat tactical reconnaissance aircraft for the USAF is rolled out at Palmdale, California.

July 17 A first flight is made by the prototype Piper T-1040 turboprop-powered commuter airliner developed from the Piper Chieftain, which is to be marketed by Piper's new Airline Division established on June 4, 1981.

July 23 A new altitude record for helicopters in the FAI sub-class E-I-d is set by an Agusta A 109A piloted by Charles Praether at Philadelphia, Pennsylvania. The 6,096 m (20,000 ft) record is later ratified by the FAI.

July 31 The Japanese Maritime Self-Defence Agency signs a contract with Grumman Corporation for the supply of four additional E-2C Hawkeye AEW aircraft; two are scheduled for delivery in 1984 and two in 1985.

August 1 Japan Air Lines celebrates the 30th anniversary of its foundation as a private airline.

A first flight is made by the Lockheed TR-1A tactical reconnaissance aircraft.

August 3 The Boeing Company attains a new production milestone with the delivery of its 4,000th jetliner, a 727-200 for Ansett Airlines of Australia.

August 4 The first Boeing Model 767 prototype (N767BA) is rolled-out at Everett, Washington.

August 14 The second Boeing E-3A Sentry AWACS aircraft for service with NATO is delivered to Dornier at Oberpfaffenhofen for installation of its AEW avionics.

A Defence White Paper prepared by the Japanese Defence Agency claims that the Soviet Union is deploying 2,210 tactical aircraft in the Far East. The total includes some 1,600 fighters/fighter-bombers.

August 15 A McDonnell Douglas DC-8 Srs 71, resulting from conversion of a DC-8 Super Sixty to have a more efficient CFM-56 turbofan power plant, makes its first flight of 5 hours.

August 25 NASA's Voyager 2 spacecraft makes its closest approach to the planet Saturn, returning spectacular pictures of its moons and rings. Next rendezvous for Voyager 2 is with Uranus, in January 1986.

August 26 A first flight is recorded by the first McDonnell Douglas F-15J Eagle to be assembled by Mitsubishi in Japan from US-built components.

August 28 The US Defense Department announces that McDonnell Douglas is selected as prime contractor for development of the proposed CX transport aircraft.

August 31 A McDonnell Douglas DC-10 makes its first flight with drag-reducing winglets installed in a programme to evaluate their effect on fuel consumption.

September 3 McDonnell Douglas delivers its 1,000th DC-9, a Super 80 (HB-INO) for Swissair.

The British Aerospace 146 Series 100 prototype (G-SSSH) makes a successful first flight at Hatfield, Hertfordshire.

September 7 Edwin A. Link, inventor of the Link trainer, dies at the age of 77. His ground-based flight trainer was the first stepping-stone towards the sophisticated flight simulators now used for a major portion of all flight training.

September 13 The 50th anniversary of the flight by Flt Lt John Boothman, in a Supermarine S.6B, which won the Schneider Trophy outright for the UK.

September 15 The 494th Tactical Fighter Squadron, based at RAF Lakenheath, Suffolk becomes the first US Air Force squadron to be operational with the Pave Tack weapons delivery system. Pave Tack comprises a pod housing a laser transmitter/receiver and a precision optical sight.

September 17 Flygvapen's C-in-C states that following evaluation of the F-5S version of the Tigershark, F-16 Fighting Falcon, F-18 Hornet and the Mirage 2000, the Saab 2105 contender for the Swedish Air Force's JAS (Jakt/Attack/Spanning: fighter/attack/reconnaissance) multi-role combat aircraft requirement is the most suitable for Flygvapen's needs.

September 20 A first flight is made by a Jaguar with a fly-by-wire control system developed by Marconi Avionics/Dowty. This is a quadruplex-redundant electrically-signalled flight control system with no mechanical backup.

The People's Republic of China launches three satellites into Earth orbit with a single booster rocket. It is the nation's first multiple launch.

A new UK operator, Anglo Scottish Air Parcels, begins a twice daily small parcel delivery service between nine UK airports.

September 21 It is announced that Bell Helicopter has won the US Army's Armed Helicopter Improvement Programme (AHIP) contest. The initial $148 million contract award covers the design, modification and test of five prototypes. Subject to satisfactory evaluation Bell could gain an estimated $1,000 million contract to modify 720 OH-58A Kiowas to AHIP configuration.

September 22 An Ilyushin Il-86, captained by G. Volokhov, establishes for the Soviet Union a new world class record for speed in a 2,000 km closed circuit, carrying payloads of 35,000 to 65,000 kg, of 526.3 knots (975.3 km/h; 606.02 mph). Two days later the same aircraft/crew combination sets a new record over a 1,000 km closed circuit of 519.1 knots (962 km/h; 597.8 mph) carrying payloads from 30,000 to 80,000 kg.

September 24   A first flight is made by the Sikorsky YEH-60 prototype, a communications-jamming ECM version of the EH-60 Black Hawk.

September 25   The first production Panavia Tornado for the Italian Air Force (IT001), a dual-control trainer, makes its first flight at Caselle. It is scheduled for delivery to the Trinational Tornado Training Establishment at RAF Cottesmore in early 1982.

September 26   The first flight of the Boeing Model 767 is completed successfully at Paine Field, Everett. This 2 hr 4 min flight is made three days ahead of a target that was set in 1978.

September 28   The new Skyship 500 non-rigid airship (G-BIHN) built by Airship Industries (formerly Aerospace Developments) makes a successful two hour first flight at RAE Cardington, Bedfordshire.

September 30   The last de Havilland Comet airliner flight in the UK is made by the Srs 4C G-BOIX, flown by Dan-Air to East Fortune for the Royal Scottish Museum.

October 2   President Reagan announces that 100 Rockwell B-1B SAL (Strategic Air-launched cruise missile Launchers) are to be procured for the USAF.

October 6   The first flight is recorded of an Airbus A300 with a two-man Forward Facing Crew Cockpit (FFCC). The FFCC flight deck has advanced avionics and improved system automation, making it possible for a flight crew of two to operate this wide-body airliner.

October 9   Ascending from a site near Los Angeles, California, Fred Gorrell and John Shoecroft in the helium-filled balloon *Superchicken III* record the first non-stop trans-America flight in a balloon, landing in Georgia 55 hr 25 min after lift off.

Dornier begins flight testing a new four-blade propeller. Developed by Dornier and Hoffmann, it is anticipated that its use could offer fuel savings of up to five per cent.

October 12   Aeroflot introduces the Ilyushin Il-86 on its Moscow-Prague route.

October 15   Irish commuter airline Avair takes delivery of a new Shorts 330 (formerly SD3-30). This is used to introduce a three-times daily Belfast-Dublin service on October 26.

October 16   McDonnell Douglas rolls out the first full-scale development AV-8B Harrier II at St Louis, Missouri.

October 20   The Australian Minister of Defence states that the McDonnell Douglas F-18 Hornet has been selected to meet the RAAF's new tactical fighter requirement.

October 24   The Japan Air Self-Defence Force takes delivery from Kawasaki of its 31st and last C-1 tactical transport.

October 30   Middle East Airlines confirms with Airbus Industrie its order for five Airbus A310s plus 14 options.

November 2   Air UK inaugurates a service linking Stansted Airport, Essex with Amsterdam, Netherlands. It is the airport's first scheduled international service.

November 4   NASA's second flight by the Space Shuttle *Columbia* is aborted 31 sec before lift-off due to a computer mis-match.

Garrett Turbine Engines begins ground testing a new TFE76 engine which has been developed for the USAF's Next Generation Trainer (NGT).

November 9   The first hardened aircraft shelters in the UK are put into use at RAF Honington, Suffolk.

November 12   The NASA Space Shuttle *Columbia* on mission STS-2 makes a successful lift-off from Kennedy Space Center with Joe Engle and Richard Truly as crew. Thirty-six orbits are performed, the mission lasting for 2 days, 6h 13 minutes. A fuel cell fault halved the expected 5-day mission.

NASA makes use of two US Navy Grumman E-2C Hawkeyes to monitor the Space Shuttle launch, and intended primarily to speed tracking and recovery of the solid rocket boosters (SRBs).

November 13   Ben Abruzzo, Larry Newman, Ron Clarke and Rocky Aoki complete the first manned crossing of the Pacific by balloon. Carried in the helium-filled balloon *Double Eagle V*, their journey from Nagashima, Japan ends in a crash-landing in severe weather some 274 km (170 miles) north of San Francisco.

November 14   With its mission cut short because of a fuel cell failure, the Space Shuttle *Columbia* makes a successful landing at Rogers Lake, Edwards AFB, California.

November 17   The Austrian government postpones the planned procurement of 24 Dassault Mirage 50s to equip the nation's air force.

November 19   The US Defense Secretary announces that the British Aerospace Hawk has won the US Navy's VTX-TS trainer competition. Following this announcement British Aerospace, McDonnell Douglas and Sperry are to be awarded a contract covering the development of the Hawk as a US Navy trainer and refinement of the computer software and simulators to be provided by Sperry.

Pan American recognises the 50th anniversary of its first operation of a four-engined airliner, the Sikorsky S-40 Clipper.

November 24   Two Sikorsky S-61Ns of Bristow Helicopters, operating in winds of about 140 km/h (87 mph), rescue 48 oilmen from the production rig *Transworld 58* after it had been blown from its moorings.

November 25-26 Crewed by French balloonists Hélène Dorigny and Michel Arnould, the Cameron A-530 hot-air balloon *Semiramis* is flown from Ballina, Ireland to St Christophe-en-Boucherie, France. This is later ratified by the FAI as a new hot-air balloon distance record of 1,154.74 km (717.5 miles).

November 30 The last Westland Whirlwind helicopters on active SAR duties in the UK are retired from RAF service and replaced by the larger Wessex.

December 3 The internationally-known aviation historian, Charles Gibbs-Smith, dies in London following a heart attack.

December 4 NASA accepts the first flight-standard ERNO Spacelab module at ERNO's Bremen factory.

December 5 Jerry Mullen takes off in an aircraft named *Phoenix*, used formerly by Jim Bede as the BD-2 *Love One*, to attempt a closed-circuit distance record for piston-engined aircraft in Class C-l-d. He lands on December 8, after 73 hr 2 min in the air, having flown a distance of 8,690.3 nm (16,104.9 km; 10,007.1 miles), which considerably exceeds the previous world record.

December 7 Lockheed Corporation states that it is the company's intention to phase-out production of the L-1011 TriStar when existing firm orders have been completed.

December 9 Aérospatiale hands over to the Armée de l'Air at Toulouse the first two of 25 new-production Transall C.160 transports.

December 11 A first flight is made at Reno, Nevada of the OMAC 1, the newest contender for orders in the US business aircraft market. It is also one of the most unusual, being of canard configuration and with a fuselage-mounted turboprop engine driving a pusher propeller.

December 14 In a ceremony at Toulouse, the Armée de l'Air accepts its 200th and last SEPECAT Jaguar.

December 17 A successful first flight is made by a Hughes OH-6A helicopter which has been modified under US Army contract to NOTAR (no tail rotor) configuration. Instead of a conventional tail rotor it uses pressurised air to offset torque effect, ejected through a controllable slot in the tailboom.

December 23 A Sikorsky CH/MH-53E prototype is flown for the first time in a mine-sweeping configuration. The US Navy plans to procure an MH-53E variant of the CH-53E heavy-lift helicopter for the mine-sweeping role.

December 25 Weapon Systems Operator Lt Thomas Tiller, USAF, is picked up from a dinghy off the North Carolina coast. He had ejected from a McDonnell F-4E Phantom II on December 18 and survived seven days of exposure in the Atlantic.

1982

January 6 The aerobatic team of the Italian Air Force, the renowned Frecce Tricolori, accepts delivery of its first Aermacchi MB 339A at Venegono airfield. The team is scheduled to receive a total of 15 MB 339As to replace its Fiat G91s.

The Rolls-Royce Gem 60 turboshaft engine, which is planned to power advanced versions of the Westland 30 and Lynx helicopters, begins test-bed running.

January 8 Air Jamaica signs a contract with Airbus Industrie for the supply of two A300B4-200s for delivery in late 1982.

A Gulfstream III executive transport operated by the US National Distillers and Chemical Corporation begins a round-the-world flight. Landing on January 10 the flight, from and to Teterboro, New Jersey is completed in 47 hr 39 min, breaking three existing records and setting 10 new ones in the approriate FAI class.

January 13 The Kuwait government completes a $90 million contract with Lockheed-Georgia covering the supply of four L-100-30 Hercules transport aircraft for delivery to the Kuwait Air Force in 1983.

The first Boeing Model 757 twin-turbofan short/medium-range transport is rolled out at Renton, Washington.

January 15 The first of an initial batch of 40 General Dynamics F-16s for service with the Egyptian Air Force is handed over officially at Forth Worth, Texas.

January 22 A first fully-automatic landing by a McDonnell Douglas F-18 Hornet is made at the Naval Air Test Center, Patuxent River, Maryland. It is achieved by linking the aircraft's autopilot to a ground-based SPN-42 radar.

NATO takes delivery of its first Boeing E-3A Sentry AWACS aircraft at Oberpfaffenhofen following installation of its AEW equipment. It is flown to Geilenkirchen, West Germany on February 24.

January 26 The USAF Systems Headquarters signs a multi-year procurement contract covering the supply of 480 General Dynamics F-16s for delivery to the US Air Force durng the fiscal years 1982-85. It brings the contracted total of F-16s to 1,085, leaving procurement of only 303 of the currently planned total to be negotiated.

January 27 Cessna Aircraft Company announces delivery of its 1,000th business jet, a Citation II.

February 4 Using one of the first examples of an improved Sikorsky S-76 II, the company operates it over a period of six days to set 12 new helicopter class records, since ratified by the FAI.

February 9 The Indonesian Ambassador in Paris accepts formally the first of three new-production Transall C-160 transports; they are to be used in transmigration flights from the heavily populated island of Java.

February 11 The Armée de l'Air accepts delivery of its 100th Alpha Jet trainer at Toulouse.

February 16 The first Airbus A310 is rolled out at Toulouse, one of the ten aircraft of this version ordered by Swissair.

Boeing 757 roll-out, January 13 1982.

February 19 The Boeing Model 757 makes its first flight at Renton, Washington. The successful 2 hr 30 min flight terminates at Paine Field, Everett where it is to be based until cleared by the FAA for operation from the company's airfield at Seattle.

February 24 The Australian government confirms it is to purchase from the UK the light aircraft carrier HMS *Invincible* which is surplus to British requirements.

February 25 With the recession in airline traffic continuing, American Airlines cancels an order for 15 Boeing 757s plus options on 15 more.

February 26 Flight testing begins at Philadelphia, Pennsylvania, of the first production conversion of the Boeing Vertol CH-47D Chinook. Subject to satisfactory flight tests the US Army plans to convert 436 CH-47As to this improved configuration.

March 1 The first two of 27 McDonnell Douglas F-15 Eagles to equip Alaskan Air Command arrives at Elmendorf AFB near Anchorage. They are to replace the 21st Tactical Fighter Wing's F-4E Phantom IIs.

March 5 It is announced in Paris that 150 Aéro-spatiale TB 30 Epsilon primary trainers are to be procured for the Armée de l'Air, the first to be delivered in the Autumn of 1983.

March 11 Bristow Helicopters takes delivery at Marignane of the first of 12 Aérospatiale AS 332L lengthened-fuselage Super Pumas (G-BJXC). Adopting the name Tiger for these aircraft, Bristow expects all 12 to be in service by late 1982 and has 12 more on order plus options for 11.

March 12 The third and last BAe (BAC) One-Eleven to be assembled at Hurn, Hampshire, for the Romanian airline TAROM (YR-BCO) is handed over.

March 15 The Japan Air Self-Defence Force retires the last example (62-7497) of 479 North American F-86 Sabres received since 1956.

March 16 First deliveries are made of EMBRAER EMB-121 Xingu general-purpose transport/training aircraft for service with the French Navy and Air Force, which ordered 16 and 25 respectively.

March 22 Space Shuttle *Columbia* is launched on

mission STS-3, with astronauts Jack Lousma and Charles Fullerton on board. The mission lasts for 8 days and 5 minutes, during which 129 orbits are made, an extra day being added to the flight because of a storm in the landing area.

March 25 Beech Aircraft Corporation celebrates the 35th anniversary of the start of Bonanza production. Almost 15,000 Bonanzas have been built, including some 10,400 of the V-tailed Model 35.

March 26 Funding for the Hughes AH-64A Apache armed attack helicopter for the US Army is approved by the Defence System Acquisition Review Council. Production of a first batch of 11 is planned for delivery in February 1984.

March 29 Brymon Airways of Plymouth, Devon inaugurates a Plymouth-Heathrow service operated by a de Havilland Canada DHC-7 Dash 7.

March 31 The first SEPECAT Jaguar to be assembled by Hindustan Aeronautics for the Indian Air Force makes its first flight.

The 100th Panavia Tornado for the Luftwaffe (GS+018) is handed over at Manching.

April 1 In a ceremony at Evreux, France the Armée de l'Air's Escadron 1/64 *Béarn* takes delivery of its first new-production Transall C.160 transport.

April 2 Argentine Forces invade the Falkland Islands and, on the following day, the island of South Georgia.

The Swedish carrier Linjeflyg AB celebrates the 25th anniversary of its formation.

Newly formed British Island Airways makes its first revenue flight, from Gatwick to Catania, with BAe (BAC) One-Eleven G-CIBA *Island Ensign*.

April 3 The United Nations Security Council passes Resolution 502 calling for the withdrawal of Argentine forces from the Falklands.

The first Airbus A310 (F-WZLH) makes a successful first flight of 3 hr 15 min at Toulouse.

The main elements of the British task force for operations against the Argentine forces on the Falklands sail from Portsmouth. They include the carriers HMS *Hermes* and *Invincible*.

April 6 A new Sea Harrier squadron, No 809, is formed at RNAS Yeovilton. Nos. 800, 801, 809 and 899 Sea Harrier squadrons carry out 2,376 sorties and complete 2,675 hr 25 min of operational flying during the conflict that follows.

April 7 The British government declares a 200-mile (322-km) exclusion zone around the Falkland Islands.

April 21 Two Westland Wessex helicopters of the British task force crash on South Georgia in bad weather. A third recovers the men of the SAS.

April 25 Aircraft attached to the British task force despatched to the Falklands Islands are in action for the first time. Lynx helicopters flying from the frigates HMS *Alacrity* and *Antelope* attack the Argentine submarine

Santa Fe off Grytviken harbour, South Georgia. Later that day Sea Kings escorted by Lynx helicopters land Royal Marines on South Georgia. The Marines subsequently recapture the island.

April 27 The US Navy awarded Sikorsky a $139.4 million contract for the first 18 of a planned 204 SH-60B Seahawk LAMPS Mk III helicopters.

April 28 The British government give Argentina 48 hours warning that an air blockade is to be imposed over a 200-mile (322-km) radius from the Falklands.

April 30 A contract is signed between the Swedish Defence Material Administration and the JAS Industry Group covering development and procurement of the JAS multi-role combat aircraft. (q.v. September 17, 1981)

Pilatus Britten-Norman delivers its 1,000th aircraft of the Islander/Trislander family , a maritime Islander for the Cyprus government.

Certification of Cessna's new Citation III is awarded by the US FAA.

May 1 The first British air attack against Argentine positions on the Falkland Islands is made by a single Vulcan B2 operating from Ascension Island. It requires flight refuelling on both the outward and return flights. The Vulcan bombs Port Stanley airfield, and an attack on the same airfield is made immediately afterwards by nine Sea Harriers from HMS *Hermes*. Three Sea Harriers also attack the airstrip at Goose Green. The Vulcan operation against Port Stanley from Ascension Island ranks as the longest ever operational sortie.

In the first Sea Harrier combat victory, an Argentine Mirage IIIEA is destroyed by a Sidewinder missile. Argentine losses on the same day include a second Mirage III and a Canberra bomber.

May 2 A Royal Navy ASW Sea King helicopter under fire from the Argentine patrol vessel *Alferez Sobral* reports its position to the task force. Soon afterwards the *Sobral* is damaged severely in an attack by two Lynx helicopters deploying Sea Skua missiles and an accompanying patrol vessel, the *Comodoro Somellera*, is sunk.

The Argentine Navy cruiser *General Belgrano* is sunk by the British nuclear-powered submarine *Conqueror*.

May 4 A Sea Harrier is lost during an attack on Port Stanley.

HMS *Sheffield*, a Type 42 destroyer, has to be abandoned and later sinks after being hit by an Exocet missile launched from an Argentine Navy Super Etendard.

May 5 Two British Airways L-1011 TriStars make safe touch-downs at London's Heathrow Airport in totally blind conditions. The landings are made with an absence of runway visual range and reference height measurements.

May 7 The British government declares a 'safe zone' extending 12 miles (19.3 km) from the Argentinian coast.

A new Sea King squadron, No 825, is commissioned at RNAS Culdrose. It and No 824 Squadron fly a combined 1,481 operational sorties totalling 2,528 hrs 15 m during the Falklands operations.

Two Sea Harriers from HMS *Invincible* are lost: it is believed they collided in poor visibility.

May 8 About 20 Harriers and Sea Harriers fly non-stop from RNAS Yeovilton, Somerset to Ascension Island, air refuelled several times during the 9 hr flight.

May 9 The Argentinian vessel *Narwal*, shadowing the British task force, is attacked by two Sea Harriers. Its crew surrender subsequently to a boarding party from HMS *Hermes*.

May 12 One of the largest airlines to collapse as a result of the current state of recession, Braniff International, terminates all operations.

May 13 Soyuz T-5 is launched successfully from Baikonur, carrying cosmonauts Anatoli Berezovoy and Valentin Lebedev. A successful link-up is made on May 14 with the Soviet Union's new orbiting laboratory, Salyut 7.

May 14 The British task force raids Pebble Island: three Argentinian Skyhawk bombers are lost in action.

India's combined communications and weather satellite, Insat 1A, becomes operational.

May 15 A SOCATA TB 10 Tobago lightplane makes a first flight with its Avco Lycoming engine modified to operate on liquified petroleum (LPG), offering large savings in fuel cost.

May 17 In what is believed to be the first launch of a satellite from an orbiting space station, the crew of Salyut 7 place the amateur radio satellite Iskra 2 in Earth orbit via an airlock in the space laboratory. (q.v. May 13, 1982).

May 18 The first Grumman E-2C Hawkeye AEW aircraft for service with the Japan Air Self-Defence Force (34-3451) is handed over officially at Bethpage, Long Island.

May 19 The space shuttle *Columbia* is moved into the Vehicle Assembly Building in preparation for its fourth mission, then scheduled for June 27.

May 20 Boeing Vertol hands over to the US Army the first production CH-47D Chinook.

May 21 Royal Marine Commandos and a Parachute Regiment battalion make a successful landing at Port San Carlos on the East Falklands. Royal Navy Sea Kings play a major role in this action: for example, a detachment of Sea King Mk. 4 Commando helicopters

of No 846 Squadron airlift more than 407 tons of stores and 520 troops on this day alone. The Type 21 frigate HMS *Ardent* is lost after air attack. Nine Argentine aircraft lost in action.

May 24 The last Boeing 707 in operation with British Airways makes its final flight, from Cairo to London Heathrow. The type had been in service with BOAC/British Airways since 1960.

Following several hits by rockets and bombs launched from Argentine aircraft on the previous day, the frigate HMS *Antelope* explodes and sinks. Seven Argentine aircraft are lost in action.

May 25 The Type 42 destroyer HMS *Coventry* of the British task force is hit by bombs from Argentine Skyhawks and sinks following serious fire damage. In another attack the container ship *Atlantic Conveyor* is hit by an Exocet missile launched from an Argentine Navy Super Etendard and is abandoned after serious fire damage. Twenty-four task force personnel lose their lives.

May 25 Air India confirms with Airbus Industrie its order for three Airbus A300B4-200 civil transports.

May 27 The first of five Lockheed P-3C Orions being assembled in Japan by Kawasaki is accepted at Gifu by the Maritime Self-Defence Force.

May 28 Goose Green and Darwin are retaken by British forces. Seventeen British soldiers are killed in the action.

June 3 An RAF Vulcan is intercepted in Brazilian airspace and escorted to Rio de Janeiro by Brazilian F-5Es.

June 8 Argentine aircraft attack task force ships at Bluff Cove. Fifty task force personnel lose their lives. Eleven Argentine aircraft are lost in action.

June 12 HMS *Glamorgan* is struck by a land-based Exocet fired from Port Stanley. Thirteen sailors are lost but the destroyer remains operational.

June 14 Argentine forces on the Falklands surrender. Argentine losses amount to more than 700 killed, five ships and well over 100 aircraft. British air losses total four Sea Harriers lost in accidents, two lost to ground fire, three Harrier GR Mk 3s lost to ground fire and helicopters. No Harrier/Sea Harrier have been lost in air to air combat.

June 27 Space Shuttle *Columbia* lifts off on STS-4, its last proving flight. The mission lasts 7 days 1 hr 9 min.

INDEX

NOTE: Ranks or titles are those that apply at the time of the individual's first entry in this index. Individual capital letters entered in parentheses after an index entry indicate: (A) Airship, (B) Balloon and (P) Power plant.

INDEX